HAWAII ACCESS®

Pacific Ocean

Princeville
Airport

Kauai

Lihue
Airport

Kaulakahi
Channel

Niihau

Kauai
Channel

Oahu

Honolulu
International
Airport

Orientation

Like a giant green comet blazing across the blue Pacific, the 132 tropical islands, reefs, and shoals of **Hawaii** form a graceful archipelago spanning more than 1,500 miles, yet they are so remote that even the ubiquitous seagull is unable to traverse the 2,400 miles from the nearest continent. Moving northwest on the back of a lithospheric plate at a rate of four inches per year, the island chain is in a continual state of eruption and erosion, as vast amounts of molten earth emanate upward toward the surface from a stationary "hot spot" on the ocean floor, only to be beaten back down by the merciless elements. After 42 million years of this, just eight major islands—the **Big Island, Maui, Kahoolawe, Lanai, Molokai, Oahu, Kauai,** and **Niihau**—remain and serve not only as home to 1.6 million people but also as one of the world's most treasured vacation destinations—Hawaii.

The beautiful, enchanting tropical paradise that is Hawaii has inspired writers from Mark Twain to James Michener; volumes have been written on the majestic volcanoes, golden beaches, captivating sunsets, and lush rain forests. Hawaii continues to enthrall millions of tourists each year with its numerous rainbows, magnificent waterfalls, astonishing lava flows, endless summer days, and warm starry nights. It's the unstaged backdrop for such movie classics as *Blue Hawaii* and *South Pacific,* the birthplace of regal humpback whales and playful spinner dolphins, and the home of world-famous surfing sites such as **Sunset Beach**, **Waimea Bay**, and the **Banzai Pipeline.** It's a playground for golfers, scuba divers, hikers, mountain bikers, windsurfers, snorkelers, swimmers, deep-sea anglers, and sun worshipers of all shapes and sizes. In short, Hawaii has something for everyone, whether you choose to sip a cool mai tai under a palm tree or dive into the depths of the turquoise sea. Perhaps most importantly, the slow, mellow pace that characterizes the Hawaiian lifestyle tends to ease stress and anxiety, allowing each visitor to return home with something far more valuable than any postcard or souvenir—peace of mind.

Hawaii is not without its faults. In an already overcrowded island state where indigenous Hawaiians are becoming increasingly rare (pure-blooded Hawaiians make up less than .005 percent of the population), the expanding number of immigrants from the mainland and abroad has spurred a rise in racial bitterness, occasionally culminating in violence and, more often, targeted theft. This, combined with a huge foreign investment in precious real estate (most private land, including entire islands, is owned by foreigners

Pacific Ocean

aiwi
hannel

Molokai Airport ✈ ✈ Kalaupapa Airport
Molokai

Kalohi
Channel

Kapalua-
West Maui ✈
Airport

Lanai ✈ Kahului
Airport

Lanai
Airport ✈ Auau
Channel

Maui ✈ Hana
Airport

Kealaikahiki
Channel

Kahoolawe Alalakeiki
Channel

Alenuihaha
Channel

✈
Waimea-
Kohala
Airport

Hilo
International
Airport

✈ Keahole-Kona
International
Airport

✈

**Hawaii
(The Big Island)**

...d a recent surge in ethnic Hawaiian
...ide, has done little to alleviate the
...terracial resentment that has
...isted since Captain James Cook
... foot on Hawaii in 1778.

...the 20th century comes to a close,
...owever, a new age is beginning for
...awaii. After 200 years of pursuing
...ings new, the people of Hawaii are
...assessing the value of things old. A
...awaiian renaissance of sorts is emerging,
...th renewed interest in ancient crafts,
...uals, and dances, and a rekindled
...ssion for the values of traditional island culture, including native art and
...e Hawaiian language. This renaissance is a necessity, because for Hawaii
...prosper in the next century, it must learn from past mistakes. As former
...overnor John Waihee sagaciously observed, "We need to ask ourselves how
...r ancestors did so much with so little, and why we are able to do so little
...th so much."

...guably the closest thing we have to heaven on earth, Hawaii is a priceless
...source worth preserving. It reminds us not only how beautiful the world
...n be, but also how much of that beauty can be found in life's simpler
...ings. Gaze down a mountainside, stroll barefoot along the beach, or just
...atch the sky change colors as the sun disappears behind the sea—it's not
...rd to find splendor here.

How To Read This Guide

HAWAII ACCESS® is arranged by island so you can see at a glance where you are and what is around you. The numbers next to the entries in the following chapters correspond to the numbers on the maps. The text is color-coded according to the kind of place described:

Restaurants/Clubs: Red   **Hotels:** Blue
Shops/ Outdoors: Green   **Sights/Culture:** Black
& Wheelchair accessible

Wheelchair Accessibility
An establishment (except a restaurant) is considered wheelchair accessible when a person in a wheelchair can easily enter a building (i.e., no steps, a ramp, a wide enough door) without assistance. Restaurants are deemed wheelchair accessible only if the above applies and if the rest rooms are on the same floor as the dining area and their entrances and stalls are wide enough to accommodate a wheelchair.

Rating the Restaurants and Hotels
The restaurant star ratings take into account the quality, service, atmosphere, and uniqueness of the restaurant. An expensive restaurant doesn't necessarily ensure an enjoyable evening; however, a small, relatively unknown spot could have good food, professional service, and a lovely atmosphere. Therefore, on a purely subjective basis, stars are used to judge the overall dining value (see the star ratings below). Keep in mind that chefs and owners often change, which sometimes drastically affects the quality of a restaurant. The ratings in this guidebook are based on information available at press time.

The price ratings, as categorized below, apply to restaurants and hotels. These figures describe general price-range relationships among other restaurants and hotels in the area. The restaurant price ratings are based on the average cost of an entrée for one person, excluding tax and tip. Hotel price ratings reflect the base price of a standard room for two people for one night during the peak season.

Restaurants

★	Good	
★★	Very Good	
★★★	Excellent	
★★★★	An Extraordinary Experience	
$	The Price Is Right	(less than $10)
$$	Reasonable	($10-$15)
$$$	Expensive	($15-$25)
$$$$	Big Bucks	($25 and up)

Hotels

$	The Price Is Right	(less than $75)
$$	Reasonable	($75-$150)
$$$	Expensive	($150-$225)
$$$$	Big Bucks	($225 and up)

Map Key

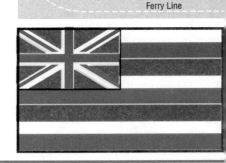

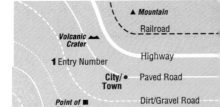

Area code 808 unless otherwise noted.

Getting to the Islands

Airports

Oahu's **Honolulu International Airport** (836.6413) is Hawaii's hub, with connections made by more than two dozen international, national, and interisland carriers. Visitors from the mainland usually fly from Los Angeles, San Francisco, or Seattle, but it is possible to book nonstop flights from other major cities, like Denver or Chicago, to Oahu, Maui, or the Big Island.

For information on other island airports, interisland flights, and local telephone numbers for airlines, see the Orientation sections of the individual island chapters.

Airlines

Aloha 484.1111, 800/367.525
American 833.7600, 800/433.730
Canada 3000 ....888/226.300
Canadian (from Vancouver) 839.224
....800/426.700
Continental 523.0000, 800/525.082

HONOLULU INTERNATIONAL AIRPORT

Mauka Viaduct
Makai Viaduct

H1

Commuter Airlines Interisland Terminal

Overseas Terminal

EWA Concourse

Central Concourse

Diamond Head Concourse

N

| km | 1/4 | 1/2 |
| mi | 1/8 | 1/4 |

Delta 833.8281, 800/221.1212

Hawaiian 838.1555, 800/367.5320

Island Air, interisland 484.2222, 800/652.6541
from the mainland 800/323.3345

Mahalo Air, interisland 833.5555, 800/277.8333
from the mainland 800/4.MAHALO

Northwest, interisland........955.2255, 800/225.2525
from the mainland 800/447.4747

Qantas 800/227.4500
in Australia 131313

Sun Country 800/752.1218

TWA 800/221.2000

United...800/241.6522

Cruise Ships

An increasing number of cruise ships are stopping in Hawaii, despite the fact that, under US law, foreign ocean liners are not permitted to travel from one US port to another. Common itineraries include stops in Ensenada, Mexico, or trips to the South Pacific, Australia, or New Zealand after a stop on the Hawaiian islands but before the ship returns to dock in San Diego or, in the case of **Cunard**'s *Queen Elizabeth 2*, Florida. **Royal Cruise Line** (800/327.7030) regularly launches voyages to Hawaii. Ports of call on the islands are: **Honolulu,** Oahu; **Kailua,** the Big Island; **Lahaina,** Maui; and **Lihue,** Kauai.

Local Lingo

In keeping with its cultural diversity, Hawaii has three languages—two official (English and Hawaiian) and one unofficial (pidgin). Virtually all islanders speak English, but it's usually infused with vernacular, sometimes to the point of incomprehensibility ("Honey, what did he just say?"). The following list includes all the Hawaiian the average tourist needs to know, plus a few words and phrases in pidgin, a hodgepodge of languages originally developed to help traders communicate. However, to avoid becoming the humorous subject of a *pau hana* talk-story session (an after-work conversation among locals), visitors should probably limit themselves to "alohas" and "mahalos."

Aloha (ah-*low*-ha) Hello, good-bye, welcome, and love

Da kine (dah-*kine*) Pidgin for "that whatchamacallit" or anything else one doesn't know the word for or location of

Diamond Head East (as in: The library is Diamond Head of Bishop Street)

Ewa (*eh*-vah) West

Grinds Pidgin for food (also used as a verb, to eat)

Hale (*hol*-ly) House

Hana (*hah*-nah) Work

Haole (*how*-lee) Pidgin for foreigner, normally used to refer to a Caucasian (sometimes in a derogatory sense)

Hawaiian time Pidgin for late (usually by about half an hour)

Heiau (*hey*-ow) Sacred temple, place of worship

J.O.J. Pidgin for tourists (stands for "Just Off the Jet")

Kamaaina (kah-mah-*eye*-nah) Native-born citizen (but usually refers to any resident or local)

Kane (*kah*-neh) Male

Kapu (kah-*poo*) Keep out, forbidden

Keiki (*kay*-key) Child

Kokua (koh-*coo*-ah) Help, assistance

Lanai (lah-*nigh*) Porch, balcony (also an island near Maui)

Lua (*lew*-ah) Bathroom

Luau (*lew*-ow) Hawaiian feast

Mahalo (muh-*hah*-low) Thank you

Makai (muh-*kigh*) Toward the sea (used when giving directions)

Mauka (*mau*-kah) Toward the mountain (used when giving directions)

No ka oi (no-kah-*oy*) Is the best (as in: Maui *no ka oi*)

Ono (*oh*-no) Delicious (also a game fish)

Pakalolo (pah-kah-*low*-low) Marijuana

Pau (*pow*) Finished

Pau hana (pow *hah*-nah) After work

Puka (*poo*-kah) Hole

Pupu (*poo*-poo) Appetizer

Talk story Casual conversation

Wahine (wah-*hee*-nay) Woman or girl

Wikiwiki (*wee*-kee-*wee*-kee) Fast

Getting Around the Islands

Driving

Except on Oahu, public transportation in Hawaii is practically nonexistent. Unless you intend to stay at your hotel or prefer chartered bus tours, plan on renting a car to get around. The largest car-rental companies have booths at the main airports. The best deals are made in advance through mainland offices or as part of a vacation package; reservations are mandatory during peak seasons. Be prepared for a $2-per-day state surcharge and an optional Collision Damage Waiver (CDW) fee. (Some credit cards and personal insurance policies automatically cover you for collision damage and liability, so be sure to check in advance.) Also, many car-rental companies prohibit renters from driving cars on certain roads. Although the companies don't actually police the roads, they won't provide assistance if you break down on one or insurance coverage if you have an accident on one. For additional information on car rentals, see the Orientation sections of the individual island chapters.

The main roads are well paved almost everywhere on the islands, but heading out on unpaved terrain is highly recommended to those renting four-wheel-drive vehicles (they're available from many island car-rental companies—check first to make sure the four-wheel-drive capacity is connected). Often the end of the road is the beginning of the journey in Hawaii, especially on the isles with large wilderness areas, like Lanai and the Big Island.

Traffic jams have become commonplace on the large islands, so try to avoid driving during rush hour, as you'll rarely find alternate routes to the main roads (most of which follow the coastlines). Also, keep in mind that it's a major faux pas to pass other cars at high speeds (some locals hate to be passed at any speed) or to honk your horn unless it's absolutely necessary (it's considered bad manners in the Aloha State). You'll also find other drivers motioning for you to go when they have the right of way (pay attention, or traffic will stop dead). And caution: Rules for yellow traffic lights are heeded and enforced.

Ferries

The only ferry operating in the Hawaiian Islands is *Expeditions* (661.3756, 800/695.2624), a shuttle between Lahaina on Maui and the island of Lanai. Each round-trip excursion is $50 for adults, $40 for children under 12; see the "Maui" or "Lanai" chapters for additional details.

Hiking

Hawaii was made for hikers. Whether you're in the heart of Honolulu or in the middle of nowhere on quiet Lanai, a trailhead is likely to be only a stone's throw away. You can climb an extinct volcano or tromp through the crater of a dormant one, hike into a desert or along a dramatic coastline, spend an hour on a well maintained trail or a fortnight in the wilds. Wherever you hike, the trail inevitably leads to the island's heart and soul.

For information on specific trails, try **Hike Maui** (PO Box 330969; Kahului, HI 96732; 879.5270), the **Molokai Ranch Outfitters Center** (PO Box 259; Maunaloa, HI 96770; 800/254.8871), or **Adventure Spirit Hawaii** (PO Box 383104; Waikoloa, HI 96738).

Taxis

Cab service is available on all the islands, but it's not cheap, so first see if there's a shuttle headed your way. You can hail a cab at the airport or look in the yellow pages for local taxi companies. The rate is usually $2 for the first eighth-mile and $2 per mile thereafter, although fares are not regulated and can vary from company to company. Some cab companies charge a flat fee for long distances.

Tours

The top tour operators in the islands are **Robert's Hawaii** (539.9400), **Pleasant Island Holidays** (922.1515), and **Trans-Hawaiian Services** (566.7420). The first two offer vacation packages to Maui, Kauai, and the Big Island from Oahu that include flights, guided bus tours, lodging, and rental cars; the third offers bus tours of Oahu, Maui, Kauai, and the Big Island, but provides no air travel, car, or lodging. Among the sights included in most tours are the active **Kilauea** volcano on the Big Island, sunrise over the dormant **Haleakala Crater** on Maui, and Kauai's dramatic **Waimea Canyon.**

For information on bus, walking, helicopter, and other types of sightseeing tours on each island, see the Orientation sections of the individual island chapters.

Walking

Hawaii's towns are well suited to walking tours. Be it Honolulu or **Kaunakakai, Hilo** or **Hanalei,** there's nowhere too big to explore in a day or two on foot. The only challenge is to slow your pace to Hawaiian time—tortoises will find more to savor in the small tropical towns than hares.

FYI

Accommodations

Peak tourist seasons are from June through August and December through February, when reservations for everything (especially hotel rooms and rental cars) are much harder to come by and more expensive. The rest of the year is considered off-season.

Rates at bed-and-breakfast establishments are often the same or less than those at average hotels, but B&Bs are far more personal and private and often are in remote locations. A prominent bed-and-breakfast referral service is **Hawaii's Best Bed & Breakfast** (Box 563, Kamuela HI 96743, 885.4550, 800/262.9912), run by longtime resident Barbara Campbell.

llas of Hawaii (735.9000) rents luxury homes on hu, Maui, the Big Island, and Kauai for as little as weekend and as long as a month. This can be a rticularly affordable lodging option for families d groups. Most of the homes are on or near cluded beaches and have all the basic amenities d then some; guests often have pools, VCRs, ater-sports equipment, exercise rooms, and tchens with everything from microwaves to arlic presses at their disposal.

ccessibility for the Disabled
he Commission on Persons with Disabilities (86.8121) distributes a guide with accessibility tings for most of the Hawaiian Islands' hotels, nopping centers, beaches, entertainment, and ajor visitor attractions. There's a nominal fee or the three-part guide. The commission also rovides addresses and telephone numbers of upport services on all the islands for visitors rith disabilities.

limate
lawaii has basically two seasons. April through lovember is the warmer period, when the mercury sually hovers in the 75- to 88-degree range although during August and September, the lottest, most humid months, temperatures requently soar into the 90s). The coldest months re December through March, when evening emperatures can dip into the high 50s. The water emperature on all the islands is about 75 to 80 legrees, five degrees cooler during the winter.

Months	Average Temperature (°F)
December-February	78
March-May	80
June-August	85
September-November	82

Drinking
The legal drinking age in Hawaii is 21. In **Waikiki** on Oahu and Lahaina on Maui, the bar action starts at about 10PM and escalates until 2AM every night of the week. Places with cabaret licenses then fill up and stay that way until 4AM. The pace is far sleepier everywhere else. Throughout most of Kauai and the Big Island, bars begin to *close* at 10PM; on Friday and Saturday nights you may find one or two places where you can hang around and sip a beer until 1AM or so—but don't count on it. Grocery and convenience stores sell beer, wine, and liquor seven days a week.

Hours
Opening and closing times for shops, attractions, coffeehouses, tearooms, etc. are listed by day(s) only if normal hours (opening between 8 and 11 AM and closing between 4 and 7 PM) apply. In all other cases, specific hours will be given (e.g., 6AM-2PM, daily 24 hours, noon-5PM).

Money
All of Hawaii's banks take traveler's checks, and most stores and restaurants accept them as cash. For the real thing, there is a plethora of 24-hour ATMs scattered throughout the islands (except on Lanai). Banks are generally open Mondays through Fridays from 8:30AM to 3PM, although some branches stay open later on some days. Common foreign currency can be exchanged at most banks.

Personal Safety
Crime is not a big issue in the islands. That said, visitors should keep in mind that it isn't uncommon for cars at the islands' beach parks to be broken into while their owners are basking on the sand or riding the waves. Also be forewarned that Honolulu's **Hotel Street** area—as close as these islands get to a red light district—is not the best place for an after-dinner stroll (although it's actually more sleazy than dangerous). Finally, be aware that local men in the **Waianae** and **Makaha** areas of western Oahu, resentful of the imposition of the American way of life on Hawaiians, can sometimes be abrasive to tourists.

Publications
The two statewide dailies are *The Honolulu Advertiser* (a morning paper) and the *Honolulu Star-Bulletin* (an afternoon paper). *USA Today* and some other major mainland newspapers are sold in Hawaii also. Visitors can pick up free copies of a handful of weekly publications targeted at them, including *This Week Magazine*, *Drive Guide*, and *Spotlight Hawaii*. Each has editions for all the major islands, available at newsstands and convenience stores.

Honolulu, Aloha, and *Hawaii* are monthly magazines available at most newsstands. The first two cater to residents with features on business, entertainment, and lifestyles; the last targets visitors, covering local festivals, adventure travel, and attractions.

The monthly magazine *Island Lifestyles* is Oahu's primary gay/lesbian publication; it contains lists of events and local resources. Pick it up at **Hula's Bar and Lei Stand** (2103 Kuhio Ave, between Lewers and Kalaimoku Sts, Waikiki, 923.0669), the central gay meeting place on Oahu.

Restaurants
Life in the islands is casual. In most restaurants, men look out of place in a jacket or tie. Reservations are recommended at elegant dining spots, however, particularly during the winter high season (December through February).

Shopping
People from everywhere but the smallest towns will probably find shopping for basic necessities cheaper and easier at home. But when it comes to locally made items, Hawaii really shines. Kona coffee, hardy tropical flower arrangements, koa wood bowls, macadamia nut candies, tropical fruit jelly, muumuus, aloha shirts, and many other locally produced items all make good gifts or souvenirs.

Smoking
No smoking is permitted in Hawaii's public buildings, elevators, or movie theaters, and sections for smokers in island restaurants are rare.

Taxes
The state sales tax, paid in shops and restaurants, is four percent. A hotel tax tacked onto the bill at all lodging places adds 6.17 percent to room rates.

Telephones
The area code for all the Hawaiian Islands is 808. For interisland telephone calls, dial "1" and the area code before the number.

Time Zone
During standard time, it's two hours earlier in Hawaii than on the West Coast and five hours earlier than on the East Coast. Hawaii does not follow Daylight Saving Time (DST), so when the mainland is on DST (the first Sunday in April to the last Sunday in October), Hawaii is three hours behind the West Coast and six hours behind the East Coast.

Tipping
Standard tips are 10 to 20 percent for waiters, waitresses, and bartenders; $2 a day for maids; 10 percent of the fare and $1 per bag for cab driver and $3 to $5 for bellhops, depending on the extent their burden.

Visitors' Information Centers
The Oahu office of the **Hawaii Visitors and Convention Bureau** (**HVCB**; 2270 Kalakaua Ave, No 801, Honolulu, HI 96815, 923.1811; fax 922.8991) is the locus of island information. It's open Mondays through Fridays from 8AM to 4:30PM. For information on other HVCB offices, see the Orientation sections of the individual island chapter

Phone Book

Emergencies
Ambulance/Fire/Police 91
AAA Emergency Road Service.............800/222.435
Poison Control 800/362.358

Visitors' Information
American Youth Hostels.........946.0591 (Oahu only
Better Business Bureau ....941.5222 (Oahu only
Handicapped Visitors' Info. ....586.8121 (Oahu only
Weather ....973.4381 (Oahu only

Parades and Pageants in Paradise

If there's one thing that **Hawaii** residents know how to do, it's celebrate. Perhaps that's because Hawaii is a melting pot of cultures and traditions, or maybe it's simply that with its endless summers, no one can think of any real reason not to. Whatever the reason, the 50th state has more official holidays than any of its 49 counterparts. Following are a few of Hawaii's biggest and brightest events. For details on happenings throughout the state, call the **Hawaii Visitors and Convention Bureau** (923.1811).

January

First Night The streets of **Honolulu** are packed with thousands of residents and visitors ringing in the New Year to the sounds of the top contemporary Hawaiian bands.

NFL Pro Bowl Early in January, the top teams from both conferences kick off the New Year with an all-star game at **Oahu**'s **Aloha Stadium.**

Chinese New Year Repair to **Chinatown** in Honolulu after the first lunar moon (between 21 January and 9 February) for lion dances, a fireworks display, and general merriment.

February

Mauna Kea Ski Meet Weather permitting, Hawaii's skiers take to the slopes of the **Big Island** volcano for this annua downhill race, held on a mid-month Saturday. Visitors may rent equipment and join in the fun. Bring your bikini.

March

Carole Kai Bed Race Teams from local restaurant bars, and businesses compete to see who can pus a bed on wheels over the **Waikiki** finish line first. The madness, which benefits area charities, usual takes place on the third Saturday of the month.

April

Merrie Monarch Festival If you want to understa the deep spirituality of the hula, this **Hilo** event is one to plan a trip around. Lasting for a week at the start of the month, it gives onlookers the chance t see both *auwana* (ancient) and *kahiko* (modern) styles of dance in an awe-inspiring series of night performances. Tickets, though inexpensive, are sc out about a year ahead, so call the **Hawaii Visitors and Convention Bureau** as far in advance as possible.

May

Lei Day "May Day is Lei Day in Hawaii," goes the singsong phrase chanted in playgrounds all over t state. The first of the month is a time to buy leis f your loved ones; the day is celebrated with pagear around the state.

Hawaii State Fair Held in Honolulu on two weeken at the end of the month, this is much like state fairs veryverywhere, except that the refreshments may be unfamiliar. Try the passion-orange-guava juice known as "POG") and *mochi* candy (a deep-fried rice-flour crackers in soy-sauce batter). It's a good opportunity to mingle with island residents on Oahu.

June

Hilo Orchid Society Show This is *the* event in the US for orchid lovers. Hundreds of different varieties is displayed in Hilo's **Edith Kamakawiwoole Stadium** during the third weekend of the month.

O Bon Japanese Festival Candlelight ceremonies and dancing are featured at this Japanese commemoration of the dead, held from the end of June into August throughout the islands. The festivities are especially colorful in **Haleiwa** on Oahu.

July

Run to the Sun Though the grueling 37-mile road race up the side of Maui's 10,023-foot **Haleakala** volcano is not a great spectator sport, it can be fun to hang out in surrounding upcountry towns and greet the hundreds of runners after their ordeal. Would-be participants should pencil in the second Saturday in July.

Parker Ranch Rodeo Hawaiian cowboys are called *paniolos,* but they ride like their mainland counterparts. They show their stuff at this rodeo, which takes place mid-month at the country's second-largest ranch in the Big Island town of **Waimea.**

Prince Lot Hula Festival If you can't attend the **Merrie Monarch Festival** held in Hilo every April, try this event at Oahu's **Moanalua Gardens** on the third Saturday of July. It isn't as big as the April festival, but tickets are easier to get, and you'll come away with insight into the Hawaiian people and their *mana* (spirit).

Volcano Wilderness Marathon The rough-and-tumble wilderness around the Big Island's **Kilauea** volcano is the venue for a marathon and a 10K race, both usually held on the last Saturday of the month. If you've never run a marathon before, we don't suggest that you start with this one.

August

Pan Am Windsurfing Pacific Cup Windsurfing competitions are held at beaches around Oahu throughout the month, depending on wind and wave conditions.

Trans-Pacific Race This LA-to-Honolulu sailboat race takes place during August in odd-numbered years. Yachts arrive throughout the month and converge on the **Ala Wai Yacht Harbor** on Oahu, where the password is "party."

Kona's Hawaiian Billfish Tournament The town of **Kona** on the Big Island teems with activity (an unusual state of affairs here) during the last week of August as sportfishers from the other islands and the West Coast compete.

September

Aloha Week This is big stuff. Buy an Aloha Week ribbon and join in the parades, luaus, pageants, presentations, and other events celebrating the spirit of aloha on all islands. The festivities generally take place in mid-September.

October

Ironman Triathlon Even if your last bike had training wheels, you can barely dog paddle, and the only thing you run is errands, watching the Big Island's **Ironman** competition, particularly at the finish line at about 10PM, is a moving experience. Senior citizens, the disabled, and couples are some of the thousands of people you'll see completing a 26.2-mile run, a 2.4-mile swim, and a 112-mile bike ride in the Kona heat on the first Saturday of the month.

November

Hard Rock Cafe's Triple Crown of Surfing The top dogs on the surf circuit are drawn to the **Banzai Pipeline** and other amazing two-story waves to vie for big money and the chance to wave at Mom on TV. If you're on Oahu for this event (usually during the third week of the month), don't miss it.

Honolulu International Film Festival If you don't mind a few subtitles, the Pacific Rim films screened throughout the islands during this annual event make novel and intermittently dazzling entertainment.

December

Honolulu Marathon The 26.2-mile race between Honolulu and **Hawaii Kai**, held on the second Saturday in December, draws the third-largest field of any marathon in the nation. This wouldn't be a bad choice for a first marathon.

Pacific Handcrafters' Fair For unique Christmas gifts, from flowered muumuus to woven mats to koa wood boxes, head for this crafts fair at **Thomas Square** in Honolulu; it takes place on one of the first two weekends of December.

The Big Island

This southernmost isle is formally known as Hawaii, although it is commonly referred to as the Big Island to avoid confusion with Hawaii, the state. Despite its relatively enormous size—4,038 square miles—this is Hawaii's least-visited major island, with only about 1.09 million tourists a year. The low turnout is probably due to rumors that the island is covered with lava, has no beaches, and offers little or nothing to do. This last may be partly true—party hounds and searching singles will fare much better on Maui or Oahu—but the rest is pure bunk. Lush vegetation covers most of the Big Island's windward side, and uncrowded white-sand beaches line the western coast. Unlike on Kauai, you can lose yourself for days here without seeing another soul; unlike on Oahu, no hordes of tourists or unsavory characters are around; unlike on Maui, nobody will want to sell you time-share deals. And because tourism has such a low impact on the resident population, which depends mostly on agriculture and livestock for income, the locals are particularly warm and receptive to visitors.

As any resident will tell you, the islands of Hawaii are vastly different from each other in character, and the Big Island is often viewed as the introverted sister, quietly earning recognition yet maintaining an unmistakable distance from the family of isles. Once understood and appreciated, however, the Big Island becomes an easy favorite among romantics, recluses, and adventurers.

The Big Island is frequently described as a miniature continent, with rain forests lining the windward coasts in the east, immense snowdrifts resting atop **Mauna Kea** volcano, grassy plains stretching around **Waimea**, and miles of desert and lava beds

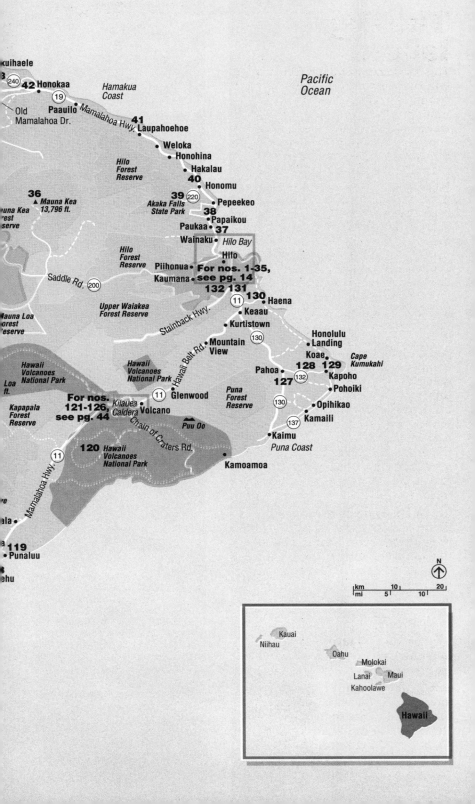

kuihaele

3 (240) **42** Honokaa

(19)

Hamakua
Coast

Pacific
Ocean

Old
Mamalahoa Dr.

Paauilo

Mamalahoa Hwy. **41**
Laupahoehoe

Weloka

Honohina

Hilo
Forest
Reserve

Hakalau

40 Honomu

36 ▲ Mauna Kea
13,796 ft.

una Kea
rest
serve

39 (220)

Akaka Falls
State Park

Pepeekeo

38

Papaikou

Paukaa **37**

Wainaku *Hilo Bay*

Hilo
Forest
Reserve

Piihonua

Hilo

**For nos. 1-35,
see pg. 14**

Kaumana

132 131

Saddle Rd. (200)

130 Haena

(11)

Keaau

Mauna Loa
orest
eserve

Upper Waiakea
Forest Reserve

Kurtistown

Honolulu
Landing

Hawaii
Volcanoes
National Park

Loa
ft.

Hawaii
Volcanoes
National Park

Mountain
View

(130)

Koae

128 129

*Cape
Kumukahi*

Kapapala
Forest
Reserve

**For nos.
121-126,
see pg. 44**

Kilauea
Caldera

Pahoa

127

(132)

Kapoho

Pohoiki

Volcano

Glenwood

Puu Oo

Puna
Forest
Reserve

(130)

Opihikao

Kamaili

(137)

(11)

120 Hawaii
Volcanoes
National Park

Kaimu

Puna Coast

Kamoamoa

(11)

Mamalahoa Hwy.

ala

119

Punaluu

ehu

N
↑

km   10   20
mi   5   10

Kauai
Niihau

Oahu

Molokai

Lanai   Maui

Kahoolawe

Hawaii

dominating the **Kohala Coast**. What is so extraordinary about this environmental diversity is that it can all be witnessed in a leisurely three-hou drive from **Hilo** to **Kailua-Kona** (towns on opposite sides of the island) acros the undeservedly maligned **Saddle Road** (which is actually a quite pleasant, albeit sometimes rough, route).

Geologically, the Big Island, with Hawaii's only active volcanoes, is still in its youth. A little more than a million years old, the landscape has become more defined with erosion yet continues to grow with every volcanic eruption. Of the five volcanoes that make up the island, Mauna Kea would be the tallest in the world if measurements were taken from the ocean floor, and **Mauna Loa,** whose last eruption was in 1984, is the world's largest active volcano. But a significantly smaller volcano, **Kilauea** (pronounced *keel*-oh-*ay*-ah), is the one that always steals the show. In a continual state of eruption since 1983, Kilauea has earned its title as the most active volcano in the world. Located within **Hawaii Volcanoes National Park**, the island's most popular attraction, Kilauea is also home to the Hawaiian fire goddess, a moody spirit known as Madame Pele.

To properly tour this island takes at least one to two weeks, with two or three days devoted to each of its six main regions. Although each section is only a short drive from the others, all six are astoundingly different in climate and scenery, making it possible to condense several unique vacations into one. Start out in Hilo, a rural city ensconced in beautiful rain forests, and don't neglect neighboring **Puna**, an area where mainland refugees and retro-hippies make their home. Then pack up and drive to rustic Waimea, an island anomaly of green pastures, grazing cattle, weathered Hawaiian cowboys, and a few excellent restaurants and shops. Explore quaint and quiet **North Kohala**, then continue down the Kohala Coast to Kona, poking about the dozens of ancient ruins near the most sun-drenched beaches in the country. Head south to remote **Kau**, where the beaches are windswept and dramatic. For a grand finale, explore the Kilauea volcano and stay overnight in the charming town of **Volcano**.

Area code 808 unless otherwise noted.

Getting to the Big Island

Airports

Hilo International Airport

Five miles east of downtown Hilo, this is a small, island-style airport with three attached buildings forming a single terminal. About 65 flights arrive and depart daily; no nonstop mainland flights land here.

Airport Services

Airport Emergencies	934.5801
Information	934.5839
Parking	969.6642

Airlines

Aloha Airlines	935.5771, 800/367.5250
Hawaiian Airlines	326.5615, 800/367.5320

In the 1820s the Hawaiian kingdom's greatest source of revenue was the whaling industry.

Getting to and from Hilo International Airport

By Bus

No public buses or hotel shuttles serve the airport.

By Car

The airport is a 10-minute drive from the heart of Hilo. Upon leaving the airport, turn right on Highway 11 to reach the downtown area; taking a left on **Waianuenue Avenue** will bring you to a handful of streets lined with restaurants and shops. Traffic isn't a problem.

The following car-rental companies have counters at **Hilo International Airport.** They stay open until about a half hour after the last flight of the day lands.

Alamo	961.3343, 800/327.9633
Avis	935.1290, 800/331.1212
Budget	935.6878, 800/527.0700
Dollar	961.6059, 800/421.6868
Hertz	935.2896, 800/654.3131
National/Interrent	935.0891, 800/227.7368

By Taxi
Cabs wait in front of the baggage claim area. Alternatively, call **Ace One Taxi** (935.8303) or **Hilo Harry's Taxi** (935.7091). The fare to Hilo is about $10.

Keahole-Kona International Airport
About 10 miles north of **Kona** on the west side of the island, **Keahole-Kona International Airport** is a typical island airport: slightly larger than a postage stamp and slightly busier than a deserted island. The airport handles about 60 flights a day, most interisland.

Airport Services
Airport Emergencies	329.2855
Information	329.3423
Lost and Found	329.5073
Parking	329.5790

Airlines
Aloha Airlines	935.5771, 800/367.5250
Hawaiian Airlines	326.5615, 800/367.5320
Mahalo Air, interisland	800/277.8333
from the mainland	800/4.MAHALO
United Airlines	800/241.6522

Getting to and from Keahole-Kona International Airport

By Bus
No public buses serve the small airport, but some **Waikoloa** hotels provide transportation for guests.

By Car
After leaving the airport, take a right on **Highway 19** to go south into Kailua-Kona; take a left on Highway 19 to head north to the Waikoloa resorts. Kona is a 15-minute drive away; Waikoloa, 25 minutes. There is no traffic.

The following car-rental companies have counters at **Keahole-Kona International Airport**. They stay open until about a half hour after the last flight of the day lands.

Alamo	329.8896, 800/327.9633
Avis	327.3000, 800/331.1212
Budget	329.8511, 800/527.0700
Dollar	329.3161, 800/421.6868
Hertz	329.3566, 800/654.3131
National/Interrent	329.1674, 800/227.7368

By Taxi
Cabs wait in front of the baggage claim. The fare to Kona is about $20; to Waikoloa, about $40.

Interisland Carriers
Aloha Airlines and **Hawaiian Airlines** offer service between the Big Island and Oahu and Kahului on Maui. **Mahalo Air** has flights between Kona on the Big Island and Oahu and, once a day, Kahului, Maui.

Getting Around the Big Island

Bicycles and Mopeds
Mopeds aren't very common on the Big Island. The shoulders of the roads are very narrow or nonexistent, so be sure you are willing to keep up with traffic (at least 30 mph) on the road that circles the island before checking into the offerings at **DJ's Rentals** (75-5663 Palani Rd, between Alii Dr and Kuakini Hwy, Kailua-Kona, 329.1700). DJ's also rents motorcycles, for $125 a day. **Hawaiian Pedals** (Kona Inn Shopping Village, Kona, 329.2294) rents mountain bikes for $20 to $30 per day. For a cycling vacation, contact **Backroads Bicycle Touring** (801 Cedar St, Berkeley, CA 94710, 510/527.1555).

Buses
The **Hele-On Bus** (961.8744) operates daily from 7AM to 6PM, running from Hilo to **Honokaa**, Waimea, Kau, and Kailua-Kona. Between Hilo and Kona the one-way fare is $5.25; the cost to travel across town is a mere 75 cents. But bus service is very infrequent and inconvenient here—even residents don't use it.

Driving
The Big Island's major roads are smoothly paved and inviting. The main "highway" (if you can call it that) circles the island, with many of the side roads accessible to four-wheel-drive vehicles only. Those who use such a vehicle (available through many island car-rental companies) will have no limits to their explorations. **Saddle Road**, a shortcut across the island, isn't maintained and is designated as off-limits in most car-rental contracts, although the federal government has committed to repaving the road in the next couple of years. Kona has one main street, **Alii Drive**, which runs along the coast; Hilo, a less tourist-oriented town, is set up in a grid pattern. Unless you're four-wheeling, it's hard to get lost on this island. Car-rental companies at the airports are listed above.

Hiking
The prime destination for savvy hikers and backpackers is **Waipio Valley** on the island's north shore and neighboring **Waimanu Valley,** where the number of waterfalls usually exceeds the number of people around to gaze at them. Waimanu Valley is accessible only by foot or kayak, the latter only in the late summer when the sea is gentle. Less ambitious forays may be enjoyed in every corner of the Big Island, including **Hawaii Volcanoes National Park,** whose trails offer varying degrees of exertion and exhilaration.

Limousines
Few people take limos on the island because of its large size and casual atmosphere, but some firms do offer tours, including **A Touch of Class Limousines** (325.0775). Their rate is $83 an hour with a two-hour minimum.

Parking
Parking is no challenge on the Big Island. Metered parking spots cost between 25¢ and $1 per hour in

the towns large enough to warrant them (there's no charge on Sundays). Rarely will drivers need to use metered spaces, though; free parking is available nearly everywhere.

Taxis

It's difficult to hail a taxi here; call **Aloha Taxi** (325.5448) on the Kona or Kohala coasts or **Ace One Taxi** (935.8303) in the Hilo area. The rate is $1.50 when the flag drops and $1.50 for each mile thereafter. Be sure to call at least a half hour before you want to depart—cab drivers run on "Hawaiian time."

Tours

Paradise Safaris (322.2366) runs daily seven-hour tours of the Mauna Kea volcano. A daylong tour that circles the entire Big Island and covers its most popular attractions—**Puuhonua O Honaunau** (Place of Refuge National Park), a coffee plantation, Mauna Kea, a sugarcane plantation, the Kona Coast, **Punaluu Black Sand Beach Park, Parker Ranch,** and a macadamia nut factory—is offered by **Robert's Hawaii** (329.1688). **Kayak Discovery Tours** (328.8911) offers half-day, full-day, and multiday kayak trips along the island's rugged western coastline, as well as boat rental. Alternatively, **Hiilawe Hiking Tours** (327.7842) leads adventurers on three-hour treks through remote Waipio Valley to a thousand-foot waterfall and its sacred pool. **Waipio Valley Shuttle** (775.7121) runs an hour-and-a-half driving tour of the valley in a four-wheel-drive vehicle. **Hawaiian Walkways** (885.7759) offers a variety of daylong hiking tours, including treks in **Hawaii Volcanoes National Park** and the **North Kohala** region. Custom hikes also can be arranged.

Contact **Captain Zodiac** (329.3199) for a four-hour cruise from **Honokohau Harbor** to **Kealakekua Bay.** The boat hugs the coast, giving passengers a chance to see caves and the **Captain Cook Monument** before it stops for snorkeling.

Blue Hawaiian Helicopters (961.5600) at **Hilo International Airport** and **Hawaii Helicopters** (329.4700) at **Keahole-Kona International Airport** offer bird's-eye views of the island. For information on horseback tours of the Big Island, see "Sights from the Saddle" on page 36.

Walking

All towns on the Big Island are small enough to be explored end to end in a day or less. No real hills get in the walker's way either, though the midday heat in the height of summer can make lengthy walks exhausting and unpleasant.

FYI

Shopping

The shop-'til-you-drop strip in Kona is **Alii Drive,** a road that runs for several miles along the coast. There you'll find a collection of coffee and fruit vendors; booths offering muumuus and other alohawear; salespeople hawking tours and excursions; real estate offices; restaurants; and surf shops, T-shirt shops, and shops selling fashions made everywhere from Bali to Tibet.

Hilo's charms are less apparent, but no less engaging. **Prince Kuhio Plaza** on Highway 11 is a shopping mall in the **Waldenbooks/Radio Shack/Orange Julius** tradition. Unless you want a Walkman or a paperback, meander by the souvenir shops and more unusual stores of the bayfront instead. There, in out-of-the-way nooks like **Elsie's Fountain Service** (339 Keawe St, 935.8681), a rustic, century-old lunch counter, you'll get a sense of the elusive real Hawaii.

Tickets

Tickets for most cultural events on the Big Island are available at **Mele Kai Music** in Kona (74-5467 Kaiwi St, between Kuakini and Queen Kaahumanu Hwys, 329.1454) and **Tempo Music** (Prince Kuhio Plaza, Hwy 11, 959.4599) in Hilo.

Visitors' Information Centers

Offices of the **Hawaii Visitors and Convention Bureau (HVCB)** in Hilo (250 Keawe St, at Haili St,

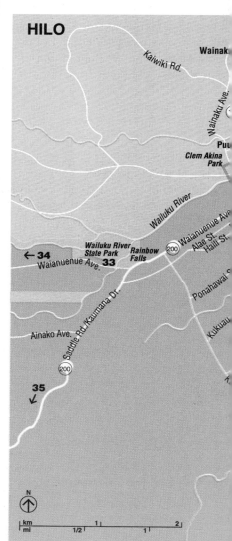

...1.5797; fax 961.2126) and in Kailua-Kona (Kona ...aza, 75-5719 W Alii Dr, between Hualalai and ...lani Rds, 329.7787; fax 326.7563). Both are open ...M to 4:30PM Mondays through Fridays.

...hone Book

...mergencies

...mbulance/Fire/Police	911
...AA Emergency Road Service	800/222.4357
...lo Hospital	961.4111
...ona Hospital	322.9311
...ocksmith	961.3305, 329.8206
...harmacy	959.4508, 329.1632
...olice (nonemergency)	935.3311
...oison Control	800/362.3585

Visitors' Information

Better Business Bureau	941.5222
Handicapped Visitors' Info.	961.8211, 329.5226
Time	961.0212

Hilo

The beaches are small, the shores are rocky, and the climate is wet, but this town—the island's largest, as well as the county seat—is full of beautiful, exotic blooms, has a lively seaport, and is the site of the Merrie Monarch Festival (see "Parades and Pageants in Paradise" on page 8). Hilo has been hit hard twice by tidal waves—in 1946 and in 1960—that heavily damaged the waterfront district. Some of the old architecture remains, however, and a number of new shops have opened over the past few years. In fact, Hilo may be Hawaii's next hot spot.

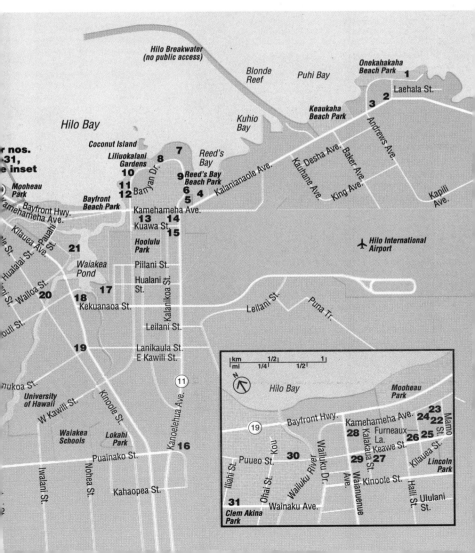

1 Onekahakaha Beach Park With lifeguards, safe swimming (it's protected by a breakwater), small tidal pools, picnic and camping facilities, and plenty of parking, this is the nicest beach in Hilo (especially for small children)—which isn't saying much. On the downside are dingy gray sand and a contingent of local homeless people. True beach lovers will head south for the Puna Coast, but this will do in a pinch. ♦ Onekahakaha Rd (off Kalanianaole Ave)

2 Arnott's Lodge $ Although it isn't listed with American Youth Hostels, this is mainly a backpackers' lodge. Close to the beaches but a long walk from shops and restaurants, the clean and friendly place has three three-bedroom dormitories (one for men, one for women, and one co-ed) that sleep a dozen people each, plus six suites (including kitchens) that sleep three. All rooms and suites have shared baths; none have TVs or phones. There's no restaurant, but guests have free rein of the shared kitchen, a bonus for budget-conscious travelers. ♦ 98 Apapane (between Kalanianaole Ave and Lihikai St). 969.7097, 800/368.8752; fax 961.9638 &

3 Hilo Homemade Ice Cream Ice cream featuring island ingredients is sold here; try the green tea flavor. ♦ 1477 Kalanianaole Ave (near Keokea Loop). 959.5959

4 Harrington's ★★$$$ Local seafood enthusiasts who come for the chowder, catch of the day, or fresh shellfish also get to admire the view of tranquil Reed's Bay. For Hilo, this is as romantic as it gets. ♦ Seafood ♦ Daily dinner. 135 Kalanianaole Ave (between Huipu St and Banyan Dr). 961.4966 &

5 Hilo Seaside Hotel $$ The nicer of the 135 rooms have private lanais overlooking a picturesque lagoon. Nothing fancy here, but the pleasant accommodations have cable TVs and refrigerators. Some rooms are air-conditioned, and there's a good, inexpensive restaurant. ♦ 126 Banyan Way (between Kalanianaole Ave and Banyan Dr). 935.0821, 800/367.7000; fax 969.9195 &

6 Banyan Drive Named for the numerous banyan trees planted here by dignitaries and celebrities during the 1930s, the drive fronts a chain of hotels along Hilo Bay. Plaques at the bases of the trees reveal names such as Babe Ruth and Amelia Earhart. ♦ Between Kamehameha Ave and Lihiwai St

7 Hawaii Naniloa Hotel $$ The best of the limited choices in Hilo, this hotel commands a fine location on Banyan Drive, with views of Hilo Bay. Three wings contain 306 rooms and 19 suites, a health spa, three lounges, and one continental and one Chinese restaurant. The decor is Japanese, with lots of pink marble. ♦ 93 Banyan Dr (between Kamehameha Ave and Kilohana St). 969.3333, 800/367.5360; fax 969.6622 &

7 Uncle Billy's Hilo Bay Hotel $$ Uncle Billy Kimi (who also runs **Uncle Billy's Kona Bay Hotel,** see page 36) believes in keeping prices down at the expense of ambience, hence the lobby video games. The 140 rooms serve their purpose; all have TVs, air-conditioning, and phones. There's a pool, restaurant, and shops. ♦ 87 Banyan Dr (at Kilohana St). 961.5818, 800/442.5841 in Hawaii, 800/367.5102; fax 935.7903 &

8 Hilo Hawaiian Hotel $$ The views from the private lanais of the 268 rooms and 17 suites here are the best in Hilo, and the seafood buffet on Fridays and Saturdays is worth checking out. Baseball legend Babe Ruth planted the banyan tree in front of the hotel. Amenities include a pool, a restaurant, a bar, and shops. ♦ 71 Banyan Dr (between Kilohana and Lihiwai Sts). 935.9361, 800/272.5275 in Hawaii, 800/367.5004; fax 935.4936 &

9 Naniloa Country Club This flat, nine-hole course (par 35, 3,156 yards) is across from the **Hawaii Naniloa Hotel,** whose guests may take advantage of a substantial discount. ♦ Inexpensive greens fees. Daily; call ahead for weekend starting times. 120 Banyan Dr. 935.3000

10 Liliuokalani Gardens Meditation mavens will find solace and harmony in this elaborate 30-acre Japanese garden, a popular picnic site. The manicured grounds contain pagodas, stone lanterns, bridges, and tidal pools. Follow the footpath to tiny Coconut Island for a sweeping view of Hilo Bay. ♦ Lihiwai St (between Kamehameha Ave and Banyan Dr)

11 Nihon Restaurant and Cultural Center ★$$$ Although this authentically decorated Japanese restaurant and art gallery serves decent meals, your best bet is a round of sake and sushi at the lanai bar overlooking Hilo Bay, **Mauna Kea, Mauna Loa,** and **Liliuokalani Gardens.** ♦ Japanese ♦ M-Sa lunch and dinner. Reservations recommended. 123 Lihiwai St (between Kamehameha Ave and Banyan Dr). 969.1133 &

12 Suisan Fish Market Early risers can watch Hilo's fishing fleet unload its catch at what old-timers know as Sampan Harbor. The auctioneer uses a patois of English, Hawaiian, Japanese, and a bit of pidgin. Set the alarm and come experience a thriving bastion of local color. ♦ Free. M-Sa; auction 8AM. Lihiwai St (between Kamehameha Ave and Banyan Dr)

13 K. K. Tei ★$$ This is the Japanese restaurant of choice among many local residents. If you have more than six people in your party, reserve one of the *ozashiki* rooms overlooking the bonsai garden. Try the sukiyaki or the seafood specialties. Entrées range from good to gourmet, so consult your waiter before ordering. ♦ Japanese ♦ Daily dinner. Reservations recommended. 1550 Kamehameha Ave (at Manono St). 961.3791 &

14 Ken's Pancake House ★$$ Located on the way to the airport, this reliable place is the only 24-hour restaurant in Hilo. Have the macadamia-nut pancakes or one of the wild waffle combinations—ask for an order with bananas and macadamia nuts (they're mixed right into the batter). ♦ Cafeteria ♦ Daily 24 hours. 1730 Kamehameha Ave (at Kanoelehua Ave). 935.8711 &

15 Fiasco's $$ The large selection of Mexican, American, Chinese, and Italian food available here should take care of just about any craving you might have, though the quality of the food is touch and go. Treat yourself to one of the house-specialty fajitas. ♦ International ♦ Daily lunch and dinner. Waiakea Square, 200 Kanoelehua Ave (at Kuawa St). 935.7666 &

16 Prince Kuhio Plaza Fashion is a relative term at this $47.5-million shopping complex, which includes **Liberty House, Sears, Hilo Hattie, Safeway, Longs,** and many other retailers. There's not much typically Hawaiian here; this shoppers' haven could be any mainland mall. ♦ Daily. 111 E Puainako St (at Kanoelehua Ave). 959.3555 &

Within Prince Kuhio Plaza:

Dick's Coffee House ★$ In an atmosphere best described as kitschy American with a Hawaiian twist, decent grinds (food) at unbelievably low prices attract a steady stream of local residents. Almost all of the breakfast dishes, including the hefty steak-and-eggs plate, go for less than five bucks. ♦ Coffeehouse ♦ M-Sa breakfast, lunch, and dinner; Su breakfast and lunch. 959.4401 &

Home Style Japanese Cooking

17 Miyo's ★★$ Local Japanese-food aficionados (and Hilo is the town for them) assemble at this popular restaurant at the edge of **Waiakea Pond.** The dining room overlooks the pond, with parks and curved bridges in the distance. Specialties include *soba* (buckwheat noodles), *shabu-shabu* (a cook-it-yourself soup in an earthenware pot), sesame chicken, and broiled salmon. ♦ Japanese ♦ Tu-Sa lunch

and dinner. No reservations. No credit cards accepted. Waiakea Villas, 400 Hualani St (at Mililani St). 935.2273

18 Restaurant Miwa ★★★$$ One of Hilo's best Japanese restaurants is in one of the worst locations—in the corner of dilapidated **Hilo Shopping Center.** The seasonal menu includes Kona crab, Bangkok shrimp, *shabu-shabu* (cook-it-yourself soup), sake-flavored steamed clams, and sushi. Sweet tooths will love the *haupia* (coconut) cream pie. ♦ Japanese ♦ M-Sa lunch and dinner; Su dinner. Hilo Shopping Center, 1261 Kilauea Ave (at Kekuanaoa St). 961.4454

19 Scruffles $ For a real taste of local cuisine, stop at this drive-in, take-out, sit-down eatery where Hilo families and business people munch fish tempura and Korean teriyaki steak. ♦ Oriental/American ♦ Daily breakfast, lunch, and dinner. 1438 Kilauea St (at W Lanikaula St). 935.6664 &

20 Sun Sun Lau ★$ Cantonese fare, including shrimp Canton, cake noodle, and fresh abalone soup, is served in a building optimistically designed for droves of customers. Extensive is the operative word for the dinner menu as well as the selection of "crackseed," a Chinese snack of preserved and seasoned fruits and seeds that's a favorite with local kids. ♦ Chinese ♦ Th-Tu lunch and dinner. 1055 Kinoole St (between Mohouli and Barenaba Sts). 935.2808 &

21 Wailoa Visitor Center At this 10-sided building, the friendly staff will advise you on local activities. Then check out the 24 changing exhibitions on Hawaiian art, history, and culture, and the permanent photographic display of post-tsunami Hilo. ♦ Free. M-F. 200 Piopio St (off Kamehameha Ave). 933.4360 &

22 Royal Siam ★★$ This spotlessly clean, unpretentious little restaurant offers more than 50 consistently good Thai dishes at every spice level from mild to aaaahhhh! The basil chicken and yellow curry beef are especially good. ♦ Thai ♦ M-Sa lunch and dinner. 70 Mamo St (between Kamehameha Ave and Keawe St). 961.6100 &

23 Hilo Farmers Market Local color abounds at this festive fair. Come early for the best buys on fresh vegetables, flowers and plants, baked goods, and arts and crafts from more than 80 vendors. Truly an ethnic bonanza, the market offers *malasadas* (Portuguese doughnuts), pickled turnips, *warabi* (fern shoots), orchids, winged beans, papayas, and various other exotic items. A number of well-known Big Island artists got their start right here. ♦ W, Sa 6AM-2PM. Kamehameha Ave and Mamo St &

24 Reuben's Mexican Restaurant ★$ When you gotta have it, you gotta have it. Hilo's only Mexican restaurant serves such classic south-of-the-border fare as chicken *flautas* (fried corn tortillas) and steak ranchero. With festive posters on the walls and colorful tissue paper covering the ceiling, every day here is a fiesta. ♦ Mexican ♦ Daily lunch and dinner. 336 Kamehameha Ave (between Mamo St and Furneaux La). 961.2552

24 Cafe Pesto ★★★$$ Pro-tourism Hilo bureaucrats would like to see more of these. A chic yuppie pizzeria, this restaurant has all the trimmings, including an open kitchen, wood-fired oven, black-and-white decor, and an outstanding menu. Try the artichoke pizza with fresh shiitake and oyster mushrooms and rosemary-gorgonzola sauce. If you're celebrating, splurge on an order of chili-anise-glazed chicken. ♦ Pacific Regional ♦ Daily lunch and dinner. 308 Kamehameha Ave (between Mamo St and Furneaux La). 969.6640 &. Also at: Kawaihae Center (off Hwy 270), Kawaihae. 882.1071 &

25 Pescatore ★★$$$ Upscale Northern Italian dishes are served at upscale prices. Start with the *calamari fritti* (fried squid) and then dive into the *fra diavolo* (shrimp, clams, and fresh fish in a garlic and basil marinara sauce). Oil paintings and chandeliers add character to the intimate setting. ♦ Northern Italian/Seafood ♦ Daily lunch and dinner. Reservations recommended. 235 Keawe St (at Furneaux La). 969.9090 &

26 Spencer's Fitness Center Has wet weather spoiled your jogging schedule? Sweat out your frustration on Spencer's treadmills or Stairmasters, then lift some weights—and hit the beach to recover. ♦ M-F 5AM-9PM, Sa 5AM-3PM, Su 6AM-noon. 197 Keawe St (at Haili St). 969.1511

27 Satsuki ★$ The Japanese/Hawaiian cuisine here is done with better taste than the interior decorating, but at such low prices, who cares? Always packed with locals (an auspicious sign at any restaurant), this is a sure bet for oxtail soup fans. ♦ Japanese/Hawaiian ♦ W-Sa lunch; M, W-Su dinner. 168 Keawe St (between Haili and Kalakaua Sts). 935.7880 &

28 Sig Zane Designs Designer Sig Zane takes simple Hawaiian motifs such as ti, breadfruit, or taro leaves and prints them on fabrics to create islandwear that is both elegant and educational. Each T-shirt, aloha shirt, muumuu, and pareu (wraparound skirt) imparts the spirit of Hawaii. Zane's wife, Nalani Kanaka'ole, is a revered hula master. Two dozen artists also exhibit their work at this blue-awninged shop. ♦ M-Sa. 122 Kamehameha Ave (at Kalakaua St). 935.7077 &

28 Lehua's Bay City Bar & Grill ★★$$ This is Hilo's hippest gathering place (which isn't saying much) for lunch, dinner, and after hours. The friendly staff delivers excellent soups (especially the clam chowder) and burgers to your table at lunch. And for dinner there's spinach lasagna, grilled prawns and chicken, fresh fish, scampi, and vegetarian entrées. The nightclub offers occasional live entertainment, mostly on weekends, and now offers Internet access to patrons. ♦ American ♦ Daily lunch and dinner. 90 Kamehameha Ave (at Waianuenue Ave). 935.8055 &

29 Bears' Coffee ★$ Always bustling, this classic establishment (pictured above) offers Belgian waffles, eggs, croissants, muffins, bagels, deli sandwiches, and salads, along with espresso and other coffee favorites. You'll be in good company if you begin your morning here. ♦ Coffeehouse ♦ M-Th 7AM-5PM, F-Sa 7AM-10:30PM. 106 Keawe St (at Waianuenue Ave). 935.0708 &

30 Wild Ginger Inn $ Simple, clean, and inexpensive, this hotel offers 22 rooms and two suites, coin-operated washers and dryers, and a complimentary breakfast buffet, but no restaurant, pool, or TVs (except in the suites). It's conveniently located two blocks from downtown Hilo. No smoking is allowed. ♦ No credit cards accepted. 100 Puueo St (between the Wailuku River and Kou). 935.5556, 800/882.1887; fax 969.1225 &

31 Dolphin Bay Hotel $ Economical and clean, this 19-unit hotel (including one two-bedroom suite) is one of Hilo's best-kept secrets. The rooms are plain but inviting, and the grounds feature a dense tropical forest and a profusion of banana trees, orchids, and ginger plants. There are four types of units in the two-story walk-up, most with a full kitchen, an *ofuro*-type bathtub (deep, with a seat), a TV set, and fans. Although there's no air-conditioning or restaurant, and the telephone is in the lobby, you'll love the convenient location, intimate ambience, and friendly banter with owners Margaret, John, and Larry Alexander. ♦ 333 Iliahi St (between Puueo St and Wainaku Ave). 935.1466; fax 935.1523 &

Lyman Museum and Mission House

32 Lyman Museum and Mission House
Built in 1839 for the Reverend David Lyman and his wife, Sarah, the **Mission House** (pictured above) was among the first wood-frame structures in Hilo. You can see the Lymans' 19th-century furnishings and clothing on guided tours offered seven times daily. The adjoining **Lyman Museum** ♿, completed in 1971, is one of Hawaii's least exhausting museums. One gallery features a *pili*-grass house, *kapa* (bark cloth), and artifacts of Hawaii's ethnic groups; another room displays volcanic and mineral formations, including land shells. There's a 15-minute video about the **Mission House. ♦** Admission. M-Sa. 276 Haili St (at Kapiolani St). 935.5021

33 Rainbow Falls Early risers can watch as the sun peeks over the mango trees, forming a rainbow in the mist of the thundering falls that cascade 80 feet into the Wailuku River gorge. With an average discharge of 300 million gallons a day, it's the No. 1 waterfall in terms of sheer water production/volume in the state. The path to the left of the parking lot leads to a secluded overlook. ♦ Wailuku River State Park, Rainbow Dr (off Waianuenue Ave)

34 Boiling Pots The spectacular collection of small waterfalls and pools on the way to Rainbow Falls is worth at least one picture. Take the short (but steep) footpath to the right of the point for a closer look, but resist the temptation to swim—many have drowned here. ♦ Wailuku River State Park, Peepee Falls St (off Waianuenue Ave), Piihonua

35 Kaumana Caves In 1881 a huge lava flow from Mauna Loa cooled on the surface and crusted over a flowing tube of molten lava. When the eruption ceased, the lava tube drained and these caves (supposedly radiation-proof) were the result. Seasoned spelunkers will bring flashlights to examine the modern-day petroglyphs, while the timid turn around at the mouth of the caves to gawk at the view looking out. ♦ Kaumana Dr (Hwy 200, between Akala and Akolea Rds), Kaumana

Between Hilo and Waimea

36 Mauna Kea A dormant volcano, "White Mountain" rises 13,796 feet above sea level (and is the tallest mountain in the world when measured from the ocean floor). Inactive for more than 4,000 years, its peak now boasts the cleanest, most rarefied air on earth. The entire northern sky and more than 90 percent of the southern sky can be viewed from this spot, which is why nine countries have observatories here (it's the largest concentration of observatories in the world).

The uppermost slopes are generally covered with snow from January through May. Weather permitting, it's quite possible to ski the mountain early in the day and return to your hotel in time for a sunset swim. There's even a **Ski Association of Hawaii** (no phone), whose members you'll recognize by their "Ski Hawaii" T-shirts. You won't find lift lines here—there are no ski lifts. Instead, skiers drive 20 miles up a paved road through black lava and cinder cones to reach the snow (which generally starts at 11,000 feet) and then continue on foot about a half mile to the start of several trails. Skiers must arrange to have a vehicle meet them at the bottom of one of the three- to five-mile runs, so they can get back up the mountain again.

Mainland skiers note: Not only are there no lifts, there's no snow-covered lodge with après-ski drinking here. The gritty texture of the snow is a lot like sand; locals call it "pineapple powder." The long and fast ski runs are natural, with snow depths generally ranging from five to six feet. Hardly a technical challenge for experienced skiers, but not a beginner's mountain either because of the high altitude and unique (sometimes rocky/crusty/steep) terrain, the volcano is skied simply because it's there. **Poi Bowl,** a quarter-mile-wide stretch starting at the summit, is excellent for beginners, while the other runs are steeper and more challenging. If you're interested in skiing a volcano, contact **Ski Guides Hawaii** (Box

1954, Kamuela, HI 96743, 885.4188) for guides, transportation, and equipment rental.

The **Mauna Kea Observatory** offers free tours at the summit on Saturday and Sunday afternoons at 2PM (participants must be at least 16 years of age). Reservations are not required, but you'll need a four-wheel-drive vehicle to get to the observatory. Call **Mauna Kea Support Services** (935.3371) on weekdays for information. If you don't have the requisite vehicle, you can visit the **Onizuka Visitor Center** (961.2180), 9,000 feet up Mauna Kea, Thursdays through Tuesdays at 7PM for a free lecture and a chance to look through an 11-inch telescope. ♦ Off Saddle Rd (Hwy 200)

37 Mamalahoa Highway Scenic Drive If you're not in a rush, take this scenic drive into the past. Beginning at Wainaku Avenue on the north side of Hilo, occasional signs will direct you to the old wooden-bridged road called the Mamalahoa Highway (Hwy 19). Pass the hot surfing spot called Honolii, then turn onto the four-mile Onomea Bay Scenic Route, overlooking the bay where sailing ships anchored during the 19th century. At one time, sugarcane trains and bullock carts going to markets and mills were the main vehicles on this rural road. Before you get back on the main highway and head north along the Hamakua Coast toward Waimea, linger at Akaka Falls (see page 21), a 420-foot waterfall into a verdant gorge just off Route 220, near the delightfully archaic town of Honomu, once a hub of the sugar industry. The distance from Hilo to Waimea is about 60 miles, approximately an hour and 15 minutes driving time.

38 Hawaii Tropical Botanical Gardens Some say this 20-acre rain forest and nature preserve is the most beautiful place in Hawaii; take the self-guided walking tour on the 1.25-mile trail to decide for yourself. Daniel J. Lutkenhouse, a retired California trucking executive who had long been charmed by Hilo's rain forests, bought the property, which was a junkyard, and formally opened the gardens to the public in 1984. The tour takes between one and two hours, with labels providing informative trivia about some of the 2,000 endemic and imported plants; visitors also can simply stroll around the large lily and koi (carp) pond, giant mango trees, pungent guava orchard, or the huge Alexander palms. The exotic plants come from as far away as Fiji, Peru, Madagascar, and Indonesia. Cars are not allowed inside the gardens—a shuttle bus transports nature lovers from the visitors' center to the entrance every 20 minutes from 9:10AM to 4:30PM. A gift shop on the property is open from 8:30AM to 5PM on weekdays. Parking and rest rooms are available, but bring mosquito repellent and wear comfortable shoes. ♦ Admission. M-F. Onomea Bay Scenic Rte (off Mamalahoa Hwy), Onomea. 964.5233

Go Fish!

Unlike many deep-sea fishing excursions, which take hours to reach prime fishing spots, the action begins minutes after your boat departs the dock at **Kailua-Kona,** since some of the best fishing waters in Hawaii are within a mile or two off the **Kona** coast. On charter trips, no previous experience is necessary, since the captain provides all the equipment, plus expert advice and cheerful assistance for even the most inept of anglers. All you need to bring is food, drink, and sunscreen (fishing licenses aren't necessary). And leave the fish bag at home—the captain has first choice of the catch, and he usually sells it at the market. (What would you do with a hundred-pound tuna?) Half-day charters leave just after sunrise and return by noon; all-day trips are back in time for cocktails. Parties of up to six people can hire charters (with a captain and first mate) for their exclusive use, or you can share boats by paying on a per-person basis.

One excellent service (and the island's oldest) is the **Kona Charter Skippers Association** (75-5663 Palani Rd, at Alii Dr, Kailua-Kona. 329.3600, 800/762.7541; fax 334.0941), which books 30- to 54-foot boats.

Other reliable charter-boat companies include **Kona Activities Center** (329.3171, 800/367.5288; fax 326.7664) and **Charter Locker** (326.2553; fax 329.7590).

39 Akaka Falls State Park What sets the 420-foot **Akaka Falls** and its 100-foot companion, **Kahuna Falls,** apart from other waterfalls is the lush 65-acre park that surrounds them, an area celebrated in ancient chants and contemporary love songs. Plants and flowers from all over the world—sprays of orchids, groves of bamboo, carpets of moss, bougainvillea bushes, gingers, azaleas, ferns, and countless other exotic plants—create the dense rain forest atmosphere. The moist air and soothing roar of the waterfalls accompany you on the 20-minute walk along the paved circular path. ♦ At the end of Hwy 220 (off Hwy 19)

40 Kolekole Beach Park Follow the sign on Highway 19 to **Kolekole Beach Park** (turn off on the *mauka,* or mountain, side), and your reward will be a cool (make that cold) freshwater pond fed by **Kolekole Falls.** Also on hand are a playing field and two picnic pavilions; camping is allowed, but a permit is required (call 961.8311). ♦ Off Hwy 19 (just north of Honomu)

41 Laupahoehoe Beach Park On this pleasant, grassy peninsula is a memorial to the 20 students and four teachers who lost their lives here in the 1946 tidal wave. The park is on the former site of Laupahoehoe village, which was moved to higher ground overlooking the point. Picnics and camping are allowed but there's no swimming. ♦ Off Hwy 19 (Laupahoehoe Point exit)

42 Honokaa Trading Company Browse through this 2,200-square-foot emporium of Hawaiiana, and you never know, you may come away with anything from a $4 Kona Bottling Works bottle to a $1,600 set of menus used on the first steamship trips to the islands. ♦ Daily. Mamane St (off Mamalahoa Hwy), Honokaa. 775.0808

42 Hotel Honokaa Club ★$ Big Islanders dine at the club (pictured above) when lobsters are in season, since the succulent crustaceans are fresh and inexpensive here. The other fare is decent and standard—steak, seafood platters—but the decor doesn't get much fancier than vinyl tablecloths and a TV in the corner. This is not the most chic place (it's strangely lit and generally weird, as is the hotel of the same name), but it's very affordable and loaded with local color. ♦ Local/Seafood ♦ Tu-Su breakfast, lunch, and dinner. No reservations. Mamane St (off Mamalahoa Hwy), Honokaa. 775.0678

42 Tex Drive Inn ★$ You'd probably drive right by this place if you didn't know how good the *malasadas* are here. These Portuguese doughnuts from heaven are best eaten hot, so don't procrastinate. If you're still hungry, try the pork plate with mashed potatoes; the meat is so tender you can cut it with a plastic fork. ♦ Country-style ♦ Daily breakfast, lunch, and dinner. Pakalana St (between Mamalahoa Hwy and Mamane St), Honokaa. 775.0598 Ꮿ

42 Big Island Macadamia Nut Co. Watch through the large windows of this processing plant as macadamia nuts are made into various snacks. The kernels are separated from their hard brown shells, roasted in coconut oil, and then packed (unless, that is, they're first smothered in chocolate, baked into cookies, or blended into jams). ♦ Free. Daily. Lehua St (three-quarters of a mile north of Mamane St), Haina. 775.7743

43 Waipio Valley Artworks A showcase for 100 Big Island artists, this shop offers a pleasing mix of paintings, native-wood carvings and bowls, sculpture, furniture, and crafts. The hand-painted T-shirts and other works employ Hawaiian motifs. The adjoining cafe specializes in ice cream. ♦ Daily. Old Government Rd, Kukuihaele. 775.0958, 800/492.4746

44 Waipio Valley The Hamakua Coast ends at the Big Island's largest valley, which has a resident population of about 40. According to oral tradition, this valley was once home to 40,000 Hawaiians. Before Captain Cook arrived, it was the cultural and political hub of the island. Some locals know it as the "Valley of the Kings" or "The Land of Curving Water." Ancient temple sites, stone terraces, waterfalls, and steep valley walls make this an inspiring stop for those with four-wheel-drive vehicles or the tenacity to hike down and back. Make friends with the locals and they may take you to Hiilawe, the awesome waterfall at the back of the valley. The few taro farmers who remain, survivors of the 1946 tsunami, proudly cling to a lifestyle immortalized in the songs and chants of ancient Hawaii. ♦ Hwy 240 (just west of Kukuihaele)

44 Waipio Hotel $ Whether you're a bank executive or a Deadhead, nothing equals the original Waipio Valley hostelry if you like roughing it. Octogenarian Tom Araki's barrackslike "hotel" is a five-room haven without phones, hot water, or even electricity. Bring your own food (there's no restaurant); everything else is provided—gas lamps, taro fields, waterfalls, wild horses, and the pleasure of Tom's company (alone worth the price of your stay). ♦ No credit cards accepted. Waipio Valley. 775.0368

For an up-to-date report on Kilauea's lava flow, call the Big Island Park Service's information line at 967.7977.

44 Waipio Treehouse $$$ Linda Beech's establishment is an exotic lodging option: a one-room cabin suspended 30 feet above ground in a monkeypod tree (pictured above), with one double and one single bed, a refrigerator, hot plates, electricity, and running water . . . all the comforts of a tree house. A waterfall and mountain pool are just down the trail, and a Japanese hot tub bubbles nearby. Standard rental cars can't make it down to the Waipio Valley, but transportation is provided. One warning: For a couple of days every year the cottage is inaccessible because of high river water. If guests are stranded, their accommodations during the delay are complimentary. This is a good base for wagon and horseback-riding tours. No TV or telephones. Another unit, a three-bedroom house on the ground, also is available. ♦ Off Hwy 240, Waipio Valley. 775.7160; fax 775.7160

45 Old Mamalahoa Drive If you have some leisure time, take this little-known scenic drive parallel to Highway 19. The extreme diversity of vegetation that can be seen in the 12 miles from east to west provides a splendid overview of the island's plant life. ♦ From Honokaa, take the Ahualoa exit off Hwy 19

Kona coffee, named for the Big Island region it's primarily harvested in, is the only java grown commercially in the United States. Like Hawaii's sugarcane and pineapple planters, however, Kona coffee growers are slowly succumbing to cheaper labor costs overseas. There are about 650 small farms in Kailua-Kona (producing $4 million a year in revenue), but in Napoopoo, where several coffee mills and competing wholesalers used to thrive, only one mill remains in operation. Because of the high cost of picking beans by hand and the limited number of places with suitable growing conditions, connoisseurs anticipating a cup of real Kona coffee may be disappointed to find that it's relatively expensive and frequently a blend, even in the islands.

Restaurants/Clubs: Red
Shops/ ♀ Outdoors: Green
Hotels: Blue
Sights/Culture: Black

Waimea

Checkered with funky-looking buildings, grazing horses and cattle, and stately homes of the landed gentry, Waimea is a friendly town. Its 2,500-foot elevation provides a cool, crisp climate that's refreshing after the hot beaches of **West Hawaii**. **Mauna Kea** looms in the distance, flower and vegetable farms abound, and *paniolos* (cowboys) in boots and hats add a real Western flavor. Volcanic cinder cones long covered by greenery are dotted with livestock. Few people realize that Hawaii's *paniolos* (the word is derived from *"español"*) predate the American West, having come from Spain and Mexico at the request of Kamehameha III in the 1830s to teach Hawaiians how to ride, rope, and herd cattle. Today, Hawaiian cowboys may be Filipino, Portuguese, Chinese, Japanese, or a mixture of some or all of the above.

Waimea is cowboy country thanks to John Parker, a seaman from New England who jumped ship in 1809, settled on the Big Island, and domesticated a herd of wild cattle that belonged to Kamehameha the Great. The king, who gave Parker some land in return, had a granddaughter whom Parker conveniently married and voilà—the **Parker Ranch** dynasty was born. Today the ranch, which is open to visitors, consists of 225,000 acres with more than 55,000 head of cattle.

Note: To avoid confusion with the town of Waimea on Kauai, the post office address for this town is **Kamuela**, Hawaiian for Samuel (after John Parker's grandson Samuel). To get to Waimea from **Kona** take Highway 19 or 190 north for 39 miles; from Hilo take Highway 19 north for 59 miles.

46 Parker Ranch Visitor Center and Museum A video shows the history of the 225,000-acre **Parker Ranch,** the second-largest ranch in the US, and describes the life of the Hawaiian cowboys. Parker family memorabilia and photographs are on display. You can tour the ranch, visit its original two-acre homestead, or walk through owner Richard Smart's historic 1947 home, **Puuopelu**, where his extensive art collection is displayed. ♦ Admission. Daily. Parker Ranch Shopping Center (off Mamalahoa Hwy, near Kawaihae Rd). 885.7655 ♿

47 Waimea Country Lodge $$ This hostelry—the closest thing to a motor lodge in the islands—has 21 spartan rooms, five equipped with kitchenettes. There's no restaurant or pool. ♦ 65-1210 Kawaihae Rd (just west of Mamalahoa Hwy). 885.4100; fax 885.6711 ♿

48 Edelweiss ★★$$$ Chef/owner Hans-Peter Hager's restaurant is a small place (only 15 tables) in a *paniolo*-style setting of open beams, but on any given night the 14 to 18 house specials range from roast duck to venison to a superb rack of lamb basted in garlic, mustard, and herbs. Also recommended is the Wiener schnitzel. Homemade Bavarian pudding, cheesecake, and fruit pies are worthy finales. No reservations are accepted, so expect long lines. ♦ Continental ♦ Tu-Sa lunch and dinner. Kawaihae Rd (between Lindsey and Opelo Rds). 885.6800

49 Parker Square Browsing through the shops in this mini-mall without making a purchase is virtually impossible. Start at **Gallery of Great Things** (885.7706), with its wild collection of museum-quality artifacts from Hawaii, Indonesia, Papua New Guinea, and elsewhere in the Pacific, including tribal jade carvings, chopsticks made of exotic woods, Indonesian baskets, koa furniture, coconut-fiber hats, and handmade jewelry. Work your way toward **Bentleys** (885.5565), a shop that specializes in ceramics and tableware (the Christmas display is unbelievable) but also carries gifts and accessories from around the world. Save some room on your credit card for the **Waimea General Store** (885.4479), which carries patterns for Hawaiian quilts and needlepoint, as well as pillow kits, yarn, and how-to books. ♦ Daily. Kawaihae Rd (between Lindsey and Opelo Rds)

50 Kamuela Inn $ This is definitely the nicer of the two hotels in Waimea and less expensive to boot. Each of the 32 cozy rooms and suites has a private bath and cable TV; some have telephones. The best rooms have full kitchens. Complimentary continental breakfast is served on the hotel's lanai. Although there's no restaurant, the other amenities combine to make this inn a nice place to lay over in Waimea. ♦ 65-1300 Kawaihae Rd (at Opelo Rd). 885.4243, 800/555-8968; fax 885.8857

Merriman's

51 Merriman's ★★★$$$ The atmosphere here is tropical, with floral-patterned carpet and a banana tree mural. Owner and former chef Peter Merriman pioneered Hawaii's regional cuisine, and his innovative use of seaweed and Big Island–raised beef, lamb, and veal is legendary. The mahimahi and *ono* (wahoo) are in his kitchen soon after they're caught; the veal is raised in Waimea, the goat cheese made in Puna, and the strawberries and tomatoes grown down the road. Specialties include wok-charred *ahi* (tuna), Kahua lamb, *lokelani* ("rose from heaven") tomato salad, and passion-fruit mousse. ♦ Hawaiian ♦ M-F lunch; daily dinner. Reservations recommended. Opelo Plaza, Kawaihae Rd (at Opelo Rd). 885.6822 ♿

52 Waimea Garden Cottage $$ Owner/host Barbara Campbell (who worked for more than 20 years at the **Kona Village Resort**) has perfected the art of hospitality in her lovely two-room bed-and-breakfast establishment overlooking the Waimea hillsides. A longtime resident of Waimea, she has surrounded her streamside cottage with geraniums, ferns, roses, and day lilies. A graceful willow tree stands in the front yard, and a small henhouse sits across the lawn. There's also a fireplace and a full kitchen with a stocked refrigerator. Although not for the budget traveler, this is definitely one of the nicest bed-and-breakfasts on the island. ♦ No credit cards accepted. A three-night minimum stay is required. Off Kawaihae Rd (just past the 59-mile marker). 885.4550, 800/262.9912; fax 885.0559

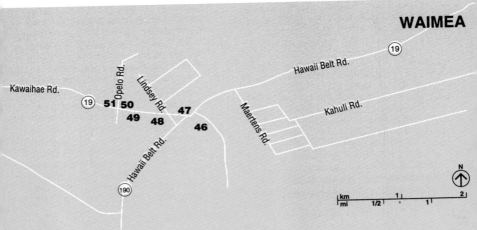

WAIMEA

An Island Gone Nuts

A native of Queensland, Australia, the macadamia was originally known as the "bush nut" and was generally considered more trouble than it was worth to eat (because of its tough shell). The nut was named after Australian chemist John Macadam by his friend Baron Mueller, the botanist who first identified the genus in 1857. The tree that produces the nut was first brought to Hawaii in the late 1800s. At that time, the trees were valued for their ornamental aspects (many species have spiked leaves, similar to holly, that are used as holiday decorations). By 1921 the macadamia's commercial potential as a snack food was seen, and the first plantation was established near **Honolulu**. Sixty years later, over 29 million pounds of nuts were being harvested on the islands annually—almost all for export.

The macadamia tree, a subtropical evergreen that can grow as tall as 100 feet, is slow to bear fruit.

The first harvest appears in five years, and the tree reaches its peak of productivity in 15 years, when it yields an average of 25 to 30 pounds of nuts (in the shell) each season.

The meat of a macadamia nut is protected by two layers: a green, oval outer covering lined with a shell s tough it's hard to break without crushing the tender nut. Its long maturation period and limited supply contribute to the macadamia's steep price, but the crisp, white nut holds its own among snack-nut competitors. In recent years it has become an increasingly popular ingredient in candies, cookies, and ice cream.

For a firsthand look at how macadamias are made into various treats, visit the **Big Island Macadamia Nut Co.** in Haina on the Bi Island. They'll even give you free, freshly roasted samples (see page 21 for details).

53 Kamuela Museum Hawaii's largest privately owned and most unorthodox museum was founded by Big Island native Albert K. Solomon, who claims that when he was eight years old his grandmother predicted he would open a museum. It took several decades, but he proved her right. Opened in 1968 by the former Honolulu policeman and his wife, Harriet, the museum ranks somewhere between an institution and a weekend flea market. Undocumented and unorganized, there's everything from Japanese machine guns to ancient Hawaiian feather money and even an old Model-T tire remover. ◆ Admission. Daily. Kawaihae Rd (at Kohala Mountain Rd), Waiaka. 885.4724

North Kohala

Remote and quiet, this small peninsula has the kind of tiny towns with quaint, tumbledown buildings that capture the imagination and give you a sense of how the Big Island once was. This is rain forest country, with plenty of chilly, wet days. But when the sun shines, there's no place finer.

54 Ohana Pizza and Beer Garden $ The highlight here isn't the food, which is okay at best, but the customers. For a real taste of life in Hawi, grab a stool, order a draft and a slice, and watch. Even better, if you're there late on a weekend, hang out at the bar, open until 1AM. ◆ Pizzeria ◆ Daily dinner. No reservations. Hwy 270 (near Kohala Mountain Rd), Hawi. 889.5888

54 Bamboo Restaurant and Gallery ★★ $$$ One of those spots the locals won't tell

you about, fearing its ruination, Bamboo is ar outpost of island ambience not often found in the 50th state. Hawaiian "aunties" make diners feel at home in the wood-paneled, flower-filled restaurant, which shares a storefront with an enticing art gallery. This is a fine dining establishment Hawaiian style, featuring such entrées as blackened *ahi* (tuna and chicken skewers. ◆ Hawaiian Regional ◆ Tu-Sa lunch and dinner, Su brunch. Try to go on a night when a local hula *halau* (school performs free from 7PM to 8PM. Off Hwy 27 Hawi. 889.5555 ら

55 Original King Kamehameha I Statue This statue may have a less dazzling setting than the replica across from **Iolani Palace** on Oahu, but its history is much richer. For $10,000, American sculptor Thomas R. Gould was commissioned in 1878 by the Hawaiian legislature to create a statue of the mighty warrior king for the centennial of Captain Cook's arrival in Hawaii. As the model for Kamehameha, Gould used a photograph of Honolulu businessman John Baker, a close friend of King Kalakaua, who posed in loincloth feather cloak, spear, and helmet.

Gould's clay figure was finished in Florence, Italy; sent to Paris for bronze casting; and eventually shipped to Hawaii. As it neared Cap Horn, the ship burned and sank, carrying the statue to the bottom of the sea. Gould agreed to make another statue for $7,500. This one reached Honolulu intact and was unveiled on 14 February 1883, during Kalakaua's coronation. A few weeks later, the original Kamehameha statue arrived in Honolulu on a

British ship whose skipper had bought it for $500 from a salvage yard. The skipper's asking price was $1,500. Since one hand was broken off and the spear was missing, Kalakaua talked him down to $875 and then had the statue repaired and sent to the sleepy town of Kapaau, where Kamehameha was born. The Honolulu statue is more fanciful, but many think the original is a more appropriate homage to the great Kamehameha. ◆ Off Hwy 270 (in front of the Kapaau Courthouse), Kapaau

56 Keokea Beach Park This picturesque white-sand beach is popular on weekends but during the week is usually vacant. The surf is good for swimming when the tide is low. There are picnic facilities. ◆ Off Hwy 270 (3.5 miles east of Kapaau), Niulii

57 Pololu Valley Lookout and Trail The view of a taro farming valley is surpassed only by the switchback trail (a 15-minute walk) through tunnels of *pandani* shrubs to a black-sand beach. Good swimmers will love the waves, but there are no lifeguards or facilities. ◆ At the end of Hwy 270, Makapala

58 Lapakahi State Historical Park This semirestored fishing village dates back 600 years. Take the self-guided tour among the stone-house sites, canoe sheds, fishing shrines, and stone games. Learn about local legends, fishing customs and techniques, salt gathering, and the prosperous, simple life of Hawaiians centuries ago. ◆ Free. Daily. Just west of Hwy 270, Mahukona

59 Kawaihae Center This collection of boutiques makes a great rest stop on your way to Kona or Hawi. Stop by the **Tres Hombres Beach Grill** (882.1031) any day at lunch or dinner for a margarita and Mexican appetizers after browsing through the unusual clothing, much of it Indonesian batik, at **Borderlines** (882.1577) and before spending an hour or so perusing the paintings and sculpture in the upscale **Kohala Kollection** (882.1510). ◆ Daily. Off Hwy 270, Kawaihae

59 Puukohola Heiau National Historic Site Measuring 224 feet by 100 feet, this fortress-like structure is the largest *heiau* (temple) in Hawaii. It is a marvel of engineering, with waterworn lava rocks and boulders set together without mortar. Built in 1790 by King Kamehameha, it's a powerful reminder of the role of human sacrifice in the ancient Hawaiian religion. A prophecy of the time held that Kamehameha would conquer and unite the islands if he erected a temple to his family war god on the hill at Kawaihae, a prophecy fulfilled after the erection of **Puukohola.** Kamehameha invited his arch rival to the temple's dedication ceremony in 1791, and then offered him up as a sacrifice. The *heiau* itself is not accessible, but visitors can walk around the 77-acre site and stop at the visitors' center. ◆ Free. Daily. Off Hwy 270 (just north of Hwy 19). 882.7218

Within the Puukohola Heiau National Historic Site:

Samuel M. Spencer Beach Park This white-sand beach offers the best and safest swimming along the North Kohala Coast, as well as good snorkeling and spearfishing. Picnic, camping, and tennis facilities make this a popular spot for families.

Kohala Coast

The northwest edge of the Big Island, the Kohala Coast has something of a split personality. It has some of the most beautiful white-sand beaches on the island, but there are also barren fields of black lava that come as a surprise to many vacationers, although some come to understand and appreciate their stark beauty. This is also called the **Gold Coast,** as numerous tourists flock to the hotels that line the shore.

60 Mauna Kea Beach Hotel $$$$ On his first visit here, Merv Griffin proclaimed, "Now I know where old Republicans come to die." Built in 1965 by Laurance Rockefeller, this property set the standard for super-luxury resorts along the Kohala Coast; more recently a $30-million renovation upgraded the resort to rival any competitor. The refurbished property, now owned by Prince Hotel Corp., has 300 rooms and 10 suites on a whopping 1,839-acre site. Two of the strongest selling points here are nearby Kaunaoa Beach, among the nicest on the island, and the legendary **Mauna Kea Golf Course** (see page 26). The spacious grounds and courtyards, alive with more than a half-million plants of nearly 200 varieties, are also part of the appeal. There are six restaurants, 10 Plexipave tennis courts, and no TVs (so the real world can't intrude). ◆ 1 Mauna Kea Beach Dr (off Queen Kaahumanu Hwy). 882.7222, 800/882.6060; fax 880.3112 ⴄ

Within the Mauna Kea Beach Hotel:

Mauna Kea Buddha A 1,500-pound pink granite sculpture, this seventh-century Indian Buddha (illustrated below) sits on a solid block of Canadian black granite in the shade of a *bodhi* tree.

Mauna Kea Buddha

The Batik ★★$$$$ Batiks hang from the walls of this cozy, two-tiered dining room, which specializes in European dishes like grilled tenderloin of beef sliced on caper-and-onion mashed potatoes with sauce poivrade and fresh snapper with lobster mushroom ragout. ♦ Continental ♦ Daily dinner. Reservations, jacket required. 882.7222 ఉ

The Pavilion ★★$$$$ Atmosphere and cuisine vie for top honors in this expensive dining room, where floor-to-ceiling windows and a drop-dead ocean view rival satay marinated chicken on a skewer with jasmine rice, bok choy, and spicy peanut sauce, and sautéed garlic prawns with fettucine, leafy greens, and pesto. The big winner might just be a soufflé—*lilikoi* (passion fruit), orange, or chocolate. ♦ Pacific Rim. ♦ M-Sa lunch buffet, Su brunch, daily dinner. Reservations recommended. 882.7222 ఉ

Mauna Kea Luau ★★$$ Hawaiian delicacies are served on the grassy oceanside gardens at this very upscale luau held on the grounds of the **Mauna Kea Beach Hotel**. The feast includes *hulihuli* (spit-roasted) chicken, *kalua* pig on special occasions, poi, *lomilomi* salmon, and baked taro, as well as steak, chicken, ribs, and crab claws. ♦ Luau ♦ Tu 7-9PM. 882.5801 ఉ

Mauna Kea Golf Course Designed by Robert Trent Jones Sr., this reclaimed ancient lava flow is widely hailed as Hawaii's toughest course. Though a few refinements cater to fair-weather golfers, the 18-hole course (par 72, 6,737 yards) remains an ego bruiser for even the above-average player. Its beautiful layout has the ocean always in sight. Ranked among America's hundred greatest golf courses and regularly designated "Hawaii's finest" by *Golf Digest*, the course hosts two tournaments annually: the **Pro-Am** in July and an **Invitational** in early December. ♦ Expensive greens fees. Daily. Preferred starting times and rates for **Mauna Kea Beach Hotel** guests. 880.3480

61 Hapuna Beach Prince Hotel $$$$ Because of its location on one of Hawaii's most gorgeous white-sand beaches, local residents vehemently (though unsuccessfully) fought the construction of the 62-acre resort. This sister hotel to the **Mauna Kea Beach Hotel** has 314 rooms and 36 suites, all with lanais and wide-angle ocean views, three restaurants, and a pool. Its top attractions are the two surrounding 18-hole golf courses (the **Hapuna** and the **Mauna Kea**) and a 13-court

tennis center a short shuttle away at the **Mauna Kea Beach Hotel**. The catch is that the property is pretty far from anyplace else. ♦ 62-100 Kauna'oa Dr (off Queen Kaahumanu Hwy). 880.1111, 800/882.6060; fax 880.311

Within the Hapuna Beach Prince Hotel:

The Coast Grille ★★★$$$$ The hotel's circular signature restaurant has an ocean view that won't quit. Dishes include Parker Ranch steak and fresh lobster, clams, oyster and jumbo shrimp. ♦ Hawaiian Regional ♦ Daily dinner. Reservations recommended. 880.1111

Hapuna Golf Course This 18-hole public course (par 70, 6,534 yards) was designed by Arnold Palmer and Ed Seay for the **Hapuna Beach Prince Hotel**. The environmentally conscious design uses half the land acreage of a regular 18-hole course and is landscaped with native Hawaiian grasses and trees. Hawaiian birds and waterfowl came gratis. ♦ Expensive greens fees. Daily. 882.1035

61 Hapuna Beach State Park This is one of the nicest white-sand beaches on the Big Island. The bodysurfing is primo, but go between 9AM and 5PM when the lifeguards are on duty, as currents can be hazardous, particularly when the surf's up. There are also picnic tables perfect for family gatherings. ♦ Off Queen Kaahumanu Hwy (just south of the Hapuna Beach Prince Hotel)

62 Puako Petroglyph Archaeological Park Site of one of the largest clusters of petroglyphs in Hawaii, this public park at the north end of the **Orchid at Mauna Lani** property was officially placed on the Hawaii and National Historic Registers in 1982. The stone carvings (such as the ones illustrated above) were created by ancient Hawaiians more than 400 years ago. The **Orchid** established the park to protect the petroglyphs after some were damaged by vandalism, the foot traffic, and even bulldozers (cleaning up after fires in the area). A natural trail system posted with signs leads to the petroglyphs, which are at the **Holoholokai Beach Park**. Don't make rubbings from the stone carvings (replica petroglyphs are provided for this purpose) and don't step on them. Damaged petroglyphs are displayed so visitors can see the consequences of mistreating these treasures. ♦ Off Mauna Lani Dr (at the entrance to the Orchid at Mauna Lani)

62 The Orchid at Mauna Lani $$$$ In 1994 this hotel (formerly the **Ritz-Carlton**) was ranked No. 3 among tropical resorts in the world by *Condé Nast Traveler*. Exceptionally professional and courteous service complements the elegant Old World decor with its signature cobalt-blue vases (filled with crimson roses specially cultivated in Waimea) and antique armoires displaying rare china. More than a thousand works of art grace the walls and hallways. The dining rooms and hallways have silk brocade wall coverings, koa paneling, Italian marble, and Renaissance-inspired upholstery, with chandeliers of Baccarat and quartz crystal. The two six-story wings face the ocean, and 539 large, luxurious rooms have peach and light blue walls and marble bathrooms. Outside you'll find a 10,000-square-foot swimming pool adjacent to a man-made white-sand lagoon. The 32-acre grounds feature myriad native plants. The **Club** level has its own lounge, tea service, elevator key, and other extras. Tennis buffs can choose from 10 courts, and golfers have special privileges at the **Mauna Lani/Francis H. Ii Brown Golf Course** (see page 28). ♦ 1 N Kaniku Dr (off Queen Kaahumanu Hwy). 885.2000, 800/845.9905; fax 885.1064 ♿

Within the Orchid at Mauna Lani:

The Grill ★★★$$$$ The clubby atmosphere, enhanced by the rich glow of koa paneling, suits the continental menu, which features such items as herb-marinated *opakapaka* (pink snapper) with Asian risotto, tropical fruit salsa, and hot and sour papaya puree, and pepper-crusted prime rib. A plush private room is available for parties of up to 14 people. ♦ Continental ♦ Daily dinner. Reservations recommended. 885.2000 ♿

The Orchid Court Restaurant ★★★ $$$$ The fare here features Hawaiian Regional dishes such as sesame wok-charred *ahi* (tuna) with a miso-shoyu sauce and saffron fettuccine with shrimp and bay scallops. There's a casual dining room and alfresco seating. ♦ Hawaiian Regional ♦ Daily breakfast and dinner. 885.2000 ♿

63 Mauna Lani Bay Hotel and Bungalows $$$$ This hotel on 29 oceanfront acres has been winning awards for its historic preservation, golf course, and overall excellence for more than a decade. A distinctively Hawaiian landmark, it embodies the highest standards of local hospitality: grace, style, architectural excellence, and aloha spirit. In the blue-tile courtyard, a waterfall leads to the **Grand Atrium**, filled with fish ponds and orchids. Rooms (built at a cost of $200,000 each) feature teak and rattan furnishings, color TVs in armoires, roomy baths with twin vanities, and private lanais. Almost all of the 341 rooms and suites have ocean views; 27 face the Mauna Kea and Mauna Loa mountains. Guests with deep pockets can opt for one of five 4,000-square-foot bungalows with private pools and 24-hour butler service; families may prefer the luxurious one- and two-bedroom ocean villas.

The grounds feature prehistoric fish ponds and a 16th-century lava flow with caves and petroglyphs. Golfers enjoy the nearby 36-hole **Mauna Lani/Francis H. Ii Brown Golf Course,** and there's a pool and a championship 10-court **Tennis Garden.** Activities include windsurfing, canoeing, scuba diving, and aqua-aerobics. The hotel was awarded five diamonds by **AAA** in 1996, and *Condé Nast Traveler* ranked it No. 5 among the best tropical resorts in the world in 1995. ♦ 1 Mauna Lani Dr (off Queen Kaahumanu Hwy). 885.6622, 800/367.2323; fax 885.1483 ♿

Within the Mauna Lani Bay Hotel and Bungalows:

The Canoe House ★★★★$$$$ Here is a rare match of ambience and impressive cuisine. Dine indoors, where a koa canoe hangs from the high ceiling, or outdoors, where the breaking waves are lit by the setting sun. Specialties include seared peppered *ahi* (tuna) with crispy slaw and grilled *opakapaka* (pink snapper) with chili-garlic–black bean sauce. ♦ Pacific Rim ♦ Daily dinner. Reservations recommended. 885.6622

Bay Terrace ★★★$$$$ Stop here for pleasant American/Regional fare for breakfast or dinner. There are *malasadas* (Portuguese doughnuts) to start the day, and candlelight and a three-piece band make for romantic dinners. On Friday and Saturday nights the place really dazzles, with an all-you-can-eat buffet that includes crab legs, made-to-order tempura and pasta, prime rib, and more, presented in the most elegant manner imaginable. ♦ American/Regional ♦ Daily breakfast and dinner; Sunday brunch. Reservations recommended. 885.6622

The Gallery ★★$$$$ A fairly standard golf club restaurant at lunch, this place becomes an intimate, candlelit venue at dusk. The fare is mostly American, emphasizing fresh seafood from the Big Island. Daily fish selections are prepared one of three ways, including crusted with macadamia nuts and covered in a lobster brandy sauce. New York steak and roasted rack of lamb also rank high on the list. ♦ Steak/Seafood ♦ Tu-Sa dinner. Reservations recommended. 885.7777

The Ironman: A Triathlon Tradition

The western side of the Big Island is renowned for sportfishing, resorts, gourmet coffee, and potent marijuana (called *pakalolo* here). **Kona** has also garnered plenty of attention as the site of the world's most prestigious triathlon, the **Ironman Triathlon World Championship.**

Launched in 1978 by long-distance runner and swimmer John Collins, this highly competitive race consists of three major endurance events: a 2.4-mile rough-water ocean swim, a 112-mile bicycle ride, and a 26.2-mile run. Every October, about 1,500 competitors from around the world begin swimming en masse in **Kailua Bay**, then ride bicycles from Kona to **Hawi** and back again, and finally dismount from their bikes at **Keauhou** and run back to **Kailua Pier.** This grueling test of strength and endurance is a major event on the Big Island, with year-round preparation, major sponsors, and coverage by "NBC Sports." For more information, contact the **Ironman Triathlon** (75-127 Lunapule Rd, #11, Kailua-Kona, HI 96740, 329.0063).

63 Mauna Lani/Francis H. Ii Brown Golf Course Since the course opened in 1981, these emerald fairways and greens have received worldwide attention, with *Golf Magazine* bestowing top honors on them in 1996. Carved out of a 16th-century lava flow, the **North Course** (18 holes, par 72, 6,601 yards) and the **South Course** (18 holes, par 72, 6,436 yards) flow bright green through the black *a'a* and *pahoehoe* lava fields, sculptured masterpieces lined by groves of twisted *kiawe* trees. Ocean views are almost secondary. The **Mauna Lani Beach Club,** a popular watering hole for mai tai lovers, is a short walk past the pro shop. ♦ Expensive greens fees. Daily. Preferred starting times and rates for **Mauna Lani Bay Hotel** guests. 68-1050 Makaiwa Dr (off Queen Kaahumanu Hwy). 885.6655

64 Kings Course Designed by Tom Weiskopf and Jay Morris, this challenging 18-hole, par 72, 7,074-yard course has six lakes, nine acres of water, 83 sand traps, and a 25,000-square-foot clubhouse. ♦ Expensive greens fees; discounts for guests of the **Royal Waikoloan.** Daily. 69-600 Waikoloa Beach Dr (off Queen Kaahumanu Hwy). 885.4647

64 Beach Course The fairways are adorned with tropical flowers, while the rough is black lava at this 18-hole, par 70, 6,566-yard course created by Robert Trent Jones Jr. A driving range is on site. ♦ Expensive greens fees; discounts for **Royal Waikoloan** guests. Daily. Off Queen Kaahumanu Hwy. 885.6060

64 Anaehoomalu Bay Ideal for windsurfing, scuba diving, walking, swimming, and sunning, this crescent-shaped white-sand beach fronts the **Royal Waikoloan.** The ancient royal fish ponds behind the beach are preserved by the hotel. Parking and public access are available at the south end of the beach. ♦ Off Queen Kaahumanu Hwy

64 Royal Waikoloan $$ Smaller and more modest than its neighbor, the flamboyant **Hilton Waikoloa Village,** this 547-room hotel is for those who favor an intimate Hawaiian ambience at a more reasonable price. The wide Anaehoomalu Bay is a key attraction; other special features of this first-rate resort include the **Royal Cabana Club,** a 15-room, two-story structure on the lagoon; Wednesday and Sunday luaus; a fitness center; six tennis courts; a pool; and two nearby championship golf courses. ♦ 69-275 Waikoloa Beach Dr (off Queen Kaahumanu Hwy), Anaehoomalu. 885.6789, 800/922.5533; fax 885.7852 ♿

Within the Royal Waikoloan:

Tiare Room ★$$$ An elegant setting of rich woods, etched glass, and crystal enhances the menu, which may include steak and local prawns over pasta or lamb chops with a cracked peppercorn glaze. ♦ Pacific Rim ♦ Th-Tu dinner. Reservations required. 885.6789

64 Hilton Waikoloa Village $$$$ Described as "Disney-esque" by those who favor more intimate settings, this 62-acre super resort has more than a mile of waterways with a dozen 24-passenger canal boats, a mile-long museum walkway, and an air-conditioned electric tram. Hardly a potted palm has changed position since the gargantuan resort metamorphosed from Hyatt to Hilton in 1993, though a $24-million renovation included new high-end oceanfront cabanas, perhaps to keep pace with the neighboring **Mauna Lani Bay Hotel and Bungalows.** The $360-million hotel is more like a small city, with 1,241 rooms, 56 suites, 2,000 employees, two main swimming pools, waterfalls, water slides, 19 meeting rooms, 20,000 square feet of shopping space, and eight tennis and two racquetball courts. The 25,000-square-foot spa offers European herbal treatments, fitness classes, nutrition counseling, steam rooms, saunas, whirlpools, and Jacuzzis. The hotel has six restaurants and eight lounges, but the most popular attraction by far is **Dolphin Quest** (see below), the 2.5-million-gallon home of 10 Atlantic bottle-nosed dolphins. Even if you have no intention of staying at the resort, drop by to gawk at American excess at its best. ♦ 69-425 Waikoloa Beach Dr (off Queen Kaahumanu Hwy), Anaehoomalu. 885.1234, 800/HILTONS; fax 885.2902 &

Within the Hilton Waikoloa Village:

Kamuela Provision Co. ★★★$$$
This is one of Hawaii's most attractive dining rooms, with six seating areas (including one alfresco), dozens of windows overlooking the sea and pool, and elegant, glass-topped tables. Diners seeking a languorous evening should start with a sunset mai tai overlooking the ocean, progress to the seafood mixed grill, Keahole lobster, or filet mignon, and finish with a Kona Sampler—a dish piled with items like banana-chocolate sandwiches, guava sorbet, Kona coffee mousse, and Big Island brulée. ♦ Steak/Seafood ♦ Daily dinner. Reservations required. 885.1234 &

Donatoni's ★★★$$$$ One of Hawaii's outstanding Italian restaurants, this is the place to savor Northern Italian favorites: tender *calamari fritti;* linguine *al pescatore* with mussels, scallops, and clams; and osso buco *alla milanese* (veal shanks with vegetables, white wine, and tomatoes). There are three drop-dead-gorgeous dining rooms, two inside and one outside, all featuring inspiring sunset views over the lagoon and the Pacific Ocean. The ambience is all elegance; the service, impeccable. ♦ Northern Italian ♦ Daily dinner. Reservations, jackets required. 885.1234 &

Dolphin Quest This is what vacation memories are made of. Here's the drill: Pick up dolphin lottery tickets at the hotel's front desk daily by 3:30PM; check back after 5:30PM to see if your number was chosen. Reservations for children and teens must be made two months in advance; otherwise, cross your fingers. Fifteen winners between ages 5 and 12 will spend half an hour in the dolphin pool watching the playful creatures do tricks. The peak experience belongs to teenagers between ages 13 and 19, who act as trainer's helpers and get a firsthand glimpse at how dolphins learn to respond to humans. ♦ Fee; most of the proceeds go

toward marine research. Daily: 2PM for teens, 3PM for younger kids; 9:30AM, 11AM, 11:45AM, and 4PM for adults. 885.2875 &

64 **The Kings' Shops at Waikoloa** This upscale collection of shops, located near the Big Island's finest resorts, is gathering some of its best restaurants and lounges. ♦ Waikoloa Beach Dr, Anaehoomalu

Within the Kings' Shops:

Big Island Steak House ★★★$$$$
The filet mignon is unsurpassed here, as are creative entrées such as the coconut prawns, but this place's popularity derives from having the closest thing in the county to nightlife. After 10PM on Fridays and Saturdays, it becomes the Merry Wahine nightclub; the bartender doubles as a disc jockey spinning techno-pop for an upscale crowd of neighboring hotel guests and local residents. ♦ Steaks/Seafood ♦ Daily dinner. 885.8805

Noa Noa Stop to admire the unique hand-painted clothing and handbags designed by longtime resident and shop owner Joan Simon and made in Indonesia. ♦ Daily 9:30AM-9:30PM. 885.5449

Roy's Waikoloa Bar and Grill ★★★$$$
This trendy bistro is the eleventh in Roy Yamaguchi's string of "in" places. Blackened *ahi* (tuna), hibachi-style salmon, and Szechuan baby back ribs are just the beginning. ♦ Euro-Asian ♦ Tu-Sa lunch, daily dinner. Reservations recommended. 885.4321 &

65 **Waikoloa Village Course** At an elevation of 1,200 feet, this 18-holer sometimes has the advantage of being cooler than its oceanfront counterparts. Designed by Robert Trent Jones Jr. and the site of the Waikoloa Open every fall, the course (par 72, 6,970 yards) also features spectacular views of the Mauna Kea and Mauna Loa volcanoes. ♦ Expensive greens fees. Daily. Waikoloa Rd (6 miles east of Queen Kaahumanu Hwy). 883.9621

65 **Roussel's Waikoloa Village** ★★★$$$
This elegant French/Creole restaurant owned by Herbert Roussel and New Orleans–born Spencer Oliver offers views of all three of Hawaii's volcanoes. Chef Spencer is a genius with fresh Hawaiian fish, oyster shrimp gumbo, shrimp creole, and soft-shell crab meunière. The Cajun-style blackened fish is legendary, and the lemon mousse is a must. ♦ French/Creole ♦ Daily lunch; dinner Tu-Sa. Reservations recommended. 68-1792 Malia St, Waikoloa Village. 883.9644

Sweet Talk

When the Polynesians first sailed to Hawaii some 1,500 years ago, they used the thick stalks of sugarcane to hold water for the long journey. The rich lava soil and wet climate, coupled with abundant sunshine, proved fertile ground for sugarcane. In 1835, the first commercial sugarcane plantation was established on the island of Kauai, but it wasn't until the end of Hawaii's whaling era in the 1860s that sugar was relied upon as a cash crop. The islands' unrefined sugar was first exported to America during the gold rush, when Northern California's sudden population boom made sugar a profitable commodity.

From 1953 to 1986, Hawaiian fields yielded about a million tons of sugar a year (more than 12 percent of the entire country's product) and strengthened Hawaii's economy by $353 million annually. The sugar industry was also primarily responsible for Hawaii's diverse racial mixture. Laborers from China, Japan, Korea, Portugal, South America, and many other lands were brought in to harvest the crop.

But times are changing in Hawaii, and high operational costs and stiff competition has led to the phasing out of the sugar industry on Hawaii (a fate that has also befallen the state's pineapple industry).

Soon Hawaii's economy will be based almost exclusively on military operations and tourism, and the verdant cane fields that for generations symbolized Hawaiian prosperity will be plowed under for good.

66 Four Seasons Hualalai $$$$ Each new hotel in Hawaii seems more lavish and resplendent than the last, and the latest addition to the Big Island's repertoire is no exception. Two hundred and twelve rooms and 31 suites on 35 acres of oceanfront property designed to recall Hawaii in the 19th century will bedazzle most vacationers. Rooms, done in mahogany and muted natural shades, feature petroglyph and banana prints, Jacuzzi tubs, four-poster beds—the works. A 16,000-square-foot spa, two restaurants, three stores, eight tennis courts, and 18 holes of golf designed by Jack Nicklaus round out the offerings. ◆ 100 Kaupulehu Dr (off Queen Kaahumanu Hwy). 325.800, 888.3405; fax 325.8053 &

Mauna Kea on the Big Island is the only place in the tropical Pacific that was at one time a glacier—the entire summit was once buried beneath 500 feet of ice.

67 Kona Village Resort $$$$ This is the ultimate "get away from it all" resort, once so remote guests had to be flown in (now they can drive up Hwy 19). What sets this all-inclusive property apart is what it lacks—telephones, TV sets, radios, suits and ties, or neighbors. The watchwords are luxury, simplicity, and peace and quiet. Aside from a few tennis courts, nothing here even vaguely resembles the standard hotel experience. The 125 individual thatch bungalows (illustrated above), sprawling over 82 acres, are replicas of New Zealand, Samoan, Tahitian, Hawaiian and other Polynesian structures. Guests are greeted with flower leis and rum punch, then set free to play with the toys, including canoes, sailboats, and snorkeling gear; ride in a glass-bottom boat; and attend cocktail parties, luaus, guided petroglyph tours, lei-making classes, and scuba dives. Meals are included in the rate. ◆ Kaupulehu Dr (off Queen Kaahumanu Hwy), Kaupulehu. 325.5555, 800/367.5290; fax 325.5124 &

Within the Kona Village Resort:

Hale Moana ★★★$$$$ Chef Glenn Alos has made this restaurant his own creative playground. The luncheon buffet, with elegant samplings of Big Island favorites, is a memorable seaside repast. Dinner selections include fresh *opakapaka* (pink snapper) broiled with saffron and orange butter, *ono* (wahoo) sautéed with lime and macadamia nut beurre blanc, and boneless quail in Cajun spices. Five panels in this high-ceilinged Polynesian *hale* (house) depict Captain Cook's voyages to Hawaii. The panels, entitled *Les Sauvages de la Mer Pacifique*, are made of 18th-century French wallpaper; they were rolled up and stored in a Paris attic for more than a hundred years before an American collector discovered them. ◆ Hawaiian Regional ◆ Daily breakfast, lunch, and dinner. Reservations required for nonguests; no shorts allowed. 325.5555

Kona Village Luau ★★★★$$$$ The best luau in Hawaii begins with a tour of the grounds, where you will witness the unveiling of the *imu* (an earthen oven where the pig and sweet potatoes are roasted). It's a dramatic event, with *malo*-clad men chipping away at the *imu* and steam rising from the pit. The feast is as authentic as a commercial luau gets, with *opihi* (limpets, a Hawaiian delicacy)

Hale Samoa

banana pudding, sushi, *laulau* (steamed pork with taro leaves), *poki* (raw fish), and a host of delicacies from Hawaii and the South Pacific. The program, held across a lagoon from the luau pavilion, is fiery and beautifully lit, with chants of Pele, Hawaii's volcano goddess, and ancient and modern dances. Look for Hawaiian artist Herb Kane's brilliant paintings on the back wall of the pavilion. ♦ Hawaiian ♦ F 6PM. Reservations required. 325.5555

Hale Samoa ★★$$$$ The fancier of the two dining rooms at the **Kona Village Resort** is highly recommended whether you're a guest or not. The menu includes grilled Indonesian lobster tail, broiled buffalo tail, and fresh *opakapaka* (pink snapper) served in a romantic room. ♦ Continental ♦ M-Tu, Th, Sa-Su dinner. Reservations required for nonguests; guests pay a surcharge to dine here. 325.5555

68 Kona Coast State Park A bumpy mile-and-a-half drive through an eerie lava field (worth the trip in itself) leads to Kaelehuluhulu Beach, with picnic tables and great snorkeling. Interesting ruins lie in the lava fields behind the 6.5 acres of coarse coral sand. ♦ Th-Tu 9AM-8PM. Off Queen Kaahumanu Hwy (about 4 miles north of Keahole-Kona International Airport)

69 Natural Energy Lab of Hawaiian Authority (NEL) Taking advantage of Keahole's unique geographical location, which receives more sunshine than any other US coastal location and has deep water relatively close to shore, the **Natural Energy Lab of Hawaiian Authority** pumps up to 28,400 gallons of seawater per minute from depths of 50 feet and 2,000 feet. The temperature difference between the deep and shallow water is then used to run heat exchangers, which in turn produce energy (it's something like a reverse refrigerator, making electricity instead of using it). The almost pathogen-free seawater also is used for all sorts of clever aquacultural ideas, including the controlled growth of specialty food products such as Maine lobster and *hirame* (a flounder prized for sashimi); a Tahitian black pearl research lab; and a *spirulina* (spiral-shaped micro-algae sold in health-food stores) farm. ♦ Free. Self-guided tours. Reservations recommended. 73-4460 Queen Kaahumanu Hwy (1 mile south of Keahole Airport Rd). 329.7341; fax 326.3262

69 Wawaloli Beach Park This long stretch of golden sand is a favorite with scuba divers and swimmers. Statistically, this is the sunniest beach in the US. There are bathroom and shower facilities. ♦ Off Natural Energy Rd (south of Keahole Point)

70 Kona to Hawi Drive Don't miss this drive through cattle country, lava fields, and mountains. Done right, it's an all-day trip—and a magnificent one. From Kona take Highway 190 (Mamalahoa Highway) north to Waimea. Turn left, and continue northwest on Highway 250 (Kohala Mountain Rd) to Hawi. Turn left again and take the coastal road (Highways 270 and 19) back to Kona.

The Big Island's Mauna Loa volcano, at 10,000 cubic miles in mass, is the largest such feature anywhere in the solar system between the sun and the planet Mars.

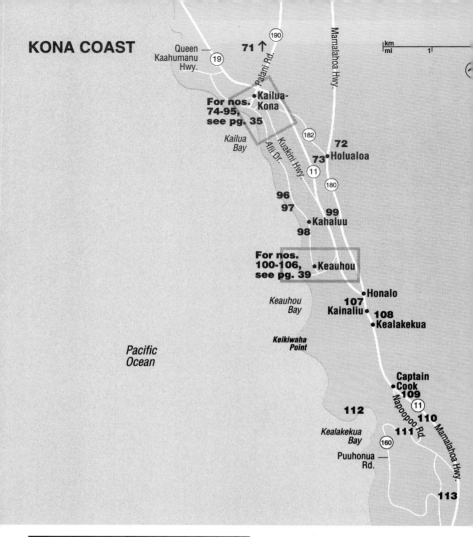

KONA COAST

Queen
Kaahumanu
Hwy. ⑲

71 ↑ ⑲⁰

Palani Rd.

Mamalahoa Hwy.

km
mi   1'

**For nos.
74-95,
see pg. 35**

• **Kailua-
Kona**

*Kailua
Bay*

Alii Dr.   Kuakini Hwy.

⑱²

72

73• **Holualoa**

⑪

⑱⁰

96
97

99
• **Kahaluu**

98

**For nos.
100-106,
see pg. 39**   • **Keauhou**

*Keauhou
Bay*

107
Kainaliu •

• **Honalo**

108
• **Kealakekua**

*Keikiwaha
Point*

*Pacific
Ocean*

Captain
• **Cook**
109

112

⑪

110

*Kealakekua
Bay*

111 •

Napoopoo Rd.

Mamalahoa Hwy.

⑯⁰

*Puuhonua —
Rd.*

113

Kona Coast

Great beaches, fabulous diving, and almost
guaranteed sunshine draw folks to the Kona Coast on
the western side of the Big Island. After a day of sand
and surf you can stroll through the sleepy tourist
town of **Kailua-Kona** (also called **Kailua, Kailua
Village,** or just **Kona**), where there are stores to
explore, restaurants to sample, and cocktails to be
sipped oceanside while watching the sun swiftly slide
below the horizon, ending the day with a fiery glow.

71 Holualoa Drive If you're staying on the
Kona Coast, set aside an afternoon for this
panoramic drive, easily the best in the area.
Start from Palani Road (Highway 190) in
Kailua-Kona and head north. After four miles,
look for a nursery on the right and turn right
onto Mamalahoa Highway (Highway 180).
Take a slow cruise south on Highway 180,
stopping in quaint Holualoa to browse among
the galleries and shops until sunset, then drive
a half mile down the road to the Hualalai Road

turnoff (Highway 182). Descending this roa
at sunset into Kona is what Hawaii is all abo

72 Kona Hotel $ A Holualoa landmark for
more than 70 years, this ramshackle pink
building attracts a steady stream of artists,
hikers, sportfishers, students, and
adventurers. Methodically disorganized and
undeniably charming, it features the world's
most scenic outhouse, 11 spartan rooms
without phones, very inexpensive rates, and
locals dozing on the front porch. Even if you
don't stay, stop by for a "how's it going?"
There's no restaurant. ♦ No credit cards
accepted. 76-5908 Mamalahoa Hwy,
Holualoa. 324.1155

72 Studio 7 Owned by artist Hiroke Morinoue
this gallery is small and serene, with a quali
much like a Zen garden or a tasteful, unpretentious Japanese inn. Morinoue's own
paintings and prints share space with the Bi
Island's best in all media. ♦ Tu-Sa. 76-5920
Mamalahoa Hwy, Holualoa. 324.1335

INN

72 Holualoa Inn $$ One of the finest bed-and-breakfasts on the Big Island, this inn has a spectacular view of the Kona Coast from its immaculate, open-beamed living room. The two suites and four guestrooms have Polynesian- and Asian-inspired decors, with careful attention to detail and artwork; a tiled pool and deck beckon outside. The location—on 40 acres in the quiet, charming town of Holualoa—is another major plus. There's no restaurant. ◆ 76-5932 Mamalahoa Hwy (the gravel driveway is just left of Paul's Place country store), Holualoa. 324.1121, 800/392.1812; fax 322.2472 &

73 Kimura Lauhala Shop Tsuruyo Kimura has been making and selling *lauhala* (items made from woven pandanus) since the days when *hala* trees were abundant in Kona and the Kimuras traveled around the island bartering. The 50-odd-year-old shop is awash in woven fiber goods from Hawaii and the South Pacific—hats, mats, kitchen goods, purses, and wall hangings. Ask for the Kona *lauhala;* it's the best. ◆ M-Sa. 77-9961 Hualalai Rd (at Mamalahoa Hwy), Holualoa. 324.0053 &

74 Kailua Candy Company Considered by many to make the best chocolate in Hawaii, this small but prolific candy factory uses only fresh ingredients. Grab a handful of free samples and watch the workers do their thing behind the glass windows of the factory, then send 30 pounds of sweets to your dietetic enemies all over the world. ◆ Daily. 74-5563 Kaiwi St (at Pawai Pl), Kailua-Kona. 329.2522, 800/622.2462 &

75 Buns In The Sun ★$ Start your day munching on pastries and sipping freshly brewed coffee out on the sunny patio. Order a sandwich to go, and you're set for a picnic lunch at the beach. ◆ Coffeehouse ◆ Daily breakfast and lunch. No reservations. Lanihau Shopping Center, 75-5595 Palani Rd (between Kuakini and Mamalahoa Hwys), Kailua-Kona. 326.2774 &

76 Kona Ranch House $$ The patio bar and homey atmosphere of this plantation-style restaurant make it popular with local families. There are two dining rooms: the country-style **Paniolo Room** inside, and the **Plantation Lanai,** filled with wicker furnishings. The menu focuses on Big Island beef (try the ribs), fresh fish, and local specialties, but the food tends to be pricey. ◆ American ◆ Daily breakfast, lunch, and dinner. Reservations

recommended. 75-5653 Ololi Rd (off Kuakini Hwy just south of Palani Rd), Kailua-Kona. 329.7061 &

77 Kona Seaside Hotel $ The best choice in town for the budget traveler, this hotel features two swimming pools and 224 rooms with big beds, air-conditioning, cable TV, refrigerators, phones, and private lanais. While the location is ideal for shopaholics, it's not recommended for anyone trying to get away from it all. There's a restaurant on the property, but it's not recommended. ◆ 75-5646 Palani Rd (at Kuakini Hwy), Kailua-Kona. 329.2455, 800/367.7000; fax 329.6157

78 Quinn's ★$$ A favorite with local restaurant staffers seeking a bite after their evening shifts (it serves dinner until 2AM), this hideaway around the corner from Alii Drive serves salads and sandwiches, vegetarian specialties, fresh fish, and beef in a patio setting. ◆ American ◆ Daily lunch and dinner. No reservations. 75-5655 Palani Rd (between Alii Dr and Kuakini Hwy), Kailua-Kona. 329.3822 &

79 King Kamehameha's Kona Beach Hotel $$ If shopping and sightseeing are more important to you than secluded white-sand beaches, look no further. The "King Kam" is located at the head of Kailua-Kona's main street, Alii Drive, in easy walking distance of **Kailua Pier** (see page 34) and the town's shops, restaurants, and historic sites. The hotel's twin buildings have 451 rooms and suites with lanais, TVs, air-conditioning, phones, and refrigerators. Adjoining the lobby is the Kona Coast's only fully air-conditioned mall, containing 15 shops. The hotel offers guests and nonguests free tours of the grounds. Ask about the outstanding **Hula Experience,** which traces the history of the ancient dance. A pool, four tennis courts, and a strand of beach run along Kailua Bay. ◆ 75-5660 Blani Dr (off Palani Rd), Kailua-Kona. 329.2911, 800/367.6060; fax 329.4602 &

Within King Kamehameha's Kona Beach Hotel:

Kona Beach Restaurant ★$$ The deal here is the prime rib and seafood buffet (Fridays and Saturdays from 5:30 to 9PM). The daily breakfast buffet and Sunday brunch are also commendable. ◆ American ◆ M-Sa breakfast, lunch, and dinner; Sunday brunch and dinner. 329.2911 &

Island Breeze Luau ★$$$$ The beauty of the historical grounds gives this, your average hotel luau, added appeal and atmosphere. ◆ Luau ◆ Tu-Th, Su 5:30PM. Reservations required. 326.4969

80 Ahuena Heiau In his final years, Kamehameha the Great ruled the newly united Hawaiian kingdom from this cove along Kamakahonu ("Eye of the Turtle") Bay. Dedicated to Lono, the Hawaiian god of fertility, this was an area of peace and prosperity. Kamehameha died here in 1819, and his body was taken to a secret resting place. Today the remains of royal fishponds and a compound of buildings, including an oracle tower and the historic **Ahuena Heiau** (Ahuena Temple), the king's refuge in his final days, are found at this picturesque historic site, which was restored by the **King Kamehameha's Kona Beach Hotel** under the direction of the **Bishop Museum** of Honolulu. ◆ Free. A free 45-minute tour is given at 1:30PM daily. 24 hours, except Tu-Th and Su 6PM-10PM. Behind King Kamehameha's Kona Beach Hotel, Kailua-Kona

81 Kailua Pier Every water activity in downtown Kona, including sportfishing, **Atlantis** and **Nautilus** rides, parasailing, dinner cruises, day cruises, diving trips, and late-afternoon outrigger **Canoe Club** practices, starts and finishes here. ◆ Off Alii Dr (across from King Kamehameha's Kona Beach Hotel), Kailua-Kona

Activities on the Kailua Pier:

Atlantis Submarines The hour-long excursion, from launch craft to sub and back again, is a tightly organized act, starting with a photo-shoot and finishing with an official certificate of completion (hokey but cute). The 48-passenger air-conditioned craft is impressive —65 feet long, 17.5 feet tall, and weighing in at 80 tons, with a silent cruising speed of 1.5 knots. The dives range from 100 feet to 115 feet, depending on the location, and all trips include an on-board commentator. What you see through the 21-inch view-ports depends on where you are; lucky passengers may see sharks, manta rays, dolphins, moray eels, and possibly whales. It's expensive, but sometimes it's worth it. ◆ Fee. Daily 10AM-3PM. 326.7939. Also at: Pioneer Inn, 658 Wharf St, Lahaina, Maui, 667.2224; Hilton Hawaiian Village, 2005 Kalia Rd (between Paoa Pl and Ala Moana Blvd), Waikiki, Oahu, 973.9811

Nautilus Semi-Submersible Not to be confused with **Atlantis Submarines** (see above), which dives completely underwater, the **Nautilus Semi-Submersible** remains partially above the surface. The comfortable passenger area, six to eight feet below the water line, has air-conditioning, padded seats, stereo music, and a video monitor. You'll get an up-close view of coral gardens and their denizens from the view-ports. Divers, swimming with the sub, bring up creatures from the bottom, while a knowledgeable commentator answers questions. Ideal for those who hate getting wet, **Nautilus** provides a chance to see Hawaii at its finest. The best times to go are before or around noon, when the sunlight penetrates the water and visibility is best. ◆ Fee. Daily 9:30AM, 10:30AM, 11:30AM, 1:30PM, 2:30PM. 326.2003. Also at: Lahaina Harbor, Maui, 667.2133

Captain Beans' Dinner Cruise This is basically a floating luau on a crimson double-hulled barge. Despite the mediocre food and two hours of touristy entertainment, participants always seem to enjoy themselves. ◆ Fee. Daily 5:15PM. Reservations required. 329.2955, 800/831.5541

Body Glove The pseudo-sailboat takes the booby prize for beauty, but it's the best dive boat out of Kona for beginners. The day trip to **Pawai Bay Marine Preserve** includes breakfast and lunch—and kids will love the 15-foot slide and high dive on the deck. ◆ Fee. Daily 9AM-1:30PM. Reservations required. 326.7122

82 Ocean View Inn ★$ If Kona had a truck stop, this would be it. There's an ocean view (if you look *really* hard through the louvered windows), but since 1935, when dinner cost 50¢, the big attraction at this landmark hotel restaurant has been home cooking at nontourist prices (not, repeat, *not* speedy service). The menu's eclectic mix of Hawaiian, American, Japanese, and Chinese standards has attracted the likes of Lucille Ball, Jimmy Stewart, and Lloyd Bridges. There's even an old soda fountain that looks like it was shipped intact from the "Happy Days" set. Wander next door to the **Hawaiian Angel Coffee** stand for the cheapest (and biggest) cups of café au lait and cappuccino in town. ◆ Hawaiian/American/Asian ◆ Tu-Su breakfast, lunch, and dinner. (Closed the month of September.) No reservations. No credit cards accepted. 75-5683 Alii Dr (across from Kailua Pier), Kailua-Kona. 329.9998 &

Astronomers atop Mauna Kea on the Big Island are urged to come down to sea level every four days because the thin air supposedly makes them more prone to absentmindedness.

KAILUA-KONA

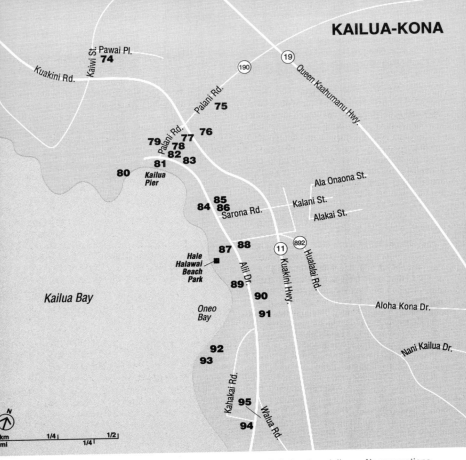

Kailua Bay

Oneo Bay

N

km 1/4 1/2
ml 1/4

83 Kona Arts & Crafts Gallery
An oasis of originality among the throng of tourist traps, this shop is run by eight charming women who consider it "the only pure Hawaiiana shop in Kona." Every item is handcrafted by a local artist or sculptor; some of the merchandise that you may not see anywhere else includes banana-bark art, petroglyph pottery, and *makaleka* dolls. Also sold are native koa and milo woodcarvings, scrimshaw, musical instruments, and black coral jewelry. ◆ Daily 9AM-9PM. 75-5699 Alii Dr (between Likana La and Palani Rd), Kailua-Kona. 329.5590 ♿

83 Cafe Sibu ★★$ Affordable and well-prepared Indonesian cuisine, served both indoors and outdoors, makes this small cafe an excellent lunch spot. It's casual and pleasant, with a variety of piquant curries, satay dishes with spicy peanut sauces, and barbecued meats and vegetables. The classic *gado gado* (vegetable) salad with peanut and lime dressing has a big following, as do the vegetarian stir-frys. Balinese artifacts adorn this tiny but atmospheric place. ◆ Indonesian

◆ Daily lunch and dinner. No reservations. No credit cards accepted. Kona Banyan Ct, 75-5695 Alii Dr (between Likana La and Palani Rd), Kailua-Kona. 329.1112

84 Hulihee Palace Members of the Hawaiian *alii* (royalty) spent their summer vacations at this Victorian-style, coral-and-lava structure built in 1838 by Big Island governor John Adams Kuakini, brother-in-law of King Kamehameha. Operated as a museum by the **Daughters of Hawaii** since 1924, it is simple but impressive, with a massive koa dining table, Queen Kapiolani's four-poster bed, and fabulous 19th-century cabinetry and mementos. ◆ Admission. Daily. 75-5718 Alii Dr (between Kona Inn Shopping Center and Palani Rd), Kailua-Kona. 329.1877

85 Mokuaikaua Church Built in 1836 by the first missionaries, this is the oldest Christian church in Hawaii. Its 112-foot steeple is still the tallest structure in town. The lava-rock walls were mortared with a mixture of crushed, burnt coral and *kukui* nut oil. ◆ Alii Dr (between Sarona Rd and Likana La), Kailua-Kona

Restaurants/Clubs: Red   **Hotels:** Blue
Shops/ Outdoors: Green   **Sights/Culture:** Black

Sights from the Saddle

If you want to experience the Big Island's *paniolo* (cowboy) country, there's no better way than to saddle up a horse. **Waipio Na'alapa Trail Rides** (109 Mamane St, off Mamalahoa Hwy, Honokaa, 775.0419) offers horseback tours along the valley's rivers and streams toward stunning Hiilawe waterfall. Your adventure begins at **Waipio Valley Artworks** (775.0958) in the tiny town of **Kukuihaele;** a four-wheel-drive vehicle transports you a thousand feet down (on a treacherously steep road) and across the valley to the stables. The two-and-a-half-hour ride goes deep into the valley. Tours are offered Mondays through Saturdays.

Kings' Trail Rides O' Kona (323.2890), in the country town of **Kealakekua,** offers both beach and mountain rides for all levels of equestrians and prepares picnic lunches for customers on half-day rides. Daily by reservation only.

86 Middle Earth Bookshoppe Who would expect a haven for the literati among the tourist shops of Kailua-Kona? This is a bookstore for browsers, with a cornucopia of travel guides, children's books, Hawaiiana, maps, calendars, and art magazines, as well as the standard fiction and nonfiction. Bibliophiles, give yourself at least an hour . ◆ Kona Plaza Shopping Arcade, 75-5719 Alii Dr (at Sarona Rd), Kailua-Kona. 329.2123

87 Hula Heaven It's a treasure trove of kitschy Hawaiian collectibles from the 1920s to the 1950s, those halcyon days of raffia-skirted hula dolls, hand-painted neckties, Mundorff prints, and Matson cruise-liner menus. The hula girl lamps, silk aloha shirts, and muumuus can cost hundreds of dollars, but the charm bracelets, salt-and-pepper shakers,

and reproductions go for much less. This pla is hard to resist. ◆ Kona Inn Shopping Village 75-5744 Alii Dr (just north of Hale Halawai Beach Park), Kailua-Kona. 329.7885 ♿

87 Kona Inn Restaurant ★★$$$ The building is fondly remembered as the site of t wonderful old **Kona Inn,** which, unfortunately was torn down in favor of yet another shoppir center. This restaurant got the best of the deal—it overlooks the manicured lawns with million-dollar ocean view. The proprietors did the site justice by building a beautiful bar, a patio area (great for sunset cocktails), and an open-air dining room with lots of rich koa wood. Less imagination went into the menu, which relies on the unfailingly repetitive catch of the day (expensive here), other seafood dishes such as Kailua prawns and kabobs, plu steak and prime rib. ◆ Steaks/ Seafood ◆ Dail lunch and dinner. Reservations recommende Kona Inn Shopping Village, 75-5744 Alii Dr (just north of Hale Halawai Beach Park), Kailu Kona. 329.4455

87 Don Drysdale's Club 53 ★$ The late Lo Angeles Dodger pitching great opened this b and eatery, a local favorite. With indoor and outdoor tables, it's known for its relaxed atmosphere, ocean view, cheap drinks, good service, and 747 cheeseburgers (some say they're Kona's best). This is a lively spot where folks nosh on soups, nachos, and buffalo burgers while watching sports events on TV. ◆ American ◆ Daily lunch and dinner. Kona Inn Shopping Village, 75-5744 Alii Dr (just north of Hale Halawai Beach Park), Kailua-Kona. 329.6651. Also at: Keauhou Shopping Village, 78-6831 Alii Dr (just north of Kamehameha III Rd), Keauhou. 322.0070

88 Uncle Billy's Kona Bay Hotel $$ This one-time annex to the old **Kona Inn** was converted into a 145-room hotel run by bargain-minded Uncle Billy Kimi (who has 11 kids). The rooms are spartan but clean and air-conditioned, and the property has a pool. Kailua Village's shopping and historic attractions are right outside the front door, and the **Banana Bay Buffet** restaurant offers unspectacular but reasonably priced food. ◆ 75-5739 Alii Dr (at Hualalai Rd), Kailua-Kona. 329.1393, 800/367.5102; fax 329.921

89 Waterfront Row A half-dozen take-out joints selling everything from coffee to sushi are complemented by three real restaurants here. The lanai dining area on the first floor is a major plus. ◆ 75-5770 Alii Dr (south of Hale Halawai Beach Park), Kailua-Kona

Within Waterfront Row:

Chart House ★★$$$ The first Chart House opened in Aspen, Colorado, more thar 30 years ago. This ocean-view outpost is No. 66 in the chain and provides selections that mainland Chart Houses lack, like *poki* (raw fish)—a favorite island appetizer—and grille *ono* (wahoo). ♦ Steak/Seafood ♦ Daily dinner. Reservations recommended. 329.2451 &

Jolly Roger Restaurant ★$$ The best things about this branch of the island-style cafeteria chain are its oceanside location, (relatively) low prices, and Sunday brunch, where the steak and eggs Benedict and orange French toast are standouts. The place also morphs into a mini dance bar on weekend nights; the crowd is young. ♦ Tropical American ♦ M-Sa breakfast, lunch, and dinner; Su brunch and dinner. No reservations. 329.1344

Michaelangelo's ★$$ The alfresco oceanfront atmosphere draws folks to this casual dining room, and the all-you-can-eat spaghetti, scampi, and dozens of other choices keep them coming back. Two-for-one dinner coupons are often handed out on the sidewalk in front of **Waterfront Row**. ♦ Italian ♦ Daily lunch and dinner. Reservations recommended. 329.4436

90 **Island Lava Java** ★$ The hip scene in Kona begins and ends at this alfresco cafe. Order a cup of java and a warm scone and enjoy the show. Local musicians perform here nightly—though the acts are more "Gong Show" than Hootie and the Blowfish. ♦ Coffeehouse ♦ Daily 7AM-10PM. No reservations. Alii Sunset Plaza, 75-5799 Alii Dr (between Walua and Hualalai Rds), Kailua-Kona. 327.2161 &

PALM CAFE

91 **Palm Cafe** ★★★$$$$ This open-air restaurant is a must-do. Large rattan chairs, green and white decor, and a spectacular view of Kailua Bay mesh well with the consistently impressive if trendy cuisine. Small portions feature innovative uses of herbs and unusual sauces and "healthful" cooking methods. Try the Kona tomato relish and the oven-baked *ono* (wahoo) in an almond-sesame crust with ginger-lime sauce and papaya. There is also a commendable vegetarian menu. ♦ New American ♦ Daily dinner. Reservations recommended. 75-5819 Alii Dr (between Walua and Hualalai Rds), Kailua-Kona. 329.7765

91 **Under the Palm** ★★★$ One of the happening new ocean-view eateries in town, it's a kinder, gentler, and more affordable offshoot of the upscale, upstairs establishment. The food runs to gourmet pizza and sandwiches, while the full bar features exotic coffee drinks. ♦ Pacific Regional ♦ Daily breakfast, lunch, and dinner. 75-5819 Alii Dr (between Walua and Hualalai Rds), Kailua-Kona. 329.7366 &

92 **Huggo's** ★$$$ This oceanside restaurant is yet another where the setting surpasses the food, though the entrées have improved in the past few years. Fortunately, if you don't like your entrée, you can feed it to the manta rays that play in the floodlights right outside. The lunch fare centers around sandwiches and such, with prime rib, steaks, and seafood (including, when available, fresh lobster and prawns) for dinner. This is also a great place for sunset cocktails. ♦ Steaks/Seafood ♦ M-F lunch, daily dinner. Reservations recommended. 75-5828 Kahakai Rd (off Alii Dr), Kailua-Kona. 329.1493 &

93 **Royal Kona Resort** $$$ It's hard not to like this place. With its landmark saltwater lagoon and lava peninsula, it manages to be romantic even though it's a somewhat large hotel. The 444 rooms and eight suites are in three towers at the south end of Kona, with private lanais landscaped with bougainville a looking out at the ocean, mountains, or village. Amenities include four tennis courts (three lighted), a pool, and a small beach nearby. There are two restaurants: **Tropics Cafe**, an open-air dining room with a sweeping view of the Kailua coastline, and the **Windjammer Lounge**, a lunch spot and lounge. The hotel's luau is held oceanside on Monday, Friday, and Saturday nights from 5:30 to 8:30PM. The close proximity to Kailua Village is another plus. ♦ 75-5852 Alii Dr (on Kahakai Rd), Kailua-Kona. 329.3111, 800/222.5642; fax 329.9532

94 **Kona Reef** $$ The big advantage of this condominium resort is its location; within easy walking distance of the shops and restaurants, it solves the problem of having to find a parking place. The 58 one-, two-, and three-bedroom units come loaded with all the comforts of home (fully equipped kitchens, washer/dryers, air-conditioning, cable TV, telephones), and there's even daily maid service, but no restaurant. ♦ 75-5888 Alii Dr (just south of Kahakai Rd), Kailua-Kona. 329.2959; 800/367.5004; fax 329.2762

95 **Tom Bombadil's Food & Drink** ★$ Named after a character in J.R.R. Tolkien's Lord of the Rings trilogy, this watering hole is a favorite hangout for local fisherfolk and triathletes. The anglers are partial to the strong mai tais, while the hardbodies who converge each October for the **Ironman Triathlon** come here for low-priced carbo-loading. The bill of fare offers pasta, pizza, beer, and the fish, chicken, and meat specials. The broasted chicken is legendary. ♦ American ♦ Daily lunch and dinner. 75-5864 Walua Rd (at Alii Dr), Kailua-Kona. 329.1292 &

Fresh Fruit that's Free to Boot

Tired of spending your hard-earned vacation dollars on food that's mediocre at best? Then keep your eyes open as you pass the many tropical fruit trees that thrive on Hawaii's isles. Chances are you've already overlooked numerous trees bearing ripe (and free) bananas, avocados, breadfruit, mangoes, papayas, guavas, coconuts, apples, and more. In general, it's okay to pick wild fruit for personal consumption, although private property is off limits and you can't take uncertified plants and fruit off the island. Grab a pocketknife and take a look at the greenery around you; you'll soon discover what the locals have always known—some of the best things in Hawaii are free.

Coconuts

Cursed with a tough, hairy shell within a smooth, oblong outer husk, the coconut is the ugly stepsister of the fruit family. Yet, however unattractive, its tough exterior protects the creamy milk and sweet meat that was an island staple for centuries. The Polynesians brought coconut trees to Hawaii, planting them immediately upon arrival. The trees were an integral part of their daily life, and they used every part of them: trunks for building homes and *heiaus* (temples); husks for bowls, utensils, and jewelry; and husk fiber for *aha* (the most saltwater-resistant natural rope ever made). When a child was born, a coconut tree was planted to provide him or her with a lifelong source of fruit. Sailors, explorers, and traders also kept coconuts on hand for food.

Today, fresh and packaged coconut are still important island staples. For visitors, they also make a fun gift to mail to family and friends. Simply write the address on the brown shell of a whole coconut, affix the appropriate amount of postage, and drop it into a mailbox; coconuts are on the certified list of fruits that may be taken off the island.

Papayas

In 1778 Captain James Cook offered a handful of seeds to a Hawaiian king, and soon papaya trees prospered on the islands. The mellow fruit became a favorite among Hawaiian rulers, who exchanged papayas as gifts.

The papaya's rosy, golden meat is reminiscent of the cantaloupe and peach, yet it has its own exotic flavor. The fruit grows in clusters on tall trees that look like a cross between breadfruit trees and palms. Each tree is either male, female, or hermaphrodite. The hermaphrodite fruit combines the juiciness of the female fruit with the leanness of the male fruit and has the best flavor. Papayas are also commercially important to Hawaii; millions are grown every year in sprawling groves and sold whole or puréed as a multiuse pulp that's low in calories and rich in vitamins. The enzyme papain, found in the juice of unripe papayas, is used to manufacture digestives and meat tenderizers.

Pineapples

No one knows when the first pineapple arrived in Hawaii, but a Spaniard wrote about the fruit (then called *halakahiki*) on his first visit to Hawaii in 1813. By the end of the 19th century, James Dole had seized on the pineapple's popularity and organized commercial production by establishing the very successful Hawaiian Pineapple Company. The company's advertisements introducing the pineapple to mainland America explained, "You eat it with a spoon like a peach."

The pineapple has since come a long way, although after a hundred years as one of the state's leading industries, its presence has diminished greatly. Hawaii's pineapples must compete in the marketplace with those grown in the Philippines, Taiwan, Thailand, and other countries where labor costs are cheaper.

The plant itself grows two to four feet tall, and takes about 18 to 20 months to produce a four- to five-pound fruit. The first harvest yields one pineapple per plant, and the second and third harvests yield one or two. After three seasons the plants no longer produce marketable fruit.

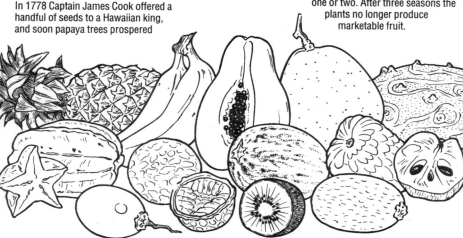

96 Aston Royal Sea Cliff Resort $$$
Families who prefer to be self-sufficient will
absolutely love the large, attractive units in this
condominium complex. The stark, angular
white structure stands out along the lava
coastline (there's no beach) and includes 150
studios and one- and two-bedroom suites with
lanais, washer/dryers, cable TV, daily maid
service, air-conditioning, and full kitchens
with dishwashers and microwaves. There are
two pools, a Jacuzzi, a sauna, and a tennis
court on the premises, but no restaurant.
Five oceanfront villas also are available. ♦ 75-
6040 Alii Dr (a mile south of Kailua-Kona).
329.8021, 800/922.7866; fax 326.1887 ♿

97 Aston Kona by the Sea $$$ There's no
real beach nearby, but the view is spectacular
from the 73 one- and two-bedroom suites.
The accommodations in this four-story resort
come with kitchens and daily maid service;
there's also a pool and Jacuzzi, but no restaurant. ♦ 75-6106 Alii Dr (a mile south of Kailua-
Kona). 327.2300, 800/922.7866; fax 327.2333

98 Jameson's by the Sea ★★$$$ One of
the few oceanside restaurants that relies on
its food instead of its view (which is quite
impressive), this is also one of the only places
in town that serves oysters on the half shell.
Fresh *opakapaka* (pink snapper), mahimahi,
and *ono* (wahoo), along with scallops, pasta,
and an especially delicious scampi, highlight
the menu. ♦ Seafood ♦ M-F lunch, daily
dinner. Reservations recommended. 77-6452
Alii Dr, Kahaluu. 329.3195

98 White Sands Beach Around November, this
beach does a disappearing act, leaving a rocky
shoreline (hence its nicknames, "Disappearing
Sands Beach" and "Magic Sands Beach"). It's
great for swimming when the waves are low,
bodysurfing when they're high, and whale
sighting during the winter. ♦ Off Alii Dr (at
Jameson's by the Sea), Kahaluu

99 La Bourgogne ★★★$$$ Owner/chef Ron
Gallaher proffers Gallic pleasures like rack of
lamb with rosemary butter and classically
prepared game in an intimate atmosphere of
hushed tones and velvet banquettes. There
are only 10 tables in this tiny dining spot.
♦ Country French ♦ M-Sa dinner. Reservations
recommended. Kuakini Plaza South, 77-6400
Nalani St (at Hwy 11). 329.6711

100 Little Blue Church Built in 1889 and
officially named **St. Peter's Catholic Church**,
this tiny tabernacle got its nickname from its
blue tin roof. ♦ Alii Dr (just north of Kahaluu
Beach Park), Keauhou

With an elevation of 13,020 feet, Lake Waiau, on
Mauna Kea on the Big Island, is the third-highest
lake in the country and the highest in Hawaii.
Nihau's Halalii Lake is the largest in the state.

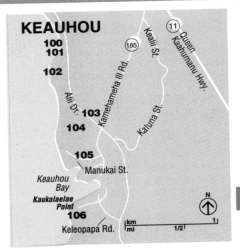

KEAUHOU

101 Kahaluu Beach Park Local fishing
enthusiasts have found this to be a worthwhile
spot, and the white-sand beach is great for
families and amateur snorkelers, since public
bathrooms are available. But stay well within
the protective bay; more rescues are made
here than on any other beach in Kona. ♦ Off
Alii Dr (just north of the Keauhou Beach
Hotel), Keauhou

102 Keauhou Beach Hotel $$ The most
historic and genuinely Hawaiian of the Kona
hotels is located in an area that used to be a
playground of Hawaii's monarchs. The beauty
of the setting hasn't changed much since
then. The seven-story, 316-room hostelry,
adorned with cascading bougainvillea, is set
in a coconut grove. The grounds feature tall,
stately monkeypods, lush plants and bushes,
stone idols, petroglyphs, a pond where King
Kalakaua once bathed, and a replica of the
king's former home. Be sure to ask for a room
in the renovated wing (garden rooms are all
unrenovated). Check out the Sunday brunch
and affordable seafood and Chinese buffets
served in the ground-floor **Kuakini Terrace**
restaurant, popular among the local folk.
♦ 78-6740 Alii Dr (just south of Kahaluu
Beach Park), Keauhou. 322.3441,
800/367.6025; fax 322.6586 ♿

103 Alapaki's The shining gem in an otherwise
dull shopping mall, this charming store won
the 1990 Kahili Award from the **Hawaii
Visitors and Convention Bureau** for
"perpetuating the essence of Hawaii." Many
items sold here, including koa wood jewelry

and bowls, *kukui* nut and coral jewelry, fine original art, wooden *konane* board games (similar to checkers), and Hawaiian hula instruments, are handmade by 168 local artists and craftspeople. ♦ Daily. Keauhou Shopping Village, 78-6831 Alii Dr (just north of Kamehameha III Rd), Keauhou. 322.2007

104 Kona Country Club Golfers staying in the Kona and Keauhou Bay areas will find this 18-hole course (par 72, 6,579 yards) a convenient place to play. Magnificent ocean views and some of Hawaii's most consistently sunny weather make the layout, cut out of black lava rock, a sure bet. Just across the road is the 18-hole **Alii Country Club** course (par 72, 6,470 yards), which is under the same management. ♦ Expensive greens fees. Preferred starting times and rates for **Kona Surf Resort** and **Keauhou Beach Hotel** guests. 78-7000 Alii Dr (between Kamehameha III Rd and Kahaluu Beach Park), Keauhou. 322.2595

105 Kanaloa at Kona $$$ These low-rise villas, with full kitchens and private lanais, rank among the most spacious accommodations in Kona. They're a good value for self-sufficient families or groups who want to share a unit. The resort, slightly off the beaten track, is extremely quiet, comfortable, and well managed, with 166 villas sprawled over 14 acres in a cul-de-sac near Keauhou Bay. Some of the split-level units have great views of the ocean, golf course, or mountains. Ceiling fans compensate for the lack of air-conditioning in some units, and the two- and three-bedroom oceanfront units have Jacuzzis and bathrooms with double vanities and separate showers with double heads. On-site extras include two lighted tennis courts and three pools, as well as a commendable terrace restaurant, **Edward's at Kanaloa**, which overlooks Heeia Bay. ♦ A two-night minimum stay is required. 78-261 Manukai St (off Alii Dr), Keauhou. 322.2272, 800/688.7444; fax 322.3818

106 Kona Surf Resort $$ A striking example of hotel architecture, this resort (illustrated below) is all the more impressive because its five four- and six-story wings were erected on rugged lava fields formed centuries ago at the ocean's edge. Unfortunately, the resort looks a little rough around the edges, as it's in need of renovations that are slow in coming. The 530 rooms are large, though, and the lack of a sandy beach is eased by the exquisite ocean view and the manta rays that gather nightly at the point. Amenities include two swimming pools (one of which is saltwater), a massage room, the **Kona Country Club Golf Course,** three lighted tennis courts, and several shops. ♦ 78-128 Ehukai St (off Keleopapa Rd), Keauhou. 322.3411, 800/367.8011; fax 322.3245

Kona Surf Resort

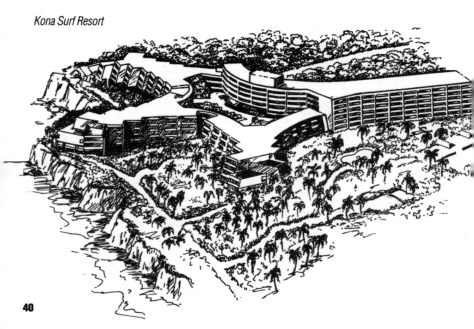

Within the Kona Surf Resort:

Pele's Court Dining Room $$$
Chicken, pasta, fish, and steak are the standards in this very standard restaurant. The Friday night prime rib and seafood buffet is good, and there's a free Polynesian show Tuesday through Friday evenings. ♦ American ♦ Daily breakfast, lunch, and dinner. 322.3411 &

07 Aloha Theater Cafe ★★$$ This is the kind of cafe you wish you had at home. Big, homemade breakfasts of French toast and omelettes with corn bread and muffins start the day. Huge, healthy sandwiches crammed with bean sprouts and such follow for lunch, and grilled fish and a rotating selection of gourmet specials are on line for dinner. The menu is pseudo-vegetarian, with an emphasis on homegrown freshness. It's definitely worth the drive from Kona, particularly when combined with a show at the **Aloha Theater** (322.9924) in the same building. ♦ Cafe ♦ M-Sa breakfast, lunch, and dinner; Su brunch. No reservations. Off Mamalahoa Hwy, Kainaliu. 322.3383

08 Bad Ass Coffee Company You'll know by the blue awning and aroma of fresh-brewed joe that you're in the right place. Quality coffee—espresso, cappuccino, and other variations—is ground and brewed on the premises. Drop in for a free sample. ♦ Daily 7AM-9PM. Off Hwy 11, Kainaliu. 322.9196

09 Manago Hotel $ Shabby but clean, this hotel offers lots of character, a great view, and a restaurant that boasts an island-wide following. More than three-quarters of a century old and still going strong, the hostelry is now run by a third generation of Managos. Cheap and quiet, the rooms come with private or shared baths but without TVs or telephones. ♦ 82-6155 Mamalahoa Hwy, Captain Cook. 323.2642

Within the Manago Hotel:

Manago Hotel Dining Room ★$ Locals come from up and down the coast for Mrs. Manago's fresh fish and pork chops. Budget prices, a deluxe view, and Japanese-style home cooking make this one of West Hawaii's landmarks. ♦ Japanese/American ♦ Tu-Su breakfast, lunch, and dinner. No reservations. 323.2642

King Kamehameha V and Prince Lunalilo were both bachelors when they died.

Metal was such a novelty to Hawaiians that when Captian Cook first landed on Kauai he was able to swap a single nail for enough fresh pork, potatoes, and taro to feed his ship's entire crew for a day.

110 Bong Brothers The sign in front of this establishment should say "Island Institution." Many visitors pass by this roadside coffee shack. Don't make that mistake. Pull over for a free cup of some of the best Kona coffee the region has to offer; if you're hungry, grab a homemade sandwich or salad to go. ♦ Daily. Mamalahoa Hwy (a mile south of Captain Cook Post Office), Honaunau. 328.9289; fax 328.8112 &

111 Royal Aloha Coffee Mill and Museum Taste the brew that made Kona famous and take a 15-minute tour of the old mill and the museum. Old equipment and photographs of past harvests are on display. ♦ Free. Daily. Middle Keei Rd (between Painted Church and Puuhonua Rds). 328.2511 &

112 Captain Cook Monument Ancient Hawaiians' first contact with Europeans occurred on 17 January 1779, when the British ships *Resolution* and *Discovery* laid anchor in this bay. Given a royal welcome by the awe-struck Hawaiians, Captain James Cook and his crew later suffered tragic consequences over the supposed theft of the *Discovery*'s rowboat. Cook, who unwisely took the local chief hostage, was beaten to death at the water's edge, then burned and dismembered, as was the custom. Four crew members met similar fates. The site is marked by a 27-foot-high white pillar, accessible by boat or arduous hiking trail, but visible from the south shore of Kealakekua Bay, a popular marine preserve. ♦ From Mamalahoa Hwy (Hwy 11), take the Napoopoo Rd turnoff (just north of Captain Cook)

113 The Painted Church Officially christened **St. Benedict's Church,** this petite place of worship got its popular name from the biblical scenes that were painted on the walls and ceiling circa 1900. For Hawaiians who couldn't read or write, Father John Berchman Velghe of Belgium illustrated Christianity with images not unlike those in the cathedral of Burgos, Spain. ♦ Painted Church Rd (between Keala O Keawe and Middle Keei Rds), Honaunau

114 Puuhonua O Honaunau (Place of Refuge National Park) When ancient Hawaiians broke *kapu* (sacred law) or were fleeing an enemy in times of war, their only escape was to run and/or swim to the nearest *puuhonua* (place of refuge), where they were exonerated by a *kahuna pule* (priest). Because breaking *kapu* was believed to anger the gods and cause mass death and destruction (lava flows, tsunamis, floods, famine, and the like), offenders were often literally running for their lives, hiding out until things calmed down a bit. This *puuhonua* was the largest in Hawaii, resting on a 20-acre peninsula of lava, and is now part of the 180-acre national historical park. Dominating the site is the **Great Wall**, a massive, mortarless barrier of lava rock—1,000 feet long, 10 feet high, and 17 feet wide—constructed around two *heiau* (temples). Also here are thatch-roofed huts, wooden idols, royal fish ponds, a trail to cliffs and lava tubes, a visitors' center, picnic area, rest rooms, petroglyphs, and palace grounds. ♦ Admission. Daily 7:30AM-8PM. Off Hwy 160, Honaunau Bay. 328.2326

115 Hookena Beach Park Although it's hard to believe when you see it, Hookena was once the main port in South Kona. Now it's a backwater community adjacent to a salt-and-pepper (black and white sand) beach favored by local families. Although the swimming, snorkeling, and bodysurfing here are excellent, the road to the shore is narrow and steep—a trial for those prone to car sickness. Camping is allowed by permit. ♦ At the end of Hookena Rd (off Mamalahoa Hwy), Hookena

Slip-Slidin' Away

There's no need to panic just yet, but geologists and seismologists recently have determined through satellite measurements that a well-populated southern flank of the Big Island, which includes the entire southern half of **Hawaii Volcanoes National Park**, is rapidly sliding into the ocean. **Kilauea**, the most active volcano on earth, now has been proclaimed the fastest-sinking volcano in the world, disappearing at a rate of several inches per year. More ominously, scientists predict that any time in the next 100,000 years the volcanic rift zone (illustrated below) could break off and tumble into the Pacific, resulting in one of the greatest natural catastrophes of all time.

Kau District

The southernmost section of the Big Island and the site of the southernmost point in the United States, the Kau District is a remote and dramatic place. Her green pastureland rolls to a coastline of windswept beaches and striking cliffs that tower above the sea. There are few tourist attractions, and relatively few tourists, but a drive through the region is sure to be memorable. Turn off the main roads to find deserted beaches, incredible views, and a glimpse into the rural lifestyle of the local residents.

116 Ka Lae (South Point) It's only 11 miles from Mamalahoa Highway (Hwy 11), but it feels like you're driving to the end of the earth. Once barely passable, the road is now paved, making the trip thoroughly enjoyable. Besides being the southernmost point in the US, this area is believed to be where the first Polynesian discoverers of Hawaii landed circa AD 150. Be sure to stop at the **Kamaoa Wind Farm**, a fenced-in field of windmills, and listen to the eerie symphony of 37 Mitsubishi wind turbine generators playing before a captive bovine audience. ♦ At the end of South Point Rd (off Mamalahoa Hwy)

117 Green Sands Beach Volcanic olivine crystals created the color and inspired the name of this secluded beach on Mahana Bay. Accessible only by four-wheel-drive vehicle or by hiking or mountain biking, it's definitely a jaunt for the adventurous at heart. Once you get there, swim only if the water is calm; currents can be treacherous, and the next stop is Antarctica—7,500 miles away! ♦ 2 miles east of Ka Lae (South Point)

118 Naalehu There's not a lot to do in this burg except check out the locals at the **Naalehu Fruit Stand** (and be checked out in turn), but you can tell your friends back home you've been to the southernmost community in the United States. ♦ Mamalahoa Hwy (6 miles east of South Point Rd)

119 SeaMountain Resort & Golf Course $$ The key word at this 76-unit condominium complex is seclusion. Halfway between Hilo and Kona, the place is so remote that it often appears vacant, and the championship 18-hole golf course (par 72) is virtually deserted. The 23 studios, 41 one-bedroom units, and 18 two-bedroom units have full kitchens and washers and dryers; the grounds feature a pool, a Jacuzzi, and four tennis courts, but no restaurant. It's not the fanciest of resorts, but for the price, seclusion, and amenities, it's a deal. ♦ 95-789 Ninole Loop Rd (off Mamalahoa Hwy), Punaluu. 928.6200, 800/344.7675; fax 928.8075 ♦

119 Punaluu Black Sand Beach Park One of the Big Island's best-known black-sand beaches, this park offers picnic and camping facilities and a broad bay with concrete foundations—vestiges of its former days as a

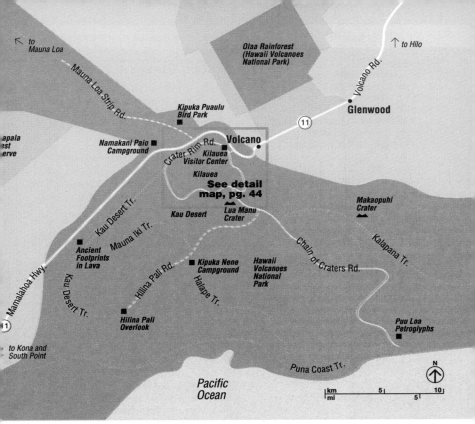

Map labels:
← to Mauna Loa
↑ to Hilo
Olaa Rainforest (Hawaii Volcanoes National Park)
Mauna Loa Strip Rd.
Kipuka Puaulu Bird Park
Volcano Rd.
Glenwood
11
apala est erve
Namakani Paio Campground
Crater Rim Rd.
Volcano
Kilauea Visitor Center
Kilauea
See detail map, pg. 44
Makaopuhi Crater
Kau Desert Tr.
Kau Desert
Lua Manu Crater
Kalapana Tr.
Mauna Iki Tr.
Ancient Footprints in Lava
Hilina Pali Rd.
Kipuka Nene Campground
Hawaii Volcanoes National Park
Chain of Craters Rd.
Mamalanoa Hwy.
Kau Desert Tr.
Halape Tr.
1
Hilina Pali Overlook
Puu Loa Petroglyphs
to Kona and South Point
Puna Coast Tr.
N
Pacific Ocean
km / mi   5   10   5

---

significant shipping point for Kau. Palm trees and spring-fed lagoons add to the beauty here, but the rocky bay is not recommended for swimming. ♦ Off Ninole Loop Rd (just past SeaMountain Resort & Golf Course), Punaluu

olcano

e tiny village of Volcano has a few places to eat, a of bed-and-breakfast places to stay in, and an ectic population of artsy types and adventurous rees from the mainland that makes for interesting ple watching. Thanks to the extremely wet ather, the vegetation is lush and diverse, and on rare dry day the scenery is gorgeous. Travelers in rch of a remote hideaway (with the added bonus an active volcano nearby) happily vacation here.

20 Hawaii Volcanoes National Park
Established in 1916, the 377-square-mile park begins at Mauna Loa near the island's center, narrows eastward, then fans south around Kilauea to the coast near what was the town of Kalapana before lava swallowed it up. Although Mauna Loa is the most obvious landmark, most tourist attractions revolve around Kilauea, the volcano that just won't quit.

Done right, a trip to the park should take all day and part of the night (when the lava glows, an unforgettable sight). Bring binoculars, a flashlight, a camera, a jacket, sturdy shoes or boots, and a stocked picnic basket. Start your day at the **Kilauea Visitors Center** (967.7311), taking the half-hour self-guided tour to familiarize yourself with the area and watching the 25-minute video of the last major eruption (shown on the hour), then grab a free guide and ask the ranger to point out where the lava flows (if any) are. Continue counterclockwise on the 11-mile Crater Rim Road, making sure to stop at the **Thomas A. Jaggar Museum** (967.7643); this one-room display of volcano-related things—including Pele's tears and different types of lava—is open daily.

Once you've circumnavigated Kilauea, the park's network of roads leads you to dozens of interesting sites that can be explored on foot. **Kipuka Puaulu Bird Park** has an easily traveled 1.2-mile unpaved path through forest and meadows filled with birds and some of the last indigenous fauna and flora in Hawaii. The **Halemaumau Trail** into the Kilauea caldera, leading across fresh lava flows, is for the hardier hiker. The 6.4-mile trek takes five hours round-trip, or you can meet a friend with a car at the Halemaumau parking area to avoid the hike back. **Mauna Iki** is a more moderate 3.6-mile, two-hour round-trip (take the **Kau Desert Trail,** between the 37- and 38-mile markers on Hwy 11). The paved path over a 400-year-old lava flow crosses the Kau Desert and leads to footprints made by warriors who unsuccessfully attempted to flee Kilauea's eruption of 1790.

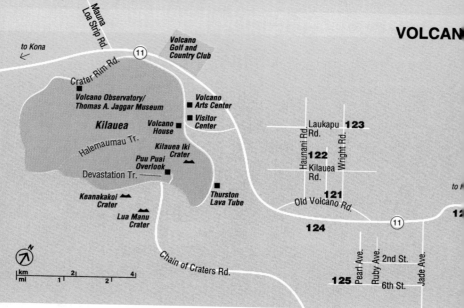

Map labels:
to Kona
Mauna Loa Strip Rd.
11
Volcano Golf and Country Club
Crater Rim Rd.
Volcano Observatory/ Thomas A. Jaggar Museum
Volcano Arts Center
Kilauea
Volcano House
Visitor Center
Halemaumau Tr.
Kilauea Iki Crater
Puu Puai Overlook
Devastation Tr.
Keanakakoi Crater
Lua Manu Crater
Thurston Lava Tube
Laukapu Rd. **123**
Haunani Rd.
Wright Rd.
122
Kilauea Rd.
121
Old Volcano Rd.
to
124
11
Chain of Craters Rd.
Pearl Ave.
Ruby Ave.
2nd St.
Jade Ave.
6th St.
125
km
mi

Chain of Craters Road, which used to continue into Puna, leads toward the famous lava flows that have been oozing from Puu Oo since 1983, ending abruptly 20 miles from Crater Rim Road. The active vent is on state land and off-limits to the public, but people hike here at night anyway to watch the bright red rivers of lava flow into the ocean. (This is extremely dangerous—if you decide to go be very careful and bring a flashlight.) You can also view the vent from the air by helicopter. Worthy stops on the return trip include the **Puu Loa Petroglyphs** and the **Hilina Pali Overlook** (at the end of Hilina Pali Rd, 18 miles round-trip). Warning: Pele, the volcano goddess, doesn't like visitors taking lava rocks home as souvenirs (it's also against the law); the park annually receives returned lava chunks in the mail from rock thieves besieged with bad luck. ◆ Admission. Visitors Center daily 7:45AM-5PM. Crater Rim Rd (off Mamalahoa Hwy). Volcano eruption information 967.7977

Within the Hawaii Volcanoes National Park:

Kilauea This volcano's record-breaking eruptive phase has destroyed 182 homes and numerous prominent landmarks since January 1983. A 1977 eruption sent lava less than half a mile from the now devastated Kalapana, while in 1960 the town of Kapoho was destroyed. That eruption added some 500 acres to the island, and Kapoho's lavascape served as a training ground for the astronauts who walked on the moon. Only one person has been killed by an eruption in modern times (an amateur photographer who got too close to a steam explosion in 1924). At press time Kilauea was still putting on a show at the end of Chain of Craters Road, but it's a hit-or-miss production.

Mauna Loa Sixty miles by 30 miles, "Long Mountain" is taller than Mount Everest and is heavier than the entire Sierra Nevada mountain range. Measured from the seafloor it is the most immense mountain on earth in total mass (although 117 feet shorter than neighboring Mauna Kea). Having spent two million years of its three-million-year existence reaching the ocean surface, this volcano sleeps for long spells between eruptions, the last of which was in 1984. Fortunately, the chances of being incinerated in a surprise lava flow are slim to none, since it is a shield volcano, not the Mount St. Helens variety that erupts violently without notice. The **Volcano Observatory** keeps a constant watch on the area; metal barricades on Crater Rim Road can be erected to stop motorists within minutes of an alert. Although reaching the summit of the volcano is possible with a three- to four-day hike (take Mauna Loa Strip Rd), the trip exceeds the boundaries of recreational tourism.

Thurston Lava Tube Tubes form when a crust of lava hardens and a river of lava continues to flow beneath the surface. A 1975 earthquake temporarily closed this lava tube when a boulder blocked the entrance. It is named for Lorrin A. Thurston, the publisher who pushed for a **Hawaii Volcanoes National Park** and was on the expedition that discovered this tube. ◆ Off Crater Rim Rd

Devastation Trail This eerie landscape looks like a science-fiction film set. Dead ohia trees, burned clean of their leaves by cinders from a 1959 Kilauea eruption, stand like skeletons in a bed of black pumice. A half-mile paved pathway crosses the region, ending at the Devastation parking area. ◆ Trailhead on Crater Rim Rd at the Puu Puai Overlook

Volcano Golf and Country Club Talk about an unusual location! With the hottest bunker on earth, this high-altitude course (par 72, 18 holes, 6,503 yards) is laid out on the rim of an active volcano—a splendid treat for golfers seeking novel experiences. ♦ Moderate greens fees. Daily. Reservations recommended a week in advance. Off Mamalahoa Hwy (a half mile east of Mauna Loa Strip Rd). 967.7331

Volcano House $$ There have been a succession of **Volcano Houses** since 1846, and all have offered something no other inn in the world can match: the opportunity to eat, drink, and sleep on the rim of an active volcano. Kilauea volcano is the hotel's backyard, best seen with a cocktail in hand at **Uncle George's Lounge** (named for George Lycurgus, who won the inn in a poker game and owned and operated it from 1895 to 1960). The service here has declined, something several changes in management have not been able to remedy, and the 42-room inn and restaurant are eclipsed by the bed-and-breakfasts in the area. The main structure has the feel of a hunting lodge, with a floor-to-ceiling lava rock fireplace whose fire has burned continuously since 1847. ♦ Crater Rim Tr (off Crater Rim Rd). 967.7321; fax 967.8428 &

Within the Volcano House:

Ka Ohelo Dining Room $$$ The best thing about this restaurant is the view of Halemaumau Crater, a spectacular sight that far outshines the food served daily to mobs of tourists brought in on charter buses. Try breakfast or early dinner to avoid the rush, but don't expect gourmet fare. ♦ American ♦ Daily breakfast buffet, lunch buffet, and dinner. Reservations recommended. 967.7321 &

Volcano Arts Center Built in 1877, this structure served as the **Volcano House Lodge** until the present lodge was completed in 1941. It now houses a variety of locally created artwork—paintings, sculptures, pottery, and photographs—by more than 200 artists. Check out the lavascapes by veteran volcano photographer G. Brad Lewis. ♦ Daily. Off Crater Rim Rd (near the Visitor Center). 967.7511 &

121 Kilauea Lodge $$ Built in 1938 as a camp lodge for the YMCA, this charming 10-acre estate is, for quality and price, the best deal on the island. All 13 uniquely decorated units, including two cottages (ideal for families) and a suite, have private bathrooms, and some also are furnished with a fireplace and a queen-size bed (be sure to ask). Gravel walkways lead through lush, impeccable landscaping to the best dining spot in the area, the **Kilauea Lodge Restaurant,** which overlooks a large manorial front yard abloom with blue hydrangeas. Considering the location, accommodations, and fare, this lodge is simply an unbeatable value. Full American breakfast is included in the rate. ♦ Old Volcano Rd (between Wright and Haunani Rds), Volcano. 967.7366; fax 967.7367 &

Within the Kilauea Lodge:

Kilauea Lodge Restaurant ★★★$$$ Easily the best in town, this gourmet continental restaurant offers first-rate cuisine, ambience, and service. The large, high-ceilinged dining room was the gathering place of the YMCA, which left its mark in an "International Fireplace of Friendship," built with rocks, coins, and memorabilia from civic and youth groups around the world. Of greater interest, however, are the beef, chicken, and seafood specialties and wonderful soups concocted by owner/chef Albert Jeyte, which attract diners from all over east Hawaii. If you're anywhere in the vicinity (which includes Hilo), stop in for duck à l'orange or seafood Mauna Kea. ♦ Continental ♦ Daily dinner. Reservations recommended. 967.7366

122 Hale Kilauea $$ The four guest rooms here are named after the siblings of owner Morris Thomas, who built this two-story structure (illustrated above) on three acres. All the spacious guest rooms face the fern and ohia forests, but the corner room (named Heidi) has a balcony and the best view. It's not the nicest bed-and-breakfast in the area (there are no phones or TVs), but what it lacks in character is made up for in price and friendly service. ♦ Off Kilauea Rd (between Haunani and Wright Rds). 967.7591

123 Chalet Kilauea $$ One of the most creative and charming bed-and-breakfasts on the island, this two-story cedar-shingle home in the misty Volcano forest is run by Brian and Lisha Crawford, an engaging young couple with exquisite taste in interior decorating. There are four fanciful theme rooms—the **Out of Africa Room,** the **Oriental Jade Room,** the **Continental Lace Suite,** and the **Treehouse Suite.** Afternoon tea is served in the large communal living room (stocked with hundreds of CDs), which is surrounded by ohia trees, *hapuu* ferns, and brilliant hydrangeas. Gourmet breakfasts (complimentary for guests) are served on fine china and linen in a cheerful Art Deco dining room, just down the hall from the Jacuzzi and the only communal bathroom you'll ever regret leaving. If you seek absolute privacy, the Crawfords also have six vacation homes, all with full kitchens, tasteful furnishings, optional gourmet breakfasts, and interesting settings. Either choice is highly recommended. ♦ Off Wright Rd (at Laukapu Rd), Volcano. 967.7786, 800/937.7786; fax 967.8660

124 Hale Ohia Bed and Breakfast $ Bed-and-breakfasts are becoming as plentiful in chilly, rainy, lush Volcano as orchid blossoms, but this retreat, made up of three suites in the main residence and three free-standing cottages, is definitely not of the standard variety. Rooms and cottages offer one-of-a-kind amenities such as lava-rock fireplaces, private gardens, and skylights. There is no restaurant, though several are nearby, and no air-conditioning, though none is needed. ♦ 11-3968 Hale Ohia Rd (off Hwy 11), Volcano. 967.7986, 800/455.3803; fax 967.8610 &

125 Carsons' Volcano Cottage $$ A short path winds through lush foliage to the English cottage and three connected studios that compose this small place. The Victorian decor is enhanced with old Hawaiian photographs, fresh flowers, and large windows looking out to the pine and plum trees. There's a veranda, and hosts Tom and Brenda Carson have equipped the rooms with coffeemakers, small refrigerators, heaters, and electric blankets (yes, these are used even in Hawaii). ♦ Sixth St (west of Pearl Ave). 967.7683, 800/845.LAVA; fax 967.8094

On a typical day in Hawaii, 171,000 people hang out at the beach, 25,000 go fishing, 22,000 ride the waves, 20,000 scuba dive, and 3,000 paddle canoes.

126 Akatsuka Orchid Gardens If you like orchids, you'll love this touristy display. All sizes, varieties, colors, and prices can be found, and pre-certified plants and cut flowers can be shipped home immediately. Stop by to use the clean rest room and receive a free orchid. ♦ Free. Hwy 11 (22.5 miles southwest of Hilo). 967.8234

Puna District

South of **Hilo,** the Puna District towns have a funky, down-at-the-heels rural charm, although some efforts at gentrification can be seen. The effects of the most recent eruptions of the **Kilauea** volcano are far more obvious, however. In the southern section of the district the lush rain forest suddenly gives way to barren lava rock, and lava flowing to the sea has blocked the road along the coast.

127 Puna Coast Drive Depending on the time of the year, the weather, and just plain luck, this can be one of the most interesting drives on the Big Island. Start at the old mill town of Pahoa, on Highway 130, staying just long enough to buy fresh fruit for the trip. Then head down Highway 132 through the stunning gauntlet of trees in **Nanawale Forest Reserve,** taking a side trip to **Lava Tree State Park.** Continue on to Cape Kumukahi and see the world's luckiest lighthouse in Kapoho; local lore says it was spared from the volcanic explosion because its kindly keeper was the only one in town to share his food with an old beggar woman (Madame Pele in her favorite disguise). Also on this route you'll have the opportunity to stop at **Isaac Hale Beach Park,** where the kids can swim off the boat ramp and chow on shave ice; the thermal warm ponds down the road, where the water will relax tight muscles; and the tidepools, a well-kept secret where you can see rare blue coral and a denser population of tropical fish than you'll find at many aquariums. Head southwest on Highway 137 along the *pandani* and palm-lined Puna Coast, keeping an eye out for whales (in season) and dolphins, until the road stops, blocked by lava from several early 1987 eruptions. With Kilauea still active, it is unlikely that the road will be open to through traffic anytime soon, so to get back to your starting point, turn around and retrace the route.

127 Paolo's Bistro ★★$$ The town of Pahoa is an odd place to find a high-caliber dining room—crowded as it is with old hippies, New Agers, and the nose-ring contingent—but this bistro is top-notch, serving mouth-watering dishes like *cioppino* (seafood stew) and pasta with prawns, clams, calamari, and mussels. Stop here for a feast after a drive through Puna—and try for a seat in the gazebo. ♦ Italian Tu-Su dinner. 333 Government Rd, Pahoa. 965.7033 ⑥

28 Lava Tree State Park Fast-flowing lava from the 1790 eruption smothered this ohia forest, and while moisture from the trees cooled the lava and formed a hard outer shell, huge fissures in the earth were busy reclaiming the surrounding lava. The result is this captivating gaggle of ghoulish tree molds. ♦ Daily. Hwy 132 (2.7 miles east of Pahoa)

29 Pamalu Hawaiian Country House $ Arguably one of the most restful places to stay in the islands, this bed-and-breakfast features koa-wood paneling in the common area, four rooms with queen-size beds and baths, a hammock, a pool, complimentary breakfasts, access to a poolside barbecue, and the attention of a convivial host. There is no air-conditioning, but ceiling fans do the job. The site also is near Pahoa's thermal ponds, tidepools, and a little-known spot called Green Lake. ♦ Off Hwy 132, Kapoho. 965.0830; fax 965.6198

Mauna Loa. Macadamia Nut Corp.

30 Mauna Loa Macadamia Nut Corporation Owned by **C. Brewer & Company of Honolulu,** this is the world's largest producer and marketer of the macadamia nut. The visitors' center offers a slide show, viewing stations of the mill's

processing and packing machines, and a few free samples. But don't make the mistake of thinking you can save money by buying macadamias from the source; you can usually get the nuts cheaper at a convenience store. ♦ Free. Daily 8:30AM-5PM. Macadamia Rd (off Kanoelehua Ave, about 6 miles south of Hilo). 966.9301

131 Nani Mau Gardens If Walt Disney had been a botanist, this would be his park. More than 2,000 varieties of Big Island flowers, shrubs, and trees fill the 20 acres of theme gardens. Take the narrated tram tour or stroll along the paved walkways with a map from the gift shop. It's touristy, but an orchid is an orchid is an orchid. ♦ Admission. Daily. 421 Makalika St (between Railroad Ave and Awa St). 959.3541 ⑥

132 Panaewa Rainforest Zoo Even if you're not a zoo person, you'll like this one. Set deep in the lush rain forest, it's a pseudo-natural environment for its resident birds, plants, and animals, most of which are indigenous to equatorial climates (which eases the inevitable "poor fella" syndrome). In fact, after viewing the tiger playground, you start to wonder who's being fenced in. Come on a weekday, and you'll have the zoo to yourself, allowing for private time with t he squirrel monkeys, tapirs, giant anteaters, and the zoobiquitous peacock. ♦ Free. Daily. Stainback Hwy (just west of Kanoelehua Ave). 959.7224 ⑥

Bests

Peter Merriman
Owner, Merriman's, the Big Island; Chef/Partner, Hula Grill, Maui

...breakfast of granola and fresh Hayden mangoes.

Mai tais in the afternoon at the **Mauna Lani Beach Club.**

Kalua pig at the **Ocean View Inn** in **Kailua-Kona**.

Barbara Campbell
Owner, Waimea Garden Cottage, the Big Island

Bird Park in the town of **Volcano.** Beautiful, quiet, peaceful . . . a great way to spend an hour or so.

Hulihee Palace in **Kona**.

Brian and Lisha Crawford
Owners, Chalet Kilauea, the Big Island

Watching lava flow into the ocean at sunset at **Kilauea;** hiking the **Mauna Iki Trail** in **Hawaii Volcanoes National Park.**

Swimming in the thermal tide pools at **Kapoho.**

Visiting the observatories and skiing atop **Mauna Kea**.

Noelani Whittington
Executive Director, Kona-Kohala Coast Resort Association, the Big Island

Volcano, a quaint village just outside **Hawaii Volcanoes National Park,** must be about 3,000 feet above sea level. Nights are great for curling up with a good book or enjoying lively conversations around a fire; days give way to picking *ohelo* berries in the native forests, bicycling, and spending money on local art.

Four-wheel-drive treks with members of the **Kona Historical Society** into very inaccessible areas. Their historian's narration is superb—I always come away with a deeper appreciation of the **Big Island.**

Horseback riding in the **North Kohala Mountains,** beautiful Big Island country.

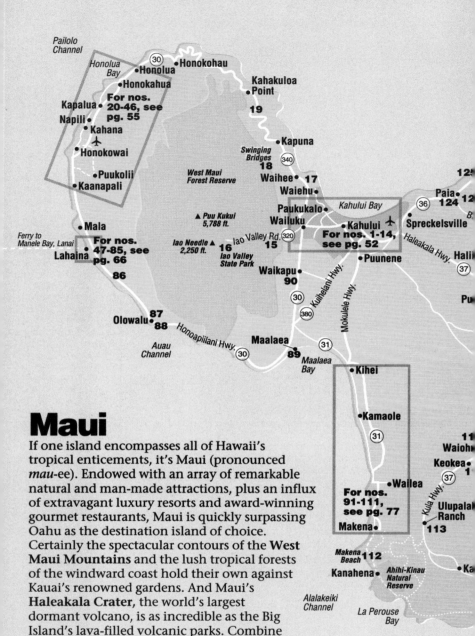

Maui

If one island encompasses all of Hawaii's tropical enticements, it's Maui (pronounced *mau*-ee). Endowed with an array of remarkable natural and man-made attractions, plus an influx of extravagant luxury resorts and award-winning gourmet restaurants, Maui is quickly surpassing Oahu as the destination island of choice. Certainly the spectacular contours of the **West Maui Mountains** and the lush tropical forests of the windward coast hold their own against Kauai's renowned gardens. And Maui's **Haleakala Crater**, the world's largest dormant volcano, is as incredible as the Big Island's lava-filled volcanic parks. Combine all this with stellar beaches, stunning rain forests, picture-perfect sunsets, and the annual humpback whale migration to Maui's coastal waters, an awe-inspiring event that takes place from December to May, and it's easy to see why tourists and residents alike agree that Maui *no ka oi*—is just the best.

Hawaii's second-largest island can be divided into five general regions: **Central Maui**, the center of commerce and government, encompassing the towns of **Kahului** and **Wailuku** and the main airport; **West Maui**, containin the up-and-coming hotel community of **Kapalua**, the glamorous beach reso area called **Kaanapali**, the bustling old whaling port of **Lahaina**, and the highest concentration of tourists; **Southwest Maui**, anchored by the **Kihei**

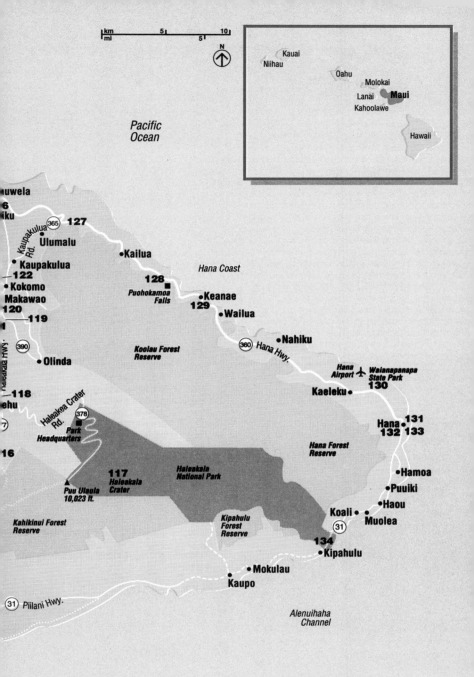

km
mi
5 | 10
5 |

N

Pacific
Ocean

Kauai
Niihau
Oahu
Molokai
Lanai **Maui**
Kahoolawe

Hawaii

uwela
6
iku
127
(365)
Kaupakulua Rd.
Ulumalu
Kailua
Hana Coast
Kaupakulua
122
128
Kokomo
Puohokamoa Falls
Keanae
Makawao
129
120
Wailua
119
390
Koolau Forest Reserve
Nahiku
Olinda
(360) *Hana Hwy.*
Hana Airport
Waianapanapa State Park
130
118
Haleakea Crater Rd.
Kaeleku
ehu
378
Hana 131
Park Headquarters
132 133
7
Hana Forest Reserve
16
117 *Haleakala Crater*
Haleakala National Park
Hamoa
Puu Ulaula 10,023 ft.
Puuiki
Haou
Kahikinui Forest Reserve
Kipahulu Forest Reserve
Koali
Muolea
134
(31)
Kipahulu
Mokulau
Kaupo
(31) *Piilani Hwy.*
Alenuihaha Channel

rip of condominiums and the posh, 1,500-acre **Wailea** luxury resort;
pcountry Maui, a rustic farming and ranching region on the grassy
opes of Haleakala and home of Maui's Kula onions as well as Hawaii's
nly winery; and the verdant **Hana Coast,** located on Maui's rugged,
unning eastern shores and accessed by the most scenic drive in all of
lawaii, the **Hana Highway.** While the majority of resorts line the sunny
eward coasts of West and Southwest Maui, the most spectacular
ttractions—the Hana Highway, Haleakala Crater, and the upcountry—
re spread across the island, so schedule a few days to explore them all.

After landing at **Kahului Airport,** most of Maui's 2.5 million annual visitors are shuffled off toward the western shoreline, where the weather is considerably better and the beaches are more accessible. While Kaanapali—a self-contained megaresort with a profusion of hotels and condominiums ranging from basic to super-luxurious—accommodates a larger percentage of tourists, the more affluent travelers tend to stay at the exclusive Kapalua and Wailea resorts. Often viewed as a playground for the rich, Maui has a higher percentage of millionaires than the French Riviera or Palm Springs, but even starving college students enjoy the island's natural beauty and easygoing Jimmy Buffett lifestyle.

Of course, Maui is not without its faults. Because of the island's popularity, traffic is becoming a nightmarish problem, as are increasing incidents of vandalism, theft, and "time-share victimization." Unbridled resort development (Maui's white-collar crime) has turned Kihei into a Condos-R-Us complex and Lahaina into a tropical Knott's Berry Farm; skyrocketing property values mean that local residents (particularly indigenous Hawaiians) can't afford to own homes. Despite these shortcomings, Maui continues to reign as Hawaii's top all-around destination, with more attractions and tourist activities—from championship golf courses to a historic steam-engine railroad to exciting whale-watching excursions—than any other Hawaiian island. It's no wonder that a significant number of Maui residents are tourists who decided to come back for good.

Area code 808 unless otherwise noted.

Getting to Maui

Airports

Kahului Airport

Kahului Airport (872.3880), two miles east of the center of Kahului, is Maui's major airport, with about 120 flights a day departing from and landing on its windy runway. There's a small, two-story terminal.

Airport Services

Information	872.3893
Lost and Found	872.3821
Parking	871.0610

Airlines

Aloha Airlines	244.9071, 800/367.5250
American Airlines	244.5522, 800/433.7300
American Trans Air	800/225.2995
Delta Airlines	871.0882, 800/221.1212
Hawaiian Airlines	871.6132, 800/367.5320
Island Air, interisland	877.5755, 800/652.6541
from the mainland	800/323.3345
Mahalo Air, interisland	877.7444, 800/277.8333
from the mainland	800/4.MAHALO
United Airlines	800/241.6522

Getting to and from Kahului Airport

By Bus

There is no public transportation system on Maui, but several companies operate shuttles to the resort areas. **Trans-Hawaiian Shuttle** (877.7308, 800/231.6984) transports people between **Kahului Airport** and the Kaanapali resorts daily from 10AM to 4PM. The shuttle leaves hourly; the cost is $13 one way. No reservations are needed for pickups at the airport, but they're recommended for departure from Kaanapali; call to make a reservation at least one day before your flight. **Trans-Hawaiian** also provides transportation to and from the airport and other areas in West Maui; reservations are required. **Speedy Shuttle** (875.8070) takes passengers between the airport and West Maui and Kihei from 5AM to 10PM by reservation; the cost ranges from $8 to $20 one way. **Island Shuttle** (875.6389) matches those prices, but uses limousines and may be reserved between 4AM and 11PM.

By Car

Kahului Airport is about a mile northeast of **Haleakala Highway;** prominent signs point the way both into and out of the airfield. The following car-rental companies have counters at the airport.

Alamo	871.6235, 800/327.9633
Avis	871.7575, 800/331.1212
Budget	871.8811, 800/527.0700
Dollar	877.2731, 800/421.6868
Hertz	877.5167, 800/654.3131
National/Interrent	871.8851, 800/227.7368

By Taxi

Cabs wait at the curb across from the baggage-claim area. Otherwise, call **Yellow Cab of Maui** (877.7000). The fare to Kapalua should be under $65; to Kaanapali, under $55; to Wailea, under $35.

...ana Airport

...st minutes west of **Hana, Hana Airport** (248.8208) ...nsists of an airstrip and a one-room terminal ...ilding. Four flights a day service this out-of-the-...y facility.

...rlines
...and Air, interisland 248.8328, 800/652.6541
...rom the mainland 800/323.3345

...etting to and from Hana Airport

Bus
...ere is no public bus system. The **Hotel Hana-Maui** ...d some bed-and-breakfast establishments provide ...port transportation for their guests free of charge. ...ll your lodging place to make arrangements ...forehand.

Car
...ollar Rent-a-Car (248.8237, 800/800.4000) is the ...ly firm that rents cars in Hana. Anything from ...nvertibles to four-wheel-drive vehicles can be ...cked up at the airport by prior arrangement.

Taxi
...ere are no cabs in this part of Maui.

...apalua–West Maui Airport

...he **Kapalua–West Maui Airport** (669.0255) was ...ilt by Hawaiian Airlines in 1987 and promptly sold ...the state, which now maintains the two-story ...rminal and 3,000-foot runway. Fourteen flights a ...ay fly in and out of the small, windy airport located ...etween the Kaanapali and Kapalua resorts.

...irlines
...sland Air, interisland 877.5755, 800/652.6541
...from the mainland 800/323.3345

...etting to and from ...apalua–West Maui Airport

By Bus
...free shuttle connects the airport with the **Westin ...otel** and the **Embassy Suites Resort** in Kaanapali. ...irport Shuttle** (667.2605) also offers transportation ...o anywhere on the island between 5AM and ...1:30PM; prices vary.

By Car
...he **Kapalua–West Maui Airport** is equidistant from ...apalua and Kaanapali, off Honoapiilani Highway ...Highway 30). There are no car-rental booths at the ...irport.

By Taxi
...abs generally await passengers in front of baggage ...claim. If you don't see any, call **Resorts and ...Kaanapali Taxi** (661.5285) or **Alii Cab** (661.3688). ...The fare to Kapalua is about $10; to Kaanapali, $13; ...to Wailea, about $55.

...nterisland Carriers
Aloha Airlines and **Hawaiian Airlines** make regular hops to **Kahului Airport** from **Hilo International**

Airport and **Keahole-Kona International Airport** on the Big Island, **Lihue Airport** on Kauai, **Lanai Airport** on Lanai, **Molokai Airport** on Molokai, and **Honolulu International Airport** on Oahu. **Island Air** flies to **Kapalua–West Maui Airport** and **Hana Airport** on Maui from Honolulu and **Princeville Airport** on Kauai. **Mahalo Air** flies into **Kahului Airport** from Honolulu, **Keahole-Kona International Airport** on the Big Island, and **Molokai Airport** on Molokai, and into **Kapalua–West Maui Airport** from Honolulu.

Ferries
Expeditions (661.3756, 800/695.2624) is a ferry between **Lahaina** on Maui and the island of Lanai. It crosses the channel to Lanai and back five times daily between 6:45AM and 5:45PM. A round-trip excursion is $50 for adults, $40 for children under 12. This is more for fun than transportation, as the round-trip passage takes a couple of hours.

Getting Around Maui

Bicycles and Mopeds
Maui is a good place for two-wheeled travel, although the big hill in the narrow part of the island between West Maui and East Maui is a little tricky to negotiate. Mopeds as well as mountain bikes are available at A&B Moped Rental (3481 Lower Honoapiilani Rd, between Honoapiilani Hwy and Olali St, Honokowai, 669.0027); mopeds are $24 for 8 hours, mountain bikes $5 for 24 hours. The Kukui Activity Center (Kukui Mall, 1819 S Kihei Rd, at Kupuna St, Kihei, 875.1151) rents mountain bikes for $12.50 a day, $65 a week.

Buses
There is no public bus system on Maui.

Driving
Two things to keep in mind when driving on Maui: **Highway 30** from **Kahului Airport** to Lahaina can be treacherous during the whale migration season (December through May), when the entire road becomes a parking lot every time someone spots a whale spouting or breaching. Also, many car-rental companies prohibit renters from driving on certain roads (for example, **Highway 31** between Hana and Upcountry Maui). Driving on prohibited roads nullifies your rental-car insurance policy, so you're liable for any damage incurred there. Car-rental companies at island airports are listed above.

Hiking
The most popular trek on the island is in the moon-like crater of **Haleakala National Park.** The trail is of medium difficulty, with options to make it longer or shorter, harder or easier. **Hike Maui** (879.5270) is a valuable resource on this trek or any other; the 15-year-old firm, operated by naturalist Ken Schmidt, offers guided natural history hikes and information on all the Maui wilderness has to offer.

Parking
It's easy to find parking spots on Maui streets. If you don't find a space on **Front Street** in **Lahaina,** you're

sure to get one on the side streets. Metered street parking is usually 25¢ for half an hour.

Taxis
Call **Resorts and Kaanapali Taxi** (661.5285) in West Maui or **Yellow Cab of Maui** (877.7000) elsewhere. Rates are $1.75 when the flag drops and $1.75 per mile.

Tours
Robert's Hawaii (871.6226) offers a half-day tour of **Haleakala Crater** and a full-day intinerary that includes the crater, **Iao Valley**, and Lahaina. **Rascal Charters** (874.8633) runs four-, six-, and eight-hour fishing trips from **Maalaea Harbor.** Breathtaking aerial tours are offered by **Alexair Helicopters** (877.4354) and **Blue Hawaiian Helicopters** (871.8844). For information on horseback riding tours, see "Maui's Mane Attraction" on page 75; for details on bicycle rides down Haleakala Crater, see "Braking Away: Maui by Bike" on page 78.

Walking
Perhaps the nicest place to take a walk on Maui is the beach at Kaanapali. It's long and white, and the hotels are set back from the shore. Front Street in Lahaina is pleasant to explore on foot—there are nice shops to inspect and plenty of people to watch. It's very hot in Lahaina, but there are lots of places to stop for refreshments. The Upcountry towns of **Makawao** and **Paia** are also good strolling spots, with shops in which to poke and browse.

FYI

Shopping
There are five major shopping destinations on Maui. For scrimshaw, head for the old whaling port of Lahaina, where standard souvenirs are also plentiful. Paia in Upcountry Maui is the place for ultracool surf stuff—boards, clothing, stickers, photos of Duke Kahanamoku, and other gear. Makawao, also in the upcountry, has the best selection of Hawaiian crafts. **Kaahumanu Center** in Kahului has the same upscale shops as your mall back home. And the **Maui**

Marketplace, also in Kahului, houses more than 30 outlet stores: nirvana for bargain shoppers, purgatory for everybody else.

Visitors' Information Centers
The **Maui Visitors Bureau** (MVB; 1727 Wili Pa Loo off Imi Kala St, Wailuku, 244.3530; fax 244.1337) is open Mondays through Fridays from 8AM to 4:30PM. The **Lahaina Visitors' Center** (667.9193) at 648 Wharf St is open daily from 9AM to 5PM.

Phone Book

Emergencies
Ambulance/Fire/Police	91
Dental Emergency	874.541
Hospital (Maui Memorial Hospital)	244.905
Locksmith (24-hour)	877.030
Pharmacy	875.469
Police (nonemergency)	244.640
Poison Control	800/362.358

Wailuku/Kahului and Environs

In the past the sister towns of Wailuku and Kahului on the northern coast of Maui's central valley, have focused on business. Wailuku is the administrative center and the county seat of **Maui County,** and Kahului is a commercial center, site of the island's only jet airport and deepwater seaport. Maui's greatest concentration of population is in or near these towns (40,000 of the 100,000 residents), and it is here that much of the island's work is done.

In recent years, however, the towns have shown a greater desire to cater to visitors, reflected in the construction of huge malls in the area. As well as shopping, visitors enjoy the historical sites, includi the 19th-century **Bailey House** and the **Alexander Baldwin Sugar Museum.** Also of note to vacatione is the scenic **Iao Valley State Park,** set amidst the majestic **West Maui Mountains** just west of Wailuk

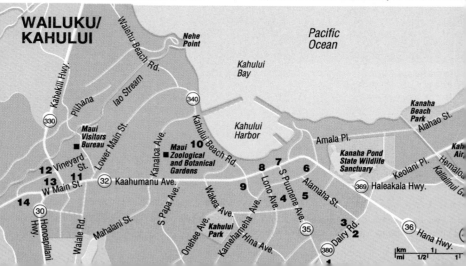

1 Alexander & Baldwin Sugar Museum Located in a restored plantation manager's house next to a working sugar mill, this small museum documents the history of sugarcane in Hawaii, from its introduction as a crop to its key role in expanding the islands' ethnic diversity with the arrival of workers from Japan, the Philippines, and elsewhere. Photo murals, century-old artifacts, and a working scale model of sugar-factory machinery make this one museum worth checking out. ◆ Admission. M-Sa. 3957 Hansen Rd (at Hwy 35), Puunene. 871.8058 ὣ

2 Maui Marketplace Built to resemble Oahu's wildly successful **Waikele Center**, this new 300,000-square-foot collection of 30 outlet stores includes **The Rack** by Liberty House, **Sports Authority**, and **Eagle Hardware**. ◆ Daily. 270 Dairy Rd (between S Puunene Ave and Hana Hwy), Kahului. No phone ὣ

3 Best of Maui Cassette Tours If you really want to do the Hana Coast or Haleakala right, stop at the shack with the yellow awning and the flashing light (located just before the Hana Highway turnoff in Kahului) and pick up a tour tape. A worthwhile investment, this high-quality, well-researched package of audiocassette tours includes a tape, cassette player, Hana Highway guidebook, bird and flower field guides, and a detailed map. The narrator has flawless Hawaiian pronunciation, and the tour is timed perfectly, describing landmarks as you pass them. Highlights include atmospheric music, professional sound quality, pertinent historical background, and tips on where to stop for a snack or picnic. The tapes are also available at **Kmart** (424 Dairy Rd, Kahului, 871.8553), **Picnics** (37 Baldwin Ave, Kahului, 579.8021), **Sub-Paradise** (395-E Dairy Rd, Kahului, 877.8779), and **Windriggers Maui** (261 Dairy Rd, Kahului, 871.7753). ◆ Fee. Daily 6:30AM-1:30PM. 333 Dairy Rd (Hwy 380, between S Puunene Ave and Alamaha St), Kahului. 871.1555

4 Maui Swap Meet Haggle over new and used handicrafts, clothes, fresh fruit, baked goods, and assorted odds and ends at this down-to-earth flea market. ◆ Nominal admission. Sa 5:30AM-noon. 142 S Puunene Ave (between W Wakea and Kamehameha Aves), Kahului. 877.3100 ὣ

5 Ming Yuen ★★$ One of Maui's top Chinese restaurants boasts an enormous menu of Cantonese and Northern Chinese dishes; don't miss the lemon chicken, Szechuan eggplant, and chilled litchi dessert. Despite the huge dining room, there's a long wait on weekends and sometimes a two-day backup on reservations, so book early; also call ahead to request the Peking or stuffed duck (both require 24-hour notice). ◆ Chinese ◆ Daily lunch and dinner. Reservations recommended Friday and Saturday nights; reservations required for parties of six or more. 162 Alamaha St (between Dairy Rd and E Kamehameha Ave), Kahului. 871.7787 ὣ

6 Stanton's of Maui ★★$ A mecca for java lovers, this coffeehouse offers such healthy fare as breakfast burritos, Kula green salads, and tofu burgers, as well as a wide selection of gourmet coffees ready to be shipped and both tropical and coffee drinks. ◆ Coffeehouse ◆ M-Sa breakfast, lunch, and dinner; Su breakfast and lunch. Maui Mall, E Kamehameha Ave and Hana Hwy, Kahului. 877.3711. ὣ

7 Chart House ★$$$ The view could use some work, but you'll find substantial portions of steaks and fresh fish at this local outpost of the national chain. This restaurant was launched by the same people who used to own upcountry Maui's best surf-and-turf place, the **Makawao Steak House**, but now it is owned by a mainland firm. The Lahaina **Chart House** has a much nicer view. ◆ Steaks/ Seafood ◆ Daily dinner. Reservations recommended. 500 N Puunene Ave (at Kaahumanu Ave), Kahului. 877.2476. Also at: 1450 Front St (at Honoapiilani Hwy), Lahaina. 661.0937; 100 Wailea Ike Dr (at Wailea Alanui Dr), Wailea. 879.2875

8 Maui Seaside Hotel $ Businesspeople from other islands frequent this three-story hotel because of its proximity to **Kahului Airport** and to the business hubs of Kahului and Wailuku. (Plus it's cheap.) There are 183 sparse but pleasant air-conditioned rooms, as well as a restaurant, central pool, and small beach. If you're traveling on a tight budget, this is the place to stay. ◆ 100 W Kaahumanu Ave (between N Puunene Ave and Kahului Beach Rd), Kahului. 877.3311, 800/367.7000; fax 871.4618 ὣ

8 Maui Palms Hotel $ Although not likely to win any awards for its architecture or interior design, this two-story, 98-room hotel is a Maui staple, and with a pool on the property and public tennis courts nearby, it's not a bad place to lay your head. Some rooms are air-conditioned, all have TVs, but none have phones. The large dining room serves American food at lunch, Chinese food at dinner. ◆ 150 Kaahumanu Ave (between N Puunene Ave and Kahului Beach Rd), Kahului. 877.0071, 800/367.5004; fax 871.5797

Restaurants/Clubs: Red   **Hotels:** Blue
Shops/ 🍴Outdoors: Green   **Sights/Culture:** Black

53

9 Kaahumanu Center Local residents have mixed feelings on the subject, but like it or not, the renovation of this trendy, two-story multimillion-dollar shopping mall is complete. Visitors who remember the days when the handful of shops here were half-empty will marvel at the Maui masses that come to see double-, triple-, and quadruple-features at the new six-plex cinema or to pick up the latest surfwear at **Local Motion** (871.7873). ◆ Daily. 275 W Kaahumanu Ave (between Kane St and S Wakea Ave), Kahului. 877.3369 Ꮯ

Within the Kaahumanu Center:

Waldenbooks This member of the national chain has more than 30,000 volumes, the largest fiction section of any Maui bookstore, and an extensive Hawaiiana section for those interested in local history, guidebooks, flora, fauna, and other island-related topics. ◆ Daily. 871.6112. Ꮯ Also at: Kukui Mall, 1819 S Kihei Rd (at Kupuna St), Kihei. 874.3688; The Cannery Mall, 1221 Honoapiilani Hwy (at Kapunakea St), Lahaina. 667.6172

10 Maui Arts and Cultural Center Maui's $75-million performing arts center opened in 1994. Designed by architect **John Hara,** the large, modern building stands on 10 acres of land and comprises a main and studio theaters, an amphitheater, classrooms, and an art gallery. A variety of groups have taken the stage here, including Santana, the Moscow Ballet, and the theater company of the **Maui Academy of Performing Arts.** ◆ Box office M-F; Sa 1PM-5PM; show times vary. N Wakea Ave (off Kahului Beach Rd), Kahului. 242.7469 Ꮯ

11 Chums ★$ A diner atmosphere and local fare make this eatery a Wailuku institution. Early risers will like the hours (it opens at 6:30AM) and budget watchers the prices. Hotcakes, omelettes, and French toast round out the breakfast menu; saimin (noodles), Portuguese bean soup, oxtail soup, teriyaki chicken, and cheeseburgers are offered the rest of the day. The poached mahimahi in white wine sauce for less than $7 is a real find. ◆ Hawaiian/American ◆ Daily breakfast, lunch, and dinner. No alcohol. 1900 Main St (at Central St), Wailuku. 244.1000 Ꮯ

12 Siam Thai ★★$$ There's nothing fancy about this restaurant, just friendly service and great spicy Thai food like curried shrimp and steamed lobster. When current owner Phillip

Daniels took over, he upgraded the interior, which features white brick walls and Thai artifacts, and kept the quality of the food high. ◆ Thai ◆ M-F lunch and dinner; Sa-Su dinner 123 N Market St (at W Vineyard St), Wailuku. 244.3817

13 Northshore Inn $ Sequestered in this shabby corner of Wailuku is a clean, cordial, hotel/youth hostel ideal for backpackers, windsurfers, and international budget travelers. There are 18 rooms (with single, double, or bunk beds), clean shared bathrooms, a common kitchen and laundry room, a small TV lounge, and a genial atmosphere, but no restaurant or air-conditioning. The proprietor often takes guests hiking, windsurfing, or to the beach for volleyball and barbecues. "Come as guests, leave as friends" is the motto. ◆ 2080 W Vineyard St (between N Market and Ilina Sts) Wailuku. 242.8999; fax 244.5004 Ꮯ

14 Bailey House Missionaries Edward and Caroline Bailey came to Maui in 1840 to teach at the **Wailuku Female Seminary,** founded in 1833 by Reverend Jonathan Green. Closed in 1858 due to lack of funding, it was home to the Bailey family for more than 40 years. Upon moving to California in 1885, the family dedicated the building to the display of Hawaiian artifacts. The collection includes quilts, tapa cloth, the island's largest collection of relics from the days before Captain Cook (such as stone and shell implements and an outrigger canoe), and more (don't miss Duke Kahanamoku's redwood surfboard). The **Maui Historical Society** operates the museum and shop, a worthy stop. ◆ Admission. M-Sa. 2375-A E Main St (between Hwy 30 and Alu Rd), Wailuku. 244.3326

15 Kepaniwai Park and Heritage Gardens When the sun's out, you can't beat the drive into this valley setting. The elevated park pays tribute to Maui's various ethnic groups with exhibition pavilions and gardens reflecting the cultures of the Hawaiians, Japanese, Chinese, Filipinos, and Portuguese. Kids love the children's swimming pool (daily in summer; Sa, Su other months) and the picnic pavilions ◆ Off Iao Valley Rd, between Alu Rd and Iao Valley State Park. 243.7408

16 Iao Valley State Park A 2,250-foot-high pillar of stone called the **Iao Needle** marks the spot where, in 1790, King Kamehameha the Great conquered the island of Maui in one of the bloodiest battles in Hawaiian history. The dead, legend has it, filled nearby Iao Stream until the water ran red. The Iao Needle is surrounded by sharp cliffs and overlooks lush, verdant Iao Valley, where the ancients buried their *alii* (royalty) in caves to protect the bones—believed to have spiritual powers—from damage or misuse. Iao's beauty is as stunning as its history is haunting; there's a hiking trail and many secluded spots for picnicking. ♦ Free. Daily. At the end of Iao Valley Rd. 243.7408

17 Waiehu Municipal Golf Course It's hard to reserve a tee time at this 18-hole course (par 72, 6,330 yards) because it's so reasonably priced. Local golfers and those seeking an alternative to the expensive resorts, where greens fees are four times what they are here, keep the place busy. ♦ Inexpensive greens fees. Daily. Call at least two days in advance for reservations. Hwy 340 (2 miles north of Wailuku. 243.7400

18 Swinging Bridges One of the best and least-known day hikes on Maui is on the windward side of the West Maui Mountains, just beyond the town of Waihee. Here you'll find a moderate trail winding through guava, mango, and passion-fruit trees; past bamboo forests, streams, and aqueducts; and across two seemingly perilous (but quite sturdy) swinging bridges. The reward at the end of the 40-minute hike: a first-rate swimming hole fed by a man-made waterfall. Launch yourself off the rope swing and take a dip behind the fall (yes, the water is cold) for a once-in-a-lifetime experience. Warning: Don't attempt this hike if it's raining—flash floods are frequent and sometimes deadly in the area. ♦ Park at the end of Waihee Valley Rd (off Hwy 340, about a mile past Waihee). On foot, turn right at the sign "Private Road, No Parking" and stay on the main trail.

19 Highway 340 Although the highway is technically for residents only, dozens of adventurous tourists tackle this eroded pass every day in all sorts of cars. The problem used to be that the road wasn't paved; now that's been taken care of, but it's barely one lane wide, so you may find yourself backing up and pulling off the road as much as going forward. From Wailuku to Honokohau it's about an hour-and-a-half drive.

Kapalua and Environs

the mid-1970s Colin C. Cameron, a descendant missionaries who presides over his family's Maui nd & Pineapple Company, commissioned a team resort specialists to build the consummate luxury estination on a sizable portion of his pineapple npire. He wasn't disappointed. Set against a ectacular backdrop of West Maui hills near one the region's most extraordinary bays, Kapalua, 1,500-acre resort community, now boasts three st-rate golf courses, two hotels, and several staurants. The 194-room **Kapalua Bay Hotel Villas** was the development's flagship hotel, though in recent years it has been slightly eclipsed y the **Ritz-Carlton Kapalua**. Access to this sun vers' Shangri-la has been much easier since the apalua–West Maui Airport opened off onoapiilani Highway (Highway 30) in 1987.

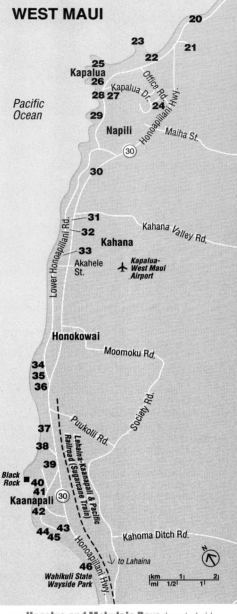

WEST MAUI

Pacific Ocean

Kapalua
Kapalua Dr.
Office Rd.
Honoapiilani Hwy.
Napili
Maiha St.
30

Lower Honoapiilani Rd.
Kahana Valley Rd.
Kahana
Akahele St.
Kapalua-West Maui Airport

Honokowai
Moomoku Rd.
Society Rd.

Puukolii Rd.
Lahaina-Kaanapali & Pacific Railroad (Sugarcane Train)

Black Rock
Kaanapali
30

Kahoma Ditch Rd.
to Lahaina
Honoapiilani Hwy.
Wahikuli State Wayside Park

km 1 2
ml 1/2 1

20 Honolua and Mokuleia Bays Located side by side just north of Kapalua, Mokuleia Bay (known by surfers as "Slaughterhouse") and Honolua Bay together make up a **Marine Life Conservation District,** a legally protected underwater preserve where the fish are fearless. Mokuleia Bay has a gorgeous white-sand beach that's relatively uncrowded, while Honolua Bay attracts snorkelers when the surf's calm. ♦ Honolua Bay: Off Honoapiilani Hwy (look for the "Marine Life Conservation District" sign and the gaggle of parked rental cars), Honolua. Mokuleia Bay: Off Honoapiilani Hwy (just west of Honolua Bay)

21 Kapalua Golf Club These three prestigious layouts—the **Bay, Village,** and **Plantation**—have for many years been the site of the nationally televised **Lincoln-Mercury International Golf Tournament.** The Ed Seay and Arnold Palmer–designed **Village Course** (18 holes, par 71, 6,001 yards) and Arnold Palmer and Francis Dwayne **Bay Course** (18 holes, par 72, 6,051 yards) have received numerous awards—*Golf* magazine rated this golf resort among the 12 best in the US. Cut into the base of a 23,000-acre pineapple plantation, these two layouts offer an ocean view from almost every fairway. The **Village Course** presents the greater test; its valleys, ridges, lake, and ironwood and eucalyptus trees make it spectacularly scenic. The newest of the three, the massive 240-acre **Plantation Course** (18 holes, par 73, 6,547 yards), designed by Ben Crenshaw and Bill Coore, includes such natural features as gradual slopes, deep valleys, native grasses, and long, generous fairways, and is also reaping various accolades. One drawback: This site is often windy, and there's a greater chance of mist and rain here than at Kaanapali or Wailea courses. ◆ Expensive greens fees. Daily. Reservations recommended at least four days in advance. Lessons are available. Preferred starting times and fees extended to **Kapalua Bay Hotel & Villas** and **Ritz-Carlton Kapalua** guests. 300 Kapalua Dr (off Lower Honoapiilani Rd), Kapalua. 669.8044

Within the Kapalua Golf Club:

Plantation House Restaurant ★★★ $$$$ Thanks to its elevated setting, open-air lanai seating, regional fare, and stunning vistas, this award-winning restaurant has developed a devoted following. Chef Alex Stanislaw blends island flavors with Euro-Asian and Mediterranean influences; his repertoire includes such entrées as honey-guava scallops and Cajun-seasoned sashimi, along with more traditional New York steak and poultry dishes. Breakfast, besides being surprisingly affordable, is simply unbeatable, especially when you're seated on the lanai and feasting on fresh pineapple dipped in a light cinnamon–sour cream sauce. ◆ Seafood/Mediterranean ◆ Daily breakfast, lunch, and dinner. Reservations recommended. Plantation Course Clubhouse, 2000 Plantation Club Dr (off Honoapiilani Hwy). 669.6299 &

More than 30 percent of the people on Maui at any one time are tourists.

Restaurants/Clubs: Red   Hotels: Blue
Shops/ 🍸 Outdoors: Green   **Sights/Culture: Black**

22 D. T. Fleming Beach Park Named for a manager of the Kapalua Plantation, this popular surfing, bodysurfing, swimming, and snorkeling beach extends from **Kapalua Golf Club**'s 16th hole to the cliffs beyond. Use caution: The steep shoreline is subject to strong riptides. Picnic and public facilities are available. ◆ Off Honoapiilani Hwy (east of Kapalua)

23 Ritz-Carlton Kapalua $$$$ Recently named the No. 1 hotel in Hawaii by *Travel & Leisure* magazine, this member of the Ritz-Carlton family has been bustling since it opened in 1992. Set on 10 acres of gently sloping beachfront, it was designed to allow maximum coastal views with minimal disturbance to the contour of the land. The 450 garden- and ocean-view rooms and suites all feature spacious lanais, twice-daily maid service, and 24-hour room service. Other amenities include a white-sand beach, boutiques, a 10,000-square-foot pool and a whirlpool, 10 tennis courts, a fitness center, host of noteworthy restaurants, and Kapalua's three championship golf courses. As the **Ritz-Carlton Mauna Lani** has done on the Big Island, this stunningly appointed property has raised the competition among Maui's luxury-class accommodations to a new level. ◆ 1 Ritz-Carlton Dr (off Lower Honoapiilani Rd), Kapalua. 669.6200, 800/262.8400; fax 665.0026 &

Within the Ritz-Carlton Kapalua:

Anuenue Room ★★★$$$$ The **Ritz**'s signature restaurant offers guests a night to remember. As soon as they enter the elegant wood-paneled dining room, with its book-lined walls, subdued lighting, and clubby atmosphere, diners know they're in for something special. The house specialties—herb-crusted *onaga* (red snapper) fillet, carmelized salmon with an orange *shoyu* (soy sauce) glaze, and seared venison chops—are highly recommended. ◆ Pacific Rim ◆ M-Sa dinner. Reservations required; collared shirt required for men. 669.9200 &

The Terrace ★★$$ The hotel's come-as-you-are eatery overlooks the pool and is accented by marble columns and silk tapestries. The bill of fare features gourmet entrées such as spicy shrimp pizza and Peking duck. Theme buffets are held on most nights. An extravagant breakfast buffet, with such highlights as sweet bread French toast, blintzes, island fruits, and Kona coffee, is served daily. ◆ Pacific Rim/American ◆ Daily breakfast and dinner. Reservations recommended. 669.6200

24 Pineapple Hill ★$$$ Located in former plantation manager D. T. Fleming's home high above Kapalua's golf courses and pineapple fields, this touristy restaurant is popular chiefly because of the panoramic view and the undeniable flavor of Hawaii's rich plantation history. The unremarkable fare includes such dishes as grilled peppercorn steak, prawns Tahitian (baked in the shell and seasoned with herbs, parmesan cheese, and dry vermouth), and Papeete steamed fish. ♦ Continental and Polynesian ♦ Daily dinner. Reservations recommended. 2000 Pineapple Hill Rd (off Office Rd), Kapalua. 669.6129 ♿

25 Kapalua Bay Hotel & Villas $$$$
This Kapalua resort is the venue for several world-renowned sporting and cultural events. The hotel has a spectacular natural setting (see below) amid 19th-century pine trees and pineapple fields, with views of the ocean and the West Maui Mountains. The 194 air-conditioned rooms feature such extras as private lanais, TV sets and VCRs, refrigerators, and marble bathrooms with separate showers and tubs, double vanities, and telephones. It's a haven for guests who prefer golf, tennis, or relaxing on the beach or by the pool to wandering in the wilderness. There are three award-winning golf courses, 10 Plexipave courts in the **Tennis Garden,** one of the US's best beaches, an excellent scuba program, and three restaurants with ocean views. Each summer, this is the site of such international gatherings as the **Kapalua Music Festival** and the **Kapalua Wine Symposium,** a noteworthy food-and-wine event. The hotel management company also manages and rents 130 privately owned villas. Luxurious and self-sufficient, the villas appeal to families, celebrities seeking privacy, and people who prefer full kitchens, a lot of space, and all the features of home. ♦ 1 Kapalua Bay La (off Lower Honoapiilani Rd), Kapalua. 669.5656, 800/367.8000; fax 669.4605 ♿

Within the Kapalua Bay Hotel & Villas:

The Bay Club ★★★$$$$ The brief shuttle ride or walk to this restaurant from the **Kapalua Bay Hotel** is especially enjoyable at sunset or on a clear, starry night. The sunset view from a promontory over the ocean is framed by palm trees beyond the veranda and the island of Lanai on the horizon. The dining room's sophisticated ambience blends superbly with soft Maui evenings. Fresh mahimahi, *opakapaka* (pink snapper), and *ahi* (tuna) are prepared a half-dozen ways, and the bouillabaisse is excellent. There's also a piano bar. ♦ Continental/ Seafood ♦ Daily lunch and dinner. Reservations recommended. 669.8008 ♿

Kapalua Bay Hotel & Villas

Seashells by the Seashore

Hawaii is a mecca for serious shell collectors and the island of Maui is their motherlode, for its shores hide some of the world's rarest and most valuable shells, including the prized checkered cowrie. The island is home to ingenious and dedicated treasure hunters who check the daily tide charts in their local newspaper, then scavenge tide pools to study the shells' habitats and camouflages. Many also snorkel or skin-dive to search for their prize.

To the uninitiated, nothing seems simpler than strolling the shores and pocketing the occasional lustrous find. But the amateur sheller should bear in mind that much more is involved than meets the eye. For starters, reefs prevent most shells from reaching the shore wholly intact, making it necessary to search in deeper water, where inexperienced snorkelers may find themselves on the "Tahitian Current Express." To compound the danger, many shelled animals, namely those found in cone shells, have powerful bites or stings that can cause serious illness. Finally, novice shell seekers should keep in mind that a shell is not just another pretty rock, it's the home of a living sea animal better suited to its own ecological circle than to your living-room bookshelf. To avoid depleting the waters of special specimens, leave shells where you find them if the original owner is still inside.

Knobby Spindle *(Latirus nodus)* This common pink shell houses a bright red sea creature. Some local divers break the end off this shell to keep others from removing it for their collections.

Tile Miter *(Mitra incompta)* Miters are not generally prized by collectors, since the four-inch-long, rough-textured shells are fairly common. They live among coral beds 30 to 80 feet deep.

Lettered Miter *(Mitra litterata)* These tiny carnivores have a poisonous sting they use to capture worms for dinner. Only one inch long, they hide under loose coral at the water's surface.

Green-Mouthed Spindle *(Peristernia chlorostome)* More yellow than green, this common one-half- to three-quarter-inch shell is found in coral along the shore.

Triton's Trumpet *(Charonia tritonis)* These rare shells, which grow up to 18 inches in length, fasten themselves to coral in deep water.

Fringed Cowrie *(Cypraea fimbriata)* This orange cowrie chooses orange coral as camouflage in depths of 2 to 60 feet.

Marlin Spike Auger *(Terebra maculata)* Found in depths of more than 10 feet, these grow up to 10 inches long and are the largest augers on earth.

Blood-Spotted Triton *(Bursa cruentata)* This lovely, common triton has an inner rim ranging from white to pale violet.

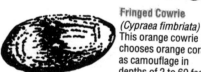

Crenulated Auger *(Terebra crenulata)* These spiny pink or blue shells are commonly found in shallow water. They are carnivores, usually about five inches long, with spiral rings distinguishing them from other island augers.

Pimpled Basket *(Nassarius papillosus)* A scavenger that hops along on a single muscle (or "foot"), its shell grows from one inch to 2.25 inches long.

awaiian Limpet *(Petella sandwichensis)* This xclusively Hawaiian animal is an edible delicacy alled *opihi* by locals. It grows up to two inches ng and is found in shallow water or on rocks xposed to waves.

olden Yellow Cone *(Conus flavidus)* These 2.5-ich-long shells range from white to greenish ellow. Like other cones, they often have an outer yer of thick *periostracum,* a substance that bscures the shells' fine colors until removed.

Brilliant Drupe *(Drupa rubusidaeus)* Long spines and a pinkish mouth distinguish this 1.5-inch-long shell.

nakehead Cowrie *(Cypraea aputserpentis)* awaii's most ommon cowrie is a erbivorous night eeder that grows up o 1.5 inches in length.

Checkered Cowrie *(Cypraea tessellata)* This rare and beautiful prize is native only to Hawaii. The tiny three-quarter- to 1.5-inch-long shell hides in about 50 feet of water.

Tiger Cowrie *(Cypraea igris)* This two- to three-inch-long shell is only ound in Hawaii and is ommonly sold in gift hops with designs carved nto its surface.

Knobbed Drupe *(Drupa nodus)* A common shell found in shallow water —look for a lavender mouth and black spikes on a white background.

Rough Periwinkle *(Littorina scabra)* This edible animal lives in shoreline coral.

Murex *(Murex pele)* These rough, craggy carnivores use their spiky surfaces as spears to capture other mollusks. Found only in Hawaii, they hide in coral at depths of 40 feet.

Horned Helmet *(Cassis cornuta)* Growing as long as a foot, this is among the largest of the Hawaiian shells.

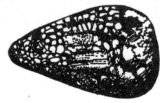

Penniform Cone *(Conus Pennaceua)* Inhabitants of these cones fire darts to stun their prey; some species are even dangerous to humans. But the common three-inch-long cones are safe as well as beautiful, with an intricate and varied design. They live buried in sand on the ocean floor.

Reticulated Cowrie *(Cypaea maculifera)* This cowrie shell is prized by world collectors. Hawaiians use the shells as jewelry and decoration. The smooth, colorful specimens are found under rocks or on coral near the shore.

The Garden Restaurant ★★$$$$ Open air and contemporary, this eatery features such items as sugarmill chicken, wild boar wok, and Maui masala, a spicy vegetable curry with chutney and salsa. Or try the restaurant's signature drink, the Kapalua Butterfly. ◆ Pacific Rim ◆ Daily dinner (F, Sa buffets), Su brunch. Reservations recommended. 669.8008 &

26 Kapalua Beach Along with Napili Bay, this is the safest swimming beach in West Maui and a longtime local favorite. Rated No. 1 in the country by University of Maryland's Coastal Research Lab, this place has it all—perfect sand, incredible views, great snorkeling, and a first-rate scuba program (including rentals, introductory dives, and lessons). The beach shack rents snorkel gear and sells assorted sundries, and an adjacent grassy area lined with palm trees is perfect for picnicking. Showers and rest rooms are available, and a bar and cafe are nearby at the **Kapalua Bay Hotel.** ◆ Parking and public access are at the south end of Kapalua (take a right after the Kapalua Bay Hotel, park your car, and walk toward the rest rooms and through the tunnels to the beach)

27 The Grill & Bar ★★$$$ This handsome bar and dining room, long popular with residents, has changed hands and chefs, but still is serving some of Kapalua's most tempting grinds (pidgin for "food"). The dining room overlooks the **Kapalua Golf Club** and parts of Napili Bay; the sophisticated menu includes fresh *opakapaka* (pink snapper), prime rib, and baked artichokes supreme. ◆ Steak/Seafood ◆ Daily lunch and dinner. Reservations recommended. 200 Kapalua Dr (between the Tennis Garden and the golf club), Kapalua. 669.5653 &

28 Napili Kai Beach Club $$$ This is the kind of seasoned, classic Hawaiian-style resort that is increasingly rare on the islands, so it's no wonder that up to 40 percent of its clientele are repeat guests. The tastefully landscaped grounds, bordered by a stone pathway fringed with hibiscus and *naupaka* bushes, adjoin one of Hawaii's finest bays. Decks, barbecue areas, outdoor bars, and complimentary mai tai and coffee parties make this a convivial vacation spot where guests become friends, returning to savor the fabulous sunsets together again and again. The 165 units spread out unobtrusively over 11 acres; the **Lahaina Wing** is closest to the

beach. All the units front the ocean and have TVs and phones, most have air-conditioning and nearly all have full kitchens. Ask the friendly staff about the **Napili Foundation**, which sponsors a hula and Hawaiian arts program for the children of West Maui; program participants perform here on Friday nights. Other amenities include four pools, a huge Jacuzzi, public access to the Napili Bay and Kapalua beaches, excellent snorkeling, a fitness center, and the **Sea House** restaurant. ◆ 5900 Lower Honoapiilani Rd, Napili. 669.6271, 800/367.5030; fax 669.0086 &

28 Napili Bay Lined with low-rise hotels and condos and featuring a long, sandy beach between two rocky points, this bay offers excellent swimming, snorkeling, and bodysurfing (watch out for the coral, though. Surfing can be good in the winter, provided the waves are high enough. ◆ Public access off Lower Honoapiilani Rd (turn at the Napili Shores sign and park anywhere), Napili

29 Napili Shores Resort $$ Choose from roomy, pleasant studios or one-bedroom condominiums with lanais and kitchens at the 152-unit complex on six acres fronting Napili Beach. Two pools and two restaurants complete the picture. This is an excellent choice for a quiet, relaxing vacation. ◆ 5315 Lower Honoapiilani Rd, Napili. 669.8061, 800/777.1700; fax 669.5407 &

Within the Napili Shores Resort:

Orient Express ★$$$ Good Chinese food on Maui is rare, so this restaurant can get away with its high-priced menu of Chinese and Thai cuisine. Signature dishes include coconut chicken soup, spinach duck, Mandarin fish clay pot, and an eponymous hot beef and seafood dish. The stuffed chicken wings and Thai noodle soup are first-rate. ◆ Chinese/Thai/Sushi ◆ Daily dinner. Reservations recommended. 669.8077 &

30 Coastline between Napili and Kaanapali West Maui's most prominent eyesore is a mile or so of shoreline on the Honoapiilani Highway (Highway 30) between Napili and Kaanapali. Overdeveloped with condominiums of garish color and design, this stretch is the antithesis of beauty and serenity. Not surprisingly, accommodations here are cheaper than elsewhere along this coast. Some of the older condominiums are comfortable, but the new high-rises are less appealing (units next to the highway get a lot of traffic noise). With very few exceptions, the beaches here range from poor to middling.

Although some condominiums advertise their proximity to the water, their beaches may be unsuitable for swimming. In addition, the area is a good distance from West Maui's best restaurants (aside from **Roy's Kahana Bar & Grill** and **Roy's Nicolina**), so you'll have to drive to Kapalua, Kaanapali, or Lahaina to get decent food. ◆ Honoapiilani Hwy (Hwy 30)

31 Roy's Kahana Bar & Grill ★★★$$$ The only reason to drive to Kahana is to eat here. If you haven't already sampled Euro-Asian cuisine at one of Roy Yamaguchi's 11 other restaurants, you're in for a treat: to the delight of Maui's gastronomes, the celebrity chef has created a copy of his original restaurant in Hawaii Kai on Oahu. Although the shopping-center location lacks a view, and the noise is cacaphonous during the rush hours, the high-ceilinged restaurant is packed with diners who faithfully *ooh* and *aah* at the sight of Mongolian grilled pork loin with ginger-pineapple sauce, blackened *ahi* (tuna), and every other dish that comes from the signature stainless-steel-and-copper open kitchen. This restaurant easily ranks as one of Maui's finest, awkward location notwithstanding. ◆ Euro-Asian ◆ Daily dinner. Reservations recommended. Kahana Gateway Plaza, Lower Honoapiilani Rd (at Hoohui Rd), Kahana. 669.6999 &

31 Roy's Nicolina ★★★$$$ A variation on the Roy's restaurant theme, this fine establishment, named after chef/owner Roy Yamaguchi's daughter Nicole, is a touch more casual than the next-door **Roy's Kahana Bar & Grill** (see above). The kitchen turns out Euro-Asian dishes and such American options as sourdough pizza and grilled Southwestern chicken with smoked tomato sauce and tortillas. ◆ Euro-Asian ◆ Daily dinner. Reservations required. Kahana Gateway Plaza, Lower Honoapiilani Rd (at Hoohui Rd), Kahana. 669.5000 &

32 Dollies $ If you're on a tight budget or in search of a particular imported beer, this pizzeria is the place for you. There are nearly 40 brands of brew on hand, and no item on the menu is over $10. It has long been the hangout spot for West Maui *kamaaina* (locals), possibly because of the wide variety of drink specials. ◆ Pizza ◆ M-Sa lunch and dinner, Su brunch and dinner. 4310 Lower Honoapiilani Rd (just south of Hoohui Rd), Kahana. 669.0266 &

33 Erik's Seafood Grotto ★$$$$ This rustic, woody dining room offers an enormous selection of fresh island and mainland fish, plus good ocean views. You can choose from 11 fish dishes, several kinds of shellfish, and an award-winning bouillabaisse. If it's available, try the fresh island lobster stuffed with seafood and flame broiled. It's popular with tourists and the early-bird-special crowd. ◆ Seafood ◆ Daily lunch and dinner. Reservations

recommended. 4242 Lower Honoapiilani Rd (at Aekai Pl), Kahana. 669.4806 &

34 Papakea Resort $$$ Although it won't win any awards, this 13-acre resort offers a perfectly enjoyable family vacation, with all the amenities of the big-name resorts. Located right on the beach, it boasts two pools, two Jacuzzis, a sauna, two putting greens, three tennis courts, and a host of water sports, but no restaurant. All 364 studios and one- and two-bedroom condo suites have complete kitchens, washers and dryers, telephones, TVs, and daily maid service. A two-night minimum stay is required. ◆ 3543 Lower Honoapiilani Rd (north of Kaanapali Shores La), Honokowai. 669.0061, 800/367.7052; fax 669.0061 &

Kaanapali and Environs

In the early 1950s, Amfac Corporation of Honolulu began planning a resort community that would give Waikiki a run for its money. This development, the first master-planned destination resort in Hawaii, was created on a chunk of barren land too dry for sugar cultivation yet lined with three miles of white-sand beaches too inviting to ignore. After Kaanapali's unveiling in 1962, Maui began to attract a volume of business previously seen only by Oahu.

Today Kaanapali is the site of six hotels, seven condominium complexes, two golf courses, 37 tennis courts, a shopping center, and an excellent whaling museum, all arranged along three miles of sandy shore. Kaanapali is Hawaii's largest resort area, occupying some 1,200 acres, less than half of which are developed. A free van takes guests around the grounds, or visitors can travel to **Lahaina**, six miles away, aboard a rebuilt sugarcane train or by shuttle bus. The planners of Kaanapali, aware that tourism would grow on Maui, designed a resort that would be secluded from the rest of the island; instead of dispersing the visitors among randomly located hotels and condos, the aim was to encourage staying in a self-contained environment. This plan has worked fairly well, although Kaanapali's proximity to Lahaina has turned that once-sleepy town into a major tourist attraction.

35 Aston Kaanapali Shores $$$$ This super-deluxe 469-room beachfront condominium resort has a range of lodging options, from simple studios to two-bedroom, two-bath suites with luxurious kitchens, large lanais, and ocean views. The property's **Beach Club** is open daily for breakfast, lunch, and dinner. There are two swimming pools, and kids enjoy **Aston's Camp Kaanapali,** which offers various educational activities. ◆ 3445 Honoapiilani Hwy (off Lower Honoapiilani Rd), Honokowai. 667.2211, 800/922.7866; fax 661.0836 &

Restaurants/Clubs: Red   **Hotels:** Blue

Shops/ ❦ Outdoors: Green   **Sights/Culture:** Black

35 Embassy Suites Resort $$$$ From the highway you can't miss this pink monstrosity, an enormous all-suites hotel occupying 14 oceanfront acres at the northern edge of Kaanapali Beach. The 413 one- and two-bedroom luxury suites abound with amenities: A typical one-bedroom suite occupies 820 square feet and includes a queen-size sofa bed, 35-inch TV, partial kitchen, oversized bath with two marble vanities, a lanai, plus views of Lanai and Molokai. Suite rates include full breakfast and a two-hour complimentary cocktail time at sunset. There's a health club, a miniature golf course, and two pools (one of which is an acre in size and has water slides). The oceanfront restaurant offers fine dining, while the poolside grill and the deli in the lobby offer lighter fare. The hotel is in bankruptcy though, so be wary. ♦ 104 Kaanapali Shores La (off Lower Honoapiilani Rd), Honokowai. 661.2000, 800/362.2779; fax 667.5821 ♿

36 Mahana at Kaanapali Condominium $$ Managed by Aston Resorts, this beachfront complex has two 12-story towers with 240 units and a good swimming beach a hundred yards away. There are studios and one- and two-bedroom units, all of which face the ocean and feature fully equipped kitchens, TV sets with VCRs, and daily maid service. A pool, poolside grill, and two tennis courts round out the amenities. For families and groups, it's a decent choice, though a three-night minimum stay is required. ♦ 110 Kaanapali Shores La (off Lower Honoapiilani Rd), Honokowai. 661.8751, 800/922.7866; fax 661.5510

37 Kahekili Park This white-sand beach is distinguished from all of Kaanapali's others by its ample free parking. The small, grassy expanse and sheltered tables are perfect for picnicking, and there are public facilities. ♦ Off Aston Maui La (take the Puukolii Rd exit off Honoapiilani Hwy)

Miffed whalers brought the first mosquitoes to Hawaii, intentionally planting larvae in the freshwater ponds surrounding the home of Reverend Baldwin in Lahaina, Maui. The reverend's unpopularity stemmed from his stand against "philandering" with the local women.

37 Maui Kaanapali Villas $$$$ About 200 of the 253 huge studios and one- and two-bedroom units in this complex, managed by Aston Hotels and Resorts and various independents, are available for vacation rental. The AAA three-diamond resort on 10 acres of prime Kaanapali beachfront has three pools and nearby golf and tennis. There's a restaurant where guests can get breakfast and dinner. A two-night minimum is required. ♦ Management office: 45 Kai Ala Dr (at Puukolii Rd), Kaanapali. 667.7791, 800/321.2558; fax 667.0366

Royal Lahaina Resort

38 Royal Lahaina Resort $$$ One of Maui's larger complexes offers 522 rooms and cottages in a variety of sizes, from two-story seaside cottages to oceanfront suites in the 12-story **Lahaina Kai** tower. The mix of low- and high-rise buildings is enhanced by 27 acres of tropical landscaping, bordered by the ocean, a golf course, and meandering walkways. There is more of everything here: two dining rooms and lounges, three swimming pools and a whirlpool spa, and 11 tennis courts (including a stadium court). The **Royal Lahaina Luau** (held nightly) is a pleasant outdoor dining affair, with a program bolstered by *kumu hula* (hula teacher) Frank Kawaikapuokalani Hewitt, one of Hawaii's luminaries. All rooms have private lanais and refrigerators, while the suites have full kitchens. ♦ 2780 Kekaa Dr (off Kaanapali Pkwy), Kaanapali. 661.3611, 800/447.6925; fax 661.6150 ♿

39 Maui Eldorado Condominiums $$ These attractive apartments sit on 12 acres between the highway and the beach, alongside a golf course. More than half of the 204 units are available for vacation rentals and, although not on the water, the resort has its own private beach club within walking distance. Three pools and two golf courses are on the property, but there's no restaurant. ♦ 2661 Kekaa Dr (off Kaanapali Pkwy), Kaanapali. 661.0021, 800/777.1700; fax 667.7039

40 Kaanapali Beach Sort of a mini-Waikiki, this beautiful, mostly uncrowded three-mile stretch of white sand is the perfect spot for swimming, tanning, and people watching. Just about any water-related activity can be found here, from scuba and windsurfing lessons to Hobie Cat rentals, and some great bars are right on the beach. The ocean is

generally calm; hotels post red flags when swimming is too dangerous. Still, keep an eye on the kids; the sandy bottom drops off abruptly. Free parking is available, but it usually fills up before noon. ◆ Off Kaanapali Pkwy (directly in front of the hotels), Kaanapali

40 Sheraton Maui $$$$ An exhaustive $170-million renovation has turned this Kaanapali institution into one of the area's top hotels. Two brand-new towers contain 510 rooms, all with drop-dead views of the Pacific and of Black Rock promontory, where a cliff diver practices his art nightly at 5:30. The 23-acre site has three restaurants, a lagoon and a pool, three tennis courts, and a health spa. ◆ 2605 Kaanapali Pkwy (north of Whalers Village), Kaanapali. 661.0031, 800/325.3535; fax 661.0458 ♿

41 Kaanapali Beach Hotel $$$ Built in the shape of a horseshoe, this hotel features 416 rooms facing a center courtyard that opens to the beach. The whale-shaped pool is only a few yards from the ocean, and the complex's immediate neighbor is **Whalers Village,** where you'll find an excellent collection of restaurants and shops. All rooms have refrigerators, TVs, phones, and private lanais. A golf course is nearby. ◆ 2525 Kaanapali Pkwy (just north of Whalers Village), Kaanapali. 661.0011, 800/262.8450; fax 667.1963 ♿

Within the Kaanapali Beach Hotel:

Tiki Terrace $$$ It's still known for its Sunday champagne brunch, complete with a 24-foot-long pastry table and omelette station, but the seafood and Polynesian cuisine are unspectacular. The dinner specialty is *kiawe*-roasted prime rib; other entrées include fresh fish and teriyaki chicken. There's standard American fare as well. ◆ Pacific Rim/American ◆ M-Sa breakfast and dinner; Su brunch and dinner. Reservations recommended. 661.0011 ♿

41 Whaler Condominium $$$ These twin high-rise towers, 360 units total, sit on an excellent stretch of beach next to **Whalers Village.** It's a simple yet comfortable place, with daily maid service, spacious studios, and the requisite television and telephone. Guests may use the pool, sauna, Jacuzzi, exercise room, and five tennis courts. However, there is no restaurant. ◆ A minimum stay of two nights is required. 2481 Kaanapali Pkwy (just north of Whalers Village), Kaanapali. 661.4861, 800/367.7052; fax 661.8315 ♿

42 Whalers Village This mix of casual restaurants and upscale shops attracts most visitors at one time or another during their stay. Here you'll find **Tiffany and Co.** and **Wyland Galleries** (661.8255), among dozens of other shops. There also are a number of casual eateries (see below). ◆ 2435 Kaanapali Pkwy (north of Nohea Kai Dr), Kaanapali. 661.4567 ♿

Within Whalers Village:

Leilani's on the Beach ★★$$$ When residents want to check out the beach scene and "talk story" with friends, they come here. There's something about a place run by TS Enterprises (which owns **Kimo's, Duke's Canoe Club,** the **Hula Grill,** and other popular restaurants in Hawaii and California) that appeals to everyone. The food is always very good, and the ambience friendly and relaxing—people spend more time here than they mean to. The regular menu has fresh Hawaiian fish, broiled steaks, and smoked ribs and chicken; for smaller appetites, there's a seafood bar called the **Beachside Grill** next to the cocktail lounge on the beach. ◆ Seafood ◆ Daily lunch and dinner. 661.4495

Hula Grill ★★★$$$$ Somehow TS Enterprises has managed to create a place that's more Hawaiian than Hawaii itself. Canoes and surfboards are everywhere in this open-air beachside dining room, and the fare too is regional. Peter Merriman, owner and former chef at **Merriman's** on the Big Island, serves up seared *ahi* (tuna), mahimahi, and swordfish, as well as Black Angus steaks with garlic mashed potatoes and Maui onion strings. Hawaiian entertainment is featured every night, with local musicians and hula shows in the bar. ◆ Hawaiian Regional/Seafood ◆ Daily lunch and dinner. Reservations recommended. 667.2777 ♿

Rusty Harpoon $$$ If you're seriously into fresh fruit daiquiris, this is a great place to get one. The restaurant refers to itself as the "daiquiri capital of the world." However, the menu offers only unremarkable

standards, such as teriyaki chicken and shrimp scampi—without the sunset view. The owners are new though, so things may improve. ♦ American ♦ Daily breakfast, lunch, and dinner. 661.3123 ♿

42 Westin Maui $$$$ After selling the **Hyatt Regency Maui** in 1987, developer Chris Hemmeter turned right around and went into direct competition, taking over the **Maui Surf** a few doors away and turning it into the **Westin Maui.** The $155-million resort is full of Hemmeter trademarks: a fantasy water complex consisting of five free-form, multilevel swimming pools, waterfalls, water slides, and meandering streams; a $2.5-million collection of Pacific and Asian art; exotic wildlife; and eight restaurants and lounges. The 12-acre resort has two 11-story towers containing 741 rooms and suites; the top two floors of the **Beach Tower** are reserved for the **Royal Beach Club**—28 ultraelegant rooms and such extras as a private elevator, a breakfast buffet, and reserved poolside seating. ♦ 2365 Kaanapali Pkwy (off Honoapiilani Hwy), Kaanapali. 667.2525, 800/228.3000; fax 661.5764 ♿

Within the Westin Maui:

Sound of the Falls ★★★$$ The high-ceilinged, open-air dining room features distant views of Lanai and Molokai and an elegant setting highlighted by exotic birds gliding along the facing lagoon. The menu has more than 140 items, including Belgian waffles, smoked seafood, and mounds of fresh fruit, and the $25 set price includes entertainment. ♦ Continental ♦ Su brunch. Reservations recommended. 667.2525 ♿

Villa Restaurant ★★$$$$ The hotel's sprawling lagoons, gardens, and waterfalls accent this dining spot's casual setting. Seafood is the staple here, and the nightly special is usually outstanding. The crab cakes are superlative, as are the tangled tiger prawns and Kona lobster. ♦ Seafood/Pacific Rim ♦ Daily dinner. Reservations recommended. 667.2525 ♿

Cook's at the Beach ★$$$ This poolside eatery is two cuts above the typical hotel coffee shop, serving such island specialties as *ahi* (tuna) and shrimp scampi, healthful entrées like "Fruit Fantasy" (fruit salad), and a nightly prime rib buffet (not for the health conscious) for $26.95. A hula show, presented on Mondays, Wednesdays, and Fridays, is free. ♦ Continental/Cafe ♦ Daily breakfast buffet, lunch, and dinner. 667.2525 ♿

43 Kaanapali Golf Course Designed in the 1960s by Robert Trent Jones Jr., the 18-hole **North Course** (par 71, 6,136 yards) offers spectacular views of the West Maui Mountains, the ocean, and the islands of Molokai and Lanai across the channel. It's a good golf test, with numerous water risks.

The **South Course** (18 holes, par 72, 6,067 yards), a former executive course extended to championship class, also has ocean views but is less exciting. Kaanapali can be windy, especially in the late afternoon, which is why the greens fees are lower after 2:30PM on the North course, noon on the South. Lessons are available. ♦ Expensive greens fees. Daily. Preferred starting times for guests at Kaanapali hotels. Reservations at least four days ahead are required. Kaanapali Pkwy (at Honoapiilani Hwy), Kaanapali. 661.3691

44 Maui Marriott $$$$ With its beautiful landscaping, cascading waterfalls, running streams, coconut grove, and trade-wind-touched lobby, this hotel reflects the Marriott chain's attempt to upgrade its image. However, critics say the two nine-story buildings on the 15-acre site look too much like the Marriotts typically found near airports. Nevertheless, the property's swimming pool fronts Kaanapali Beach, and all 720 rooms and suites have private lanais, some of which face the ocean. Amenities include five tennis courts and a resident pro, a children's pool, two Jacuzzis, a championship golf course next door, catamarans, an exercise room, and a whole lot more. ♦ 100 Nohea Kai Dr (off Kaanapali Pkwy), Kaanapali. 667.1200, 800/763.1333; fax 667.8192 ♿

Within the Maui Marriott:

Moana Terrace ★$$$$ The resort's main dining room opens onto gardens and is terraced to provide maximum ocean views, with alfresco seating the most desirable. It's a nice atmosphere for gorging on chicken Caesar salad, chicken Santa Cruz sandwiches, or grilled sugarcane shrimp on noodles. There's even a kids' corner that features videos. ♦ American ♦ Daily lunch and dinner. 667.1200 ♿

Nikko Steak House ★★$$$$ Marriott's smartest move in Hawaii was opening this Japanese *teppanyaki* (tableside cooking) steak house. It filled a void in West Maui, where exceptional ethnic restaurants are rare. After the house soup, try out the *teppanyaki* selections and the savory sauces, but save room for the fried ice cream (cake filled with ice cream and deep-fried). Tables seat eight, so other diners fill any empty seats, and a 15 percent gratuity is added to the check. ♦ Japanese ♦ Daily dinner. Reservations recommended. 667.1200 ♿

Lokelani Room ★$$$ The decor in this restaurant (named after Maui's official flower) is nautical, and the menu—a mixture of American and Polynesian—has a seafaring theme as well. ♦ Seafood/Hawaiian Regional ♦ W-Su dinner. 667.1200

Makai Bar ★★$ Known for its *pupus* (appetizers), this open-air appetizer bar at the southern end of the lobby overlooks the beach from its elevated vantage point. The decor includes six 150-gallon fish tanks and 30 stools along a circular bar. The serious eating begins after 10:30PM, when some dishes, such as sushi, egg rolls, and *poki* (chopped, seasoned raw fish), are half-price. These *pupus* have won culinary awards for three years running. No one under 21 is admitted. ♦ Appetizers ♦ Daily 4:30PM-12:30AM. No reservations. 667.1200 ♿

45 Hyatt Regency Maui $$$$ Developer Chris Hemmeter built this super-deluxe "Disneyland for adults" in 1980 for $80 million. Seven years later, Kokusai Jidosha, a Japanese company, bought it for $319 million (approximately $391,000 per room), throwing in $12 million for renovations in 1990 and another $16 million in 1995. The hotel consists of three 19-story connecting towers on 40 oceanside acres, with 884 rooms and suites. Custom-designed wall coverings, upholstery, and furniture, as well as Italian marble countertops and terra-cotta tile floors, are among luxurious touches added by Kokusai Jidosha. Hemmeter, however, should still be credited for the lavish collection of Asian and Pacific art, including John Young paintings, Hawaiian quilts, Cambodian Buddhas, Ming Dynasty wine pots, and battle shields from Papua New Guinea. Outside, a 154-foot enclosed water slide empties into the 1.5-acre swimming pool. Mexican artists designed the 14-karat-gold tiles that embellish the sprawling pool's mosaic. There's also a swinging rope bridge and a swim-up **Grotto Bar**, set between two waterfalls. Flamingos, swans, penguins, peacocks, and ducks add to the hotel's flamboyantly exotic flavor. The **Regency Club** offers such extras as concierge service, breakfast, and sunset cocktails and appetizers. ♦ 200 Nohea Kai Dr (off Kaanapali Pkwy), Kaanapali. 661.1234, 800/233.1234; fax 667.4714 ♿

Within the Hyatt Regency Maui:

Lahaina Provision Company ★★$$$$ Paella, filet mignon, and fresh local fish like *ono* (wahoo) and *ahi* (tuna) are served in a garden setting with nautical touches. The lavish Chocoholic Bar, a dessert buffet featured nightly, has its fans—and rightly so. ♦ Steaks/Seafood ♦ Daily lunch and dinner. 661.1234 ♿

Swan Court ★★★$$$$ The large, elegant dining room of this award-winning restaurant overlooks a lagoon with a flotilla of gliding swans. Soft piano music enhances the stunning view of the waterfalls and the sun setting between Lanai and Molokai. The menu is different each night. The fresh fish and roast duckling are excellent choices when they're offered, or try the rack of lamb, chateaubriand, or lobster in puff pastry. The wine list is long—and expensive. In the mornings, a lovely breakfast buffet with pancakes, French toast, and crepes is laid out. Unlike most restaurants, this one encourages cigar smoking. ♦ Continental ♦ Daily breakfast and dinner. Reservations recommended. 661.1234 ♿

Spats Trattoria ★$$$ In its present incarnation, this place offers a decent selection of dishes such as seafood grill over fettuccine Alfredo and chicken parmigiana. ♦ Italian/Seafood ♦ Daily dinner. Reservations recommended. 661.1234 ♿

Drums of the Pacific ★$$$ An extravagant (if antiseptic) South Seas show accompanies a lavish all-you-can-eat buffet. Main dishes include *kalua* pork (baked in ti leaves), *shoyu* chicken (in soy sauce), and coconut beef. ♦ Luau ♦ Daily dinner. Reservations recommended. 661.1234 ♿

46 Wahikuli State Wayside Park This popular recreation site has picnic pavilions, public facilities, and nearby tennis courts. There's also a beach, but it's very small, usually damp, and covered with debris. ♦ Honoapiilani Hwy (Hwy 30), between Mala and Kaanapali

"No alien land in all the world has any deep, strong charm for me but [Hawaii]; no other land could so longingly and so beseechingly haunt me sleeping and waking, through half a lifetime, as that one has done. Other things leave me, but it abides; others change, but it remains the same. For me its balmy airs are always blowing, its summer seas flashing in the sun, the pulsing of its surf-beat is in my ear; I can see its sugarlanded crags, its leaping cascades, its plumy palms drowsing by the shore, its remote summits floating like islands above the cloud rack; I can feel the spirit of its woodland solitudes, I can hear the splash of its brooks; in my nostrils still lives the breath of flowers that perished 20 years ago."

Mark Twain, 1889

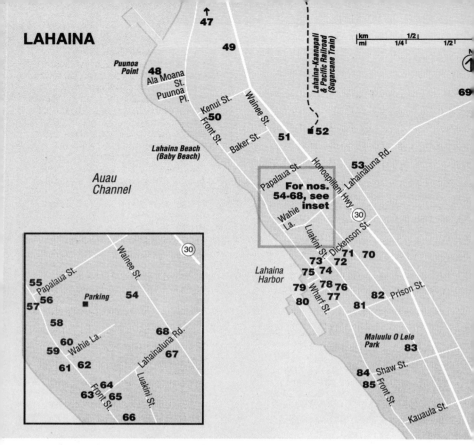

Lahaina

In the course of its history, this waterfront town has had three distinct identities. Under Kamehameha the Great, it was an early political center of the united Hawaiian kingdom. From approximately 1820 to 1860, it served as the most important provisioning stop for America's entire Pacific whaling fleet, and as such was the site of a struggle between sailors dedicated to debauchery and Protestant missionaries trying to save souls. Designated as a National Historic Landmark in 1962, Lahaina has since entered a third incarnation—this town of 10,000 people has become West Maui's main tourist attraction, with attractive shops, fine restaurants, and nightclubs appealing to a young crowd.

The town is only a few blocks deep, and most of the points of interest are on or just off a half-mile stretch of **Front Street,** which has undergone extensive renovation and beautification in the past few years. Sightseeing should take two to three hours or so (a bit more for dedicated shoppers), but for optimum comfort, plan your excursion for the morning or evening—the town is deserving of its name, *lahaina,* which means "merciless sun."

47 Chart House ★$$$ The idea behind its high perch at the northern end of Lahaina was to give diners a great sunset and ocean view, which it does. The restaurant's long-standing reputation for good steak and fish

holds firm here, but if you're short on cash, the Caesar salad makes a fine meal. ◆ Steaks/Seafood ◆ Daily dinner. Reservations recommended. 1450 Front St (between Kapunakea St and Honoapiilani Hwy). 661.0937. Also at: 500 N Puunene Av (at Kaahumanu Ave), Kahului. 877.2476; 10 Wailea Ike Dr (at Wailea Alanui Dr), Wailea. 879.2875

48 Jodo Mission Lahaina's Buddhist temple, which consists of the Amida Buddha (Great Buddha), temple bell, main temple, and pagoda, was completed in 1970 to commemorate the centennial of the first Japanese immigration to Hawaii, as well as to memorialize loved ones who passed away in the last one hundred years. The Amida Buddha, at 12 feet and 3.5 tons, is the largest of its kind outside of Japan. ◆ 12 Ala Moana St (off Front St)

49 Lahaina Cannery Mall Whatever you need, from beach chairs to Dramamine, you'll find it here for less. The center, a pineapple cannery from 1918 to 1963, has two anchor stores (**Longs** and **Safeway**), 48 shops and food stands, special events such as lei-making and pineapple-slicing demonstrations and an adorable *keiki* (kids') hula show every Sunday at 1PM. It's an unusual mall in an unusual location (too far to walk from Front Street, too close to justify losing your parking space), but it's blissfully air-conditioned. A free shuttle from Lahaina Harbor runs all day. ◆ Daily. 1221 Honoapiilani Hwy (at Kapunakea St). 661.5304 &

50 Seamen's Hospital During Lahaina's wild whaling days in the mid-1800s, thousands of sailors were left behind on Maui by American and British whaling ships seeking to lighten their loads before embarking on trading trips to Canton. Many of the sailors subsequently died of a "disreputable disease" at this two-story hospital; in fact, at the time the care of sick sailors in Lahaina and Honolulu used up half the budget appropriated by Congress for the care of all US seamen. Ironically, the place was sold to a group of nuns in 1865 and served as a Catholic school for some 20 years and then as an Episcopalian vicarage for 30 years; it was abandoned in 1908. In 1982, through a unique arrangement between the **Lahaina Restoration Foundation** and architect **Uwe Schultz**, the deteriorating eyesore was completely restored. The building is not currently in use and is closed to the public. ◆ Front St (at Kenui St)

51 Scaroles ★★★$$$ Northern Italian cuisine is served in a tiny, stylish setting off the beaten track. From fresh-baked onion rolls to seafood pasta and veal Scaroles (with eggplant and prosciutto), the food is superb. Other pluses: nightly specials, a famous tiramisù, and Maui's only collection of Italian opera music. This place shouldn't be missed. Note: There's no liquor license, so bring your own wine. ◆ Northern Italian ◆ M-F lunch and dinner; Sa-Su dinner. Reservations recommended. 930 Wainee St (between Papalaua and Kenui Sts, directly behind the Hard Rock Cafe). 661.4466 &

52 Lahaina-Kaanapali & Pacific Railroad (Sugarcane Train) Children and train buffs will especially enjoy the Sugarcane Train: a rebuilt little-train-that-could that chugs six miles between Lahaina and Kaanapali. Puffing beside original narrow-gauge track used by the **Pioneer Sugar Mill** since 1890, this steam locomotive (pictured above) with whistle and open-air passenger cars recalls a bygone era. Buy one-way or round-trip tickets, or choose a package that includes **The Hawaii Experience Dome Theater** movie or a museum tour. A

free bus runs between the Lahaina depot and town; a jitney links the Kaanapali station with hotels; and there's a boarding platform across the footbridge at the north end of the Kaanapali resort. The narrated trip (about 25 minutes each way) takes passengers past cane fields, mountains, and the shore, and features a singing conductor. ◆ Fee. Six round-trips daily. Three stations: Lahaina Station (Hinau St, off Honoapiilani Hwy, just north of the Pioneer Sugar Mill); Kaanapali Station (Honoapiilani Hwy, at the Kekaa Dr exit, no parking available); Puukoli Station (Puukoli Rd, off Honoapiilani Hwy, Kaanapali). 661.0089

53 Pioneer Sugar Mill Built by sugar magnate James Campbell, the Pioneer Mill Company thrived as others folded and went on to become a kingpin of Maui sugar production, providing generations of Mauians with employment. The mill's smokestack is as familiar a part of the Lahaina landscape as the cane fields and boat harbors. The building is closed to the public. ◆ Lahainaluna Rd (at Mill St)

54 House of Saimin ★$ If you haven't tried a bowl of saimin yet, do so here. Basically a fancier version of ramen noodles with extras (such as fish cakes and wontons), it's served in a huge bowl with chopsticks and a soup spoon. More than a cheap, healthy lunch, saimin is a cultural experience. The best side dish on this restaurant's succinct menu is the chicken sticks—so good you'll probably put in a second order while feeding the jukebox. ◆ Local ◆ M-Sa lunch. No reservations. Lahaina Shopping Center, 845 Wainee St (between Lahainaluna Rd and Papalaua St). 667.7572

54 Golden Palace $ Chinese restaurants are about as plentiful on Maui as ski resorts, and the few that do exist usually are hard to find. This restaurant is no exception; it will only be of interest to those who are seriously in the mood for Chinese food. Takeout is available. ◆ Cantonese ◆ Daily lunch and dinner. Lahaina Shopping Center, 845 Wainee St (between Lahainaluna Rd and Papalaua St). 661.3126 &

55 Lahaina Center This shopping center has the personality and charm of a refrigerator, but it continues to receive busloads of tourists, and parking is no longer free, so the stores here must be prospering. The major outlets include **Liberty House** department store (661.4451), which sells high-end Hawaiian print fashions, and **Hilo Hattie** (667.7911), which sells low-end Hawaiian print fashions. ♦ Daily. 900 Front St (at Papalaua St). 667.9216 &

Within the Lahaina Center:

Hard Rock Cafe ★★$$ It's said that familiarity breeds contempt, but for the Hard Rock chain, all it breeds is success. As usual, the rock music is loud, the walls are adorned with rock and surf memorabilia, and there's always a line to buy T-shirts. The food, if unexceptional, is good enough to draw even the locals, who come for the six-ounce burgers and Texas-style ribs. Yes, it's predictable and very touristy, but you'd be hard-pressed to have a bad time. ♦ American ♦ Daily lunch and dinner. 667.7400 &

World Cafe $ If you're looking to spend a high-energy night in Lahaina, this is the place. The ocean-view spot has dancing upstairs and down to local and mainland bands like Willy Ko and Fishbone, as well as country nights, DJs spinning everything from techno to hip hop—and an enormous menu featuring items like three-cheese lasagna and Mexican plates, available until 1AM. ♦ American ♦ Daily noon-2AM. Cover. No reservations. 661.1515 &

Longhi's

56 Longhi's ★$$$ When this restaurant tripled in size a number of years ago, the service (somewhat predictably) declined—a problem for a place where the servers are known for reciting the menus. Only the most seasoned waiters can remember the extensive and complicated choices and still provide service that isn't spotty or hurried. Don't be afraid to ask the waiter to slow down, and be sure to ask the prices. Portions are large, so be careful about overordering, especially if you plan on trying one of the trademark homemade desserts. The cuisine has an

Italian flair, with dishes like pasta Lombardi (with snow peas, prosciutto, and cream), lobster Longhi (with pasta, calamari, clams, and mussels in a marinara sauce), seafood, and enormous sandwiches. Eclipsed by new restaurants down the street, this is no longer *the* Lahaina dining spot, but it remains a local landmark and a breakfast favorite, and it books some stellar jazz bands on weekend nights. ♦ Continental/Italian ♦ Daily breakfast, lunch, and dinner. Reservations required. 888 Front St (at Papalaua St). 667.2288 &

57 Lahaina Broiler $$$ The proprietors say this is the biggest restaurant in Lahaina, but its real claim to fame is the 100-year-old monkeypod tree growing out of the roof. The food, mainly steak, seafood, and chicken, is fairly standard. The best reason to come is the superb setting overlooking the water. The view of Molokai and Lanai and the sunset mai tai special are both memorable. ♦ American ♦ Daily lunch and dinner. 889 Front St (across from Longhi's). 661.3111 &

58 Wo Hing Temple In 1909 Chinese laborers brought here to work in West Maui's sugarcane fields formed the **Wo Hing Society,** a mid-Pacific chapter of a 17th-century Chinese fraternal organization. Three years later the group built a hall with a separate cookhouse in downtown Lahaina. In 1983 the **Lahaina Restoration Foundation** turned the building into a museum, preserving a chapter in the history of one of Hawaii's significant ethnic groups. Among the items on display in the cookhouse are Chinese utensils and fire pits once fueled with *kiawe* wood for oversize woks. Films of turn-of-the-century Hawaii made by Thomas Edison are also shown. ♦ Donation. Daily. Front St (between Wahie La and Papalaua St). 661.3262

59 Kimo's ★★$$$ Two young men who made a fortune with the Rusty Scupper chain on the mainland built this popular oceanfront restaurant and bar (pictured below) on Front Street, with views of Molokai and Lanai from the outside deck. The food isn't anything to

Kimo's

write home about, but it's consistently good, including your basic fresh fish, a huge cut of prime rib, steaks, and island specials such as *koloa* (plum-sauce–glazed) pork ribs and Polynesian chicken. On Friday and Saturday afternoons a local singer puts on a show, but the best entertainment for locals and visitors alike is the spectacular sunset. ♦ Steaks/Seafood ♦ Daily lunch and dinner. 845 Front St (across from Mariner's Alley). 661.4811 &

60 Avalon ★★★$$$$ Some of chef/owner Mark Ellman's imaginative Pacific Rim creations, such as Australian barbecued lamb chop and seared *tiki* salad (a mix of potatoes, salmon, mango, eggplant, greens, and tomato salsa with plum-vinaigrette dressing), are truly exceptional. The setting is comfortable, with wood floors and a brick courtyard. The presumptuous attitude of the staff in this trendy restaurant is a detraction; nevertheless, this remains one of the island's finest dining rooms. ♦ Pacific Rim ♦ Daily lunch and dinner. Reservations recommended. Mariner's Alley, 844 Front St (at Wahie La). 667.5559 &

60 Moose McGillycuddy's ★$$ Part of the chain that extends from Oahu to California, this restaurant lacks originality but makes up for it in practicality. By offering a variety of reasonably good food at low prices, it plays a much-needed role in Lahaina. Menu items include prime rib, mahimahi, chicken, steak and lobster, Mexican food (especially the fish tacos), and giant salads. There's also a kids' menu. The breakfasts are huge (all the cops start their day with the $1.99 special), and the bar has nightly specials and live dance music. The cheapest dinners in town are the early-bird specials served from 4:30PM to 5:30PM (try the prime rib or steak and lobster). At the other end of the spectrum is the $22.95 all-you-can-eat king crab extravaganza. ♦ American ♦ Daily breakfast, lunch, and dinner. Mariner's Alley, 844 Front St (at Wahie La). 667.7758 &

61 Lahaina Fish Co. ★$$$ If you're confused by the names and pronunciations of the fish served in restaurants all over Hawaii, this fish house will set you straight. Comprehensive menus translate the Hawaiian word for each fish, and there's also a wall-mounted guide to island game fish. Although the cuisine isn't particularly memorable, the setting is—an open-air lanai overlooking Lahaina Harbor, Lanai, and Molokai. Prices for the Cajun mahimahi, shrimp Salvador, and the catch of the day are very reasonable, considering the million-dollar sunset that accompanies your meal. If you're not a fan of fish, opt for the popular stir-fry. ♦ Seafood ♦ Daily lunch and dinner. 831 Front St (across from The Hawaii Experience Dome Theater). 661.3472 &

62 The Hawaii Experience Dome Theater Admittedly, there's something weird about sitting in a theater watching a film of a volcanic eruption, a school of fish being chased by a bigger fish, or a whale breaching, when that's what you came to Hawaii to see close up. But this 180°, three-story-high screen gives you a closer view than you'll ever get in real life. ♦ Admission. Daily 10AM-10PM; hourly shows. 824 Front St (between Lahainaluna Rd and Wahie La). 661.8314

CHEESE 🌴 BURGER
·I·N· P·A·R·A·D·I·S·E·

63 Cheeseburger In Paradise ★$ Yes, the name comes from the popular Jimmy Buffett tune, which is of the same genre as the continuous background music, live and taped, played at this open-air burger joint. It's cheap, it's pretty good, and it's always jumping. But no, Jimmy never eats here, though a lively local band does belt out Buffett-style hits on weekend evenings. ♦ Burgers ♦ Daily lunch and dinner. 811 Front St (near Lahainaluna Rd). 661.4855 &

Lahaina Inn

64 Lahaina Inn $$ In the 1860s, when Lahaina was the whaling mecca of the world, this hotel housed the whalers who came to port. When the whaling era ended, the hostelry, then called the **Lahainaluna Hotel,** became a gathering place for genteel travelers and local power brokers. The building later served as a general store, and then business offices (destroyed by fire in the mid-1960s). Today it's a two-story, 15-room inn (including three suites) refurbished in old-style grandeur by its current owner, entrepreneur, preservationist, and antiques collector Rick Ralston (of **Crazy Shirts** fame). Luxurious turn-of-the-century touches include beautiful armoires, leaded-glass lamps, floral wall coverings, rocking chairs on the lanais, and lace curtains. No children under 15 are allowed, there are no TVs, and smokers are encouraged to use the lanai. The rooms have air-conditioning and telephones, and continental breakfast is included in the rate. ♦ 127 Lahainaluna Rd (at Front St). 661.0577, 800/669.3444; fax 667.9480

When the Eagles sing "Jesus is Coming" in their song, "The Last Resort," they're referring to a large sign that has been posted for decades outside a Lahaina church.

69

Gecko Roamin'

The wall-walking Pacific gecko (or *gekkonidae peropus mutilatus*) is Maui's favorite pet, leaving felines and canines in a distant second place. Why? For starters, these four- to six-inch-long lizards are free (they set up shop in people's homes, whether they're wanted or not). Plus, they don't need any maintenance; superstition holds that they bring good luck to the household; they feast on bugs, especially cockroaches; they're fascinating to watch, particularly when feeding or mating; they're completely harmless and nonpoisonous; they make cute clucking noises; they usually remain hidden until sunset, when they start scurrying along the walls; and they are just downright adorable.

Not indigenous to Hawaii, the first geckos (*mo'o* in Hawaiian) probably arrived by boat, although geckologists agree that their eggs could have been carried on organic flotsam, incubating during the journey. Without many natural predators (i.e., snakes), the gecko population quickly found its niche in the households of Hawaii, particularly in Maui, and easily surpassed the television for home-entertainment value (granted, the competition was weak). Quick to seize the opportunity to make a buck, souvenir retailers jumped on the reptilian bandwagon and, by the mid-1980s, geckomania was in full swing with gecko T-shirts, toys, tattoos, towels, and even jewelry (gold gecko pins sell for more than $275) dominating the stock of many tourist shops. In just a few short years, modern marketing catapulted this shy, innocuous reptile into the elite ranks of Mickey Mouse and Bugs Bunny—heady stuff for a little lizard.

The best location for gecko-gawking is in **Lahaina, Maui,** at **Lahaina Coolers,** where the hungry (and horny) wall-walkers do their thing at dusk under the neon sign just over the bar. For the price of a beer, it's some of the best entertainment in town.

Within the Lahaina Inn:

David Paul's Lahaina Grill ★★★$$$$
Once a seedy barroom on the ground floor of the former **Lahainaluna Hotel,** this star on the local culinary scene possesses the same turn-of-the-century ambience as the hotel. The large, airy dining room retains the feel of a classy Victorian barroom, with a long wooden bar, ceiling fans, and white tablecloths; it accommodates 122 people and one baby grand piano. The wine list is extensive and the fare, says part-owner and celebrated chef David Paul, features "flavors from around the world perfectly blended with local ingredients." A few examples: tequila shrimp with firecracker rice, Kona coffee–roasted lamb, and *kalua* duck—and triple berry pie for dessert. ◆ International ◆ Daily dinner. Reservations recommended. 667.5117 ♿

65 Lahaina Marketplace The impeccable landscaping distinguishes this open-air shopping arcade filled with jewelry and souvenir kiosks. Head toward the back and admire the sentinel-like fan palms, towering hedges, brick patio, and formidable foliage tiki. ◆ Front St (at Lahainaluna Rd)

66 Planet Hollywood ★★$$$ Taking the **Hard Rock Cafe** concept (see page 68) and applying it to the world of the silver screen, this chain features movie memorabilia, clips from upcoming films, and other scraps of Hollywood culture (an oxymoron, we know). The food is American—burgers, steaks, chicken, ribs, etc. ◆ American ◆ Daily lunch and dinner. No Reservations. 744 Front St (between Dickenson St and Lahainaluna Rd). 667.7877; fax 667.5965 ♿

67 Plantation Inn $$ A group of private investors took over three residential lots in the center of Lahaina and came up with this luxurious, elegant, and surprisingly affordable hotel. The 19 rooms and suites all have an intimate, plantation-style ambience, with French doors, brass four-poster beds and other antique furniture, verandas, stained glass, wainscoting and floral wallpaper, and hardwood floors scattered with area rugs. Modern amenities include air-conditioning, TV sets, VCRs, a swimming pool, and a Jacuzzi. A buffet breakfast comes gratis. Adjacent to the inn is **Gerard's,** the best French restaurant in Maui (if not Hawaii), and only a block away are the shops and galleries of Lahaina's bustling Front Street. ◆ 174 Lahainaluna Rd (between Wainee and Luakini Sts). 667.9225, 800/433.6815; fax 667.9293

Adjacent to the Plantation Inn:

Gerard's ★★★★$$$$ An apprentice chef in France at age 14, Gerard Reversade trained with four French culinary masters, acquiring the expertise that makes him one of Hawaii's top chefs. After moving to Hawaii in 1973, Gerard worked in the finest French restaurants in the state and in 1982 established his own place in downtown Lahaina—a small, charmingly unpretentious adjunct to the stately **Plantation Inn.** The decor recalls Provence; the entrées, including rack of lamb and roasted Hawaiian snapper, are impeccably prepared. True to his French roots, Reversade has a policy of using fresh local ingredients. Yes, it's expensive, but it's also the best. (*Wine Spectator* magazine gave the restaurant its top award in 1994, '95, and '96.) Guests of the **Plantation Inn** receive a discount. ◆ French ◆ Daily dinner. Reservations recommended. 661.8939 &

68 **West Maui Cycle and Sports** Looking to rent mountain bikes, snorkel sets, boogie boards, surfboards, or baby joggers? This is the place. The price is right, too—it's less than $10 to borrow either a surfboard or a bike for 24 hours. ◆ Daily. 193 Lahainaluna Rd (at Wainee St). 661.9005

69 **Hale Pai (House of Printing)** This structure is the only original building still standing on the **Lahainaluna High School** campus—the first American school established west of the Rocky Mountains. Founded in 1831 by Protestant missionaries as a means of spreading the Christian gospel to the Hawaiian people, the school used a secondhand press to print Hawaii's first newspaper in Hawaiian, *Ka Lama Hawaii* (The Torch of Hawaii), in 1834. The press, brought by the missionaries on their journey around Cape Horn, also turned out translations, history texts, and even Hawaiian currency.

The building has been fully restored by the Lahaina Restoration Foundation. ◆ Donation. M-F 10AM-3PM. At the end of Lahainaluna Rd. 661.3262 &

70 **Maui Islander** $$ Lush tropical plants and quiet surroundings distinguish this unobtrusive, 9-acre complex of two-story structures. Banana trees, ancient palms, plumeria, papaya, and large torch gingers transform this otherwise plain establishment into a cool oasis in the middle of simmering Lahaina. Its 350 clean but unspectacular rooms and suites have the usual comforts: TVs, telephones, air-conditioning, and lanais for the two- and three-bedroom suites. There's no restaurant, but for the price, location (a short walk from everything), and casual ambience, it's a fairly good choice for lodging in Lahaina. ◆ 660 Wainee St (between Prison and Dickenson Sts). 667.9766, 800/367.5226; fax 661.3733 &

71 **Lahaina Coolers** ★★$$ Very few dining establishments make it onto the locals' favorite-hangout list, but the informal atmosphere and friendly staff make this open-air restaurant and bar *the* place in Lahaina to unwind with a Lahaina cooler cocktail and a curry chicken and pasta appetizer. The restaurant offers a host of daily specials in addition to its eclectic menu; it's hard to go wrong with the Molokai sweet bread French toast or a handmade pizza. Free entertainment is usually provided by the resident gecko family, which performs nightly under the neon lights. ◆ American ◆ Daily breakfast, lunch, and dinner. Reservations recommended. Dickenson Square, 180 Dickenson St (between Wainee and Luakini Sts). 661.7082 &

72 **Kobe Steak House** ★★$$$ Lahaina's best sushi bar is located here among the *teppanyaki* (tableside cooking) grills and the human Veg-o-Matics, whose culinary skills are as good as the food. The service is always friendly, the sushi always fresh, and the bill always higher than you think it'll be. For something different and unbelievably good, try the *unagi* (freshwater eel) and *dynamite* (baked scallops), with a Purple Haze (fortified sake) to wash it all down. ◆ Japanese ◆ Daily dinner. 136 Dickenson St (at Luakini St). 667.5555 &

Restaurants/Clubs: Red   Hotels: Blue
Shops/ ♥ Outdoors: Green   **Sights/Culture:** Black

Banyan Tree

73 Take Home Maui The irony of this produce and deli shop is that it's obviously geared toward tourists (with pineapples, coconuts, Maui onions, papayas, macadamia nuts, and other delicacies to send home to loved ones), but it's always filled with locals, who come for the coffee, smoothies, pastries, and deli items. Before you spend the day driving around Maui, grab a table and enjoy a cup of mac-nut or chocolate-raspberry Kona coffee, then get a Moon Box lunch—a sandwich, a piece of fruit, a side of pasta or potato salad, and a cookie or chips—to go. Yes, the resident bird talks ("ah*row*ha"), and no, it does not bite (well, not often). ♦ Daily. 121 Dickenson St (at Luakini St). 661.8067

74 Village Galleries In a town where marine art is big business, Lynn Shue's gallery offers a refreshing change of genre. It has pieces by Hawaii's finest artists, including George Allan and Pamela Andelin, with works in all media. ♦ Daily. 120 Dickenson St (at Luakini St). 661.4402. Ꮬ Also at: Dickenson Square, 180 Dickenson St (between Wainee and Luakini Sts), Lahaina, 661.4402 Ꮬ; Ritz-Carlton Kapalua, 1 Ritz-Carlton Dr (off Lower Honoapiilani Rd), Kapalua, 669.1800 Ꮬ

74 Baldwin House The Reverend Dwight Baldwin, a medical missionary, relocated from the mainland to Lahaina in 1835 for the sake of his own health, then wound up attending to the medical needs of the Hawaiians who gathered daily on his doorstep. In 1853 he singlehandedly fought to save Maui, Molokai, and Lanai from a smallpox epidemic. Until he moved to Honolulu in 1868, the Reverend lived with his family in this white two-story house made of coral, stone, and hand-hewn timbers. He received both royalty and ship captains here, providing them with a seamen's chapel and Christian reading room. The **Lahaina Restoration Foundation** now operates the house—the oldest standing building in Lahaina—as a museum and also has its administrative offices here. ♦ Admission. Daily. Front St (between Prison and Dickenson Sts). 661.3262

75 Sunrise Cafe ★$ A popular hangout for philosophical locals who enjoy deliberating over cappuccino and pastry, this cafe serves light baked goods for breakfast, and sandwiches, quiche, homemade soup, some heartier dishes like mahimahi, and daily specials for lunch and dinner. If you miss your cafe back home, this will do in a pinch. Open at 6AM, it's also a good wake-up stop to make before an early-morning drive or boat trip. Take note, though: Service is refreshingly slow. ♦ Cafe ♦ Daily breakfast, lunch, and dinner. 693-A Front St (at Market St). 661.8558

76 Wharf Cinema Center This complex is touristy beyond belief, housing some of Lahaina's most mediocre shops and restaurants. But it does have a movie theater and when it gets really hot in Lahaina, even the worst flicks can be worth suffering through for 90 minutes of air-conditioned comfort. ♦ Daily. 658 Front St (between Prison and Dickenson Sts)

77 Banyan Tree It's hard to believe that this huge banyan—nearly a block in size including its roots and overhanging branches—stood a mere eight feet when it was brought to Lahaina from India. Planted in 1873 by Sheriff William Owen Smith to commemorate the 50th anniversary of Lahaina's first Protestant Christian mission, the venerable tree (pictured on page 72) is now among the oldest and largest in the islands and is listed on the state register of exceptional trees. It reaches up more than 50 feet and stretches outward over a 200-square-foot area, shading two-thirds of an acre in the town's landmark courthouse square. ♦ Front St (between Canal and Hotel Sts)

77 Lahaina Courthouse The courthouse and palace of King Kamehameha III once stood near the site of this semidilapidated structure, but they were leveled in 1858 by gale-force winds. In 1859 the stones from the destroyed building were used to build the present courthouse, which at one time was the governmental center of Maui County. Now it's the center for the **Lahaina Arts Society,** as well as the **Lahaina Visitors' Center,** the **Old Jail Gallery,** and the **Banyan Tree Gallery.** Both galleries showcase the work of island artists with exhibits that change monthly. ♦ Daily. 649 Wharf St (between Canal and Hotel Sts). 661.0111

77 Waterfront Fort In 1831 a legal battle raged between the whalers, who were accustomed to some immediate R&R with the locals when their ships pulled into harbor, and the missionaries, who regarded the whole affair with disgust. A law was passed prohibiting local women from swimming out to greet the incoming ships, which prompted the rowdy whalers to fire cannons at the missionary complex. At Queen Keopuolani's orders, a one-acre area was then walled off to protect the citizens, with huge coral blocks hacked from the reef fronting the Lahaina shores. The fort was torn down in 1854 and the stones used to build Lahaina's prison. When Lahaina became a historical landmark, a heap of coral blocks was put together to resemble a corner of the fort—and that's about what it looks like today. ♦ Wharf St (at Canal St)

78 Pioneer Inn $$ George Freeland, a member of the Royal Canadian Mounted Police who fell in love with Lahaina after following a criminal to the area, built this inn at the turn of the century. Once weathered and run-down, this funky haunt has been spruced up with a $5-million renovation—though the service is still hit-or-miss. Thirty-two rooms and two suites are available for those who don't mind the noise from the saloon downstairs, which stays open until 4AM. The rooms have air-conditioning, but no TV sets, and there's no pool on the premises. Located right next to the wharf, this is precisely the place not to get away from it all. ♦ 658 Wharf St (between Hotel and Papelekane Sts). 661.3636, 800/457.5457; fax 667.5708

Within the Pioneer Inn:

The Grill and Bar $ If you're going to spend your day in Lahaina, you might as well start it with breakfast in the **Pioneer Inn**'s courtyard. After breakfast, it's usually too hot to eat or drink here until the late afternoon, when entertainer Trevor Jones sings the same salty numbers he's sung for a decade (3:00PM to 7:30PM every day but Friday). Although the food is not memorable (teriyaki chicken burgers, shrimp salad, submarine sandwiches, and the like), the energy level

Pioneer Inn

reflects its prime location across from the wharf. And thanks to some archaic legal clause, this place doesn't stop serving alcohol when everywhere else in town does, so by 4AM everyone is looking good. ♦ American ♦ Daily breakfast, lunch, and dinner. No reservations. 661.3636

Harpooner's Lanai $$ Rest your parched, wearied bones for a spell in the courtyard of this alfresco dining room. The pompano and scallops with chervil beurre blanc and the rib eye of beef seared with blue cheese and rosemary sure are an improvement over the menu items of the years when this was just a colorful hole in the wall. ♦ American/French ♦ Daily dinner. No reservations. 661.3636 ♿

79 Brig Carthaginian The original *Carthaginian* left Lahaina for Honolulu in 1972 for dry dock but instead hit a reef and sank. This 93-foot replacement—*Carthaginian II,* the only authentically restored brig in the world—sailed here from Denmark and is operated by the **Lahaina Restoration Foundation.** Below decks, visitors can inspect a museum of whaling history and watch a program on humpback whales, which migrate to Maui waters every winter. ♦ Admission. Daily. At the wharf (across from the Pioneer Inn). 661.8527 ♿

80 Lahaina Harbor Nearly all Lahaina's water activities start and finish at the harbor. Come here to watch the hustle and bustle of what used to be one of the world's busiest whaling ports. Some activities and recommended companies: sailing with **First Class** (667.7733) or **Scotch Mist** (661.0386); fishing with **Islander II** (667.6625); scuba diving with **Hawaiian Reef Divers** (667.7647); dinner cruises with **Manutea** (661.5309); all-day sailing/snorkeling trips with **Trilogy** (661.4743); rafting with **Ocean Riders** (Mala Wharf, 661.3586); whale watching (in winter)

with **Lahaina Princess** (661.8397); submarine rides with **Atlantis** (667.2224); and rides on the **Nautilus** semisubmersible (667.2133). ♦ Off Wharf St (at Canal St)

81 Dan's Greenhouse Although it's only a half-block off Front Street, this plant and animal emporium is easily bypassed—but shouldn't be. The specialty here is certified bonsai ready to ship home, along with orchids, Maui onion seeds, sprouted coconuts, and other packaged Hawaiian plants. The showstoppers, though, are the tropical birds that love to cuddle and croon. They're also for sale, but before you get too attached, check out the price tags—ol' Prince Ele, a quixotic and enigmatic black palm cockatoo from way far away, goes for $25,000. Not for sale are the frisky tamarins caged in the parking lot around the entrance. Ask the friendly staff for a handful of Cheerios to feed them. ♦ Daily. 133 Prison St (between Luakini and Front Sts). 661.8412 ♿

82 Hale Paahao Built in 1852 by convicts, this structure was once Lahaina's prison (the name means "the stuck-in-irons house"). Most of the inmates were drunken sailors who failed to return to their ships at sundown although some were confined for desertion, working on Sunday, or dangerous horseback riding. Ball-and-chain and wall shackles further restrained troublemakers. ♦ Donation. Daily. Prison St (at Wainee St). 661.3262 ♿

83 Wainee Churchyard Both prominent and anonymous residents of early Lahaina are buried in this first Christian cemetery in Hawaii, built in 1823. Many of the graves are those of missionaries' children (infant mortality was high then); others belong to Hawaiian royalty, including Queen Keopuolani—wife of King Kamehameha I, mother of Kamehameha II and Kamehameha III, and the first Hawaiian convert to be baptized a Protestant and given a Christian burial; her daughter, Nahienaena; the last king of Kauai, King Kaumualii; high chief Hoapili, Keopuolani's second husband; and Kekauonohi, one of the five queens of Kamehameha II. To the right of the churchyard is **Waiola Church,** which stands on the site of the first stone church on Maui. The original structure, called **Wainee Church,** was built in 1832 and seated up to 3,000 on the floor. Its history is one bad luck story after another: The church lost its roof in an 1858 whirlwind; was burned down in 1894 by Hawaiians opposed to the overthrow of their monarchy; was rebuilt in 1897, only to be partly destroyed by fire in 1947; and was toppled by another whirlwind in 1951. The present church, erected after the last whirlwind, was given the name "Waiola (living waters)," in hopes of breaking the spell. Church services are held on Sundays at 8 and 10AM. 535 Wainee St (between Shaw and Luakini Sts). 661.4349

Maui's Mane Attraction

Islanders were first introduced to horses in the early 1880s when *lio* (wild mustangs) were brought over from Mexico. These animals quickly adapted to the rough terrain, and today their docile descendants can carry you on a trek through Maui's beaches, valleys, pineapple fields, volcanoes, and waterfalls. Here are a few outfitters with horses for hire:

Adventures on Horseback (Box 1419, Makawao, HI 96768, 242.7445) offers a five-and-a-half-hour tour into a rain forest, through waterfall country, and across the verdant slopes of **Haleakala Crater.** The tour, which is limited to six adults, includes a guide, continental breakfast, refreshments, and lunch. Special-occasion sunset rides for two are also a possibility.

Pony Express Tours (Box 535, Kula, HI 96790, 667.2200) takes riders on a unique all-day or half-day horseback trip into Haleakala Crater with a guide who discusses the dormant volcano's geologic history and related legends. Lunch, a jacket, and a raincoat are provided. Other options include one-

and two-hour rides on **Haleakala Ranch** lands.

Ironwood Ranch (5095 Napili Hau St, Suite 308, Lahaina, HI 96761, 669.4702) operates out of cool, scenic **Napili** with two- to four-hour rides through bamboo forests and pineapple fields. Trips vary according to the experience of the riders and can include extras like hiking; all include complimentary pickup from area hotels.

84 505 Front Street Designed to resemble a New England whaling village, this small jumble of boutiques, stores, restaurants, and a dance club actually offers more than most of the larger malls lining Front Street. And it's within easy walking distance of the town's famous banyan tree. ◆ Daily. Just south of Maluulu O Lele Park. 667.2514

Within 505 Front Street:

Old Lahaina Luau Cafe ★★$$$$
As commercial luaus go, this is West Maui's finest—a blend of exoticism, good food, and memorable entertainment. Torches and palm trees, traditionally clad performers, and an *imu* (earthen oven) roasting a 200-pound pig make for an enjoyable evening. Far from the patronizing program that characterizes many "authentic" native shows, this one includes both ancient and modern renditions of the hula, along with dramatic touches such as a torch-lit canoe offshore. The open bar and all-you-can-eat buffet, featuring such items as *shoyu* (soy sauce) lime chicken with chili sauce and filet mignon in a kukui nut butter, likewise surpass the norm.
◆ Hawaiian ◆ Daily 5:30PM-8:30PM. Reservations recommended. 667.1998

Pacifico Restaurant ★★$$$ In recent years, this place has become a favorite with local residents. Try the local fish wrapped and grilled in a banana leaf, or the rack of lamb roasted with mac nuts. The polished wood bar, with a friendly staff and a laid-back ambience, is perfect for an afternoon cocktail

or three, or drop by for live jazz on Thursday, Friday, and Saturday nights. Another reason to come here: the outside dining area with a view of the island of Lanai and some of the most beautiful sunsets on the planet.
◆ Pacific Rim ◆ Daily lunch and dinner. Reservations recommended. 667.4341 ♿

Village Pizzeria ★★$$$ There's no ocean view, no live music, and yet no question that this pizzeria serves the best pie to be found in Lahaina: clam and garlic pizza—the halitosis house special.
◆ Pizza ◆ Daily lunch and dinner. 661.8112 ♿

85 Lahaina Shores $$$ What makes this place unique is that it's the only hotel in town that's right on the beach, with a comfortable pool and a grassy sunbathing area bordering the sand. Once a rambling, plantation-style mansion, the building has been converted into a 199-room hotel with studios and one-bedrooms, and eight 1,400-square-foot penthouse suites, all with full kitchens, daily maid service, and reasonable rates. Over a complimentary continental breakfast on their first morning, new arrivals are briefed by knowledgeable staff members on the activities and sightseeing possibilities nearby. There's no restaurant, but considering the location, price, hospitality, and spacious accommodations, even the pickiest of travelers won't be disappointed.
◆ 475 Front St (just south of 505 Front Street). 661.4835, 800/628.6699; fax 661.4696

Between Lahaina and Kihei

86 Paunau Beach Park Small and unspectacular, the closest beach park to Lahaina offers fair swimming, summer surfing, and picnic facilities. The water is fairly shallow, with a rock and sand ocean floor. ♦ Public access at the end of Front St (a mile southeast of Lahaina)

87 Olowalu A nearby cliff face covered with petroglyphs indicates that the impenetrable West Maui Mountains were once traversable via an ancient trail connecting Olowalu to Iao Valley. But historians know this seaside village as the site of the 1790 Olowalu Massacre, when Captain Simon Metcalfe, seeking revenge for the loss of a sailor and a boat (presumably at the hands of local thieves), invited a group of Hawaiians to visit his American ship under the pretense of trading goods. Once the Hawaiians had gathered on the starboard side of the *Eleanora*, Metcalfe ordered the gunwales uncovered. He and his men fired down on the startled, defenseless islanders, killing more than one hundred and seriously wounding many more. ♦ Honoapiilani Hwy (Hwy 30, 5 miles southeast of Lahaina)

87 Chez Paul ★$$$$ This dining landmark in West Maui dates back 20 years to when Boston Irishman Paul Kirk and his French wife, Fernie, sold their highly successful Santa Barbara restaurant and opened a tiny French place with private dining rooms in the middle of nowhere. Their unusual operation was in a shabby building that had a certain cachet, especially when juxtaposed with the ultra-chic Kaanapali establishments. Today, an overpriced menu, featuring items like duck Tahitian and *opakapaka* (pink snapper) beurre blanc, and outdated decor make this restaurant, now run by Lucien Charbonnier, less desirable. ♦ French ♦ Daily dinner. Reservations recommended. Off Honoapiilani Hwy (Hwy 30), Olowalu. 661.3843

87 Olowalu General Store An example of a classic Hawaiian phenomenon is this old-fashioned general store (originally a plantation store owned by Pioneer Mill), which sells a little of everything you'll ever need on an island. If you're going to spend the day at Olowalu Beach, stop here first and pick up some *onolicious* (delicious) homemade local grinds, all packaged and ready to go. But watch out for the treacherous turnoff—locals don't slow down. ♦ Daily. Off Honoapiilani Hwy (Hwy 30), Olowalu. 661.3774 ♿

88 Olowalu Beach It remains a Maui mystery why so many tourists are smitten with this beach. Yes, the snorkeling is usually good, especially for beginners, but the stretch of gray sand just south of Olowalu is tiny, damp, and right off a busy highway. And there are no facilities. ♦ Off Honoapiilani Hwy (at the 14-mile marker)

89 Maalaea Harbor Unless you're told by a boat-tour operator to meet your boat here, there's no real reason to stop except to seek out a bowl of clam chowder at **Buzz's Wharf**. ♦ At the end of Maalea Rd (off Honoapiilani Hwy), Maalea

90 Maui Tropical Plantation and Country Store Sugarcane, pineapples, bananas, papayas, coffee beans, macadamia nuts, exotic flowers, and other crops can be found in this 112-acre showcase for Hawaii agriculture. The park was developed by Australians Bill and Lynn Taylor on land owned by the C. Brewer Corporation. More than a dozen fields fan out from the restaurant and market area; 40-minute narrated tram tours take visitors through 50 acres of the plantation, with stops for walking around to take a closer look. The *kapu* (Keep Out) signs posted in most agricultural areas on the islands are nowhere in sight here.

Orchids, hibiscus, and other greenhouse plants in the nursery can be shipped home, and the store sells produce grown on the property, including fruit that's been inspected and approved for shipment from the island. The **Tropical Restaurant** (244.7643) serves fresh fruit creations—try the *lilikoi* (passion fruit) and ginger parfaits; from 10:30AM until 2PM daily there's a tropical luncheon buffet. And on Tuesday, Wednesday, and Thursday evenings (5 to 7:30PM) the plantation puts on a Hawaiian country barbecue. There's *paniolo* (cowboy) entertainment and steaks, chili, a salad bar, and macadamia-nut pie. It's touristy, but enjoyable. ♦ Daily. Reservations required for the barbecue. 1670 Honoapiilani Hwy (just south of Waikapu). 244.7643 ♿

Kihei

The town of Kihei is a prime example of what happens when there's no central planning for urban development. Shamefully overbuilt and crowded and utterly lacking any cohesive form or design, this stretch of coast has just one or two selling points apart from the consistently sunny weather: less expensive accommodations than in **Lahaina**, and above-average beaches (unfortunately, most are hidden behind a ragtag assortment of hotels and condos, and they're also notoriously windy; by early afternoon, you'll give up trying to keep your beach

wel in place). For information about condominium
ntals in Kihei, call **Condominium Rentals Hawaii**
79.2778), and be sure to specify if you want a
om on the beach.

91 Surfer Joe's ★$$ This casual
indoor/outdoor tavern offers an array of
local and American favorites ranging from
teriburgers to pizza. It's a good place to stop
and relax with a Guiness on tap and a fried
zucchini appetizer. ♦ American ♦ Daily lunch
and dinner. 61 S Kihei Rd (at Uwapo Rd),
Kihei. 879.8855 ♿

92 Mai Poina Oe Lau Beach Park Although
the wind picks up in the afternoon, this is a
good swimming beach with a few rocks on
the sandy ocean bottom. You can still see
what's left of the old **Kihei Landing** at the
shoreline. Picnic and public facilities are
provided. ♦ S Kihei Rd (at Ohukai Rd), Kihei

93 Kalepolepo Beach Remains of a fishpond
create a nice wading pool for children, but
ocean swimming is trickier because of the
rocky bottom. This area was once a Hawaiian
village complete with taro patches, coconut
groves, shoreline fishponds, churches, and a
small whaling station. Picnic and barbecue
facilities are available. ♦ Off S Kihei Rd (half a
mile north of Uluniu St), Kihei

94 A Pacific Cafe Maui ★★★$$$$
Jean-Marie Josselin's fourth restaurant in
the islands presents diners with impossible
decisions, like whether to order the delicious
signature mahimahi, pan-seared with a
garlic-sesame crust and lime ginger sauce,
or the roasted half Island chicken with
grilled Japanese eggplant and garlic
mashed potatoes. The kitchen is open and
the bar set in the center of this establishment
that attracts patrons from the far reaches
of the island. ♦ Hawaiian Regional ♦ Daily
dinner. Reservations recommended. Azeka
Place Shopping Center, 1279 S Kihei Rd
(between W Lipoa and Nohokai Sts), Kihei.
879.0069 ♿

95 Kalama Beach Park This 36-acre park
is more for sports enthusiasts than beach-
goers, the prime attractions being soccer and
baseball fields; volleyball, basketball, and
tennis courts; and a children's playground.
♦ S Kihei Rd (between Iliili Rd and Kihei Fire
Station), Kihei

96 Radio Cairo ★★$$ South Cape calamari,
prawns piripiri, and ju ju sirloin are just a few
of the items on the menu at this one-of-a-kind
restaurant and club. There's nothing Hawaiian
about the place, but the $250,000 in African
art and the live music issuing from the hot
spot seven nights a week are guaranteed to
keep pleasure seekers entertained. ♦ African
♦ Daily 4PM-2AM Rainbow Mall, 2439 S Kihei
Rd (between Keonekai and Kanani Rds),
Kamaole. 879.4404 ♿

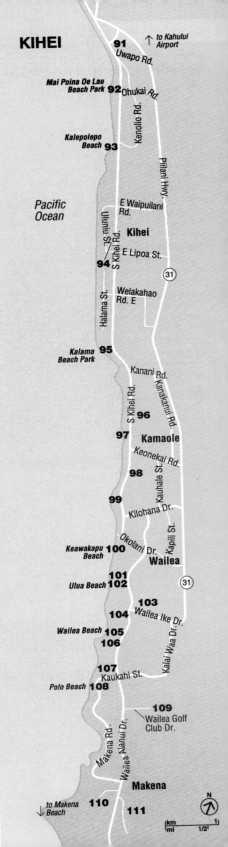

Braking Away: Maui by Bike

For those willing to wake up at an ungodly hour, head for the top of a 10,023-foot volcano, risk life and limb getting down to the bottom, and pay $100 for the privilege, a unique vacation experience awaits: biking 38 miles down the slopes of Maui's **Haleakala Crater.**

Before sunrise, a driver will pick you up at your hotel and, after coddling you with coffee and doughnuts, take you to the top of Haleakala, where you will be outfitted with a single-speed, specially designed bicycle (equipped with megabrakes), a windbreaker, gloves, and a helmet.

The chilly but pleasant ride takes about three and a half hours, cruising through cattle ranches, protea farms, and sugarcane and pineapple fields, with a stop in the picturesque town of **Kula** for lunch. The entire trip ranges from memorable to miserable depending on the unpredictable weather, but one thing is certain: It's downhill all the way.

Bicycle tours from Haleakala are offered daily by **Maui Mountain Cruisers** (871.6014, 800/232.MAUI) and **Maui Downhill** (871.2155, 800/535.BIKE).

97 Kamaole Beaches All three beach parks (marked I, II, and III) run along the south end of Kihei and have great sand, good swimming, lifeguards, and picnic and public facilities. Kamaole III also has a playground, and the reef area between II and III is good for snorkeling. ♦ S Kihei Rd (a mile south of Kalama Beach Park)

98 Kamaole Sands $$ One of the best deals on Maui, especially for families, the 440 well-managed, roomy, freshly renovated condos sit on 15 acres across the street from the Kamaole beaches, and many of the suites look out across the ocean to the islands of Molokini and Lanai. Fully equipped kitchens include dishwashers, and there are also washer/dryers and daily maid service. There's a swimming and a wading pool, two Jacuzzis, a restaurant and barbecue area, and four tennis courts. A two-night stay is required. ♦ 2695 S Kihei Rd (between Kilohana Dr and Keonekai Rd), Kamaole. 874.8700, 800/272.5275; fax 879.3273

Wailea and Environs

In 1973 no one imagined that this 1,500-acre stretch of coastline dotted with patches of scraggly *kiawe* and *wiliwili* trees would become a deluxe resort area, but Wailea had two important things going for it: great weather and white-sand beaches. Located on the dry, leeward side of **Haleakala,** the area has an average yearly rainfall of 11 inches and an average temperature of 75.15 degrees Fahrenheit. Not only is the volcano a beautiful backdrop, but it acts as a natural buffer, protecting Wailea from rain and wind.

Each of Wailea's five beaches has a smooth, sandy bottom protected by coral reefs, excellent for swimming and snorkeling.

Built in 1976, the **Aston Wailea** was the first Wailea resort hotel, followed two years later by the **Renaissance Wailea Beach Resort.** In 1990 the **Four Seasons Resort** opened, followed by the **Grand Wailea** in 1991 and then the unusual **Kea Lani Hotel.** All of this bodes well for Wailea, which is now considered a luxury resort on a par with the Big Island's Kohala Coast. Within the region you'll find 54 holes of golf, one of the largest tennis complexes on the islands, the **Wailea Shopping Village,** and several first-rate restaurants.

99 Carrelli's ★★$$$ One of the few highly commendable restaurants in the area is ideally situated right on the beach. Gourmet Italian cuisine is served in an open-air setting. Menu selections include homemade pizzas, fresh seared *ahi* (tuna) *sorrentine,* and the *specialità della casa* (specialty of the house)—*zuppa di mare cioppino,* a tempting assortment of clams, mussels, scallops, prawns, lobster, squid, and crab in a spicy tomato sauce. Factor in Maui's stunning sunsets, and it's hard not to enjoy the evening. ♦ Italian ♦ Daily dinner. Reservations recommended. 2980 S Kihei Rd (near Kilohana Dr), Wailea. 875.0001 ⅏

100 Keawakapu Beach South Kihei Road dead-ends at the parking lot of this charming beach with excellent swimming (thanks to a sandy bottom) and fair snorkeling. There are no public restrooms but there are showers. ♦ At the end of S Kihei Rd, Wailea

01 Renaissance Wailea Beach Resort
$$$$ This is a luxury resort for the traveler who likes to get away from it all, but not too far away from room service or a world-class restaurant. The secluded AAA four-diamond site is small (15.5 acres) and intimate, with dense, lush landscaping and an array of bridges and pathways that lend themselves to romance, lingering, and the occasional wedding. Many of the 333 rooms have ocean views, and all are the same size—small but very pleasant, with spacious lanais. The **Mokapu Beach Club**, a separate wing with 26 suites on the beach, offers VIP perks and services. The peaceful beach is ideal for swimming, sunning, snorkeling, or windsurfing. A pool, three Jacuzzis, and two tennis courts complete the list of amenities; there's a shuttle bus to **Wailea Golf Club.** ♦ 3550 Wailea Alanui Dr (between Wailea Ike and Okolani Drs), Wailea. 879.4900, 800/992.4532; fax 874.5370 ♿

Within the Renaissance Wailea Beach Resort:

Raffles'

Raffles' ★★★$$$$ This spacious and beautiful dining establishment was named after Sir Thomas Stamford Raffles, founder of the city of Singapore, home of the legendary Raffles Hotel. Re-created several times, the restaurant is now run by chefs Frank Laucis and Hector Morales, who prepare intriguing Hawaiian Regional and Pacific Rim specialties such as seafood paella, sugar-cured *ahi* (tuna), and Thai coconut curry. The decor is light and airy, the service impeccable, and the ambience relaxed and undeniably romantic. ♦ Hawaiian Regional/Pacific Rim ♦ Tu-Sa dinner. Reservations recommended. 879.4900 ♿

102 Ulua Beach Located in front of the **Renaissance Wailea Beach Resort,** this well-maintained stretch of white sand is the most popular of the Wailea beach quintet, and the best for bodysurfing. On calm days snorkeling is excellent because of the exceptionally clear water. Showers are available but not rest rooms. ♦ Off Wailea Alanui Dr (just south of the Renaissance Wailea Beach Resort; take the walkway from the landscaped park to the beach on the left), Wailea

103 Joe's Bar and Grill ★★★$$$$ Here's how the story goes: Bev and Joe Gannon had the successful **Halimaile General Store** in Upcountry Maui. Bev cooked; Joe made suggestions. Until one day Bev made a suggestion: "Joe," she said, "let's get you a restaurant of your own." Thus was born this popular burgundy and green venue, with sliding glass doors open on three sides and views of the golf course. Favorite menu items are grilled pork chops with sweet potatoes and dried fruit compote, lobster seafood pot pie, and penne with smoked chicken, roasted pumpkin seeds, tomatoes, scallions, and fresh spinach in a dijon cream sauce. ♦ New American. ♦ Daily dinner. Reservations recommended. 131 Wailea Ike Dr (at Wailea Alanui Dr), Wailea. 875.7767 ♿

104 Aston Wailea Resort $$$$ Flanked by crescents of white sand, this AAA four-diamond hotel has an elaborate porte cochere and a Hawaiian roofline based on the architecture of **C. W. Dickey.** It occupies 22 acres of oceanfront, with 516 rooms and suites in seven low-rise buildings and an eight-story tower. There are three swimming pools and 14 tennis courts (three grass and 11 hard courts) across the street, and guests enjoy privileges at the **Wailea Golf Club** and the small putting green alongside it. ♦ 3700 Wailea Alanui Dr (near Wailea Ike Dr), Wailea. 879.1922, 800/367.2960; fax 874.8331 ♿

Within the Aston Wailea Resort:

Hula Moons ★★★$$$$ One of the area's most popular casual eateries, this comfortable, Hawaiian-style dining room serves interesting dishes, including pork loin chop with peppered pineapple compote, Maui onion tomato relish, fig and tamarind marmalade, and *poha* (a local berry) and cranberry chutney. Other favorite features are a hula dancer and copious *pupus* (hors d'oeuvres) between 5:30 and 6:30PM nightly. ♦ Steak/Seafood ♦ Daily lunch and dinner. Reservations recommended. At the central pool. 879.1922 ♿

105 Grand Wailea Resort, Hotel and Spa
$$$$ This Disney-esque creation, which cost a whopping $600 million, features 761 rooms and suites with all the extras and 40 acres of impeccably maintained landscape and attractions, including a $15-million water playground; $30 million in museum-quality artwork from around the world, including

Colombian sculptor Fernando Botero's buxom bronzes and works by Jan Fisher, Fernand Léger, and others; a 300,000-square-foot floor of stone quarried from around the world; 12 lounges and five restaurants—including the celebrated **Cafe Kula** (see below); **Camp Grande,** a phenomenal kids' program; a 50,000-square-foot health spa; and various recreational activities, including golf, tennis, scuba diving, sailing, windsurfing, and deep-sea fishing. With rates starting at $370 and topping out at $10,000 per night, this resort obviously caters to an exclusive clientele, but nonguests are more than welcome to ogle and observe what unlimited funds and a prodigal imagination can accomplish. ◆ 3850 Wailea Alanui Dr (south of Wailea Ike Dr), Wailea. 875.1234, 800/888.6100; fax 874.2442 ♿

Within the Grand Wailea Resort, Hotel and Spa:

Cafe Kula ★★★$ This cafe offers a fine balance between health-consciousness and palate appeal; dishes such as grilled vegetables on inch-thick bread leave diners feeling both full and fit. The very casual, open-air eatery has counter service and a view of the gardens. ◆ Health food ◆ Daily breakfast and lunch. 875.1234 ♿

105 Wailea Beach Maui's longest crescent beach is popular with swimmers and snorkelers and offers both rest rooms and showers. ◆ Off Wailea Alanui Dr (just south of the Grand Wailea), Wailea

106 Four Seasons Resort $$$$ Billing itself as an island of tranquillity within an island, this eight-story, 380-room hotel offers comfortable rooms and super-deluxe, mansionlike suites on 15 acres at Wailea Beach. A $4.2-million renovation in 1996 has upgraded both common areas and rooms—as if they'd needed it. The specially commissioned works of art in the public areas are scaled to the architecture—understated yet impressive. The rooms are large and luxurious, and each has a lanai with teak interior walls, potted orchids, and thick-cushioned rattan furniture. The enormous bathrooms are all marble and mirrors, each with a deep bathtub, separate glass shower, and an eight-foot marble counter with double vanities. Most of the rooms have ocean views, and all have TVs and VCRs, fully stocked mini-bars, and twice-daily maid service. The hotel prides itself on its personal services: Attendants on the pool terrace will bring you towels and chilled Evian spritzers, gratis; your shoes can be shined while you sleep; and the general manager trots out the silver coffee urns and croissants at 5AM for jet-lagged tourists. There's an extensive fitness center and weight room. A kids' program focuses on Hawaiian culture and nature. ◆ 3900 Wailea Alanui Dr (south of Wailea Iki Dr), Wailea. 874.8000, 800/334.6284; fax 874.2222 ♿

Within the Four Seasons Resort:

Seasons ★★★★$$$$ The open-air dining room has a piano, a small dance floor, and an unforgettable menu. You can't help noticing the effort to use island ingredients in particularly innovative ways. There's salmon and *opakapaka* (pink snapper) carpaccio, *onaga* (red snapper) with a Hawaiian salt crust, and lobster with couscous—to name a few of the mindbending menu items. The extraordinary dining experience is enhanced by the crisp, cordial service. Be sure to try the scrumptious desserts (ask about the cream cheese with fruit compote) and vintage port, then end the evening by dancing cheek-to-cheek. ◆ Mediterranean/ Pacific Rim ◆ Daily dinner. Reservations and jackets required. 874.8000 ♿

107 Kea Lani Hotel $$$$ If you can get past the garish Arabian architecture (a torrent of whitewashed domes, arches, and tents), you'll find 413 of the largest suites in Hawaii (and a handful of two- and three-bedroom villas). At a minimum of 840 square feet, every unit of this luxury resort is twice the size of an average hotel room and impeccably furnished, with a marble European bathroom containing an oversize "love-tub"; an entertainment center with VCR, CD player, and wide-screen TV; a mini-fridge; and a huge bedroom with a king-size bed. Amenities include three restaurants, three pools, and white-sand beach that's excellent for snorkeling and swimming, as well as complimentary transportation to the nearby championship golf courses and tennis courts. For honeymooners who don't plan on getting out much, this is the place to stay. ◆ 4100 Wailea Alanui Dr (at Kaukahi St), Wailea. 875.4100, 800/659.4100; fax 875.1200 ♿

108 Polo Beach Club $$$$ If the **Grand Wailea Resort, Hotel and Spa** is exactly the type of place you want to avoid, you'd probably prefer this subdued condo resort. Hidden behind the **Kea Lani Hotel,** the complex has 30 well-appointed two-bedroom, two-bathroom ocean-view apartments set on a white-sand beach and available for short-term rental. The property offers a pool, spa, and sundeck, with easy access to Wailea's golf and tennis clubs, but no restaurant. ◆ 20 Makena Rd (south of Kaukahi St), Wailea. 879.1595, 800/367.5246; fax 874.3554

108 Polo Beach Because of its somewhat remote location, this white-sand beach was uncrowded until the **Kea Lani Hotel** was built right behind it. There's still public access (by law), and a parking lot in front of the **Polo Beach Club.** The sandy bottom and rock outcroppings make it a great swimming and snorkeling beach. Public facilities are provided. ◆ Off Wailea Alanui Dr (just south of the Kea Lani Hotel), Wailea

09 Wailea Golf Club One of Wailea's main attractions is a trio of carefully manicured, bone-dry golf courses on the leeward slopes of Haleakala Crater. The **Blue Course** (18 holes, par 72, 6,758 yards) is visually pleasing but less exciting than the longer **Gold Course** (18 holes, par 72, 7,070 yards), which has more hills and trees, and even ancient stone walls. The newer **Emerald Course** (18 holes, par 72, 6,825 yards) is the most challenging of all. Be prepared for strong afternoon winds. ♦ Expensive greens fees.   Preferred starting times for Wailea hotel guests. Reservations required.100 Wailea Golf Club Dr (off Wailea Alanui Dr), Wailea. 879.2966

09 SeaWatch Restaurant ★★$$$$ Chinese five-spice crab cakes, miso chili–glazed tiger prawns, filet mignon pan-seared with Japanese pepper spice and served with a red onion–Zinfandel jam—gastronomes, you're not in Kansas anymore. You're at the mercy of chef Richard Matsumoto and his staff of culinary pranksters, out to delight you in this out-of-the-way location, distinguished by high ceilings and indoor/outdoor seating that invites lingering. ♦ International ♦ Daily breakfast, lunch, and dinner. Reservations recommended. 100 Wailea Golf Club Dr (off Wailea Alanui Dr), Wailea. 875.8080; fax 875.7462 ♿

10 Maui Prince Hotel $$$$ Somewhat controversial when it opened owing to its spare, Japanese-influenced architecture and decor, this hotel has matured into a beautiful resort that many former critics have grown to appreciate. The 291 rooms and 19 suites have unobstructed ocean views encompassing the islands of Molokini and Kahoolawe. The central courtyard, with waterfalls, rock gardens, fishponds, and footpaths, is a lush, pleasing space where musicians perform. On arrival, guests are greeted with hot, almond-scented towels (the traditional *oshibori* service) to refresh them after their journey to this rather isolated location at the western end of the island. Compared to the nearby resorts, this hotel leans toward the unpretentious, capitalizing on its secluded location to attract a clientele that prefers anonymity. The resort also contains the **Makena Golf Course,** a fitness center, jogging trails, an award-winning tennis facility with six courts, and two pools. A children's program keeps youngsters happily entertained. A shuttle service transports guests throughout the resort and surrounding area. ♦ 5400 Makena Alanui Dr (near Makena Rd), Makena. 874.1111, 800/321.6284; fax 879.0082 ♿

Within the Maui Prince Hotel:

Hakone ★★★$$$$ The wood interior, slate floors, and refined ambience are well suited to the fine food and professional service. Multicourse *kaiseki* dinners consist of dainty samplings of soup, salad, appetizers, and fish—raw, boiled, grilled, or fried. The sushi is excellent, the *chawanmushi* (a light steamed custard) otherworldly, and more ordinary dishes such as tempura and noodles are cooked to perfection. ♦ Traditional Japanese ♦ Tu-Sa dinner. Reservations recommended. 874.1111 ♿

Prince Court ★★★★$$$$ At this place, listed in *Who's Who in American Restaurants,* even the appetizers—notably stuffed sashimi and sautéed crab cake with grilled Maui onion guacamole—are gustatory adventures. The world-class fare—such as *kiawe*-grilled shrimp in a lime-leaf marinade, catch of the day in avocado butter and macadamia-nut oil, swordfish and Pacific salmon in a potato crust with baby artichokes, and filet mignon with three lobster claws—is complemented by the elegant setting and sunset views. The Sunday brunch, with free-flowing champagne and hundreds of international dishes, shouldn't be missed. ♦ Hawaiian Regional ♦ Th-M dinner; Su brunch. Reservations recommended. 874.1111 ♿

If you want to experience "hog heaven" in Maui, call or stop by Island Riders (126 Hinau St, at Honoapiilani Hwy, Lahaina, 661.9966; 1794 S Kihei Rd, Kihei, 874.0311), where you can rent the Harley-Davidson of your choice, from the 883 Sportster to the 1340 Fat Boy, for a half or full day. If, instead, your fantasy is to play Motorcycle Momma for a day, hire a friendly Road Captain for a chauffeured two-up ride around Maui's sunny coast—it's an experience you won't soon forget.

Restaurants/Clubs: Red   **Hotels:** Blue

Shops/ ♥ Outdoors: Green   **Sights/Culture:** Black

111 Makena Golf Course Robert Trent Jones Jr. designed this layout, which has mountain and ocean views, tight fairways, huge greens, and enough sand for a beach. Named one of the top 10 courses in Hawaii by *Golf Digest,* it was expanded to 36 holes (the original course was divided and nine new holes were added to each half). The **North Course** is par 72, 6,914 yards; the **South Course** par 72, 7,017 yards. The 15th and 16th holes of the **South Course** (part of the original back nine) skirt the ocean, and throughout you can spot quail, panini plants, hibiscus, and the rolling hills of Ulupalakua. ♦ Fee. Daily. Reservations required. 5415 Makena Alanui Dr (south of Wailea Golf Club Dr), Makena. 879.3344

112 Makena Beach (Big Beach) More than 3,000 feet long and 100 feet wide, this is the beach of choice for Maui's *kamaaina* (locals), who have been coming here with their families and their coolers for generations. This glorious, golden stretch is commonly called Big Beach by islanders (it also has a third name, Oneloa Beach); over a hill to the right is Little Beach. Both are excellent swimming spots but must be approached with caution because of occasional steep shore breaks and riptides. Though this is unofficially thought of as a nude beach, nude sunbathing is prohibited by Hawaii state law (some visitors learn this the hard way when arrested during one of the twice-yearly raids). ♦ Off Makena Rd, south of the Maui Prince Hotel (look for the paved road and parking lot), Makena

The Mighty Mongoose

Made famous as Rikki-Tikki-Tavi in Rudyard Kipling's *The Jungle Book,* the mongoose is a small, ferocious carnivore with an equally fierce appetite. The ferret-size mammal is celebrated throughout Africa, southern Europe, and India as an effective control for small mammals and snakes (legend has it that the mongoose is immune to poisonous snake venom). In the 1880s the mongoose was imported to Hawaii to help fight a population explosion among the islands' crop-destroying rats. But the effort was an ecological disaster, because no one took into account that the rat is a nocturnal animal and the mongoose is not. The hungry mongoose instead attacked harmless small mammals, reptiles, and ground-nesting birds. Today the agile critter scampering across the road is responsible for the extinction and near-extinction of several native birds. Quite a record for such a little beast.

Upcountry

Upcountry, as the region on the western slopes of **Haleakala** is known, is a quiet rural region whose land is devoted to sugarcane, pineapple, carnations and pastureland. Thanks to the higher elevation, it's always cooler here than elsewhere on the island, with average daytime temperatures in the low 70s. Upcountry is remarkably scenic—green and hilly, with a plethora of panoramic views.

The uplands are ranch country, and Maui's largest ranch, **Ulupalakua,** with 30,000 acres and about 5,000 head of Hereford and Angus cattle and 3,000 head of deer, is located here. Also here is the **Kula District,** the center of vegetable, fruit, and flower farming on Maui. In recent years, this cool and quiet rural area has captured the imagination of folk from elsewhere on Hawaii and from the mainland, resulting in an influx of artists and entrepreneurs. The newcomers have changed the nature of some upcountry towns. The farming community of **Kula,** for example, now has a number of restaurants and bed-and-breakfasts, and **Makawao,** once a sleepy *paniolo* (cowboy) town, now boasts cafes, trendy shops, and art galleries.

113 Tedeschi Vineyards The rich volcanic soil of Ulupalakua has proved fertile ground for Hawaii's first and only commercial vineyard. The 23-acre enterprise produces a variety of wines, including Pineapple Blanc, Maui Brut Champagne Blanc de Noir, Rose Ranch Cuvee Ulupalakua Red, Plantation Red, and Maui Blush. It all began in 1974, when vintner Emil Tedeschi (te-*des*-ki) and Pardee Erdman, owner of the surrounding 30,000-acre **Ulupalakua Ranch,** experimented with numerous varieties of grapes to determine which would best adapt to the 2,000-foot elevation. They eventually chose the Carnelian grape, a cross developed at the University of California at Davis, and it seems they were right. Visitors can tour the winery, where Hawaiian royalty and visiting dignitaries used to gather for lavish parties when the property was a cattle ranch and sugar mill. Wine connoisseurs and anyone else driving through Maui's beautiful upcountry will find this an interesting side trip. ♦ Free. Guided tours daily 9:30AM-2:30PM; tasting room dai 9AM-5PM. Off Kula Hwy, Ulupalakua Ranch. 878.6058 ♿

114 Silver Cloud Ranch $$ Maui isn't all white-sand beaches and multimillion-dollar resorts, and here to prove it is a bed-and-breakfast establishment at 3,000 feet in the upcountry village of Keokea. The six guest rooms in the old ranch house are all individually decorated (one features white lace, another bamboo, another black lacquer and so on). There are also six modern studio apartments with kitchenettes. Some have TV none have phones. ♦ Off Kula Hwy, Keokea. 878.6101, 800/532.1111; fax 878.2132 ♿

4 Grandma's Maui Coffee ★★$ While he was growing up, Alfred Franco's grandmother showed him how to harvest and roast coffee from the trees on her land. She taught him well; for years Franco has been doing just that in the upcountry town of Keokea, using Grandma's 110-year-old roaster to process his lovingly tended beans. His homespun restaurant sells not only coffee, but homemade soups, sandwiches, and pastries. Try a cup of java and an I-Am-Hungry sandwich, which comes piled high with turkey, avocado, cheese, and ham. ♦ Coffeeshop ♦ Daily breakfast and lunch, F-Sa dinner. Takeout. Off Kula Hwy, Keokea. 878.2140 ♿

15 Bloom Cottage $$ Situated high on the western slopes of Haleakala overlooking Maui's picturesque leeward coast, this bed-and-breakfast is perhaps the nicest on the island. Herb and Lynne Horner's secluded guest cottage, which would be perfectly at home in the English countryside, features a four-poster bed, a fireplace, twig curtain rods, wood floors, handmade quilts, Victorian prints, and an aromatic display of fresh herbs picked from the garden. Also included in the surprisingly reasonable price is a fully stocked kitchen, an alcove with a single bed, and complete privacy. Located just off the Kula Highway, this bright, cheerful hostelry is highly recommended. ♦ No credit cards accepted. Off Kula Hwy (at Maukanani Rd, between the 15- and 16-mile markers), Kula. 878.1425

16 Halemanu $$ The lack of hotels and resorts in Kula and the town's growing popularity have spawned some terrific bed-and-breakfast operations in the area. This rural retreat is one of the best. *Halemanu* means "perch" or "birdhouse," and that's exactly what it is—an elevated, 3,600-foot aerie with a spectacular view. Maui native and newspaper columnist Carol Austin's two-story bed-and-breakfast inn is filled with collectibles from all over the world. The one guest room has a queen-size bed, private bath, and a deck with a spectacular view. If you don't mind the 40-minute drive to the beach, this is an excellent choice for a memorable vacation. ♦ 221 Kawehi Pl (off Waipoli St, east of Kekaulike Ave), Kula. 878.2729; fax 878.2729

17 Haleakala National Park The world's largest dormant volcano, Haleakala—the name means "House of the Sun"—is the showpiece of this 27,284-acre national park. High above the ubiquitous cloud layer is Haleakala's huge, moonlike crater—21 miles in circumference and 3,000 feet deep, with 30 miles of interior trails winding around nine cinder cones. Measuring 10,023 feet from the seafloor, it is Maui's highest elevation—ideal for a gorgeous sunrise or spectacular view.

Hawaiian legends flourish around this giant landmark, and modern-day spiritualists come here for inner renewal (even US Air Force research indicates that this is the strongest natural power point in America). The drive to the summit (open 24 hours daily) takes about 90 minutes from Kahului; it's a good idea to bring something warm to wear or wrap up in. If you're going to see the sunrise, bring something very warm, because it's at least 30 degrees cooler here than in the flatlands. A flashlight will also help you make your way from the parking lot up to the unattended observatory at the summit lookout. Be sure to call park information (572.7749) the night before for sunrise time and viewing conditions.

If the idea of rolling out of bed at 4AM doesn't appeal to you, there's plenty to see and do here during the day; stop at the headquarters near the park entrance for maps, information, or camping and hiking permits. En route to the summit, which is 11 miles from the entrance, are two overlooks and a **Visitors' Center,** where park rangers conduct scheduled tours. Drivers should make sure to use the lower gears when descending. For an unforgettable experience, see if you can score one of the six very inexpensive cabins in the crater. (Reserved by monthly lottery; cabin requests must be made at least 90 days in advance. Send requests with preferred and alternate days to **Haleakala National Park,** Box 369, Makawao, HI 96768, 572.9177.) Like the Grand Canyon or Niagara Falls, this volcano is something that must be seen at least once in your life. ♦ Admission per car. Park Headquarters/Visitors' Center open daily 7:30AM-4:30PM. Haleakala Visitors' Center open daily sunrise-3PM. Take Hwy 377 to Haleakala Hwy (Hwy 378) and follow it to the end. 572.9306

118 Kula Lodge $$ When the residents of Maui need a mini-vacation or a weekend of romance, they come here. Located high upon the cool grassy slopes of Maui's upcountry, this lodge is a switch from the typical Hawaiian resort: There's no sand, no program of activities, and no tropical ambience, and the temperature at 3,200 feet rarely rises above cool. The five individual chalets are small but cozy, with private lanais overlooking incredible vistas. Two of the chalets have fireplaces (romantic and practical), and four have lofts especially suitable for children. The adjoining **Kula Lodge Restaurant** has the best panorama in Maui, although the cuisine and service could stand a little improvement (fortunately, excellent restaurants are only a short drive away). Spending the day at nearby Makena Beach—one of Maui's best—and the evening by the fire watching the sun set is about as good as it gets. ♦ Off Hwy 377, Kula. 878.1535, 800/233.1535; fax 878.2518

119 Olinda Drive From Kula, follow Kula Highway (Highway 37) north to Pukalani, then take Makawao Avenue (Highway 365) to Makawao and make a right. If you continue on Baldwin Avenue (Hwy 390) past Makawao, it turns into Olinda Road, a pleasant nine-mile loop of scenic vistas, small forests, and enviable homesteads. The narrow winding road eventually returns to the main highway just below Makawao.

120 Casanova Italian Restaurant & Deli ★★★$$$ Regularly voted "Best Italian Restaurant" by readers of *The Maui News,* what started as a chic deli that sold squid-ink pasta to upscale hotels has now come of age as an extremely popular restaurant and nightclub housed in a two-story storefront on Makawao's main street. Inside the restaurant are koa tables, a koa bar, and a copper pizza station. Put together a picnic of pasta salads, cheeses, and desserts from the petite but bountiful deli, or go next door and dine on classic Italian cuisine. Fresh fish, Big Island beef, wood-oven-fired pizza, and lobster pasta are only a few of the items on the extensive menu. There's also music and dancing on Wednesdays, Fridays, and Saturdays. Part-time area resident Willie Nelson occasionally puts in an appearance. Watch the alcohol consumption; it's a long drive home to almost anywhere. ♦ Italian ♦ M-Sa lunch and dinner. 1188 Makawao Ave (at Baldwin Ave), Makawao. 572.0220

120 Komoda's This sparse yet charming half-century-old Makawao landmark is a combination old-fashioned general store and bakery that's famous throughout the islands for its monumental cream puffs. The *azuki* bean pie is popular too. ♦ M-F 7AM-5PM, Sa 7AM-2PM. 3674 Baldwin Ave (at Makawao Ave), Makawao. 572.7261

The lowest temperature ever recorded in Hawaii was in January 1961—11 degrees Fahrenheit at the summit of Haleakala Crater on Maui.

Of the 680 types of fish that live in Hawaiian waters, about 200 are found nowhere else in the world.

120 Makawao Steak House ★★★$$$ Th simple menu at Dickie and Judy Furtado's upcountry establishment, which lists the b beef, lamb, poultry, fish, and salads, gives little hint of what's in store for diners here. The straightforward bill of fare doesn't do justice to the consistently excellent dishes, which include such mouthwatering specialities as slow-cooked prime rib and stuffed chicken breast baked in wine sauce Add top-notch service and a soothing environment of flickering fireplaces, dim lighting, and polished woodwork, and you've got the best steak house on the island. ♦ Steaks ♦ Daily dinner. Reservatio recommended. 3612 Baldwin Ave (near Na St), Makawao. 572.8711 ♿

120 Viewpoints Gallery This fine arts collective is a cooperative venture dreamed up, designed, and run by two dozen Maui artists. A wide range of interesting and unusual artwork is represented, including (paintings, sculpture, pottery, watercolors, (etchings printed on Hawaiian fiber paper. ♦ Daily. 3620 Baldwin Ave (near Nakui St), Makawao. 572.5979 ♿

121 Haliimaile General Store ★★★★$$$ Bev and Joe Gannon converted an old plantation store in the middle of the pineap fields into an oasis of fine dining. High ceilings, hardwood floors, two dining room and works by noted Maui artists provide th ambience, while the kitchen produces som the best cuisine on Maui. Gastronomes fro all over the island drive to the 1,200-foot elevation for the brie-and-grape quesadilla, Bev's boboli (similar to pizza crust) with cr dip, barbecued Szechuan salmon, coconut seafood curry, and the Hunan-style rack of lamb (simply unbelievable). The wine list is outstanding, as is the chocolate–macadam nut pie. The owners' showbiz background (Joe has produced concerts for Julio Iglesi Alice Cooper, and Ringo Starr; Bev was on the road manager for Liza Minnelli and Joe Heatherton) makes this a celebrity haunt to You just never know who might show up. ♦ Pacific Rim ♦ Daily lunch and dinner. 90C Haliimaile Rd (between Haleakala Hwy and Baldwin Ave), Haliimaile. 572.2666; fax 572.7128 ♿

Cruising the Upcountry

The cattle and farming land on the fertile slopes of **Haleakala** is Maui's "upcountry," extending from the 10,023-foot summit to the island's isthmus and resting at the foot of the **West Maui Mountains.**

A drive to these parts offers a chance to explore another side of Maui—where people, including island residents, go to escape the crowded beach scene. The verdant rolling hills and cool, fresh air seem to miraculously erase tension and worry. In fact, it's common for smitten tourists to make the upcountry their new home.

The best route to the upcountry is along **Baldwin Avenue,** which begins in **Paia** just east of **Kahului Airport.** The gently ascending road is bordered by fragrant eucalyptus trees, cactus plants, brightly flowering jacarandas, and green hillsides where cattle graze among brilliant flowers. The air grows much cooler as you reach the top, so bring a jacket. And on your way, take the time to stop in Paia, once the hub of Maui's commercial scene (notice all the closed gas stations) and now just a pleasant shopping and snacking stop on

everyone's way to somewhere else; **Makawao,** an artsy little town with great shops and restaurants; and the area of **Kula,** where the scenery alone is worth the excursion.

122 Hui Noeau Visual Arts Center Noted architect **C. W. Dickey** designed this 1917 stucco mansion (pictured above) ensconced in a manorial five-acre setting. Vestiges of one of the island's first sugar mills mark the tree-lined entrance. Originally built for prominent *kamaaina* (longtime residents) Harry and Ethel Baldwin, the estate was turned into an arts center by their grandson, Colin Cameron, in the late 1970s. Today it offers ongoing exhibits, and regular classes in line drawing, printmaking, and other arts. The gift shop features earrings, paintings, ceramics, and handmade paper. ♦ Donation. M-Sa. 2841 Baldwin Ave, between Makawao and Haliimaile. 572.6560 &

123 The Vegan Restaurant ★★$ This small eatery is persuading more and more people around the island that pure vegetarian cuisine is not only wholesome and good for you, but also can be quite delicious. Bovine-free dishes include *tofucci* (lasagna without meat or dairy products), grilled basil polenta, and *banini* (banana shakes without milk or sugar). A favorite choice is the tasty vegan burger, a clever combination of wheat gluten, tempeh, and grains. ♦ Vegetarian ♦ Daily lunch and dinner. 115 Baldwin Ave (south of Hana Hwy), Paia. 579.9144

124 Picnics ★$ If you're going to make the trip to Hana, be sure to stop here and stock up on edibles. Basically a take-out counter serving hot and cold sandwiches, salads, burgers (the spinach-nut burger has fans around the world), and complete box lunches ranging from spartan to exotic, this eatery also serves espresso and cappuccino—a godsend for hungover Hana-bound drivers. The huge newsprint menu is a boon, too: on the flip side is a guide to Hana, a map of Maui, a list of the state and county parks, and a chart of distances to Hana (it even lists Hana's 56 bridges). A tablecloth, ice chest, and ice are provided for a fee. ♦ Cafe/Takeout ♦ Daily 7AM-4PM. No credit cards accepted. 30 Baldwin Ave (a half block south of Hana Hwy), Paia. 579.8021 &

125 Mama's Fish House
★★★$$$$ Despite its remote location in a converted beach house, this has been Maui's best-known fish house for nearly 30 years. Located just past Paia, it features such one-of-a-kind delicacies as *Pua Me Hua Hana*—fresh fish sauteed with bananas, coconut milk, and lime juice, served with Maui sweet potatoes. The landscaped grounds, ocean view, and rustic Polynesian decor are memorable. For dessert, try the *Hookipa* sundae: ice cream, Frangelico, Amaretto, cocoa, cream, and nuts. ◆ Seafood ◆ Daily lunch and dinner. Reservations recommended. 799 Poho Pl (off Hana Hwy), Kuau. 579.8488 &

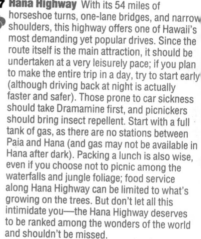

125 Mama's Vacation Rentals $$$ For almost 20 years, the owners of **Mama's Fish House** (above) have been investing in property around their restaurant in Kuau Cove, and now they've begun to rent the units—four two-bedroom oceanfront homes and two one-bedroom apartments—to families, couples, and groups. Each of the oceanfront units sleeps six, which makes them a bargain for those traveling in numbers. They also have TVs, phones, full kitchens, ceiling fans, CD players, VCRs, and Weber barbecue grills. ◆ Housekeeping surcharge for stays of less than three nights. 799 Poho Pl (off Hana Hwy), Kuau. 579.9764, 800/860.HULA; fax 579.8594

126 Pauwela Cafe ★★$ Had enough of the same old thing? Pull into this former cannery in the middle of (apologies to friendly owners Chris and Becky Speere) nowhere for a sandwich of *kalua* turkey (smoked, shredded turkey baked in ti leaves) with green chili pesto on a French roll. Local residents are already muttering that the cavernous cannery is starting to seem a bit small. ◆ Cafe ◆ Daily breakfast and lunch. 375 W Kuiaha Rd (south of Hana Hwy), Pauwela. 575.9242 &

Hana Coast

A small, remote village on Maui's eastern coast, Hana consists of little more than a post office, a couple of restaurants, and one exclusive, exceptional resort, the **Hotel Hana-Maui**. But people don't travel to Hana for a glitzy resort scene or lively nightlife—they come for the countryside, which is rural, isolated, undeveloped, tranquil, and beautiful. Thanks to more than 70 inches of rainfall annually, the region is part dense, luxuriant rain forest laced with waterfalls, and part green and open countryside. The entire district is home to only some 2,500 people, many of them pure or part Hawaiian. A number of outsiders, including many celebrities and entertainers, have homes in Hana, but they have come for the peace, quiet, and privacy, and they haven't changed Hana one bit.

This region's splendid isolation is due, more than anything, to the narrow, pitted, potholed winding country road called the **Hana Highway**. Those who want their Maui vacation to be a simple interlude in the country, with the added attraction of a few beaches (though not the best on the island), and with no nightlife and no TV, will choose to stay in Hana. For everyone else, the road to Hana itself, and the scenery along it, is the attraction.

127 Hana Highway With its 54 miles of horseshoe turns, one-lane bridges, and narrow shoulders, this highway offers one of Hawaii's most demanding yet popular drives. Since the route itself is the main attraction, it should be undertaken at a very leisurely pace; if you plan to make the entire trip in a day, try to start early (although driving back at night is actually faster and safer). Those prone to car sickness should take Dramamine first, and picnickers should bring insect repellent. Start with a full tank of gas, as there are no stations between Paia and Hana (and gas may not be available in Hana after dark). Packing a lunch is also wise, even if you choose not to picnic among the waterfalls and jungle foliage; food service along Hana Highway can be limited to what's growing on the trees. But don't let all this intimidate you—the Hana Highway deserves to be ranked among the wonders of the world and shouldn't be missed.

The drive begins near the **Kahului Airport**, where you'll see the sign: "Hana 54 miles." In fact, the road seems *much* longer—it curves, twists, curls, and pirouettes through 617 hairpin turns, passes over 56 miniature bridges, and is so narrow it's often impossible for two cars to pass unless one pulls over. The road took several years to build with pick and shovel, and several more to pave, using convict labor. Before it was paved, the road often washed out; drivers blocked from passing by mud slides were known to swap cars and then continue on their respective ways, later meeting back at the same mud slide to switch cars again for the return trip. The now-defunct **Keanae Chinese Store** provided free overnight beds for these stranded motorists.

Of course, the infamous road itself is not the only reason the drive to Hana takes so long. After all, it would be a travesty not to make an occasional stop to explore the myriad waterfalls, gardens, beaches, freshwater caves, and swimming holes. The roadside harbors a living catalog of Hawaiian plant life, with ferns and flowers vying for space among trees hung with breadfruit, mango, and guava. Picturesque rest stops include **Waikamoi**

Ridge Trail (leading to a forest perfect for picnicking), **Puohokamoa Falls** (where you can swim in a natural pool), **Keanae Lookout**, and the **Waianapanapa Black Sand Beach.** About 10 miles beyond Hana is **Oheo Gulch**, part of **Haleakala National Park.** Since it's impossible to see everything in one day, try to keep to some sort of schedule (but not too rigidly) and remember to save some energy for the trip back.

The Piilani Highway (Hwy 31), which starts at Hana and continues around Haleakala toward Kihei, is supposedly off-limits to rental cars because of the somewhat rugged terrain, but tourists drive it all the time anyway. While much of the highway was paved years ago, it's still punctured with potholes further deepened by the tour buses that careen down it regularly. Although this way back to civilization is longer and much more energy-sapping than retracing your steps on the Hana Highway, it's worth it just to witness the dichotomy of terrain within a matter of miles, from lush jungle growth to barren deserts of lava rock.

28 **Waikamoi Ridge Trail** Because it is unmarked and relatively unknown, this trail, which leads to one of the most isolated and beautiful picnic areas in Hawaii, makes for an ideal all-day excursion. Starting at the sign "QUIET—TREES AT WORK," hike for about 15 minutes up the lush, canopied ridge to a small, sun-filed oasis with a manicured lawn and a picnic table with a barbecue grill. After lunch, continue to explore the significantly narrower trail that leads through bamboo forests and passes numerous pools and waterfalls. Bring mosquito repellent. ♦ Off Hana Hwy (look for a small dirt turnoff between the 9- and 10-mile markers; a metal gate and a green post mark the trailhead)

29 **Keanae Arboretum** Don't miss this spectacular collection of native and introduced plant life that includes trees from around the world, notably a stunning collection of towering eucalyptuses. Past the taro patches irrigated by the meandering Piinaau Stream is a small trail that leads to a pleasant forest. ♦ Free. Daily. Off Hana Hwy (past the Keanae turnoff)

29 **Huelo Point Flower Farm** $$ This parcel of paradise belonged to spiritual teacher and author Shakti Gawain before the current owners, Guy Fisher and Doug Self, stumbled onto it in the mid-1980s. There's one three-bedroom house, one two-bedroom house, and a cottage for two, but wherever you stay, you'll spend a lot of time wandering from the pool to the cliffside hot tub to the private waterfall across the driveway and through the woods. This place is not recommended for socialites. There's no restaurant and there's a two-night minimum stay. ♦ No credit cards accepted. Off Hana Hwy (near Keanae). 572.1850; fax 572.1850 ♿

Shaka to Me, Baby!

First, make a fist. Next, stick out your pinkie finger. Then give the thumbs-up signal, wiggle your wrist a little, and say *shaka bra* (*shock*-ah-brah). Congratulations, you've just made the unofficial Hawaiian hand signal: the *shaka*.

Chances are you've encountered the *shaka* sign before, even if you've never been to Hawaii. Seventy million TV viewers saw it as island girl Carolyn Sapp walked the Miss America victory stroll; Johnny Carson buffs may remember Doc greeting his boss the same way after returning from a Hawaiian vacation; and sports fans saw the *shaka* flashed at the camera every time Hawaii's Russ Francis or Mosi Tatupu scored an NFL touchdown.

The *shaka* sign's origin was first pegged to a 1906 photograph featuring newsboys poised in front of a printing plant. But the boy thought to be giving the *shaka* sign turned out, upon closer examination, to be picking his nose with his pinkie. Now credit for popularizing the thumb-and-pinkie sign goes to car salesman "Lippy" Espinda, who used the expression and sign together for his 1960s TV commercials. He claims the word *shaka* originated from his childhood marble games, where any good marble shooter was called a *shaka kini* (*kini* refers to the marble). Hence, *shaka* evolved to mean anything nice or fine, like Lippy's used cars.

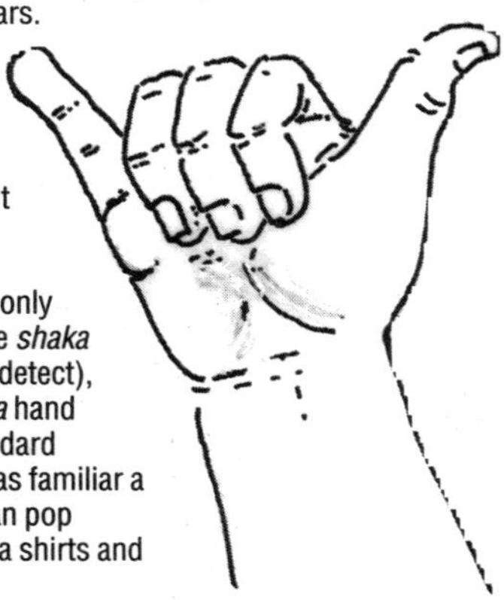

While locals often have personalized *shaka* signs (with subtle but important variations in meanings that only the most astute *shaka* signers would detect), the basic *shaka* hand signal is a standard greeting, now as familiar a part of Hawaiian pop culture as aloha shirts and plastic leis.

130 **Waianapanapa State Park** Try not to leave Hana before exploring the rugged volcanic shoreline of Waianapanapa (which means "glistening water" and refers to the cold, crystal-clear freshwater pool in a cave in the park). You can hike along an ancient three-mile trail to Hana, sunbathe at the black-sand cove (although swimming there can be treacherous), and look for turtles and seabirds from the elevated trail over the lava rock outcroppings. There are cabins and picnic facilities, and camping is available by permit (248.8061). ♦ Off Hana Hwy (3 miles northwest of Hana)

Restaurants/Clubs: Red **Hotels:** Blue
Shops/ Outdoors: Green **Sights/Culture:** Black

Hollywood and Hawaii: A Love Story

Hollywood's infatuation with the Hawaiian Islands started in 1913 with Universal Pictures' **Hawaiian Love** and **The Shark God,** came of age in 1953 with **From Here to Eternity,** and reached new heights in 1994, when on-location filming brought $70 million to state coffers and actors like Kevin Costner and Dustin Hoffman to local shores. You may be surprised at how many Hollywood stars have smiled for the cameras here . . . perhaps right where you spread your beach towel yesterday. The following are some favorite Hawaiian flicks, listed by the years they were filmed in the Aloha State:

Blue Hawaii (1961) Guy meets girl; guy woos girl the beach; guy sings "Can't Help Falling in Love"; gets girl. Elvis Presley stars in this Kauai-based classic.

Papillon (1973) An action-packed, pathos-infuse film based on Henri Charriere's novel about two escapees from Devil's Island, it features Dustin Hoffman, Steve McQueen, and **Molokai.**

King Kong (1976) Jessica Lange debuted in the remake of this 1933 classic, with scenes on the **Na Pali Coast** of Kauai.

Hawaiian Love and **The Shark God** (1913) These pre-missionary short films were shot at **Liliuokalani Park** on **Oahu.** In the first, a chief's daughter has a love affair; in the second, a Hawaiian girl is wooed by a sea captain.

The Black Camel (1931) Honolulu police detective Charlie Chan is called in to solve the murder of a movie star stabbed in Waikiki. This mystery, starring Bela Lugosi and Robert Young, was filmed in **Waikiki** and **Kailua** on Oahu.

Curly Top (1935) Based on Jean Webster's book *Daddy Long Legs,* the film, shot on Oahu, features Shirley Temple singing "Animal Crackers in My Soup."

From Here to Eternity (1953) This Oscar winner, shot on Oahu, adapted James Jones's novel of Army life in Hawaii just before the attack on **Pearl Harbor.** It stars Montgomery Clift, Frank Sinatra, Burt Lancaster, Deborah Kerr, and Donna Reed.

The Old Man and the Sea (1958) The movie version of Ernest Hemingway's tale about an aging fisherman's daily battle with the elements stars Spencer Tracy and is set on the **Big Island.**

South Pacific (1958) Mitzi Gaynor stars in a story of life, love, and music on the Pacific Isles during World War II. The Rodgers and Hammerstein favorite was filmed on **Kauai's North Shore.**

Gidget Goes Hawaiian (1961) When a beach-loving teen from California goes on a tropical vacation with her parents, anything can—and does—happen. Shot on Oahu; with Deborah Walley and James Darren.

Islands in the Stream (1977) An adaptation of the Hemingway novel, the story of an island-dwelling sculptor (George C. Scott) and his three sons was filmed on Kauai.

10 (1979) Dudley Moore plays a middle-aged songwriter smitten with scantily clad Bo Derek; sh on Oahu and Kauai.

Raiders of the Lost Ark (1980) An archaeologist/adventurer (Harrison Ford) searches the world for a unique religious artifact, finding hair-raising dan at every turn. Scenes filmed on Kauai.

Karate Kid II (1985) The sequel sees Pat Morita a Ralph Macchio traveling to Japan from Oahu to fa Morito's long-standing archenemy.

Black Widow (1985) A female investigator with th federal Justice Department (Debra Winger) becon obsessed with apprehending a woman who marrie men, then kills them. Her search leads to the Big Island.

Throw Momma from the Train (1987) Danny DeV and Billy Crystal make an agreement to kill each other's mother and wife, respectively, in this come shot on Kauai.

Lord of the Flies (1989) This remake is based on William Golding's novel about schoolboys who become savage on a remote island (played by Kau Balthazar Getty stars.

Point Break (1990) A maverick FBI agent (Keanu Reeves) goes undercover into Southern California surfing community to investigate a series of bank robberies. Patrick Swayze plays the leader of the ang and his prime suspect. The dramatic California surfing scenes were filmed on Oahu's **North Shore.**

Hook (1991) The legendary Peter Pan (Robin Williams), now grown up and a corporate lawyer, returns to Never Never Land when Captain Hook (Dustin Hoffman) kidnaps his children. Julia Roberts is Tinkerbell; Kauai is Never Never Land.

Jurassic Park (1992) In this movie based on the book by best-selling author Michael Crichton, Kauai reprises its role as a remote island, this time one turned into a dinosaur theme park. Jeff Goldblum, Laura Dern, and Sam Neill star in this special-effects blockbuster.

Outbreak (1994) Kauai is the stand-in for yet another remote island in this thriller about the spread of a deadly virus. Dustin Hoffman stars.

Waterworld (1994) Filmed on the Big Island, Kevin Costner's futuristic flick about a man-made island world cost more to produce than any other movie in filmmaking history.

131 Hotel Hana-Maui $$$$ With its secluded location, soothing atmosphere, and cordial staff, this top-notch property has attracted celebrities, VIPs, and respite-seeking world travelers for more than 40 years (it has a repeat-visitor rate of 80 percent). Just a few of its many awards: Most Romantic Resort in the World (*Romantic Hideaways*); Top 10 Resorts in the US (*Harper's Hideaway Report*); Top 10 Tropical Resorts in the US (*Condé Nast Traveler* magazine); and Best Small Hotel in Hawaii (*Aloha* magazine). Although the property has changed management three times since the mid-1980s (it's now run by the ITT Sheraton Corporation, though there have been rumors of another change), there's been no hint of decline. The 66-acre site houses 74 rooms and 19 large, luxurious suites in one-story cottages spread out across the property. Seven charming **Sea Ranch Cottages**—stained dark green like old plantation homes—skirt the shoreline with stone pillars, pitched corrugated-iron roofs, and borders of lava rock. The decor recalls an elegant Hawaiian beach cottage, with bleached hardwood floors, quilts, tiled baths that open onto private gardens, and lots of rattan, bamboo, fresh orchids, and greenery. There are many special touches (our favorite: fresh Kona coffee beans and a coffeemaker in every room), but the greatest luxuries are the four-poster bamboo beds and the huge decks with Jacuzzis and ocean views. The leisurely pace and various recreational activities give visitors ample opportunity to enjoy the natural surroundings. The **Hana Health and Fitness Retreat** offers nature walks and hikes, aerobics, yoga, and exercise and diet programs. Guests can also ride bicycles or horses, attend cookouts and picnics, and partipate in outings to the historic **Piilanihale Heiau** (a nearby stone temple) and the adjacent **Kahanu Botanical Garden.** The luau, put on every Tuesday, is among the best in Hawaii. The restored **Plantation House,** formerly the plantation manager's home on a hill away from the beach, is used for weddings, meetings, and groups of up to 25. Although the drive to the hotel from **Kahului Airport** is pleasant, most guests fly into the nearby **Hana Airport.** As expected, the rates are astronomically high, but that's the price of perfection. ◆ Hana Hwy, Hana. 248.8211, 800/321.4262; fax 248.7202

Within Hotel Hana-Maui:

Hotel Hana-Maui Dining Room ★★★

$$$$ If you want to do Hana in style, you won't pass up the chance to dine at the finest restaurant in town. In an open-beamed room best described as "Old Hawaii elegant," with polished wood floors and views of the verdant courtyard, you can enjoy meals that reflect Pacific Island, American, and Asian influences. Seared *ahi* (tuna) on saimin noodles and charbroiled mahimahi with Chinese cabbage are among the delicacies to savor. Dishes incorporate wonderful local touches—even at breakfast, the menu features macadamia nut waffles with guava, *lilikoi* (passion fruit), and coconut syrup. The kitchen also prepares fabulous picnic baskets. ♦ Pacific/ American/Asian ♦ Daily breakfast, lunch, and dinner. Reservations required for nonguests, recommended for guests. 248.8211 &

Hana Coast Gallery All of the artists (about 60) whose work is displayed here live in Hawaii. The gallery serves as a showcase of original art and master crafts (no reproductions) reflecting the beauty and heritage of the islands and their people. Pieces range from bronzes of the volcano goddess Pele and rare paintings by Herb Kane to Todd Campbell's turned-wood bowls and the lush landscape paintings of James Peter Cost. The owners are Gary Koeppel, producer of the annual **Maui Marine Art Expo,** and Carl Lindquist, a longtime prominent Hana citizen and former manager of the **Hotel Hana-Maui.** ♦ Daily. 248.8636 &

Hana Ranch Stables Although the stables are part of the **Hotel Hana-Maui**'s activities program, nonguests are welcome to participate in the hour-long horseback rides along the scenic Hana coast; these rides are available three times per day. Also possible is a two-hour Tuesday-only luau ride that goes up into the hills and back down to Hamoa Beach for the luau. Make arrangements through the **Hotel Hana-Maui**'s activities desk. ♦ Fee. M-Sa. Reservations required. 248.8211

131 Hana Cultural Center Located on the grounds of the old courthouse and jail, the center has ever-changing exhibits culled from the more than 4,000 items in its

archives. Also called **Hale Waiwai,** the center has more than 200 members who collect and display photographs, shells, quilts, and other objects and artifacts. The courthouse was built in 1878, and the adjoining jail was in use from 1871 to 1878. (Everyone in town knew when the jail held an inmate because, with groundskeeping a required prisoner task, the lawn would suddenly be mowed.) ♦ Nominal fee; seniors free. Daily. Uakea Rd (at Keawa Pl), Hana. 248.8622

131 Hana Beach Park Grab the kids and head to the safest swimming area in town. This has been a surfing spot for centuries, with the best breakers occurring in the middle of the bay. There's a pier to one side and an island, Puukii, beyond it. Picnic and public facilities are available. ♦ Off Uakea Rd, Hana

131 Tutu's at Hana Bay **$** This small take-out stand on Hana Bay hawks sandwiches, burgers, and plate lunches (called *bentos* by those in the know), but is best known for its Maui-made *haupia* (coconut pudding) ice cream. ♦ Takeout/Ice cream ♦ Daily. No credit cards accepted. 174 Hana Bay (at Hana Beach Park), Hana. 248.8224 &

132 Hana Ranch Restaurant ★**$$** This down-home, ranch-style restaurant has a take-out counter at one end that serves eggs, ham, French toast, and bacon for breakfast, and burgers, hot dogs, and teriyaki sandwiches for lunch. Dinner is served in the dining room three nights a week; take-out suppers are available the other four nights. Wednesday is pizza night. ♦ American ♦ Daily breakfast, lunch, and dinner. Reservations recommended. Hana Hwy (just south of Haouli Rd), Hana. 248.8255 &

133 Hasegawa General Store More than just a shop, this is one of Hana's main attractions, both a gathering place and a purveyor of everything from appliances to food and fishing supplies. A song has even been written about it. The Hasegawa family has created an institution by piling their store from floor to ceiling with an assortment of goods no one can live without (particularly useful is their latest addition—an automatic teller machine). The place doesn't have quite the character it did before a fire gutted it and forced the proprietors to move down the road to this building, but if you need something, chances are the Hasegawas have it (you just have to figure out where they've hidden it). ♦ Daily. 5165 Hana Hwy (just south of Haouli Rd), Hana. 248.8231 &

134 Pools at Kipahulu (Seven Sacred Pools) As a promotional scheme, an activities director at a Hana hotel nicknamed the pools at Kipahulu the "Seven Sacred Pools," which soon became a misnomer of staggering popularity (much to the dismay of Hawaiians, many of whom will sardonically respond "The seven what?" when asked about the pools). Although the pools are inspiring and beautiful, they are neither "sacred" nor do they number seven. There's more like 24 pools, but who's counting?

The long series of freshwater pools cascades down to the sea, creating a perfect setting for swimming, picnicking, and camping. A road bridge passes between the fourth and fifth pools; slightly beyond the bridge you can leave your car and either walk the trail down to the lower pools near the ocean or take the pleasant 30-minute hike to the higher pools, which are much more entertaining.

If you choose to venture upward, you'll be rewarded by the Makahiku and Waimoku

Waterfalls, a bamboo forest, and a series of interconnecting pools. Note: Before trekking uphill, it's a good idea to ask the park ranger about the anticipated weather conditions. Also, get out of the pools immediately if the water suddenly rises: On at least five occasions, when streams rose rapidly due to flash flooding, ranger Pu Bednorse has risked his life to save people from drowning—receiving a presidential citation for his heroism. (For details on **Haleakala National Park,** see page 83.) ◆ Piilani Hwy (10 miles south of Hana)

Honolulu means "sheltered bay" in Hawaiian.

ests

onnie Friedman
wner, Grapevine Productions, Maui

full-moon picnic at Maui's **Keawakapu Beach.**

riving through upcountry Maui's **Kula District** on May morning when the jacaranda trees are in full oom. The best place to end up is at **Grandma's aui Coffee** in Keokea for a cup of java.

haring a pizza at **Casanova Italian Restaurant & eli** in Makawao and a dessert and cappuccino at aliimaile General Store.

unday brunch at the **Maui Prince Hotel.**

enting a cabin at **Waianapanapa State Park** in ana, and walking the beach trail at sunrise.

atching an authentic hula.

ower leis—for me, the giving (and receiving) of is is the most beautiful of Hawaiian traditions.

tting outside on a clear, starlit night watching r moonbows (a rare phenomenon, similar to a inbow but at night), shooting stars, and *pueos* awaiian owls that symbolize good luck).

obert J. Longhi
estaurateur, Longhi's, Maui

atch a sunset from the **Kea Lani Hotel**'s beach, en listen to jazz in the lounge.

olf at **Kapalua Golf Club Village Course,** the akena Golf Course at the **Maui Prince Hotel,** r at any of the other great courses on the island.

atch the whales do their annual dance from ovember through May.

arl Lindquist
ublisher/Writer, Maui

he **Hana Coast** at sunrise provides the mystical ght and innate sense of power that accompanies e beginning of each Hana day.

Piilanihale Heiau, the largest of the ancient stone temples left standing, is a place revered for its antiquity and its *mana* (spiritual power).

Ulupalakua at sunset. Sipping wine high on the slopes of **Haleakala Crater** (the world's largest dormant volcano) as the sun fades, then taking a leisurely drive through **Kaupo** to Hana. Haleakala has the kind of grandeur and silence that puts one's life back in perspective.

John Pope
General Manager, Radio Cairo, Maui

Golf Courses:

The **Plantation** and **Village** courses at Kapalua.

Snorkeling in **Kapalua Bay.** Sailing on the *Scotch Mist.*

Nightlife:

Dining at **Avalon** in Lahaina.

Ann Fielding
Marine Biologist/Tour Director, Snorkel Maui, Maui

The naturalist-guided hikes through **Haleakala National Park** . . . free, informative, and fun!

Mark Ellman
Chef/Owner, Avalon, Maui

Whale-watching excursions . . . there are hundreds of beautiful humpbacks out there.

Breakfast at **Longhi's,** lunch at **Kimo's,** dinner at **Roy's Kahana Bar & Grill** or **Avalon** (better make a reservation), and the breakfast buffet at the **Ritz-Carlton Kapalua.**

A Sunday drive in upcountry Maui for a late lunch at the **Haliimaile General Store.**

Lying on the beach. Lying on the beach. Lying on the beach.

Kahoolawe

Although barren, dry, and, aside from a few wild goats, uninhabited, Kahoolawe (kah-*ho*-oh-*law*-vay) is one of Hawaii's most controversial islands. Located about seven miles off the southwest coast of Maui and easily visible from both Maui and Lanai, for decades this brown and green mottled promontory had the dubious honor of being the most heavily bombed island in the Pacific, used until 1990 as a practice range by the US Navy. Although title has since been signed back over to the state amid much fanfare, this 73-square-mile booby trap remains littered with unexploded bombs. The state and a Hawaiian activist group called **Protect Kahoolawe Ohana** (*ohana* means "family" in Hawaiian) have agreed that the isle will one day become a cultural reserve, but when that day will come remains unknown. The government is taking bids for an eventual cleanup, but is doing so "on Hawaiian time," that is, at about the same speed that a shell becomes sand. Currently Kahoolawe is off-limits to the public except for a few days each month, and access is possible then only if you know someone who's a member of the **Ohana**.

The smallest of Hawaii's eight major islands, Kahoolawe wasn't always deserted and lifeless. For centuries it was a sacred place inhabited by ancient Hawaiians, evidence of whose occupation is now scattered, bombed remains of ancient temples, fishing shrines, and villages. Abandoned possibly because of an unfavorable shift in climate, the island wasn't inhabited by people again until 1839, when it served unsuccessfully as an Alcatraz of sorts for convicted

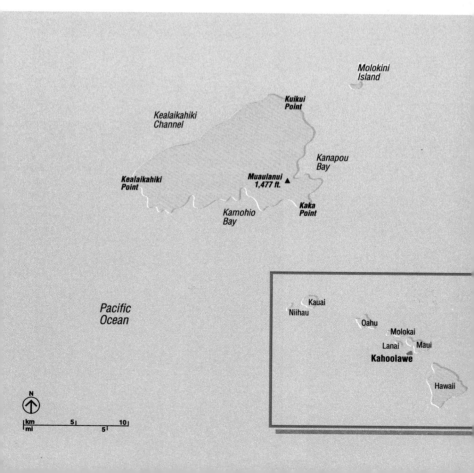

criminals. In 1858 the first of several attempts was made to turn the island into a large cattle ranch, and after a long period of trial and error, the inhabitants of Kahoolawe managed to sustain horses, cattle, fowl, and an assortment of trees and grasses. But in 1939 the ranchers made the grave error of leasing the southern end of the island to the Navy for $1 a year for target practice. After the attack at Pearl Harbor in 1941, the Navy unceremoniously booted the ranchers and their stock off Kahoolawe and turned the entire island into a gunnery range, providing an occasional pyrotechnical display for the citizens of Maui as huge battleships blasted the extinct volcano with their 16-inch guns.

But in 1991, hearings were held that led to the US government's return of the island to its rightful owner, the state of Hawaii. Few have seen Kahoolawe, since the $400-million price tag on the cleanup has resulted in reams of red tape. One way or another, though, everyone agrees that the future of this battered yet potentially profitable ex-bomb site is more promising than it was before. After all, in Hawaii, even bomb-riddled real estate is worth fighting over.

Hula Kahiko: The Return of the Traditional Hawaiian Dance

If you are watching—or learning—a hula dance, think hands, not hips. While the body sways gracefully to the rhythm of the music, the hands and facial expressions tell a story. According to a popular Hawaiian legend, the first hula was performed by Laka, the goddess of dance, to entertain her fiery sister Pele, the volcano goddess. Pele reacted by lighting up the sky with delight.

Hula kahiko (ancient hula) became a sacred part of Hawaiian religion, performed originally by men only and later by both sexes. Hundreds of interpretive dances telling stories of Hawaiian history and life have been passed on from generation to generation.

Nathaniel Emerson, author of *The Unwritten Literature of Hawaii*, called the hula "the door to the heart of the people." But when missionaries arrived in the 19th century, they were shocked by the ritual dance. They found the costumes (men in loincloths and topless women in kapa skirts) and the thrusting *opu* (pelvic) movements sexually explicit and vulgar, and promptly banned the hula.

Hawaiians responded by dancing in secret until King Kalakaua came to power in 1883 and brought the

ancient ceremony out of hiding—with a few changes. Male dancers still dressed in loincloths, but women wore long skirts under their ti-leaf skirts and long-sleeved, high-necked tops.

In the 20th century, when the hula dance became a major tourist attraction, its traditional meaning was lost somewhere between the swaying grass skirts and the ukuleles. But in the last 15 years the inner spirit of the hula has returned in full force, and the ancient dance is once again performed for historical and cultural reasons. Dance celebrations such as the **Prince Lot Hula Festival** in July at the **Moanalua Gardens** on **Oahu** and the **Merrie Monarch Festival** in April in **Hilo** on the **Big Island** are flourishing. The tradition is likewise being kept alive in public schools, where hula competitions are now almost as popular as football games. For visiting hula enthusiasts, introductory classes are offered by many of the major hotels. The popularity of the Polynesian dance is on the rise in other states and countries too; *halaus* (groups of dancers) are practicing and performing both *kahiko* (done to the beat of a drum) and the more modern *auwana* (done to music) in such far-flung locales as Fukuoka, Japan, and Chicago.

M. BLUM

93

Lanai

For nearly a century the entire island community of Lanai (lah-nah-*ee*) worked under a single employer to harvest what was once the largest pineapple plantation in the world. But in October of 1993, Castle & Cooke Properties, a subsidiary of Dole Foods, shut down the pineapple operation because of high labor costs, shifting the bulk of its operations to Thailand and the Philippines. Faced not only with immediate unemployment but with an end to a way of life, Lanai's 2,500 residents were determined to retain their strong ties to the land and the community. Hands callused from harvesting pineapples were retrained to drive shuttle buses and tend gardens as Lanai's luxury resorts, the **Manele Bay Hotel** and the **Lodge at Koele**, opened the doors to tourism on an island that had been uninhabited for hundreds of years for fear of the ghosts of the *alii* (Hawaiian royalty) buried here.

When visiting Lanai, you will immediately sense an esprit de corps among the islanders. The majority of residents live in Lanai's only town, **Lanai City**—a cool, sleepy mountain community 1,700 feet above the sea. Lightly coated with a fine, iron-rich dust and lined with majestic Norfolk and Cook Island pines, Lanai City consists mainly of multicolored tin-roofed plantation houses that reflect a bygone era. James Dole first laid out the town in 1924 after purchasing the entire island for $1.1 million, and most of Lanai City's buildings date from those early years. Residents often gather to "talk story" (Hawaiian for gossiping) while roasting local mouflon sheep or axis deer on someone's porch, perhaps sharing a case of beer brought over from Maui. It's a close-knit community, proud of its hardworking lineage and unscathed by its narrow escape from extinction—for if tourism hadn't replaced the pineapple industry, Lanai would have been returned to the restless spirits.

Three main roads trisect the 140-square-mile island, but dozens of unpaved roads lead to remote beaches, well-preserved *heiaus* (temples) and petroglyphs, misty mountaintops, and various other natural wonders, so renting a four-wheel-drive vehicle is mandatory if you want to truly explore Lanai. The island is also ideal for camping, hunting, hiking, and mountain-bike riding, and the exquisite beach at **Hulopoe Bay** (a popular playground for spinner dolphins) makes for a pleasant day trip from Maui via the *Expeditions* ferry. Whether arriving by plane or boat, make sure you've arranged to be picked up by your hotel or **Lanai City Service**, the island's only taxi/car-rental agency, since there's no public transportation from the harbor or the airport. Tourists who can't foot the $300-plus per night bill at either resort hotel will most likely be content staying at the island's only other hostelry, the **Hotel Lanai**. Once James Dole's clubhouse, it's now a cozy, unpretentious, and moderately priced inn in the heart of Lanai City. Wherever you stay, it is impossible to spend any amount of time on Lanai and not fall under the spell of the island and its people.

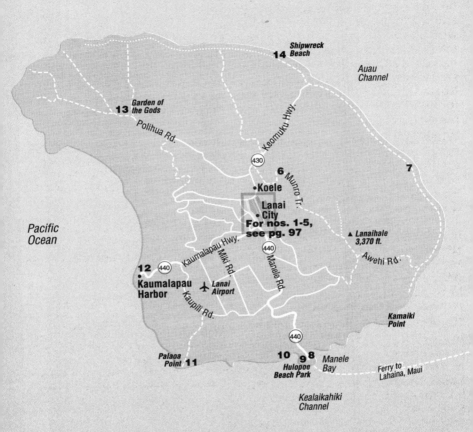

Kalohi
Channel

Pacific
Ocean

*Shipwreck
Beach* **14**

Auau
Channel

13 *Garden of
the Gods*

Polihua Rd.

Keomuku Hwy.

(430)

6 *Munro Tr.*

7

•Koele

•Lanai
City
**For nos. 1-5,
see pg. 97**

▲ *Lanaihale
3,370 ft.*

(440)

Awehi Rd.

12 (440)

•
**Kaumalapau
Harbor**

Kaumalapau Hwy.

Miki Rd.

✈ *Lanai
Airport*

Manele Rd.

*Kamaiki
Point*

Kaupili Rd.

(440)

*Palaoa
Point* **11**

10
9 **8**

*Manele
Bay*

*Hulopoe
Beach Park*

*Ferry to
Lahaina, Maui*

*Kealaikahiki
Channel*

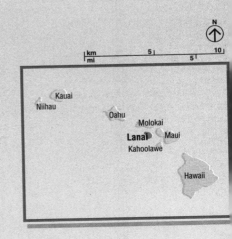

N

km
mi

5

5

10

Kauai
Niihau

Oahu

Molokai

Lanai Maui

Kahoolawe

Hawaii

Area code 808 unless otherwise noted.

Getting to Lanai

Airports

Lanai Airport

Four miles southwest of Lanai City, **Lanai Airport** (565.6757) is a runway and a one-room terminal in what used to be pineapple fields. The building is open only when flights (interisland only) are scheduled.

Airlines

Hawaiian Airlines...............565.6977, 800/367.5320

Island Air, interisland 565.6744, 800/652.6541
from the mainland 800/323.3345

Getting to and from Lanai Airport

By Bus

No public buses serve the small airport, but the **Lodge at Koele** and the **Manele Bay Hotel** provide shuttle buses for their guests.

By Car

There are no car-rental booths at the airport.

By Taxi

Lanai City Service (565.7227) provides limited taxi service, but must be called. There are no taxi stands at the airport.

Interisland Carriers

Hawaiian Airlines flies to **Lanai Airport** direct from Honolulu and Molokai. **Island Air** flies direct from Honolulu and from the **Kahului Airport** on Maui.

Ferries

Expeditions (661.3756, 800/695.2624) is the island's only ferry. The boat makes the trip from Lahaina on Maui to **Manele Bay** on Lanai and back five times daily; passage takes about an hour and can be choppy. The first ferry departs Lanai at 8AM, the last one leaves the island at 6:45PM. A round-trip excursion is $50 for adults, $40 for children under 12.

Getting Around Lanai

Bicycles

The **Lodge at Koele** (565.7300) provides mountain bikes to guests for $8 an hour, $40 a day. Mountain bikes make it possible to travel on the island's many unpaved roads. **Lanai City Service** (565.7227) rents mountain bikes for $25 per day.

Buses

There is no public bus system on Lanai.

Driving

The streets of Lanai City are on a grid system. Almost everything is on **Lanai Avenue,** which intersects streets from **Third** through **Kaumalapau Highway.** Only two "main" roads—**Highway 430 (Keomuku Highway)** and **Highway 440 (Kaumalapau Highway and Manele Road)**—cross the rest of the island; off

these branch numerous unpaved four-wheel-drive roads. There's also a network of dirt roads through pineapple fields, but visitors can easily get lost in these paths. **Lanai City Service** (1036 Lanai Ave, between 11th and 10th Sts, Lanai City, 565.7227) rents compact cars and four-wheel-drive vehicles.

Hiking

The most popular trek on Lanai is the **Munro Trail,** named for George Munro, who imported Norfolk pines from his New Zealand homeland. The hike to the top of 3,370-foot **Lanaihale Mountain** and back takes six hours. To reach the trailhead, drive north from Lanai City on Highway 430 and take the first major gravel road to the right two miles out of town; keep left and stick to the roads most traveled.

Parking

To say that parking is not a problem on Lanai would be a gross understatement. Park anywhere—there are no meters, and unless you block an entry to one of the larger hotels, you will not be ticketed or towed

Taxis

Call **Lanai City Service** (565.7227) with any transportation needs; they're the only game in town.

Tours

The **Lodge at Koele** (565.7300) offers an inexpensive ($79 per person including lunch; children half price) mini-tour in a small bus; reserve 24 hours in advance. The **Lodge** also offers one- to two-hour plantation rides on horseback for $35 to $50 per person.

Walking

Lanai City can be covered on foot in half a day. Points of interest outside the city are far-flung, so you'll also need another mode of transportation.

FYI

Shopping

It's interesting to stroll by the rustic stores on Lanai Avenue in Lanai City, but unless you're in the market for a plastic comb, you probably won't need your wallet. There are more souvenir possibilities in the gift shops at the **Lodge at Koele** and the **Manele Bay Hotel,** but you're better off buying your alohawear and koa wood bowls on one of the other islands, where the prices are lower and the selection wider.

Visitors' Information Centers

Destination Lanai (730 Lanai Ave, at Eighth St, Lanai City, 565.7600) is open by whim or appointment. The staff is very knowledgeable about the island.

Phone Book

Emergencies

Ambulance/Fire/Police 911

Hospital (Lanai Community Hospital) 565.6411

Pharmacy..565.6423

Poison Control 800/362.3585

Police (nonemergency) 565.6428

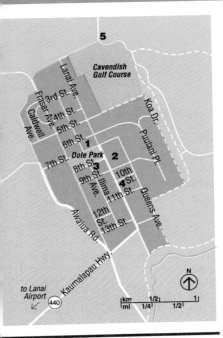

HÒTEL LANAI

2 Hotel Lanai $$ If you don't mind staying miles from the nearest beach, this hotel is an excellent choice. Built in 1923 to house guests and serve as an entertainment center for James Dole's executives, it was for decades the only hotel on the island. Now dwarfed by two super-luxury resorts, the property continues to fill a niche in Lanai's tourist industry, providing reasonably priced accommodations and affordable dining. The 10 rooms are small but tastefully decorated (a cottage is available for those who'd like more space and privacy), and the staff is friendly to a fault. There's a shaded veranda, a rustic dining room (where the complimentary continental breakfast is served), and acres of cool green lawns under Norfolk pines. Two golf courses are nearby. ◆ 828 Lanai Ave (between Ninth and Eighth Sts), Lanai City. 565.7211, 800/795.7211; fax 565.6450

Within the Hotel Lanai:

Henry Clay's Rotisserie ★★$$ The cozy fireplace, large wood tables, paintings and photographs by island artists, and the friendly staff lend a pleasant ambience. The kitchen is under new management and now serves such items as rotisserie chicken and beef as well as gourmet pizza. ◆ American Country ◆ M-F lunch; daily dinner. 565.7211 &

3 Akamai Trading and Gifts Locally grown Norfolk pines are used to create the one-of-a-kind bowls that make this small store and espresso bar a highly recommended stop on a town tour. ◆ Daily. 408 8th St (between Kiele St and Ilima Ave). 565.6587 &

Lanai City

The only town on the island is a 10-minute drive from the airport and a 25-minute drive from **Manele Harbor**. The **Hotel Lanai** is located here, as are a few very small galleries, boutiques, stores, and cafes that line the edges of a small, grassy square called **Dole Park**. The **Lodge at Koele** is on the outskirts of the tiny town.

1 Blue Ginger Cafe ★$ A great place to meet friendly locals, this restaurant is known for its good, low-priced local grinds. The cafe doubles as a bakery, serving croissant sandwiches along with omelettes, hamburgers, and pizza. ◆ Cafe ◆ Daily breakfast, lunch, and dinner. 409 Seventh St (at Jacaranda Ave), Lanai City. 565.6363

1 Tanigawa's $ Lanai City's version of a short-order diner serves island-style meals and snacks at a counter with swivel stools. The shakes are the best choice, made at an old-fashioned soda fountain that ranks as one of Lanai's favorite attractions. ◆ Diner ◆ Th-Tu breakfast, lunch, and dinner. 419 Seventh St (between Lanai and Ilima Aves), Lanai City. 565.6537

1 Lanai Playhouse Looking for after-dark entertainment on laid-back Lanai? This is about the only choice the island offers. The movies aren't exactly first-run, but if you're lucky, you can catch up on something you missed. ◆ Nominal admission. Hours vary; call for schedule. 456 Seventh St (at Ilima Ave). 565-7500

The process of burning sugarcane fields has an uncertain history. Laborers claim the first fields were torched as a form of protest. But sugar growers contend that cane was burned deliberately as a means of pest control, and that they discovered only inadvertently that it saves on labor costs; fire consumes the outer plant material, which must be removed anyway, but not the sugar-producing stalk. Now up to 70,000 acres of sugarcane go up in flames annually in Hawaii.

The Daily Grinds

Hawaii has never been hailed as one of the country's premier culinary destinations, yet thanks to the influence of Asian and Polynesian cultures, Hawaiian cuisine is a virtual smorgasbord of unique foods—some you'll never want to eat again, and some you'll remember longingly months after you've returned to the mainland. Unfortunately, what the locals eat and what's on a menu are often two different things; most restaurants cater to Western tastes, despite their exaggerated claims of serving "island specialties." The best way to experience authentic local dishes is to get an invitation to a private luau, party, or picnic (a rare treat for tourists) or to visit a county fair or an "authentic" public luau (where you'll find a smattering of local dishes among the platters of barbecued chicken and ribs). Whichever way you sample the cuisine, prepare yourself for some surprises, from grilled parrot fish (which tastes amazingly similar to lobster) to poi (a Hawaiian staple with a consistency and flavor akin to wallpaper paste). Here's a guide to the more popular local dishes:

Adobo (ah-*dough*-bo) A generic Filipino term for anything (usually pork or chicken) stewed in vinegar and garlic.

Char Siu (char-*soo*) Chinese sweet roast pork.

Chicken Long Rice Long, transparent noodles boiled with shredded chicken.

Crackseed Preserved and sweetened fruit and seeds, including papaya, watermelon, mango, and coconut. An acquired taste, crackseed makes great munchies. Sold at most stores.

Haupia (how-*pee*-uh) Custard made from fresh coconut milk and cornstarch.

Kalua (kah-*loo*-ah) **Pork** The centerpiece of any luau, the meat from a whole pig wrapped in ti and banana leaves and baked in a pit (*kalua* refers to any dish baked underground). The cooked meat is tender enough to cut with a plastic fork.

Kimchee (kim-*chee*) A Korean creation of fermented cabbage and tangy spices chopped up into a slaw.

Kona Coffee Gourmet coffee from hand-picked beans grown on the Kona coast of the Big Island. It's the only coffee grown in the United States.

Laulau (*lau*-lau) Butterfish, pork, taro leaves, and sometimes sweet potato, steamed in a bag of ti leaves.

Lilikoi (*lee*-lee-koy) Passion fruit, usually made into juice, pies, or sherbet.

Limu (*lee*-moo) Seaweed mixed with ground kukui nuts, salt, and sliced octopus or fish for a seafood salad called *poki* (*po*-kee).

Lomilomi (*low*-mee-*low*-mee) **Salmon** Salted salmon that's been shredded and kneaded with tomatoes and green onions. Served chilled.

Malasadas (mah-lah-*sah*-das) Portuguese doughnuts (without holes), served hot and covered with sugar. Sold at most bakeries.

Manapua (mah-nah-*poo*-ah) The Hawaiian version the Chinese *bao,* a steamed bun filled with pork, bea paste, and other fillings. Sold at roadside stands all over the islands.

Maui Onions Large, mild, sweet onio grown on Maui, considered by teary eyed enthusiasts to be *ono ono* (the most tasty) of all onions.

Opihi (oh-*pee*-hee) Limpets (which cling like barnacles to rocks in the surf zone) that are picked, shelled, and immediately eate (they sell for about $150 a gallon).

Pao Dolce (pawn-*deuce*) A Portuguese sweet dough loaf. Great for French toast.

Poi (*poy*) Taro root that's been cooked and pounde into a purple paste. Water is then added, the amour depending on how pasty or watery you want it. Poi traditionally eaten with one's fingers. The taste ranges from wallpaper paste to cardboard, but finger-licking locals swear by it, claiming it gives th "fo' real" carbo-buzz. New initiates should add a liberal amount of sugar.

Portuguese Bean Soup Rich soup made of various beans, vegetables, and Portuguese sausage.

Saimin (sigh-*min*) Noodle soup, usually served wit barbecued skewers chicken or beef.

Shave Ice A Hawaiian-style snow cone, with dozens of syrup flavors to choose from. Try the triple flavor combo with sweetened black azuki beans an tiny scoop of ice cream at the bottom of the cone.

Tako (*tah*-koh) Octopus. Try *tako* with *limu* (seaweed) if you're feeling adventurous—it's *onolicious.*

Taro Chips (*tar*-oh) Sliced and deep-fried taro root sold at most stores.

4 Lanai City Service Don't try shopping around for a better deal, because this is the only car-rental agency, cab company, and gas station on the island. It also does a brisk business renting four-wheel-drive Jeeps, so make reservations as far in advance as possible. ◆ Daily. 1036 Lanai Ave (between 11th and 10th Sts), Lanai City. 565.7227

5 Lodge at Koele $$$$ Once the site of Lanai's ranching operations (a big business before the pineapple industry took over), the grounds here now combine the elegance of an English manor with the rustic comfort of Old Hawaii. The riding stables, bowling lawn, croquet course, swimming pool, three tennis courts, reflecting pool, and acres of meticulously maintained lawns impart the atmosphere of a handsome English estate. This ambience attracts a large number of European guests and is a refreshing alternative to the muumuus-and-mai-tais mood of many Hawaiian resorts. The chilly upland air is equally invigorating. The aptly named **Great Hall**, with 35-foot-high ceilings and immense stone fireplaces, is an ideal place to linger with a book and a glass of port. The 102 rooms and suites are decorated in old plantation style, with hand-carved four-poster beds and oil paintings and artifacts from around the world. There's a library, a tearoom, a gameroom, and even a music room for listening to the classical selection of the day. Guests may choose from a full range of activities, from horseback riding to tennis, boating, hiking, and croquet. The 18-hole championship golf course, designed by Greg Norman and Ted Robinson, is a draw for many. ◆ Off Keomuku Hwy (just north of Lanai City). 565.7300, 800/223.7637, 800/321.4666; fax 565.4561 ♿

Within the Lodge at Koele:

Dining Room at the Lodge at Koele
★★★★$$$$ Inventive gourmet dishes are served in an elegant octagonal dining room looking out over the English gardens and pools. The cuisine is New American and the menu changes regularly, but includes such legendary dishes as local axis deer and seafood caught that day and served steamed, poached, smoked, raw, or however else you like. The vegetables and fruits are picked at an organic farm a few miles away. Although the competition is slim to none, this is unquestionably the best restaurant on the

island—and one of the best in the state. ◆ New American ◆ Daily dinner. Reservations required; jackets required. 565.7300

The Terrace at the Lodge at Koele
★★$$$ Guests at the more casual **Terrace** can request a table at the edge of the gardens and dine on lamb shank with a side of tiger prawn coleslaw as the sun sets, all the while pitying their friends back home. ◆ Hawaiian Regional ◆ Daily breakfast, lunch, and dinner. 565.7300 ♿

Elsewhere on Lanai

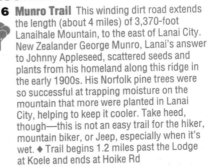

6 Munro Trail This winding dirt road extends the length (about 4 miles) of 3,370-foot Lanaihale Mountain, to the east of Lanai City. New Zealander George Munro, Lanai's answer to Johnny Appleseed, scattered seeds and plants from his homeland along this ridge in the early 1900s. His Norfolk pine trees were so successful at trapping moisture on the mountain that more were planted in Lanai City, helping to keep it cooler. Take heed, though—this is not an easy trail for the hiker, mountain biker, or Jeep, especially when it's wet. ◆ Trail begins 1.2 miles past the Lodge at Koele and ends at Hoike Rd

7 Keomuku An extreme example of what happens to a town when a nearby sugar plantation fails, Keomuku was abandoned at the turn of the century when the local commercial sugar venture collapsed. Almost all of the buildings have vanished except for the **Ka Lanakila O Ka Malamalama Church**. Built in 1903 and recently restored, it still stands as a testament to the deserted village, once home to nearly 2,000 people. ◆ 5 miles southeast of the northern end of Keomuku Hwy (Hwy 430)

8 Manele Bay Like nearby Hulopoe Bay, this was once the site of an ancient Hawaiian village. The only public harbor on the island, Manele Bay is now part of the **Marine Life Conservation District**. Swimming is unsafe here because of heavy boat traffic, so don't bother to bring your flippers. ◆ At the southern end of Manele Rd (Hwy 440)

The first flight from the mainland to Hawaii was in 1925. A two-engine PN-9 Navy seaplane left San Francisco on 25 August but ran out of gas 300 miles short of Maui and splashed down in the Pacific. The pilots improvised sails and sailed into the harbor at Kauai on 10 September. Two years later, an Army Fokker C-2-3 Wright 220 Trimeter made the first nonstop flight from Oakland, California, to Oahu.

Hawaii residents have the longest life expectancy among US citizens.

Tropical Treasures

Chances are your first introduction to the Hawaiian Islands will include a gift of flowers, since many guests are greeted with leis either at the airport or their hotel. Hawaiians take great pride in their flowers; here's a brief guide to some of their finest flora:

Anthurium *(Anthurium andraeanum)* This heart-shaped flower grows in many colors, including white, greenish white, pink, red, lavender, and pink-streaked. The surface of the bloom has a waxy shine that looks almost artificial. When anthuriums are cut and placed in a vase, they last for weeks.

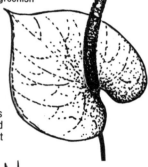

Bird of Paradise *(Strelitzia reginae)* Originally from South Africa, this ostentatious flower is easy to identify —just look for plumage (bright orange and blue petals) topping a long gray-green stalk. Each flower blooms in six stages, a new one every couple of days.

Hibiscus *(Hibiscus rosa-sinensis; Hibiscus koki'o)* Hibiscus shrubs grow easily on all the islands and come in several colors and shapes. They're rarely used in leis, because the large showy flowers are so fragile.

Lobster-claw Heliconia *(Heliconia humilis)* A member of the same family as the bird of paradise, this plant has leaves the color and shape of cooked lobster claws. Cradled within these leaves are small green flowers.

Night-blooming Cereus *(Hylocereus undatus)* A nocturnal beauty, this cactus blooms from June to October. The fragrant yellow blossoms open at dusk and close when the sun rises.

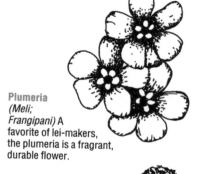

Plumeria *(Meli; Frangipani)* A favorite of lei-makers, the plumeria is a fragrant, durable flower.

Silversword *(Argyroxiphium sandwicense)* This plant grows in Maui's **Haleakala National Park** and on the **Big Island** in rocky or volcanic soil at altitudes of 6,000 to 12,000 feet. Its silver spike leaves grow on a six-foot-tall stalk, which is capped in August by tufts of flowers.

9 Hulopoe Bay The usually calm waters of the bay make this by far the nicest beach on the island for swimming and snorkeling. You can also watch spinner dolphins frolic while you sunbathe or search for the interesting marine creatures that often turn up in the tide pools. The beach is equipped with public rest rooms as well. There's a sad legend associated with Puupehe, the rock islet just off the southwest point of the bay. According to island lore, a woman named Pehe was so beautiful that her jealous husband, Makakehau, hid her in a sea cave on the isle, where she drowned during a storm. With the help of the gods, Makakehau scaled the cliff with Pehe's body and buried her at the islet's summit, now known as the Hill of Pehe. ♦ Off Manele Rd (Hwy 440)

10 Manele Bay Hotel $$$$ In direct contrast to the **Lodge at Koele**, this hotel has operated on the basic tropical resort principle since its opening; it offers the requisite expansive white-sand beach, central pool with dozens of deck chairs, and numerous water activities (sailing, fishing, snorkeling, and swimming). The decor reflects Mediterranean and Asian influences, and the grounds are lined with Hawaiian, Japanese, and Chinese gardens. There are 250 luxury villas and suites with private verandas and ocean views in the hills behind striking Hulopoe Bay, with a Jack Nicklaus–designed 18-hole golf course nearby. ♦ Off Manele Rd (Hwy 440). 565.7700, 800/321.4666; fax 565.2483 ♿

Within the Manele Bay Hotel:

Ihilani Terrace ★★$$$$ The best thing about this fine dining room is its unbelievable ocean view. Next best is either the roasted prime Colorado lamb loin or the panfried *opakapaka* (pink snapper)—both prepared with freshly caught ingredients. The decor is elegant and somewhat Asian, with Chinese vases, sculptures, paintings, and screens. ♦ French/Mediterranean ♦ Daily dinner. Reservations required. 565.7700 ♿

11 Kaunolu The fishing grounds of this well-preserved ancient Hawaiian village were Kamehameha the Great's favorite. Archaeologists have found 86 house sites, 35 stone shelters, and numerous grave markings here. The road leading to the site is difficult to find and even harder to negotiate (a four-wheel-drive vehicle is a must), but the shoreline at road's end is perfect for sunbathing and snorkeling. ♦ At the southern end of Kaunolu Tr (off Kaupili Rd, 2.7 miles west of the intersection of Kaupili and Manele Rds)

12 Kaumalapau Harbor The harbor was completed in 1926 by the Hawaiian Pineapple Company (later the Dole Company) to ship pineapples from Lanai to a cannery in Honolulu. From 1968 to the mid-1970s, when operations were in high gear during the summer months, more than a million pineapples a day were transferred from trucks to barges for the journey. It's still the principal seaport for Lanai (tourist operations use Manele Harbor), with good shore fishing. ♦ At the west end of Kaumalapau Hwy (Hwy 440)

13 Garden of the Gods The scattered assemblage of huge rocks and unusual lava formations here has the appearance of having dropped in from outer space. At sunrise and sunset, the eerie moonlike shapes are in every shade of purple, pink, and sienna. The stacked rocks signify absolutely nothing (they're stacked by tourists). The fenced-in area just before this site is a project by the **Nature Conservancy of Hawaii** aimed at maintaining Lanai's native dryland forest, one of the fastest-disappearing ecosystems in the world; the fence is to keep the axis deer out. Extremely rare species of plants, including a dryland gardenia tree, are able to survive here. ♦ Take the left turnoff just before the tennis courts at the Lodge at Koele and head about 7 miles northwest on Polihua Rd

14 Shipwreck Beach The hull of a World War II ship offshore marks the spot where many vessels from West Maui end up when they break their mooring. Timber from other unlucky vessels was used to build nearby squatters' shacks. A spectacular collection of Hawaiian petroglyphs is located a few hundred feet inland from the end of the dirt road in the direction of Molokai (north). This is a nice beach for wading and beachcombing. ♦ About 2 miles northwest of the northern end of Keomuku Hwy (Hwy 430)

Harry Truman wore them. So did Bing Crosby, Frank Sinatra, Burt Lancaster, and Montgomery Clift (though they were paid to do so in the movie *From Here to Eternity*). Olympic surfer Duke Kahanamoku was an avid collector, as is Tom Selleck. All of them sported classic Hawaiian shirts—those blindingly colorful bursts of flowers, birds, palm trees, and pineapples that are so tacky they're chic.

According to *The New York Times*, the residents of Hawaii are America's leading consumers of the canned meat Spam®.

Molokai

Compared to its neighboring islands, Molokai (moh-loh-*kah*-ee) is in a world of its own—and if its 7,000 residents have any say about it, it's going to remain that way. Molokai has a town but no stoplights. It has a resort but no fast-food chains. It even has an exotic wildlife park but no movie theater. It is an island of enigmas with a checkered history and an uncertain future. For hundreds of years Molokai was home to powerful *kahuna* (priests) who were feared throughout the island chain, and the island was given a wide berth by warring chiefs who called it "The Lonely Isle." When victims of leprosy were unceremoniously dumped on the island in the late 1800s, that reputation was sealed. In an attempt to convalesce from a rather unjustified historical drubbing, the state's fifth-largest island has retitled itself "The Friendly Isle," which, when islanders are treated with due respect, is unquestionably accurate.

Molokai is the only major Hawaiian island other than Niihau where most of the population is of native descent. Its two largest attractions are products of circumstance: **Kalaupapa**, the infamous exile colony for victims of leprosy (now called Hansen's disease), is now the subject of various tours; and the outfitters' center and wildlife preserve run by **Molokai Ranch**, which imported animals from Africa about 30 years ago as a means of controlling the mesquite brush encroaching on the ranch's grazing land, has become a 53,000-acre preserve with about a thousand free-roaming animals, from antelope to zebra. Aside from these man-made attractions, Molokai relies mostly on its natural wonders—the world's highest sea cliffs (reaching 3,000 feet) on the north shore and Hawaii's longest white-sand beach in the west—to lure visitors from the more popular destination resorts on Maui and Oahu. But this may not be the case forever, at least not if the Molokai Ranch Development Corporation has anything to say about it. The company, which owns about a third of the island, is eager to turn the sleepy town of **Maunaloa** into the Hawaiian hub of ecotourism and has spent $7 million on the endeavor to date; rumor has it that more than $100 million is earmarked. So far, the **Molokai Ranch Outfitters Center** has failed to attract swarms of intrepid Outward Bound types, but the jury is still out. Locals want things to continue at the same laid-back pace, immune to the winds of change, of course. Time will tell.

There is only one main road on the island, running from one extreme end to the other, and, unlike those on Lanai, most of the sights worth seeing don't require a four-wheel-drive vehicle. Although there are various tour companies that will shuttle you around, Molokai is best traveled by car so you can set your own pace (it's impossible to get lost here, even without a map). Don't expect any luxuries aside from peace and quiet, for the shopping is poor and most of the dining even poorer (if you're staying for more than a few days, get a room with a kitchen). Aside from the **Kaluakoi Hotel and Golf Club**, the island's only destination resort, Molokai is geared mostly toward adventurous travelers who don't mind getting a little muddy or salty from hiking, mountain biking, or swimming, and who appreciate the austerity that characterizes this unique Hawaiian isle.

Pacific
Ocean

Kalaupapa
Airport
Kalaupapa
Peninsula
Kalaupapa
Harbor
Kalaupapa
19

Limi St.
ukapele Ave.
ngton Ave.
Hoolehua
nomi Ave.
20
18
Kalae

15 17
14 16
Kualapuu
470

olokai
rport
Maunaloa Hwy
Maunahui Rd.

Haupu
Bay

Kalawao

Kalaupapa
National
Historic
Park

Waikolu
Lookout

Molokai
Forest
Reserve

▲ Kamakou
4,970 ft.

Halawa Valley
County Park
1
Halawa
Bay
Halawa

Kapuaiwa **13**
conut Grove **460**

For nos. 8-12,
see pg. 106

Kaunakakai

7 **Kamiloloa**
6
Kawela
450
Kamehameha V Hwy.

Kaluaaha 3
4
Kamalo
5
Ualapue

Pukoo
2

Waialua
Pauwalu

Pailolo
Channel

Kalohi
Channel

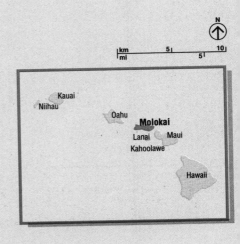

N

km
mi
5
10
5

Kauai
Niihau
Oahu
Molokai
Lanai Maui
Kahoolawe
Hawaii

Area code 808 unless otherwise noted.

Getting to Molokai

Airports

Molokai Airport

Seven miles northwest of **Kaunakakai, Molokai Airport** (567.6140) is open only when one of the 20 interisland flights a week is due to arrive or depart. The single terminal is tended by just a few employees.

Airlines

Island Air, interisland	567.6115, 800/652.6541
from the mainland	800/323.3345
Hawaiian Airlines	553.3644, 800/367.5320
Mahalo Air, interisland	567.6515, 800/277.8333
from the mainland	800/4-MAHALO
Molokai Air Shuttle	545.4988
Trans-Air	567.6319, 800/634.2094

Getting to and from Molokai Airport

By Bus

The only bus serving **Molokai Airport** is the shuttle to and from the **Kaluakoi** resort. The service is for resort guests only (552.2555); fare is $8.25 one way. The shuttle operates during business hours.

By Car

Two car-rental companies have booths at the airport: **Budget** (567.6877, 800/BUD.GET7) and **Dollar** (567.6156, 800/342.7398).

By Taxi

There are usually cabs at the airport to meet arriving travelers. The fare to Kaunakakai is about $5.

Kalaupapa Airport

Two round-trip flights per day land on the tiny airstrip at Kalaupapa. **Kalaupapa Airport** (567.6361) has no facilities except rest rooms, but travelers won't need any; they'll be whisked aboard a van that will have them in the center of town in a matter of minutes.

Airlines

Island Air, interisland	567.6115, 800/652.6541
from the mainland	800/323.3345
Molokai Air Shuttle	545.4988

Getting to and from Kalaupapa Airport

Those who fly to Kalaupapa must take the van tour run by **Damien Tours** (567.6171); there is no other way to visit the historic town.

Interisland Carriers

Hawaiian Airlines flies to **Molokai Airport** from **Honolulu International Airport. Island Air** has flights to **Molokai** and **Kalaupapa Airports** from **Honolulu** and from **Kahului** and **Kapalua-West Maui Airports** on Maui. **Mahalo Air** flies to **Molokai Airport** from **Honolulu** and **Kahului Airport** on Maui. **Molokai Air**

Shuttle flies between **Honolulu International Airport** and both **Molokai** and **Kalaupapa Airports. Trans-Air** flies to **Molokai Airport** from **Honolulu International** as well as **Kapalua-West Maui.**

Getting Around Molokai

Bicycles

Bicycles can be rented at **Fun Hogs** (552.2555) at the **Kaluakoi Hotel and Golf Club** and at **Molokai Bicycle** (553.3931; 800/709.BIKE).

Buses

There is no public bus system on the island.

Driving

Most roads on Molokai are paved and easy to travel. Four-wheel-drive vehicles are usually not necessary. Car-rental companies at **Molokai Airport** are listed above.

Hiking

The two most popular treks, to **Halawa Valley** and over the **Wailau Trail**, are both now closed—the former following a liability suit, the latter after years of disrepair. Hikers are now encouraged to check at **Molokai Ranch Outfitters Center** (552.2791) for expeditions both guided and unguided.

Parking

You can park pretty much anywhere on Molokai. There are no meters.

Taxis

Two cab companies share the Molokai business— **Kukui Tours and Limousines** (553.5133) and **Molokai Off-Road Tours and Taxi** (553.3369), both based in Kaunakakai. The state-regulated rates are comparable.

Tours

Damien Tours (567.6171) is the only tour operator that offers excursions to Kalaupapa, site of the historic leper colony. **Kukui Tours and Limousines** (553.5133) runs a half-day tour that covers the town of Maunaloa, a macadamia nut farm, coffee fields, the Kalaupapa Peninsula overlook, and Kaunakakai. **Kukui**'s full-day tour stops at all of the above, plus fishponds, a church built by Father Damien, and the Halawa Valley. A full-day tour run by the **Kaluakoi Hotel and Golf Club** (552.2555) has a similar itinerary. The resort also offers a morning snorkel tour off the coast of Kaluakoi and an excursion to Lanai aboard a 42-foot sloop. **Molokai Off-Road Tours** (553.3369) has day trips to **Waikolu** lookout.

Walking

Stroll down the wide main street of Kaunakakai, stopping to shop and snack along the way; the excursion will take about an hour if you walk slowly. The sugar town of Maunaloa is also a nice place for leisurely on-foot explorations.

> The 3,000-foot sea cliffs along the north coast of Molokai are the highest in the world.

YI

opping

unakakai is the place to buy T-shirts and other uvenirs. The town of Maunaloa has a farmers' rket, a kite shop, and gift shops.

sitors' Information Centers

e **Molokai Visitors' Association** (PO Box 960, unakakai, HI 96748, 553.3876; fax 553.5288) will swer questions and provide information over the one and now is open during business hours on ekdays at milepost O on **Kamehameha V Hwy.** I ahead to receive an extensive packet of ormation in the mail.

hone Book

ergencies

bulance/Fire/Police 911
spital (Molokai General Hospital) 553.5331
armacy...553.5790
lice (nonemergency) 553.5355

ast Molokai

1 Halawa Valley County Park The valley begins at the northeastern tip of the island, where Kamehameha V Highway (Hwy 450) ends. Hundreds of families once occupied the valley, but a tidal wave in 1946 prompted their evacuation, and only a few families returned. Remains of the once-thriving taro patches and old irrigation ditches can still be seen. Intrepid hikers used to be able to get to the waterfalls at the back of the valley, but a liability resulting from one such hiker's injury caused the area to be closed permanently. The black-sand beach, however, is gorgeous. ♦ At the end of Kamehameha V Hwy (Hwy 450)

2 Molokai Horse & Wagon Ride If you can't find a luau on the island, this will suffice nicely. Owner Junior Rawlins drives passengers from a beachside hut up into a 50-acre mango patch and straight up the mountain to a turn-of-the-century stone temple. You'll cross a stream (on the wagon), smell the wild guavas and flowers, and return to the beach, where you'll be greeted with a laid-back, Hawaiian-style barbecue. The whole deal takes about two hours. ♦ Fee. M-Sa 10:30AM. Off Kamehameha V Hwy (Hwy 450, west of the 16-mile marker). 558.8380

3 Our Lady of Seven Sorrows Church Father Damien built this white wooden structure in 1874. A statue of the priest, the island's most famous former resident, stands in the church pavilion. ♦ Off Kamehameha V Hwy (Hwy 450, west of the 15-mile marker)

4 Wavecrest Resort $ All 34 rental units in these 20-year-old wooden buildings front the ocean, which makes the individually owned but centrally managed condominiums a pretty fair bargain, though they're far from everything but the ocean. All the units have full kitchens, and a few have TV sets; none is air-conditioned. There's a pool and a snack bar on the premises. Solitude seekers, look no further. ♦ Kamehameha V Hwy (Hwy 450, across from the 13-mile marker), Ualapue. 558.8103, 800/535.0085; fax 558.8206 &

5 St. Joseph Church This small, white, wood-frame church was the last one built (in 1876) by Father Damien before his death. ♦ Off Kamehameha V Hwy (Hwy 450, west of the 11-mile marker)

6 Hotel Molokai $$
Retreat to a narrow strip of beach on Molokai's south shore, where this hotel offers 56 A-frame bungalows, equipped with swinging love seats and lanais. There's no restaurant or pool, and the rooms have no TVs, radios, or telephones, but a few overlook the ocean, and the larger units have lofts with twin-size beds. Like the island, this is a friendly place. ♦ Kamehameha V Hwy (Hwy 450, 2 miles east of Kaunakakai), Kamiloloa. 553.5347; fax 553.3928 &

7 Molokai Shores $$ A set of 101 individually owned condominiums (though only 26 are rented to visitors), this complex has long been a haven for residents of other islands. The rental units have ocean views, but the coastline is rocky and there's no beach for swimming. Units have kitchens and cable TV, but no phones or air-conditioning. A pool and a shuffleboard court are on the grounds. There's no restaurant. ♦ Kamehameha V Hwy (Hwy 450, 1 mile east of Kaunakakai), Kamiloloa. 553.5954, 800/535.0085; fax 553.5954 &

Kaunakakai

This town inspired the song "The Cock-Eyed Mayor of Kaunakakai," although, truth be told, Kaunakakai has no official mayor (Molokai is technically a part of Maui County). The town's two biggest attractions are its main street, **Ala Malama,** which looks like a Hollywood Western set in the 1920s, and the half-mile-long wharf, where local teens cruise up and down in their cars. The pace is blissfully slow.

8 Pau Hana Inn $ With lots of down-home charm and a fabulous view of the ocean, this cottage-style inn on the fringe of Kaunakakai features 39 budget-priced rooms, including

KAUNAKAKAI

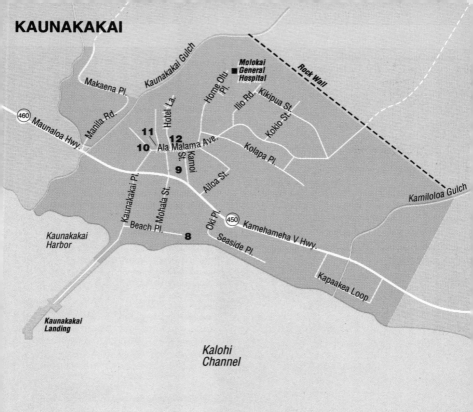

Molokai
General
Hospital

Home Olu Pl.

Rock Wall

Makaena Pl.

Kaunakakai Gulch

Manila Rd.

460 Maunaloa Hwy.

Hotel La.

Ilio Rd. Kikipua St.

Kokio St.

11

12

10 Ala Malama Ave.

Kamoi St.

Kolapa Pl.

9

Ailoa St.

Kamiloloa Gulch

Kaunakakai Pl.

Mohala St.

Beach Pl.

Oki Pl.

450 Kamehameha V Hwy.

8

Seaside Pl.

Kaunakakai
Harbor

Kapaakea Loop

Kaunakakai
Landing

Kalohi
Channel

N

km 1/2 1
mi 1/4 1/2

poolside studios with kitchenettes. *Pau Hana* means "after work," and, true to its name, the bar here is a favorite early evening gathering place for locals. The open-air **Pau Hana Inn Restaurant** offers decent continental cuisine, and the Friendly Isle Band Rhythmic Experience (FIBRE) plays on Friday and Saturday nights. Cool off in the pool after a night of dancing. There are no phones, no TVs, and no air-conditioning. ♦ Beach Pl (off Kaunakakai Pl). 553.5342, 800/423.6656; fax 553.3928 ♿

9 Molokai Drive Inn ★$ A Molokaian McDonald's of sorts, this take-out counter is a rarity. Try the fresh mahimahi, a perfect complement to the french fries. The hamburgers are also popular, as is the Japanese-style *bento* (box lunch). ♦ Takeout ♦ Daily breakfast, lunch, and dinner. Kamoi St (between Kamehameha V Hwy and Ala Malama Ave). 553.5655

10 Outpost Natural Foods ★$ A great stop for a healthy take-out snack, hot or cold, this juice bar is known for its Mexican food, smoothies, and sandwiches. The organically grown produce is mostly fresh from Molokai. ♦ Mexican/Takeout ♦ Su-F lunch. Ala Malama Ave (behind Kalama Service Station). 553.3377

11 Molokai Fish & Dive The island's only sporting goods store is also the home of the "original Molokai T-Shirts & Caps," two items you just can't be without. Snorkeling gear, boogie boards, and fishing poles are also available for rent. Stop in and check it out (what else do you have to do?). ♦ Daily. 61 Ala Malama Ave (near Manako La). 553.5926 ♿

11 Molokai Island Creations Swimwear, T-shirts, fragrances, soaps, Hawaiian note cards, original Molokai glassware and coral jewelry, and other Molokai miscellany are offered at this pleasant country boutique. ◆ Daily. 63 Ala Malama Ave (near Manako La). 553.5926 &

12 Kanemitsu Bakery Open since 1925, this bakery is a Molokai legend, with bread that appears on menus all over the island. When other islanders visit here, they inevitably take home some of the famous Molokai bread, a round white loaf that's simply delectable. You'll also find Molokai raisin-nut, onion-cheese, and wheat bread, along with doughnuts, pies, cakes, cinnamon crisps, and a first-rate *haupia* jelly roll. Try to get here early—everything tends to go fast. ◆ M, W-Su. 73 Ala Malama Ave (near Hotel La). 553.5855

West of Kaunakakai

13 Kapuaiwa Coconut Grove Kamehameha V planted a thousand palm trees here in the 1860s when he was only a prince, and several hundred of them can still be seen in one of Hawaii's last surviving royal groves. There's a shoreside park nearby for picnicking. ◆ Maunaloa Hwy (about 2 miles west of Kaunakakai), Umipaa

14 Kualapuu Reservoir The rubber-lined reservoir is the world's largest, containing 1.4 billion gallons of water. Molokai residents are very proud of it. ◆ Off Kalae Hwy (Hwy 470), Kualapuu

15 Kualapuu Cookhouse ★$ A tiny converted plantation house with an old-fashioned-diner decor, complete with Formica tables, this restaurant serves enormous omelettes, chili, saimin (noodles and spices), salads, chicken sandwiches, and quarter-pound burgers. But the real specialties are the plate lunches and homemade chocolate macadamia-nut pie. ◆ Diner ◆ Daily breakfast, lunch, and dinner. No credit cards accepted. Off Kalae Hwy (Hwy 470), Kualapuu. 567.6185

16 Coffees of Hawaii The only coffee grown commercially in Molokai is sold by Malulani Estates from their plantation store, which also displays an oddball assortment of crafts created by local artisans. ◆ Daily. Kanae Hwy (Hwy 470, east of Kualapuu). 567.9023 &

17 Ironwood Hills Golf Course The 1,500-foot elevation and majestic eucalyptus and ironwood trees make this a distinctive and enjoyable course. Play the nine championship holes twice for a full round (par 68, 6,176 yards). ◆ Fee. Daily. Off Kalae Hwy (Hwy 470, between Kalae and Kualapuu). 567.6000

18 Palaau State Park One of Molokai's few designated recreation areas, this 234-acre park forms part of the **Molokai Forest Reserve** on the north side of the island. Camping and picnic facilities are available in this forested mountain area. ◆ At the northern end of Kalae Hwy (Hwy 470)

Within Palaau State Park:

Kalaupapa Lookout The exquisite view of Kalaupapa from this 1,500-foot-high lookout is considered one of the finest sights in Hawaii. A series of displays tells the story of the settlement below.

18 Phallic Rock If you think Mother Nature lacks a sense of humor, check out this large and rather provocative stone, which has given rise to various legends, including the tale that childless women who spend the night at its base soon become pregnant. Bring the camera for this one. ◆ Just west of Kalaupapa Lookout

18 Molokai Mule Ride The popular mule ride down into the leprosy colony at Kalaupapa is up and running again; as many as 15 riders a day can saddle up and take the six-hour tour, which includes three hours of rugged riding, a two-hour tour of the settlement, and lunch. Riders must be over 15 years old, in good physical condition, and must weigh less than 245 pounds. Overnight and other packages also are available. ◆ M-Sa, 8AM check-in. Reservations required. Off Kanae Hwy (Hwy 470, at Kalaupapa National Historical Park). 567.6088, 800/567.7550; fax 567.6244

19 Kalaupapa This little town on the flat, isolated Kalaupapa Peninsula on the northern coast of Molokai figures poignantly and tragically in the history of the island. In 1866 the Hawaiian monarchy began banishing people with Hansen's disease (leprosy) to this area, separating them from families and loved ones. Lacking decent food and shelter, they lived here in great misery until their deaths. After arriving in 1873, a Belgian priest named Damien de Veuster chose to live in isolation with these people, selflessly providing them with spiritual and physical aid for the rest of his life. Father Damien contracted the disease in 1884 and died five years later, shortly after the completion of his **St. Philomena's Church** in Kalawao.

After his death, Father Damien became known as the "martyr of Molokai" for his heroic dedication to the leprosy victims. When sulfone drugs brought the disease under control in the 1940s, the patients still living here were free to go. However, since Kalaupapa had been their home since childhood, they chose to stay. Today, fewer than 80 residents remain.

A steep, zigzagging trail leads down the 1,600-foot slopes overlooking Kalaupapa, but only those with permits may hike down it, and only those on tours may visit the settlement. (For information on permits and tours contact **Damien Tours,** 567.6171.) Visitors may also fly to Kalaupapa from **Molokai Airport** (contact the **Activity Information Center,** 800/624.7771). The tours, led by a resident, include a stop at Father Damien's church, a visit to the guide's home, and a picnic lunch. ♦ In Kalaupapa National Historical Park.

20 Purdy's All-Natural Macadamia Nut Farm With heavy emphasis on the "all natural" part, friendly and vivacious Tuddie Purdy will teach you everything you ever wanted to know about macadamia nuts. You'll learn how to crack the hard inner shell of the nut without breaking your nails, how long it takes for a nut to mature (nine months), and how long macadamias have been in Hawaii (more than a hundred years). Purdy will also assure you that macadamia nuts roasted without oil have few calories and no saturated fats or cholesterol (let your conscience be your guide). You'll also learn how to open a coconut and then dip its flesh into honey. Best of all, Purdy will tell you all this just because he thinks you should know, never pressuring visitors to buy his nuts (you will anyway out of guilt). Purdy's nut farm is one of Molokai's top attractions. ♦ Daily 9AM-3:30PM. Lihi Pali Ave (behind Molokai High School), Hoolehua. 567.6601 days, 567.6495 evenings ♿

21 Molokai Ranch Outfitters Center "What's there to do on Molokai?" has long been a refrain of vacationers considering an interisland hop to the laid-back isle. In response, the Molokai Ranch Development Co. has produced a brochure that lists 54 items, all of which can be arranged through the ecotourism-oriented Outfitters Center. Adventurers can book everything from cowherding to backpacking, kayaking to nature tours. ♦ Daily. Maunaloa Hwy (Hwy 460, 1 mile north of Maunoloa). 552.2791, 800/254.8871; fax 552.2773

22 Maunaloa General Store It's the only store within miles of Maunaloa, an old plantation town, and it's now operated by Molokai Ranch Development Co., so it's a little more modern than in former years. ♦ Daily. Maunaloa Hwy (Hwy 460, across from the post office), Maunaloa. 552.2791

22 Big Wind Kite Factory and Plantation Gallery It took a windy town like Maunaloa to spawn Hawaii's only kite factory. Jonathan and Daphne Socher design and make kites with images of Diamond Head, tropical fish, giraffes, whales' tails, and other colorful Hawaiian motifs. Adjoining the kite shop is their gallery of local and Indonesian crafts—clothing, handbags, T-shirts, native wood bowls, Balinese carvings, and the like. ♦ M-Sa; Su 10AM-2PM. 120 Maunaloa Hwy (Hwy 460, next to the post office), Maunaloa. 552.2364 ♿

23 Paniolo Campsite $$ This is Molokai Ranch Development Company's answer to the baby boomer market, which, they feel, likes the benefits of camping without the liabilities. A night in a platform tent for two, including round-trip transportation from the airport, three gourmet meals a day, and one activity arranged through the **Molokai Ranch Outfitters Center** (see above), is $250. Hot and cold running water come gratis, but there are no phones or TVs. ♦ 1 mile southwest of Maunaloa. 552.2791, 800/254.8871; fax 552.2773

State Standouts

State Motto *Ua mau ke ea o ka aina i ka pono* (Hawaiian for "The life of the land is perpetuated in righteousness") was written by King Kamehameha III in 1843, when Great Britain restored Hawaiian sovereignty. It became the official state motto in 1959.

State Song *Hawaii Ponoi,* which means "Great" or "Mighty" Hawaii, was composed by King Kalakaua in 1874, with music by royal bandmaster Henri Berger. The song was written as a tribute to the great warrior king Kamehameha I.

State Tree The *kukui* (or candlenut) tree produces a quarter-size nut filled with an oil that is used as a healing aid, for dyes, and to make candles.

State Flower The Mallow Marvel, which belongs to the Malvaceae or Mallow family, is a large and showy hibiscus. This edible flower is sometimes used in salads.

State Mammal Humpback whales, which visit Hawaii's waters to breed during their annual winter migration, were named the official state mammal in 1979.

State Bird The rare and fascinating nene (pronounced *nay*-nay) is the state's largest bird, a species of goose that is able to survive in the rugged terrain of old lava beds. The nene has clawlike digits instead of webbed feet.

4 Molokai Ranch Wildlife Park Hailed as one of the country's finest natural game preserves, this African safari–like wildlife park has hundreds of exotic animals, including zebras, oryx, Indian black buck, eland, giraffe, and Barbary sheep. They're all raised on a thousand acres of fenced-in pastureland, a venture of the cattle-raising and hay-growing **Molokai Ranch**. Groups of up to 14 can picnic in the park, inevitably attracting the gregarious giraffe, who may lean over the fence to say hello. Narrated tours, which take about two hours, must be booked through the **Molokai Ranch Outfitters Center** (552.2791). ◆ Admission. Tours Tu-Sa 8AM, 10:30AM, 1:30PM; Su 10:30AM. About 4.5 miles north of Maunaloa

25 Paniolo Hale Condominiums $$$ These condos are probably the best place to stay on Molokai. Some of the 32 rental units at this six-acre property on Kepuhi Beach feature private hot tubs on the lanais; all have telephones, full kitchens, and washers and dryers. There's also a pool, and golf at the nearby **Kaluakoi** course (but no restaurant). Choose from studios and one- and two-bedroom suites. ◆ Kakaako Rd (off Kaluakoi Rd). 552.2731, 800/367.2984; fax 552.2288

25 Kaluakoi Villas $$ The villas were refurbished, and each of the 74 units now features an ocean view, plus island-style decor with rattan furnishings, ceiling fans, TV sets, kitchenettes, and private lanais. Guests can use the **Kaluakoi Hotel and Golf Club**'s facilities (see below). ◆ Kaluakoi Rd (near Kepuhi Beach). 552.2721, 800/525.1470; fax 552.2201

25 Ke Nani Kai $$ This Marc Resort property offers 120 large one- and two-bedroom suites that are well managed, clean, and set in clusters of wooden buildings. This isn't exactly a deluxe hotel, and there's no restaurant, but it's comfortable, with ocean and mountain views, large kitchens, a pool, and lanais. It's a five-minute walk to the beach. ◆ Kaluakoi Rd (near Kepuhi Beach). 552.2761, 800/535.0085; fax 552.0045

25 Kaluakoi Hotel and Golf Club $$ Molokai's top (and only) destination resort is a serene oasis for the traveler who truly wants to get away from it all. The property consists of two-story redwood and ohia structures overlooking a wide stretch of Kepuhi Beach.

There are 101 rooms with lanais, high, beamed ceilings, and fans to augment the ocean breezes. A championship golf course, 15-kilometer jogging path, a tennis court, a pool, and a volleyball court are available to guests. ◆ Kaluakoi Rd (near Kepuhi Beach). 552.2555, 800/365.6944; fax 552.2821 &

Within the Kaluakoi Hotel and Golf Club:

Ohia Lodge ★$$$ This tiered dining room gives every table a panoramic view of the beach and of Oahu in the distance. At breakfast, Molokai bread makes a splendid French toast. The dinner menu includes fresh fish, Hunan duck, Indonesian herbal chicken, rack of lamb, prime rib, and a few pasta dishes. Live music from the adjoining bar provides a nice accompaniment to dinner. ◆ Continental ◆ Daily breakfast and dinner. 552.2555 &

 Kaluakoi Golf Course A well-known joke says that people who live here lower their golf handicap by 10 strokes—meaning there's not much else to do on Molokai. Designed by Ted Robinson, the **Kaluakoi** course (par 72, 6,187 yards) is windy yet pleasant; 5 of its 18 holes border the ocean. Many golfers from Oahu consider this their getaway course, a place to enjoy the game while taking in panoramas of the Pacific and, if they're lucky, glimpsing the quail, deer, pheasant, wild turkey, and partridge that roam the 160 acres. There's also a putting green and driving range. ◆ Moderate greens fees (ask about specials). Daily. 552.2739

26 Papohaku Beach If you continue on Kaluakoi Road past the **Kaluakoi Hotel and Golf Club**, you'll see the sign for Papohaku, Hawaii's longest natural white-sand beach. The three-mile stretch is ideal for beachcombing, sunning, and swimming during the calm summer months. ◆ Off Kaluakoi Rd (south of Kepuhi Beach)

 27 Hale o Lono Harbor The best times to come here are either during Hawaii's annual **Aloha Week** (which actually lasts several weeks) in September or for the grueling 42-mile **Bankoh Molokai Hoe** (Bank of Hawaii Molokai Paddle) canoe race from Molokai to Oahu on the second Sunday in October (see "Paddlemonium!" on page 158). Founded in 1952, the race is celebrated as the world's first and foremost long-distance, open-ocean canoeing competition. It begins at southwest Molokai's little Hale o Lono Harbor, crosses the treacherous Kaiwi Channel, and ends at Duke Kahanamoku Beach in Waikiki. The women's race, **Bankoh Na Wahine O Ke Kai** (Women Against the Sea), takes place two weeks earlier. ◆ 1 mile west of Halena

Restaurants/Clubs: Red	**Hotels:** Blue
Shops/ ♥ Outdoors: Green	**Sights/Culture:** Black

Catch of the Bay

Whether you're peering through your diving mask or admiring the entrée on your plate, you will encounter a mind-boggling variety of fish in Hawaii. To make things even more confusing, each fish can have several names, including a Hawaiian name (for instance, broadbill swordfish are also called marlin and *au*). Here's a brief illustrated guide to the fish you'll find on many of Hawaii's menus (usually deepwater fish) as well as those cruising the local reefs:

Fish to Eat

Au (broadbill swordfish or marlin) An expensive delicacy that, once on the hook, puts up a legendary fight. The meat is most commonly consumed as jerky.

Ahi (yellowfin tuna) A favorite of deep-sea sportfishers for its fighting spirit, *ahi* (pictured above) weighs up to 300 pounds (the average is 80 pounds). It makes excellent sashimi and plays an important role in Hawaii's tuna industry.

Ahipalaha/Tombo Ahi (albacore) The world's premium tuna (pictured below), usually destined for mainland canneries, is a small predator that averages 40 to 80 pounds. It migrates extensively throughout the north Pacific, far away from Hawaii, and is occasionally substituted for *ahi* and *aku* in raw fish preparations.

Aku (skipjack tuna) Although the flesh of this smaller (10 to 20 pounds) tuna is less firm than that of *ahi*, it is still common on Hawaiian tables.

Mahimahi (dorado or dolphinfish) *Not* the same animal as the beloved "Flipper," the mahimahi/dorado/dolphinfish has beautiful jeweled scales of iridescent blues, lavenders, and greens that turn to dull gray the fish (pictured at the bottom of this page) dies. A playful swimmer weighing up to 25 pounds, it is often seen chasing flying fish through the waves. Mahimahi is a favorite local food sold most of the year, although availability peaks from March throu May and September through November. Frozen fill from Taiwan and Japan have made this fish availab to budget-conscious diners, while fresh mahimahi a coveted item on continental menus.

Onaga (red snapper) A popular bottom fish served upscale restaurants, *onaga* ranges from one to 18 pounds in Hawaiian waters. Availability peaks in December.

Ono (wahoo) *Ono* is Hawaiian for "good to eat"—an apt name for this fish. Its flaky white meat is served in everything from grilled sandwiches to sophisticated continental preparations. The best times to look for *ono* are summer and fall In Hawaii it typically weighs eight to 30 pounds but it can grow up to a hundred pounds.

Opah (moonfish) One of the most colorful commercial fish species in Hawaii, with crimson fins and large, gold-encircled eyes, *opah* range from 60 to 200 pounds. They are well liked for their moist, extremely flaky texture.

Opakapaka (pink snapper) Hawaii's premium table snapper is usually caught in deep water. A bottom fish, weighing 18 pounds on average, it appears on island menus year-round, although availability peaks from October through February.

Uku (gray snapper) One of Hawaii's three most popular deepwater snappers, *uku* usually weigh four to 18 pounds. They are most abundant from May through July.

Ulua (jackfish) Ranging from 15 to 100 pounds, this sport fish is a favorite among deepwater spearfishers. Its white flesh with a meaty texture is popular year-round.

sh to Meet

muhumunukunukuapuaa (triggerfish) The fame
this fairly common fish, Hawaii's state fish, comes
m its long name. *Humuhumu* means "to fit
ces together," and *nukunukuapuaa* is Hawaiian
"nose like a pig." The triggerfish (illustrated
low) is equipped with two protective devices: its
es can rotate independently, enabling it to see in
o directions at once, and when frightened it dives
its nest and locks itself in place with its dorsal

Oiliuwiuwi (fan-tailed
filefish) Yellow with black
dots, the fan-tailed filefish
(pictured above) makes grunting and squealing
noises when removed from the water (*oiliuwiuwi*
means squealing filefish). Early Hawaiians used
them as fuel to cook tastier fish since they
were too scrawny to eat.

ikihi
(oorish idol)
e breathtaking beauty
d fragility of the *kihikihi*
ictured below) places it in a class by itself. It's
ually found in small
hools, using its long
out to probe for
od in the
evices of
efs.

Uhu (parrot fish) Often
found in the waters of
Hanauma Bay off **Oahu**, this
fascinating fish scrapes algae off
the coral with its jagged beak. By day,
uhu (like the one above) flash their one- to
four-foot-long gaudy bodies covered with blue-
green, gray, and rust-colored scales. While
sleeping at night, they cover themselves in a
secretion that forms a protective bubble.
Remarkably, *uhu* can change their sex; those
born as males eventually turn into females. The
omnivores also create sand: they eat coral,
crustaceans, and mollusks, which are excreted
as grains of sand.

uwiliwili (crochet
lemon butterfly
h) The
uwiliwili
hown at
ht) is found
abundance
roughout Hawaii but
far has been seen
where else. You can
entify this fish, which grows
to six inches long, by the 11
rtical rows of spots on either side
its body.

Oahu

With its avenues of avarice, high-rise hotels, legendary beaches, historical battleships, and banzai surfers, Oahu (o-*ah*-hoo) is the nucleus of Hawaii, the island that has it all and then some. Although smaller than Maui and only slightly larger than Kauai, Oahu is where the majority of Hawaii's citizens choose to live—875,000 people, a whopping 75 percent of the state's entire population. Consequently, Oahu has more problems than any other island. It's one of the greatest ironies of tourism in Oahu that the J.O.J. (just off the jet) tourists come to Hawaii expecting to get away from it all, only to find themselves stuck in **Honolulu**'s rush-hour traffic and hopelessly lost (the one-way street system in Honolulu is comical at best). And city planners continue to approve developments, including a new convention center in **Waikiki** and the $3-billion **Koolina** resort in **Kapolei** (touted as the isle's Second City) on the **Waianae Coast**. Fortunately, Oahu's undaunted aloha spirit compensates for these excesses. Even in the major metropolis of Honolulu, this remains a friendly island whose people take great pride in their homeland. Cars here still slow down for yellow lights, warm smiles greet you at the hotels and restaurants, and there is plenty of prime beachfront space for relaxing.

In addition to having some of the most exclusive hotels (the **Royal Hawaiian**, the **Halekulani**, the **Sheraton Moana-Surfrider**, the **Kahala Mandarin Oriental**), famous attractions (**Pearl Harbor**, the **Polynesian Cultural Center**), finest restaurants (**Roy's, La Mer**), and largest shopping malls (**Ala Moana, Royal Hawaiian**) in the state, Oahu also has **TheBus**, the only public transportation system in Hawaii. These seemingly ubiquitous brown-and-yellow behemoths will, for only a buck, take you anywhere on the island—the **Greater Honolulu** area, which includes Pearl Harbor, Waikiki, and the **Diamond Head** and **Koko Head** volcanoes; the scenic windward side, from **Kahaluu** to **Makapuu Point**, site of the popular **Sea Life Park**; the **North Shore**, home of fabled **Sunset Beach**, monster waves, and insane surfers; and the Waianae Coast on the western side of the island. Aside from the mostly residential Waianae Coast, where locals prefer to remain undisturbed by tourists, all of these areas warrant exploring. The North Shore in particular makes for a pleasant day trip (not to be missed when the mammoth surfing waves come in), while the stunning views across the **Pali Highway** and around the southeastern tip of the island offer a more close-at-hand break from the cityscape.

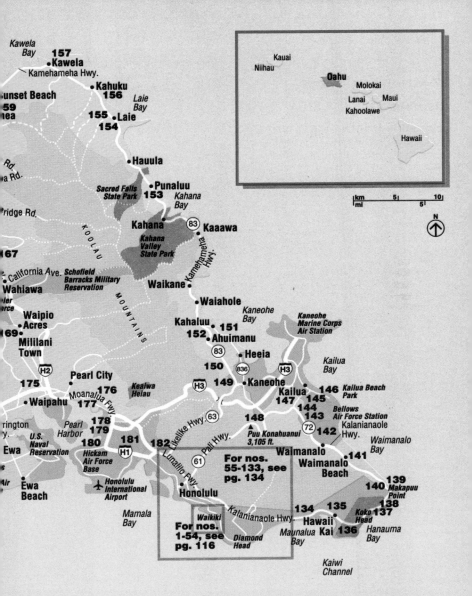

Basically, two types of tourists come to Oahu: the first-timers, who are at the mercy of their travel agents' advice; and the frequent flyers, who know exactly where to go and what to do. The former usually end up in Waikiki, which is paradise to some and a bumper-to-bumper and rump-to-rump nightmare to most others. Even after a multimillion-dollar face-lift, Waikiki still suffers from overabundance; there is simply too much of everything in too small a space, overcrowded with coupon-laden tourists purchasing cheap souvenirs and dining at overrated, overpriced restaurants. But "vacationing" is a relative term, and what some would consider as much fun as watching paint dry is a great time for others. That's the key to Oahu—there *is* something for everyone, you just have to know where to look.

Area code 808 unless otherwise noted.

Getting to Oahu

Airport

Honolulu International Airport

Hawaii's main airport has two bi-level terminals, one for domestic flights, the other for international; more than a thousand flights take off and land on its runways each day. The airport is nine miles west of Waikiki.

Airport Services

Airport Emergencies	711 on courtesy phones
Information	836.6413
Lost and Found	836.6547
Parking	861.1260
Police	836.6606

Airlines

Aloha	484.1111, 800/367.5250
American	833.7600, 800/433.7300
Canada 3000	888/226.3000
Canadian	839.2244
(from Vancouver)	800/426.7000
Continental	523.0000, 800/525.0280
Delta	833.8281, 800/221.1212
Hawaiian	838.1555, 800/367.5320
Island Air, interisland	484.2222, 800/652.6541
from the mainland	800/323.3345
Mahalo Air, interisland	833.5555, 800/277.8333
from the mainland	800/4.MAHALO
Northwest, interisland	955.2255, 800/225.2525
from the mainland	800/447.4747
Qantas	800/227.4500
in Australia	131313
Sun Country	800/752.1218
TWA	800/221.2000
United	800/241.6522

Getting to and from Honolulu International Airport

By Bus

Oahu's efficient bus system, aptly named **TheBus** (848.5555), pulls up at the curb near the baggage claim area regularly, with connections to such far-flung locations as the North Shore, Waikiki, **Windward Oahu** (the towns of **Kailua** and **Kaneohe**), Honolulu, and just about everywhere else. The fare for a ride anywhere TheBus goes is only a dollar (50 cents for students).

In addition, a program called the **Oahu Discovery Passport** enables visitors to purchase a four-day pass at any one of 30 ABC stores for only $10. The problem is that no luggage is permitted on board (taxi companies lobbied for and got this proviso so that the bus company wouldn't nab their business). Wheedling

and choking back the occasional sob may get you with a small rucksack at an off hour, but if you have the usual amount of luggage forget it.

Some Waikiki hotels offer airport shuttle service; be sure to ask when you're booking your room.

By Car

You can reach downtown Honolulu on the **H-1 Freeway**. Interstate signs are easy to follow between the city and the airport. On the return trip, stay to the right on H-1 and watch for the airport sign or you'll end up at Pearl Harbor.

The airport is usually a 20-minute drive from Honolulu, although the trip may take an hour during rush hours (weekdays 7 to 8:30AM and 4 to 6PM). On Friday afternoon traffic is even slower; you may as well stay in the airport lounge until after dinnertime. Long- and short-term parking lots are within easy walking distance of the main terminal.

The following car-rental companies have 24-hour counters at the airport:

Alamo	833.4585, 800/327.963.
Avis	834.5564, 800/331.1212
Budget	836.1700, 800/527.0700
Dollar	831.2331, 800/421.6868
Hertz	831.3500, 800/654.3131
National/Interrent	831.3800, 800/227.7368

By Limousine

A ride between the airport and downtown Honolulu via limousine costs about $85. A reputable local company is **Charley's Taxi and Tours** (531.2333).

By Taxi

Taxi stands are outside the baggage-claim area. Look for an attendant holding a radio; he will call for a cab if there isn't one waiting. A ride from the airport into Honolulu will cost about $20.

Interisland Carriers

Aloha Airlines flies to Honolulu from **Keahole-Kona International** and **Hilo International Airports** on the Big Island, **Lihue Airport** on Kauai, and **Kahului Airport** on Maui. **Hawaiian Airlines** has flights to Honolulu from those airports as well as from **Lanai Airport** on Lanai and **Molokai Airport** on Molokai. **Island Air** flies to Honolulu from the **Kahului, Kapalua-West Maui,** and **Hana Airports** on Maui; from both the **Molokai** and **Kalaupapa Airports** on Molokai; and from **Lanai Airport** on Lanai. **Mahalo Air** has flights on 48-seat, turboprop planes between **Honolulu International Airport** and **Keahole-Kona International Airport** on the Big Island, **Kahului Airport** and **Kapalua-West Maui Airport** on Maui, **Molokai Airport** on Molokai, and **Lihue Airport** on Kauai.

Getting Around Oahu

Bicycles, Mopeds, and Motorcycles

Although parts of the island are too overdeveloped for slow-moving creatures on wheels, places like

aikiki and the North Shore are tailor-made for
cycle, moped, and motorcycle riding. The folks at
ue Sky Rentals (1920 Ala Moana Blvd, between
lakaua Ave and Ena Rd, Waikiki, 947.0101) can
ovide you with rented wheels. You'll need a valid
ver's license to rent a moped and a motorcycle
ense to rent a motorcycle.

ses

hu's very efficient bus system, **TheBus**
48.5555), covers the entire island every day for one
llar one way. It's one of the best deals in Hawaii.

iving

e good news is that driving on Oahu is much the
me as driving elsewhere in the US. The bad news
that the island has the heaviest traffic in the state,
d progress can be "slow" to "no" within a 10-mile
dius of Honolulu between 7 and 8:30AM and 4 and
M on weekdays—and driving on Friday afternoons
a thoroughly hopeless proposition.

single road, known as **Farrington Highway, H-1,**
ghway 93, Kalanianaole Highway, Highway 72,
ghway 83, Kahekili Highway,** and **Kamehameha
ghway,** depending on which portion you're on,
irts the coast. Sightseers can't drive completely
ound the island, since the northwestern tip, **Kaena
int,** is accessible by four-wheel-drive vehicle only.
other highway, called **Highway 99,** Kamehameha
ghway, and **H-2** at various points, bisects the island,
eandering between Honolulu and the North Shore.
new highway, **H-3,** from Kaneohe to Honolulu, was
heduled to open as we went to press.

e main thoroughfares in Waikiki are **Kalakaua** and
hio Avenues**; traffic on Kalakaua runs east toward
amond Head, while cars on Kuhio move west
ward Honolulu. In Honolulu, cars driving east on
ng Street** arrive in Waikiki; while those moving
est on **Beretania** wind up in **Chinatown.** Keep in
ind that many downtown streets are one way, and
at there are only two ways around the **Ala Wai
anal** into Waikiki—take Kalakaua Avenue from
onolulu or **Kapahulu Avenue** from the Kahala area.

iking

ome of the most popular half-day and daylong hikes
e to the top of Diamond Head Crater, to the
aterfall at the end of the **Sacred Falls Trail** on the
orth Shore, and along one of the lush loops off
antalus Drive** in the hills overlooking Honolulu.
ring a full water bottle. For more information,
ontact the Hawaii chapter of the **Sierra Club** (212
erchant St., #201, Honolulu, 538.6616).

imousines

his isn't a big industry on Oahu, but several
ompanies will arrange transportation and tours in
xurious stretch limos, complete with televisions
nd bars. One such company is **Charley's Taxi and
ours** (531-2333), which operates 24 hours a day
nd accepts most major credit cards.

arking

nding a parking place in Honolulu and Waikiki can be
hallenging, particularly during business hours for the

former and nightclub hours for the latter. In Waikiki, try
the second-level garage at the **Royal Hawaiian
Shopping Center** (Kalakaua Ave, just east of Royal
Hawaiian Ave); parking is free with validation at one of
the center stores (no purchase necessary). In
Honolulu, try the **Bishop Square Parking Garage**
(1001 Bishop St, between N King and N Beretania Sts,
536.0127). You'll pay $3 per half hour on weekdays; on
Saturdays and Sundays the cost is $3 for the whole
day. Metered spaces on the street generally cost about
$2 an hour. A caveat: If you park on Beretania or King
Streets on a weekday, check the signs for "No Parking"
hours. All parked cars will be towed from the streets at
those times. If you forget, expect to pay at least $50.

Taxis

Don't wait for a cab to drive past—call **Charley's
Taxi** (531.1333) or **The Cab** (422.2222). Both serve
the whole island and accept credit cards. The fare
should be $2 initially and less than $2 a mile.

Tours

The top tour operators here are **Robert's Hawaii**
(539.9400), **Pleasant Island Holidays** (922.1515),
and **Trans-Hawaiian** (566.7420). All offer half- and
full-day trips by bus or van to Diamond Head, Pearl
Harbor, the **National Cemetery of the Pacific,
Hanauma Bay,** and other attractions. Specialized tours
are offered by dive companies (**Aaron's Dive Shops,**
262.2333), sailing charter firms (**Honolulu Sailing
Company,** 239.3900), helicopter operators (**Rainbow
Pacific Helicopters,** 834.1111), and others.

Honolulu Time Walks (2634 S King St #3, between
Kapiolani Blvd and University Ave, 934.0371) offers a
variety of inexpensive, entertaining three-hour tours:
a living-history tour, a crime-beat tour, a ghost tour,
a wartime Honolulu tour, a children's tour, a
Chinatown tour . . . the list goes on. Other walking
tours of Chinatown are offered by the **Hawaii
Heritage Center** (1128 Smith St, 521.2749), the
Chinatown Historical Society (1250 Maunakea St,
521.3045), and the **Chinese Chamber of Commerce**
(42 N King St, 533.3181).

Trolleys

The Waikiki Trolley (596.2199) offers narrated tours
of Waikiki and Honolulu daily from 8AM to 4:30PM.
The two-hour "Old Town Honolulu" tours depart every
15 minutes from the **Royal Hawaiian Shopping
Center** for the **Bishop Museum**; the route includes
Iolani Palace, Honolulu's historic waterfront, and
other sights. Passengers can ride all day, getting off
and on at will, for $17 ($30 for 5 days). The trolley
also shuttles between central Waikiki hotels and the
Aloha Tower Marketplace from 9AM to 2PM for $2
round-trip.

Walking

You can't see everything in a day (or a week, for that
matter), but Waikiki and Honolulu are both good
places for long, meandering walks. Both areas are
organized on a grid pattern and are easy to explore.
Kalakaua and Kuhio Avenues are the main arteries in
Waikiki; King and Beretania Streets are the main
thoroughfares in Honolulu.

FYI

Shopping

Hyper-commercial Waikiki is heaven for some shoppers, hell for others. Good buys are aloha shirts, muumuus, marine art, Hawaiian calendars, macadamia nut candy, coconut syrup, Hawaiian-print fabric, grass skirts, coconut hats, fruit jelly, Kona coffee, Hawaiian music, surf paraphernalia, T-shirts, tiki torches, and koa wood bowls.

To get a sense of your souvenir options, start by window-shopping, with Waikiki as your first target. Most stores don't close until 11PM, so take it slowly. After walking Kalakaua Avenue end to end, turn around and do Kuhio Avenue and the side streets.

Other favorite shopping stops are: the **Ala Moana Shopping Center** (1450 Ala Moana Blvd, between Atkinson Dr and Piikoi St, Honolulu, 946.2811), home of 200 stores; the alfresco **International Marketplace** (2330 Kalakaua Ave, between Kaiulani Ave and Duke's La, Waikiki); the two-story **Ward Warehouse** (1050 Ala Moana Blvd, between Kamakee St and Ward Ave, Honolulu, 591.8411); and the neighboring **Ward Centre** (1200 Ala Moana Blvd, between Auahi and Kamakee Sts, Honolulu, 591.8411).

Tickets

Looking for tickets to a cultural, musical, or athletic event? Check with the **Blaisdell Center Box Office** (777 Ward Ave, between Kapiolani Blvd and S King St, Honolulu, 591.2211) or **The Connection** (phone orders only with MasterCard, Visa, or Discover cards, 545.4000).

Visitors' Information Centers

The central office of the **Hawaii Visitors and Convention Bureau** (**HVCB;** 2270 Kalakaua Ave, No 801, Honolulu, HI 96815, 923.1811; fax 922.8991) is open Mondays through Fridays from 8AM to 4:30PM.

Phone Book

Emergencies

Ambulance/Fire/Police	911
AAA Emergency Road Service	800/222.4357
Dental Emergency	845.0686
Hospital (Queen's Medical Center)	538.9011
Locksmith (24-hour)	946.1011
Pharmacy	737.1777
Poison Control	941.4411
Police (nonemergency)	529.3111

Visitors' Information

American Youth Hostels	946.0591
Better Business Bureau	941.5222
Handicapped Visitors' Information	586.8121
TheBus	848.5555
Time	983.3211

Waikiki

Waikiki, with its long stretch of sand set against the romantic **Koolau Mountains,** has long been a favori vacation spot. Oahu's *alii* (nobility) came here to su and swim long before Kamehameha conquered the island, and hotels have catered to mainland tourists since the swampy area was drained early in this century. It was the great building boom of the 1950s, however, that made Waikiki the bustling urban resort it is today. Bounded by the **Ala Wai Canal** and **Diamond Head,** Waikiki is two miles long, a half-mile wide, and chock-full of hotels, condominiums, restaurants, and stores. There's no denying that it's commercial and crowded. But Waikiki retains its natural attractions—the mountai and Diamond Head Crater, frequent rainbows, spectacular sunsets, and of course, great beaches. Add an array of sports and activities, first-class restaurants, high-quality entertainment, and a few cultural attractions, and you will see why vacationer continue to flock to Waikiki.

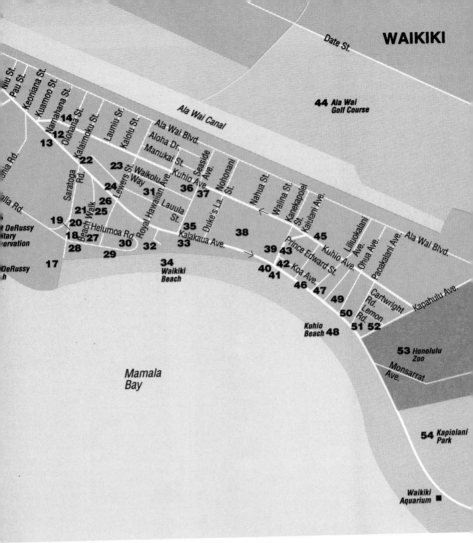

WAIKIKI

Date St.

44 Ala Wai
Golf Course

Ala Wai Canal

Niu St.
Pau St.
Keoniana St.
Kuamoo St.
Namahana St.
14 Olohana St.
12 Kalaimoku St.
13
22 Launiu St.
23 Kaiolu St.
Ala Wai Blvd.
Aloha Dr.
Manukai St.
Seaside Ave.
Nohonani St.
Saratoga Rd.
Lewers St.
24 Waikolu Way
31 Kuhio Ave.
36 37
Nahua St.
Walina St.
Kanekapolei
Kaiulani Ave.
21 26
19 20 25 Beach Walk
18 27 Helumoa Rd.
28 Royal Hawaiian Ave.
Lauula St.
35
33 Kalakaua Ave.
38
Liliuokalani Ave.
Ohua Ave.
Paoakalani Ave.
Ala Wai Blvd.
45
17 29 30 32 34
Waikiki
Beach
39 43 Prince Edward St.
42 Koa Ave.
40 41
46 47 49
Kuhio Ave.
Cartwright Rd.
Lemon Rd.
50 51 52
Kapahulu Ave.
Kuhio
Beach 48

DeRussy
Military
Reservation

DeRussy

Mamala
Bay

53 Honolulu
Zoo

Monsarrat Ave.

54 Kapiolani
Park

Waikiki
Aquarium ■

1 Hawaii Prince $$$$ Created in a meant-to-be-noticed style best described as "international opulence," this luxurious hotel boasts English slate, Spanish glass, Italian marble (some say there is too much marble), Japanese tile, and French accessories. All 521 rooms, including 57 one- and two-bedroom suites, have floor-to-ceiling windows overlooking the yacht harbor. A pool and whirlpool are on the premises as well.

Although the hotel is within walking distance of **Ala Moana Beach Park** and **Ala Moana Shopping Center,** a free shuttle service takes guests to both places and to most other attractions in Waikiki, including two nearby tennis courts and a 27-hole golf course. ◆ 100 Holomoana St (between Hobron La and Ala Moana Blvd). 956.1111, 800/321.6248; fax 800/946.0811

Within the Hawaii Prince:

Prince Court ★★★$$$$ The menu changes monthly, but it might include *keawe*-roasted pork chops, sautéed catch of the day over angel-hair pasta, and deep-sea prawns stuffed with blue crab hash with black bean, tomato, and fennel sauces. The decor is chic and modern, with a central fountain and works of fine art, including a painting by Marc Chagall. The view of the harbor is cheerful by day and romantic at night. ◆ Hawaii Regional ◆ M-Sa breakfast, lunch, and dinner; Su brunch and dinner. Reservations recommended. 956.1111

Hakone ★★★$$$$ The dishes served here are both traditional and exquisite: *kaiseki* dinners of soup, pickles, sashimi, broiled fish, and other Japanese favorites; sukiyaki; noodles; tempura; and assorted sashimi. When in season, the Kona crab is cooked to perfection. The dining room is elegant in its simplicity, with delicate Japanese paintings and carved wood furniture from Japan. ◆ Japanese ◆ Tu-Su lunch and dinner. Reservations recommended. 956.1111

2 Red Lobster ★★$$$ A **Red Lobster** is a **Red Lobster** is a **Red Lobster**. The advantage to dining here is that you know what you're getting (which can also be the disadvantage to dining here). The all-you-can-eat deals on Alaskan king crab legs, steak and lobster, and shrimp can't be beaten. The airy interior is filled with plants, wood, and bamboo. ◆ Seafood ◆ Daily lunch and dinner. 1765 Ala Moana Blvd (at Hobron La). 955.5656

3 Ilikai Hotel $$$ Located on the outer fringe of Waikiki overlooking the **Ala Wai Yacht Harbor,** this 780-room high-rise offers a compromise for people who want to be near the action but not consumed by it. Although dramatically eclipsed by the **Hawaii Prince** hotel next door, this hotel still reigns as Waikiki's acknowledged tennis center, with five courts (including a lighted court with artificial grass) and resident tennis pros. In addition there are two pools, a fitness center, and three restaurants. Nearby you'll find a placid beachfront lagoon and **Ala Moana Beach Park;** the **Ala Moana Shopping Center,** a mecca for shopping enthusiasts, is only a five-minute walk away. Many rooms include kitchens with refrigerators and mini-bars. ◆ 1777 Ala Moana Blvd (between Kalia Rd and Hobron La). 949.3811, 800/245.4524; fax 944.6373 &

Within the Ilikai Hotel:

Canoes at the Ilikai ★★$$$$ The cuisine at this high-end eatery runs to Pacific Rim dishes like rotisserie chicken, teriyaki chicken (an island favorite), and local fish prepared Polynesian style. There's a nice view of the harbor from the terrace and split-level dining room, and live entertainment in the lounge on Tuesdays, Thursdays, Saturdays, and Sundays. ◆ Pacific Rim ◆ Daily breakfast, lunch, and dinner. 949.3811 &

4 Aston Waikikian Hotel $$ The hotel's most appealing aspect is that it's everything the rest of Waikiki isn't—small (105 rooms), friendly, and Polynesian in both appearance and mood (in other words, don't expect anything fancy).

The original buildings are no more than two stories high (the separate seven-story tower was built later), with ground-level lanai room that open onto a walkway verdant with palms and ferns. Second-story rooms have lanais with partial views of the ocean, the mountain or at least the walkway. There's a pool in the central courtyard. It's an easy stroll from the hotel's Duke Kahanamoku Lagoon, which ha its own beach, to the sands of Waikiki Beach. Guests who like the **Waikikian**'s low elevatio should specify a room in the original **Banyan Wing.** ◆ 1811 Ala Moana Blvd (between Kalia Rd and Hobron La). 949.5331, 800/922.7866 fax 946.2843 &

Within the Aston Waikikian Hotel:

TAHITIAN LANA

Tahitian Lanai ★★$$$ Old-timers love this balmy poolside setting with its casual Polynesian ambience, superb breakfasts, and sing-along piano bar. Try the legendary eggs Benedict or the curried-fish dishes. ◆ Continental ◆ Daily breakfast, lunch, and dinner. Reservations recommended. 946.6541 &

5 Kobe Steak House ★$$$ Although the chefs, who give flamboyant performances at the *teppanyaki* tableside grills, contribute to the festive atmosphere, they're still serving formula Japanese cuisine—shrimp *teppanyaki,* Kobe emperor steak, and vegetable tempura. It's good, but not worth writing home about. ◆ Japanese ◆ Daily dinner. Valet parking. 1841 Ala Moana Blvd (between Kalia Rd and Hobron La). 941.4444 &

6 Hilton Hawaiian Village .$$$ With a total room count of 2,545, this is the largest hotel in the state. Just short of a self-contained village, it has more than a hundred shops, 20 restaurants and lounges, three pools (one has two tiers), beautifully landscaped gardens, banquet and convention facilities for up to 5,000 people, a six-story parking garage, a boat dock, and one of Waikiki's largest showrooms, the **Hilton Dome.** Those seeking an even more upscale stay should check into the **Alii Tower,** an exclusive hotel within the hotel, with its own separate guest reception area, concierge, private pool, and exercise room. Although a $100-million renovation changed much of the architecture of this resort in 1988, some of the original structure remains, including the garish 16,000-tile rainbow mural on the **Rainbow Tower**'s exterior (the tallest mosaic mural in the world, according to *Guinness*). Another big plus is the choice location on Waikiki Beach, with catamaran sailing, Pearl Harbor cruises, and other outdoor activities. ♦ 2005 Kalia Rd (between Paoa Pl and Ala Moana Blvd). 949.4321, 800/445.8667; fax 947.7815 ♿

Within the Hilton Hawaiian Village:

Benihana of Tokyo ★$$$ Not only is everything here cooked (making it a perfect choice for those who avoid raw fish), cooking is the main attraction. Chefs perform at the *teppanyaki* grills, slashing at beef, lobster, chicken, shrimp, and vegetables with blinding speed. ♦ Japanese ♦ Daily lunch and dinner. Reservations recommended. Rainbow Bazaar. 955.5955 ♿

Golden Dragon ★★★$$$$ A festive atmosphere prevails when chef Steve Chiang serves up Imperial beggar's chicken (spiced and cooked for most of a day; 24-hour advance notice required) and Peking duck, the signature dishes of this vermilion and black Chinese restaurant. The extensive menu also includes such traditional Cantonese dishes as lemon chicken, smoked duck, and lobster in curry sauce. ♦ Chinese ♦ Tu-Su dinner. Reservations recommended. Rainbow Tower. 946.5336 ♿

Bali by the Sea ★★$$$$ With spectacular views of Waikiki Beach and Diamond Head, this restaurant lives up to its name. A distinguished roster of visiting chefs specializes in fresh seafood and imaginative sauces—*opakapaka* (pink snapper) with basil sauce, tiger prawns on linguine, and herb-crusted rack of lamb. ♦ Continental ♦ M-Sa breakfast, lunch, and dinner. Reservations recommended. Rainbow Tower. 941.2254 ♿

Atlantis Submarines A 64-passenger submarine fitted with viewing ports has been providing two-hour excursions off Waikiki Beach for years, letting visitors in on an undersea world they might not otherwise see. Now the same company is offering a glimpse of another of Hawaii's worlds with a **Heritage Cruise and Walking Tour,** which includes a catamaran sail from the **Hilton Hawaiian Village** pier to Honolulu Harbor, a visit to the **Hawaii Maritime Center,** and a walk through Chinatown. ♦ Fee. Daily 8AM-4PM. At the hotel pier. 973.1285, 973.9811

Hawaiian Village Mini Golf Grab the kids and head for this 36-hole, 15,000-square-foot miniature golf course. Play the foliage-filled, rain forest–like **Mauka Course,** or opt for the beach-themed **Makai Course**—complete with sand, coral, seashells, and driftwood. ♦ Fee.

Daily 10AM-midnight. Behind the Hilton Dome. 941.8846

7 Wailana Coffee House $ This Honolulu institution offers typical coffeehouse fare. Nothing special here, but it's very popular among residents and tourists. (Parking is a nightmare, so use the garage in the same building and validate your ticket.) ♦ Coffeehouse ♦ Daily 24 hours. 1860 Ala Moana Blvd (at Ena Rd). 955.1764 ♿

8 California Pizza Kitchen ★★$$ The immensely popular pizza-and-pasta chain has successfully invaded Honolulu, serving oven-fired pizzas with an eclectic choice of toppings, including rosemary chicken and potato, Peking duck, and Thai chicken. The ingredients are fresh and the crusts are just perfect (try the honey-wheat dough). Even the pasta dishes stand out. If you can't decide what to order, the Sante Fe chicken pizza is a sure thing. ♦ Pizza/Italian ♦ Daily lunch and dinner. Validated parking for two hours. 1910 Ala Moana Blvd (at Ena Rd). 955.5161. Also at: Kahala Mall, 4211 Waialae Ave (at Kilauea Ave), Honolulu. 737.9446 ♿

9 Doubletree Alana Waikiki $$$$ This 19-story property (formerly the **Alana Waikiki Hotel**) is marketed mostly in Japan and is often crowded. The 313 guest rooms are decorated in a modern yet subdued manner, with meticulous attention to detail. Amenities include a pool, fitness center, business center, and conference facilities; room service is provided by the hotel's **Harlequin Restaurant.** ♦ 1956 Ala Moana Blvd (between Kalakaua Ave and Ena Rd). 941.7275, 800/367.6070; fax 949.0996 ♿

10 The Wave For Waikiki (and all of Hawaii), this is as wild as the nightlife gets. (The islands' trendy clubs are tame by mainland standards.) Strictly for the young and tireless, this hot spot features live music until late into the night and DJ-spun dance music until much, much later. ♦ Cover. Daily 9PM-4AM. 1877 Kalakaua Ave (between Ena Rd and Ala Wai Blvd). 941.0424 ♿

Eggs'n Things

11 Eggs 'n Things ★$ An institution for insomniacs, late-night party fiends, and workers getting off the graveyard shift, this is the place to come for a midnight snack or early breakfast. Try a spinach, bacon, and cheese omelette, lemon crepes, or pancakes with macadamia nuts, chocolate chips, pecans, raisins, or bananas. Fresh mahimahi, cajun swordfish, and *ono* (wahoo) straight from the owner's fishing boat are favorites, too. ◆ American ◆ Daily 11PM-2PM. Validated parking at the **Hawaiian Monarch** hotel. 1911 Kalakaua Ave (between Ala Moana Blvd and Ena Rd). 949.0820

12 Nick's Fishmarket ★★★$$$$ Nick Nickolas opened the first of his seafood palaces here, and it has since been a home away from home for many a discriminating diner, Tom Selleck notably among them. The luxurious black booths and classic seafood selections such as grilled *opakapaka* (pink snapper) and lemon-broiled *ahi* (tuna) make for a pleasant dining experience at this, one of Honolulu's premier seafood restaurants. ◆ Seafood ◆ Daily dinner. Valet parking. In the Waikiki Gateway Hotel, 2070 Kalakaua Ave (at Olohana St). 955.6333 ᕃ

13 Kyo-ya ★★★$$$$ An ultracontemporary but very Japanese structure, this restaurant is a statement in minimalist elegance—marble, glass, granite, and concrete abound. A corner of the restaurant is devoted to *soba* (noodles) and the main dining room is downstairs. The breathtaking private tatami rooms are upstairs amid tasteful Zen gardens. The food is first-rate; the sashimi is always fresh, the kaiseki (traditional multicourse dinner) de rigueur, and the fish *misoyaki* (fish soaked in a savory soybean by-product) superb. ◆ Japanese ◆ Daily dinner; M-Sa lunch. 2057 Kalakaua Ave (between Saratoga and Maluhia Rds). 947.3911 ᕃ

14 Royal Garden Hotel $$ The bad news is that the 220-room hotel isn't on the beach. The good news is that this cozy property is one of Waikiki's best-kept secrets. Splurge on a suite and lounge by the pool. Rooms are equipped with phones and TVs, and there are two restaurants. ◆ 440 Olohana St (at Kuhio Ave). 943.0202, 800/367.5666; fax 946.8777 ᕃ

15 Hale Koa Hotel $ The centerpiece of the Army's **Fort DeRussy** reservation—66 acres of prime Waikiki real estate—this military-owned high-rise is a sweet deal for military personnel and retired officers (nonmilitary folks need not apply). Located next to one of the best beaches in Waikiki, the newly renovated 14-story hotel has 814 units, three restaurants, a fitness center, and two pools. ◆ 2055 Kalia Rd (between Saratoga Rd and Paoa Pl). 955.0555, 800/367.6027; fax 955.9660

16 Fort DeRussy Beach This oasis is a favorite of residents and the military, with military personnel serving as lifeguards (talk about a cushy assignment). Picnic facilities, volleyball courts, and a snack bar complete the picture. ◆ Behind Hale Koa Hotel

17 US Army Museum of Hawaii Wartime artifacts and memorabilia are displayed inside a 1911 bunker with 22-foot-thick walls built so solidly that the Army turned it into a museum to avoid having to tear it down. Exhibits include ancient Hawaiian weapons as well as memorabilia from World War II and the Korean and Vietnam Wars. Uniforms and tanks, coastal defense artillery, and articles and photos relating to the Army in Hawaii have also been preserved. ◆ Donation. Tu-Su. Guided tours must be booked in advance, but self-guided tours are available any time. Building 32, Fort DeRussy Military Reservation (off Kalia Rd). 438.2822 ᕃ

18 Outrigger Royal Islander Hotel $$ Within walking distance of Waikiki Beach, this nicely decorated hotel is ideal for the budget-minded. There are 94 rooms and seven suites; one-third of the rooms overlook the beach, and the rest have views of the neighboring park or the city. All rooms have air-conditioning, TV sets, phones, and refrigerators. There's no pool on site, though guests have full privileges at any of the other Outrigger hotels nearby. There's a **McDonald's** on the property. ◆ 2164 Kalia Rd (at Saratoga Rd). 922.1961, 800/688.7444; fax 923.4632

19 Malihini Hotel $ Okay, so it's not the Waldorf. There's no restaurant, pool, or TVs, and only partial air-conditioning, and it's not even on the water (though it's near the beach). But for the price, this is a steal. The 28 rooms are spartan but clean, with kitchenettes, ceiling fans, and daily maid service. This low-budget hotel is very popular, so make reservations well in advance. ◆ No credit cards accepted. 217 Saratoga Rd (at Kalia Rd). 923.9644

20 The Breakers $$ Those who want to be close to the beach without paying the price of a big-name hotel should check out this two-story lodge hidden among the high-rises. It's reasonably priced, with 50 air-conditioned rooms (with kitchenettes) and 14 suites in a setting complete with the requisite palm trees and tropical plants. There's a pool, a snack shop, and a bar; daily maid service is provided. ♦ 250 Beach Walk (between Kalia Rd and Kalakaua Ave). 923.3181, 800/426.0494; fax 923.7174 ₺

21 Hawaiiana Hotel $$ Another refreshingly unpretentious low-rise located half a block from Waikiki Beach and close to Fort DeRussy Beach, this three-story hotel has 95 rooms complete with kitchenettes, air-conditioning, and connecting rooms for families. It's a good deal for Waikiki, and the mostly Hawaiian staff is unforgettable. There are two pools and complimentary Kona coffee, but no restaurant. ♦ 260 Beach Walk (between Kalia Rd and Kalakaua Ave). 923.3811, 800/535.0085; fax 926.5728 ₺

22 Popo's $$ What began as a strange architectural hodgepodge (containing even stranger restaurants) built by Japanese investors quickly folded and was bought out by the Spencecliff chain. Now it's a popular Japanese-owned Mexican restaurant (go figure) serving standard dishes, including tacos, burritos, and enchiladas. ♦ Mexican ♦ Daily lunch and dinner. 2112 Kalakaua Ave (between Lewers and Kalaimoku Sts). 923.7355 ₺

23 Waikiki Joy Hotel $$ On a small, noisy side street off the beach, this hotel has a curious charm despite the absence of views from its two towers, one with 11 floors and the other with eight. With a total of 50 rooms and 44 suites, the property is petite, but it's big on extras like Jacuzzis and state-of-the-art stereo speakers. It caters to business travelers, offering such nice touches as the **Corporate Suite Program,** with special rates for business travelers; valet parking; complimentary newspapers, breakfast, and local calls; and many business services. A pool and restaurant round out the deal. ♦ 320 Lewers St (between Lauula St and Kuhio Ave). 923.2300, 800/922.7866; fax 924.4010

The Charlie Chan mysteries of the 1920s and 1930s, written by Earl Derr Biggers, were inspired by Honolulu detective Chang Apana, who used to relax under the ancient *kiawe* tree at Halekulani's House Without a Key restaurant in Waikiki.

24 Moose McGillycuddy's ★★$$ Part of a chain, this is a yuppie-holiday kind of place, with daily drink specials, cheap breakfasts, and a popular early-bird dinner menu (try the prime rib). Rock music plays every night upstairs, and sporting events are shown via satellite. ♦ Pub ♦ Daily breakfast, lunch, and dinner. 310 Lewers St (between Kalakaua Ave and Lauula St). 923.0751. Also at: 1035 University Ave (between S King St and Varsity Pl), Honolulu. 944.5525 ₺

25 Perry's Smorgy $ Still popular with the all-you-can-eat-cheap buffet crowd, this eatery is something of an American phenomenon, where tourists are corralled toward troughs of grub to receive their wafer-thin slice of roast beef. Large windows allow spectators to witness feeding time. ♦ American ♦ Daily breakfast, lunch, and dinner. 250 Lewers St (between Helumoa Rd and Kalakaua Ave). 922.8814 ₺

26 House of Hong ★$$ Run by the Hong family, this place has suffered a severe drop in popularity due to the opening of so many other Asian eateries in the area, but for many years it was the leading Chinese restaurant in Waikiki. The large glittery dining rooms are decorated with ancient art objects; the huge Cantonese menu includes standard choices like Mongolian beef and Hong Kong shrimp. ♦ Chinese ♦ M-Sa lunch and dinner; Su dinner. 260-A Lewers St (between Helumoa Rd and Kalakaua Ave). 923.0202 ₺

27 Trattoria ★★$$$ A longtime favorite located in the **Outrigger Edgewater Hotel,** the restaurant serves lasagna, fettuccine Alfredo, and other Northern Italian classics. This is one of Waikiki's perennial, reliable restaurants—even locals eat here. ♦ Northern Italian ♦ Daily dinner. Valet parking. 2168 Kalia Rd (between Lewers St and Beach Walk). 923.8415 ₺

28 Outrigger Reef Hotel $$$ Located on Waikiki Beach, this is one of the nicest (and most expensive) hotels of the Outrigger chain. The 838 air-conditioned rooms (some with kitchenettes) and 47 suites on 17 floors encompass a wide price range. Fort DeRussy Beach, with its volleyball courts and water activities, is nearby, and there's a pool and two restaurants. Rates are more reasonable than at most beachfront hotels. ♦ 2169 Kalia Rd (just east of Fort DeRussy Military Reservation). 923.3111, 800/462.6262; fax 924.4957

Hawaii from Top to Bottom

The eight major Hawaiian islands (illustrated below) were actually tips of enormous volcanoes. Centuries ago, these submerged volcanoes erupted over and over, building up lava until they finally emerged above the ocean surface some 2,400 miles off the coast of North America. Today they cover about 400 miles of the Pacific Ocean.

Nearly all of Hawaii's population lives on these islands, although another 124 islands and atolls northwest of **Niihau** complete the Hawaiian archipelago. The summits of the islands pictured here—the youngest in the chain— range from 13,796 feet on the **Big Island** to 1,280 feet on Niihau.

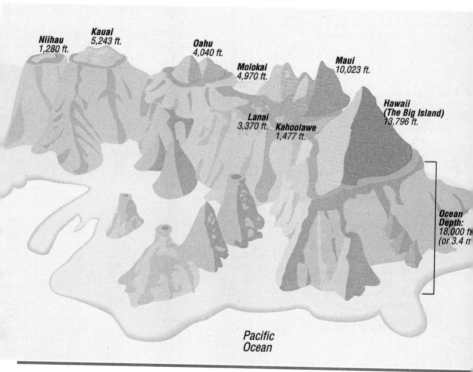

Niihau
1,280 ft.

Kauai
5,243 ft.

Oahu
4,040 ft.

Molokai
4,970 ft.

Maui
10,023 ft.

Hawaii
(The Big Island)
13,796 ft.

Lanai
3,370 ft.

Kahoolawe
1,477 ft.

Ocean
Depth:
18,000 ft
(or 3.4 m

Pacific
Ocean

Halekulani

29 Halekulani $$$$ *Halekulani* means "the house befitting heaven," and this hotel combines the standards of a first-class establishment with the gracious atmosphere of Old Hawaii. When Robert Lewers opened for business in 1907, the property consisted of quaint cottages with overhanging eaves nestled in a coconut grove. In 1981 the hotel was sold to the Halekulani Corporation, which razed the aging cottages but restored the main building and the **House Without a Key** lounge (leaving untouched an impressive beachside *kiawe* tree). Most of the 456 rooms and suites look out at the beach, each thoughtfully decorated to the smallest detail, like bathrobes and a complimentary morning paper. Another luxury is the in-room check-in service. Several restaurants and bars and a pool are on the premises. If you can afford the steep rates, this is the place to stay.
♦ 2199 Kalia Rd (east of Fort DeRussy Military Reservation). 923.2311, 800/367.2343; fax 926.8004

Within the Halekulani:

Orchids ★★★$$$$ With a terraced open-air dining room overlooking Diamond Head and the Pacific, this casually elegant dining establishment has one of Hawaii's nicest restaurant settings. The innovative Pacific Rim menu's entrées range from smoked mahimahi to steamed *onaga* (red snapper) Oriental style. Sunday brunch is the most popular production, though you may have to abuse the credit card a bit to attend. ♦ Pacific Rim ♦ M-Sa breakfast, lunch, and dinner; Su brunch and dinner. Reservations recommended. 923.2311 &

La Mer ★★★★$$$$ Serious connoisseurs dub this restaurant the finest in Hawaii. The view from the elegant dining room is incomparable, with palm trees silhouetted against the darkening ocean at sunset. The menu matches this picture-perfect setting. The signature here is fresh seafood prepared a number of imaginative ways—such as *onaga* (red snapper) poached with three-caviar sauce, and *kumu* (goatfish) *en papillote*, with seaweed and shiitake mushrooms—and a carefully gleaned selection of meat and fowl. Leave room for dessert—the fruit tulip with passion-fruit *coulis* is amazing. Yes, it's a very expensive meal, especially if you have to buy a jacket to get in, but at least you can say you've dined at the best. ♦ French ♦ Daily dinner. Reservations and jackets required. 923.2311

House Without a Key ★★$$ A key would actually be useless, as this is an open-air restaurant and cocktail bar. A full breakfast buffet, sandwiches on whole wheat bread, and hamburgers, as well as local favorites such as sashimi and saimin (noodles in broth), are served with a view of the ocean and Diamond Head. A romantic hula show under the old *kiawe* tree may inspire you to dance under the stars after knocking back a few mai tais. ♦ American ♦ Daily breakfast, lunch, and dinner. 923.2311 &

Lewers Lounge Plush with leather and teak, this cocktail spot is perfect for couples and conferring businesspeople. It's quiet except for the tinkling of the ivories at the piano bar and the voices of the fine jazz singers who perform here nightly after 9PM. ♦ Daily 8:30PM-1AM. 923.2311

30 Waikiki Parc $$$ The Halekulani Corporation built this 23-story hotel as a less expensive alternative to the **Halekulani** just across the street. If you can live with the limited ocean view and the 30-second walk to the beach, it makes sense to stay here. All 298 rooms have private lanais or balconies, fully stocked refrigerators, and mini-bars. There's also a pool and laundromat. ♦ 2233 Helumoa Rd (east of Lewers St). 921.7272, 800/422.0450; fax 923.1336 &

Within the Waikiki Parc:

Parc Cafe ★★$$$ The casual dining room here has high ceilings, tile floors, and plants abundant. The buffet is appealing in terms of price and selection, though it's not as big as those at the fancier hotels. The continental and American dishes are prepared with an island flair, and the dinner buffet is one of Honolulu's best values, with a variety of fresh fish; stir-fried vegetables; duck, leg of lamb, or chicken carved to order; and a fabulous salad bar, with everything from Peking duck salad to Kula tomatoes and charbroiled eggplant. ♦ Continental/American ♦ Daily breakfast, lunch, and dinner. 921.7272

Kacho ★★$$$$ Sushi is the specialty in this small but stunning contemporary restaurant highlighted by a long granite sushi bar. The more adventurous might try the *kaiseki* dinner (a set-menu affair) or the traditional Japanese breakfast, which includes miso soup, grilled fish, steamed rice, and a raw egg. ♦ Japanese ♦ Daily breakfast, lunch, and dinner. 924.3535

31 Duty Free Shops If you have an airline ticket to a destination outside the US, you can visit a duty-free shop at the **Honolulu International Airport** or here in Waikiki. Japanese tourists like duty-free shops because the merchandise is often less expensive than at home, but there aren't many bargains for Americans. ♦ Daily 9AM-11PM. 330 Royal Hawaiian Ave (between Lauula St and Waikolu Way). 931.2700

32 Sheraton-Waikiki $$$$ The hotel is larger than a football stadium, with 1,835 rooms and suites and more than 45,000 square feet of meeting space. But even after the much-touted millions spent on improvements in the 1980s, the lofty ocean views remain the best feature of this monstrosity, the largest resort in the world when it opened in 1971 (**Hilton Hawaiian Village** has since surpassed it). Yet another renovation has begun, however, this one projected to take five years and to upgrade the rooms and lobby. Don't blink or you'll miss the actual beachfront, which seems tiny compared to the size of the building. Your room will reflect one of a variety of decorating themes, including Art Deco, French, and Chinese. There are two pools. ♦ 2255 Kalakaua Ave (east of Lewers St). 922.4422, 800/325.3535; fax 923.8785 &

Within the Sheraton-Waikiki:

Hanohano Room ★★$$$$ Take the glass elevator up 30 floors for a panoramic view and unmatched black-tie service. Your best bets here are breakfast and sunset cocktails, but there's continental cuisine at dinner (garlic prawns and lobster medaillons with Pernod sauce are good) and dancing afterwards. ♦ Continental ♦ M-Sa breakfast and dinner; Su brunch and dinner. Reservations required. 922.4422 &

33 Royal Hawaiian Shopping Center A four-level, 175-store complex with the biggest names in international fashion: **Chanel** (923.0255), **Hermès** (971.4200), **Lancel** (971-2000), **Gianni Versace** (922.5337), and more, as well as a liberal selection of restaurants. ♦ Daily. 2201 Kalakaua Ave (east of Lewers St). 922.0588

Within the Royal Hawaiian Shopping Center:

Restaurant Suntory ★★$$$$ Suntory Ltd., the Japanese liquor producer that has built showcase restaurants all over the world, reportedly spent more than $2 million on this one. Elegance abounds, from the handsome cocktail lounge to the separate dining rooms, each devoted to a special style of Japanese cuisine: *shabu-shabu* (cook-it-yourself soup), *teppanyaki* (tableside cooking), sushi, and so on. There's also a traditional Japanese room with tatami seating (sunken areas accommodate extended legs). ♦ Japanese ♦ M-Sa lunch and dinner; Su dinner. Reservations recommended. Orchid Court, third floor. 922.5511

Paradiso Bar & Grill $$$ New York steak and fresh local seafood top the menu at this oddly located coffee shop, closely followed by pizza. The outdoor seating makes it a nice place to take a break from shopping. ♦ American ♦ Daily breakfast, lunch, and dinner. Orchid Court, ground floor. 926.2000 &

33 Royal Hawaiian Hotel $$$$ Despite high-rise neighbors, this hotel (pictured below) clings to its glory days as the "Pink Palace of the Pacific." The original Spanish-Moorish design, by **Warren & Wetmore,** had cost the Matson Navigation Company a cool $4 million by the time the hotel opened in 1927 (Matson built it to provide world-class accommodations for passengers on their luxury liners). Before World War II, the hotel was the playground of the wealthy and famous. Hollywood celebrities such as Mary Pickford and Douglas Fairbanks vacationed here, as did honeymooners Nelson Rockefeller and Henry Ford II (with their brides, that is). The halcyon days ended during World War II, when the hotel was leased to the Navy as an R&R spot for sailors from the Pacific fleet.

Sheraton bought the hotel in 1959 and added the 16-story **Royal Tower.** It's now owned by a company called Kyo-Ya (though Sheraton continues to operate it). The ornate porte cochere is impressive; chandeliered walkways leading from the spacious lobby are wide and richly carpeted. A green lawn framed by lush foliage and banyan trees leads to Waikiki Beach, where hotel guests enjoy a private stretch of sand. There's also a pool on the grounds. Though the **Royal Tower** offers modern levels of comfort, nostalgic guests will prefer to stay in the original stucco structure, still regularly repainted its traditional pink color. There are 530 rooms on the 10-acre property, all with air-conditioning, refrigerators, and pink telephones. ♦ 2259 Kalakaua Ave (east of Lewers St). 923.7311, 800/325.3535; fax 931.7840 &

Within the Royal Hawaiian Hotel:

Mai Tai Bar Watch the action on Waikiki Beach from this open-air, beachside bar. True to its name, it serves excellent (and expensive) mai tais. There's also live Hawaiian

Royal Hawaiian Hotel

entertainment by Keith and Carmen Haugen.
♦ Daily 10AM-1AM. 923.7311 ♿

Surf Room ★★$$$$ Suitors searching for the perfect place to pop the question need look no farther than this open-air, oceanside dining room. The pink tablecloths match the glow of the exquisite sunsets seen here. The *ono* (wahoo) with lobster syrup and shiitake mushrooms is recommended, as is the prime rib. ♦ Continental/Pacific Rim ♦ Daily breakfast, lunch, and dinner. 923.7311

Royal Hawaiian Luau $$$$ If you want to experience the classic hotel luau, you might as well go all out and do it here. There's no *imu* (Hawaiian oven dug into the ground) for pig roasting, however, and on the whole, the authenticity of the proceeding is questionable. ♦ Luau ♦ Expensive cover. M 6-8:30PM ♿

34 Waikiki Beach The mother of all Hawaii beaches stretches in broken segments from Ala Wai Canal to Diamond Head, absorbing the tourists and hotel facades that encroach upon its golden grains. Despite what hotel markers claim, the two-mile beach is public property up to the high-water mark (and plenty of the public takes advantage of it). Parts of the beach were widened in the mid-1980s to ease traffic, but congestion is still a problem. Swimming is safe, even for beginners, and surfboards, boogie boards, umbrellas, beach mats, snorkel gear, and more can be rented from concession stands along the beach. You can even take up surfing; several places offer lessons, including **Leahi Beach Services** (at the Reef Hotel; no phone). An hour of instruction, equipment included, costs about $15, and they guarantee you'll stand on the board (they don't say for how long). ♦ Off Kalakaua Ave (between Diamond Head and Lewers St)

35 Waikiki Beachcomber $$$ Set in the very heart of congested Waikiki, this property offers 496 air-conditioned rooms (and four suites) with balconies. There's also a pool, Hawaiian entertainment nightly in the **Surfboard Lounge,** and dining in the **Hibiscus Cafe.** Easy access to the shopping malls and Waikiki Beach is another plus. ♦ 2300 Kalakaua Ave (at Seaside Ave). 922.4646, 800/622.4646; fax 926.9973 ♿

36 Matteo's ★★$$$$ Well-known restaurateur Fred Livingston, who also owns **Trattoria** and **Tahitian Lanai** (see pages 121 and 118), as well as the **Crouching Lion** on the North Shore, uses high-backed booths, soft lighting, and amber tones to create an intimate, ambience. The osso buco, live Maine lobsters, and New York steaks are all popular with the lawyers, yuppies, and showbiz types who frequent this place. ♦ Italian/Continental ♦ Daily dinner. Reservations recommended. Valet parking. 364 Seaside Ave (at Kuhio Ave). 922.5551 ♿

37 Maharaja Somewhat uppity and pretentious, this Japanese-owned disco, which attracts mostly Japanese tourists and local businesspeople, has a dress code, a VIP room reserved for members who shell out $500 a year in dues, and a varied late-night menu (stick to the drinks and dancing). Decked out in marble and brass, with the full gamut of high-tech bells and whistles on the dance floor, it fancies itself Honolulu's hottest nightclub. Not. ♦ Cover. Daily 6PM-4AM. In the Waikiki Trade Center, 2255 Kuhio Ave (between Duke's La and Seaside Ave). 922.3030 ♿

38 International Marketplace The fancy name belies the mostly worthless merchandise scattered among 150 carts. Located across from the **Sheraton Moana Surfrider Hotel,** the open-air grounds are shaded by a huge banyan tree. The only thing remotely international about the place is the bargaining system—you can pick up souvenirs for a song if you're not afraid to haggle. ♦ Daily 9AM-11PM. 2330 Kalakaua Ave (between Kaiulani Ave and Duke's La). 923.9871 ♿

39 Princess Kaiulani Hotel $$$ This Sheraton hotel has expanded significantly since 1955, when the 11-story main building opened. The addition of a 29-story tower and three wings brought the total number of rooms to 1,150. Located across from the **King's Village** shopping center, it's only one block from Waikiki Beach. There are air-conditioned rooms in several price categories, dictated by ocean, city, or mountain views; note, however, that this is not an oceanfront hotel. A pool and several restaurants and bars are on the premises. ♦ 120 Kaiulani Ave (between Kalakaua and Kuhio Aves). 922.5811, 800/325.3535; fax 931.4526 ♿

40 Sheraton Moana Surfrider $$$$ This venerable landmark was the first hotel on Waikiki Beach. It opened in 1901, a time when Hawaiian beachboys hung out at the 300-foot Moana pier, greeting tourists with music as the sun set. Luxuries included a ballroom, saloon, billiard room, pool, roof-garden observatory, and the area's first electric elevator. Subsequent expansions, changes in ownership, and a $50-million renovation produced today's impressive property. Restored to its original design and listed in the National Register of Historic Places, the hotel is furnished with indigenous woods, four-poster beds with bamboo headboards, marble-top tables, a grand staircase, Victorian-style lamps, colonial verandas and millwork, and memorabilia. Robert Louis Stevenson *may* have penned some of his prose under the banyan tree in the courtyard. Planted in 1885, the famous tree now towers more than 75 feet, with a 150-foot span. The **Banyan Court** and **Banyan Veranda** feature sunset performances of great Hawaiian music. The 791 rooms (including 44 suites) in three towers have all the modern amenities, including air-conditioning, refrigerators, TVs, and 24-hour room service. ♦ 2365 Kalakaua Ave (across from the International Marketplace). 922.3111, 800/325.3535; fax 923.5984 &

Within the Sheraton Moana Surfrider:

Banyan Veranda ★★★$$ Since the restaurant started a Hawaiian music program, it has become a top beach attraction. Sunday performances by such Hawaiian musicians as the Puuhonua Trio and the Banyan Serenaders give a glimpse of the elusive "real Hawaii." The setting is unbeatable: rattan chairs sheltered by a banyan tree, and a view of the **Banyan Court** and the Pacific. Drinks, be warned, are hideously expensive. ♦ Continental ♦ Daily breakfast, afternoon tea, evening appetizer buffet, and Sunday brunch. 922.3111 &

Ship's Tavern ★★$$$$ This "tavern" is the **Moana**'s formal dining room, with an oceanside setting. The menu features steak and seafood such as fresh Maine lobster, poached *onaga* (red snapper), sautéed scallops, and Kahuku prawns. ♦ Steaks/Seafood ♦ Daily dinner. Reservations recommended. 922.3111 &

W. C. Peacock & Co., Ltd. ★$$$ Dine alfresco in a casual, oceanside restaurant. Th emphasis is on simple fare—chicken teriyaki broiled or baked mahimahi, and prime rib. ♦ Steaks/Seafood ♦ Daily dinner. Reservations recommended. 922.3111 &

41 **Wizard Stones** A modest outcropping in front of a bronze statue of champion Hawaiia surfer/swimmer Duke Kahanamoku, these stones look like ordinary rocks, but, like the memorial, add a quiet majesty to the spot. Hawaiian lore has it that four Tahitian kahuna (priests) who journeyed here in the 16th century gave their *mana* (healing powers) to the stones and then vanished. ♦ Waikiki Beac (east of Sheraton Moana Surfrider)

42 **Hyatt Regency Waikiki** $$$ Designed by **Wimberly, Allison, Tong and Goo** in association with **Lawton & Taylor,** the hotel (pictured below) was built in 1976 for $100 million and sold in 1987 for $300 million. Forty-story twin towers rise on both sides of the landscaped atrium lobby. There are 1,208 rooms, 25 suites, several restaurants and bars, an indoor pool, more than 70 boutiques, and a two-story waterfall. The rooms, with Asian furnishings, have private lanais and air-conditioning. Although impressive, this isn't a place to get away from it all, since it's located in the busiest part of Waikiki. ♦ 2424 Kalakaua Ave (between Uluniu and Kaiulani Ave). 923.1234, 800/233.1234; fax 923.7839 &

Hyatt Regency Waikiki

Within the Hyatt Regency Waikiki:

Musashi ★$$$$ As much attention is paid to drama and theater as to food in this Japanese restaurant, named after famous samurai Miyamoto Musashi. (His classic study of the warrior code, *A Book of Five Rings,* is the bible in Japanese business schools.) Waitresses dress in kimonos, chefs in samurai garb, and busboys in traditional street-acrobat wear. Try the duckling glazed with herb sauce and the "jewel box," a dessert of five sherbets. Diners may sit at the sushi bar, *teppanyaki* grills, or tables. ♦ Japanese ♦ Daily dinner. Reservations recommended. 923.1234 &

Furusato ★★$$$$ This dining spot predates the hotel; it was a restaurant in the **Biltmore,** which was razed to make room for the current hotel. It's remarkably good, very authentic, extremely expensive, and caters to Japanese tourists. Order *ishiyaki* steak, which is cooked on hot rocks, or sukiyaki with beef and vegetables. ♦ Japanese ♦ Daily dinner. Reservations recommended 922.4991 &

43 The Rose and Crown ★$ Styled after a London pub (an anomaly in Waikiki), this spot is very popular with the Aussies, Brits, and New Zealanders who come for the lusty sing-alongs, pub grub (grilled ham sandwiches, meatball subs, broiled chicken), dart boards, and of course, imported beer. ♦ Pub ♦ Daily Noon-2AM. 101 Kaiulani Ave (at Koa Ave). 923.5833

43 Odoriko ★$$$$ Tanks of lobsters, prawns, crabs, and oysters add living color to this authentically furnished Japanese seafood and steak house. The specialties include fish broiled or with teriyaki sauce; there's also a sushi bar. For something different, try the Japanese-style breakfast. ♦ Japanese ♦ Daily breakfast, lunch, and dinner. Kings Village, 2400 Koa Ave (at Kaiulani Ave). 923.7368

44 Ala Wai Golf Course The greens fees are relatively low, so this flat, moderately interesting 18-hole course (par 72, 6,065 yards) bordering the murky Ala Wai Canal is crowded with local players. Getting a tee-off time can be difficult. ♦ Inexpensive greens fees. Daily. 404 Kapahulu Ave (between Ala Wai Blvd and Date St). 733.7387

45 Hy's Steak House ★★$$$$ If this plush bar and dining room make you feel you're in a baron's wood-paneled library, that's because the interior actually came from a private estate in the eastern US. The dining room features a stunning gazebo, Tiffany-style glass ceiling panels, chandeliers, and a glassed-in *kiawe* broiler. The menu includes rack of lamb and beef Wellington, but steak Neptune (grilled over *kiawe* charcoal and topped with béarnaise sauce) is the best choice. ♦ Steaks ♦ Daily dinner. Valet parking. 2440 Kuhio Ave (between Kapuni and Kaiulani Aves). 922.5555

46 Aston Waikiki Beachside Hotel $$$$ If you want to be right in the middle of the action but feel as though you're in a different world, this European-style Aston hotel is the place to call. It's tiny, with 79 rooms (also tiny but well appointed) in a narrow 12-floor tower drenched in travertine marble. André and Jane Tatibouet made this their dream project, decorating it lavishly with careful attention to detail. The entrance looks like Tiffany's, with moldings galore, Oriental art and furnishings, and expensive wall coverings. Three of the eight rooms on each floor have ocean views over bustling Kalakaua Avenue, and all feature Chinese lacquered furniture, Oriental screens, and black-chrome-and-gold shower heads that cost more than a room for the night. There are none of the traditional resort accoutrements like restaurants, room service, a pool, or tennis courts. Ask about the specials on room rates. ♦ 2452 Kalakaua Ave (between Liliuokalani Ave and Uluniu). 931.2100, 800/922.7866; fax 931.2129 &

Garbage collectors in Honolulu, Oahu, have a clause in their contract that allows them to go fishing as soon as they're done with their route, which is usually just before dawn. This is part of what Hawaiians used to call the *"ukapau"* ("go fast and be done") system of receiving payment for work done instead of time spent.

Hawaiian shirts got started in the 19th century, when missionaries gave the natives plain shirts to cover their bare chests. The natives painted the shirts by hand with Hawaiian motifs, a practice that's been copied ever since.

Restaurants/Clubs: Red   Hotels: Blue
Shops/ ♟ Outdoors: Green   Sights/Culture: Black

Nature's Necklaces

When Polynesians first came to the Hawaiian Islands, leis were among the most precious keepsakes they brought from their homeland. As the islands were settled, the exotic garlands became part of daily Hawaiian life. In addition to being ornaments, the various designs indicated rank in religious and spiritual rites and reflected different backgrounds. Royalty, for example, usually preferred *lei hulu mans* (leis made of feathers, especially bright yellow ones). Today, while modern historians study ancient leis to help define emigration patterns, the custom of giving and wearing leis remains one of Hawaii's most cherished traditions.

Not all leis are made of flowers or feathers; many are fashioned from shells, seeds, or animal teeth and are either strung together by hand, braided with flowers or greens, sewn to heavy fabric, or wound with cord. Feather leis, favored by Hawaiian royalty, are still among the most precious. They're more expensive than shell or nut leis because they take more time to construct and their materials are harder to come by, especially when the feathers are from exotic birds. Handcrafted feather leis last for years, if not generations.

More temporary leis are made with fruit, vines, berries, leaves, and of course, flowers; gardenias, jasmine, pikake, plumeria, orchids, *puakinikini*, carnations, and ginger are the favorites. Leis made from the pandanus shrub have been worn since ancient times; they're considered an aphrodisiac, as well as a symbol of love and the end of bad luck.

Mokihana (pictured below) and maile leis are often worn at important ceremonies. Leis made of maile are traditionally worn for special occasions like weddings and graduations. Green mokihana berries (grown in the mountains of Kauai) are added to a lei to confer a special honor—one reserved for newly married couples or special guests. Illustrated here are a few samples of unusual leis:

Lei awapuhi melemele

Lei mauna-loa

Lei mokihana

Lei of mamane, lehua, a ali i, ukae-nene, oa, and palapalai

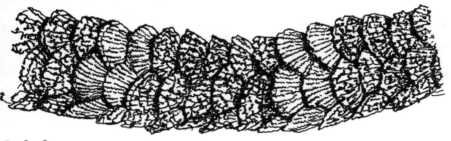

Lei olepe

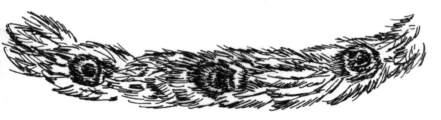

Peacock lei

Lei pupu o Niihau

Tonga lei

47 Pacific Beach Hotel $$$ The 38-story **Ocean Tower** and 17-story **Beach Tower,** across from Kuhio Beach, have 822 rooms and eight suites with ocean, city, and mountain views. Each room has a private lanai, air-conditioning, and refrigerator. Other amenities include a swimming pool, two tennis courts, a 24-hour fitness center, and a Jacuzzi. ◆ 2490 Kalakaua Ave (between Kealohilani and Liliuokalani Aves). 922.1233, 800/367.6060; fax 922.8061 ᕝ

Within the Pacific Beach Hotel:

Oceanarium Restaurant ★$$$ The big attraction is dining alongside what is claimed to be Hawaii's largest indoor oceanarium—three stories of glass holding 280,000 gallons of water and a profusion of colorful sea creatures. Otherwise, it's your basic, unexciting American menu, featuring steaks and seafood. Go for Sunday brunch, which offers more unusual items such as *poke* (raw fish), Portuguese sausages, and sashimi. ◆ Steaks/Seafood ◆ M-Sa breakfast, lunch, and dinner; Su brunch and dinner. Reservations recommended. 922.1233 ᕝ

Shogun ★$$$ This Japanese restaurant is popular among seafood lovers. Sample the shrimp tempura and the *nigiri* (raw fish rolled in sushi), or try the sukiyaki—simple ingredients (meat, broth, vegetables, noodles, eggs) yield surprising results. The trade-off is its pedestrian environment on the third floor of the hotel, with a view of a concrete building. ◆ Japanese ◆ Daily breakfast, lunch, and dinner. Reservations recommended. 922.1233 ᕝ

48 Kuhio Beach Swarming with hundreds of people, this section of Waikiki doesn't boast the clearest water in the world, but it's still great for strolling. Use caution while wading, though; large underwater holes pose an invisible danger. ◆ Off Kalakaua Ave (west of Kapahulu Ave)

49 Damien Museum Granted the museum is a dive, but it still houses some interesting pictures, artifacts, and other possessions of Father Damien. The Belgian priest dedicated his life to the physical and spiritual needs of patients with Hansen's disease (leprosy) who were confined to a colony on the island of Molokai. The museum is run by the Sacred Heart Society, an organization Damien founded. Even if you aren't interested in the displays, it's a great place to park your car for nothing. ◆ Donation. M-F 9AM-3PM. 130 Ohua Ave (between Kalakaua and Kuhio Aves). 923.2690

50 Hawaiian Regent Hotel $$$ A decent but hardly dazzling hotel, except for the impressive lobby and courtyard, this property, which is managed by Otaka Hotels and Resorts, is a sister to the nearby **Hawaiian Waikiki Beach Hotel.** There are 1,346 rooms, many with ocean views, in two towers on more than five acres. Request an oceanside room; the view is spectacular. There are six restaurants, two pools, a tennis court, a nightclub, and a shopping arcade. ◆ 2552 Kalakaua Ave (between Paoakalani and Ohua Aves). 922.6611, 800/367.5370; fax 921.5222 ᕝ

51 Hawaiian Waikiki Beach Hotel $$ For the price and location (near the **Honolulu Zoo Kapiolani Park,** and the **Waikiki Aquarium**), this is one of the better deals in town, with 675 rooms and 40 suites in two towers. After you've visited the nearby attractions, relax in the hotel's pool or take a break in the coffee shop. Rooms are clean but offer only the standard amenities and decor—TVs, phones, air-conditioning, wicker furniture. ◆ 2570 Kalakaua Ave (at Paoakalani Ave). 922.2511, 800/877.7666; fax 923.3656 ᕝ

51 Park Shore Hotel $$ Smack dab on a busy corner, with Kuhio Beach across one street and **Kapiolani Park** across the other, this hotel offers 227 guest rooms, some with kitchenettes and all with private lanais and views of Diamond Head, the park, or the ocean. There's also a small pool, two Japanese restaurants, and a **Denny's.** ◆ 2586 Kalakaua Ave (at Kapahulu Ave). 923.0411, 800/367.2377; fax 923.0311

52 Waikiki Grand Hotel $$ Taking into consideration the rooms (which have a pleasant tropical decor), the location, and the affordable price, this hotel is a bargain if you can live with the noises from the nearby **Honolulu Zoo.** It's relatively small (173 rooms, 17 suites), with a rooftop sundeck and pool and a **Jack in the Box.** ◆ 134 Kapahulu Ave (between Kalakaua Ave and Lemon Rd). 923.1511, 800/535.0085; fax 808/923.4708

53 Honolulu Zoo Building a zoo in Waikiki is like taking coals to Newcastle, but there's one here nonetheless. The usual animals peer out through cages that are covered with vegetation for a tropical jungle effect. The

Children's Zoo lets kids play with goats, llamas, chickens, and the like. Tykes also have a chance to feed Mari, the zoo's only elephant, under the supervision of zookeepers. The **Education Pavilion** stages puppet shows at noon on the first and third Saturdays of the month. Ask about the monthly moonlight walks. The main attraction during summer months is the weekly "Wildest Show in Town," featuring the best local entertainers, including Hookena and the Pandanus Club. The show is immensely popular and, even better, it's free. ◆ Admission; children 5 and under free when accompanied by an adult. Daily 9AM-4:30PM; summer shows Wednesdays at 6PM. 151 Kapahulu Ave (between Paki and Kalakaua Aves). 971.7171 ♿

Within Honolulu Zoo:

Art Mart Twice a week, local artists with varying degrees of expertise set up card tables and prop their wares against the zoo's fence. The predictable ocean sunsets and palm-fringed beaches cover most canvases, although there is the occasional snowy New England scene. It's a pleasant outing, with souvenir potential. ◆ Free. Sa-Su 10AM-4PM. Along Monsarrat Ave ♿

54 Kapiolani Park Hawaii's first public park has been popular since it opened in 1877, a gift from King Kalakaua to the people of Honolulu (in return, he asked that it be named after his wife, Queen Kapiolani). Sprawled across 220 acres in Diamond Head's shadow, it's conveniently close to Waikiki yet away from the roar of the crowd, drawing joggers, softball games, barbecues, and picnics. It also encompasses the **Waikiki Aquarium** and the **Waikiki Shell Amphitheater**. In mid-December it's the site of the finish line of the annual **Honolulu Marathon**, one of the world's largest foot races. ◆ Off Kalakaua Ave (south of Kapahulu Ave). 971.2500

Within Kapiolani Park:

Waikiki Shell Although a variety of performances are staged here, this modern, outdoor theater is best known as the home of the **Kodak Hula Show**. A Waikiki institution, the show premiered in 1937, and some of its original dancers, now in their eighties, still perform. Three mornings a week, nearly 3,000 people wait in line an hour or more for the chance to plop down on bleachers and watch a revue they've probably already seen a dozen times on TV: Hawaiians in G-rated native garb dancing to ukuleles played by *tutus* (grandmothers) wearing bright muumuus and floppy hats. Spectators who volunteer to dance with the performers inevitably provide the most entertainment. ◆ Free. Tu-Th 10AM-11:15AM. 2805 Monsarrat Ave (between Paki and Kalakaua Aves). 591.2211 ♿

WAIKIKI AQUARIUM

54 Waikiki Aquarium The revamped marine museum on 2.3 acres features a 35,000-gallon shark tank; a theater showing two 10-minute video programs; exhibits on monk seals and Hawaiian jellyfish; and the **Reef Machine,** which re-creates a living coral reef. Also here is a mahimahi hatchery, a working aquaculture research center where visitors can observe mahimahi bred on-site. Other tanks display stingrays, butterfly fish, turtles, octopi, live coral, lionfish, a seahorse, and a giant clam—a total of 350 marine species. In 1990 the aquarium became the first in the US (and second in the world) to successfully hatch a chambered nautilus. The **Nautilus Nursery** tank opened that year and furthered the aquarium's renown as a national resource on the rare mollusk. There's a wide range of children's activities, summer reef explorations, music festivals, field trips, workshops, and many other programs. ◆ Admission. Daily. 2777 Kalakaua Ave (south of Kapahulu Ave). 923.9741

55 Sans Souci Beach Park Local families often picnic here, but this crescent of sand, also called "Queen's Beach," is best known as the spot where gay men come to cruise and be cruised. ◆ Off Kalakaua Ave (south of Kapahulu Ave).

56 New Otani Kaimana Beach Hotel $$ A favorite among many repeat visitors, this modest high-rise is in the best part of Waikiki—on historic Sans Souci Beach, where Robert Louis Stevenson sunned himself in the 1890s. The small stretch of white sand offers a refreshing alternative to Waikiki congestion. Hikers and joggers have easy access to **Kapiolani Park** and to the road around the base of Diamond Head, where a lookout offers views of the surfers and windsurfers below. **Kaimana** manager Steve Boyle founded the popular **Diamond Head Climbers Hui,** a club for hikers who've made it to the top of the crater. There are 104 guest rooms and 20 beautiful suites. Some rooms are quite small, but they all have air-conditioning and refrigerators; corner suites have the best views. ◆ 2863 Kalakaua Ave (just south of Sans Souci Beach Park). 921.7017, 800/356.8264; fax 922.9404

Within the New Otani Kaimana Beach Hotel:

Hau Tree Lanai ★★$$$$ A giant 100-year-old *hau* tree serves as a canopy for this open-air dining room. Set right on the ocean's edge, it commands an extraordinary view of the Pacific—come at sunset when the seascape is exceptionally beautiful; Wednesday through Saturday from 6 to 9PM a guitarist serenades diners. Items worth trying include New York steak crusted with blue cheese and served with shiitake mushrooms and fresh *opakapaka* (pink snapper) Chinese style. ♦ American/Continental ♦ Daily breakfast, lunch, and dinner. Reservations recommended. 923.1555

Miyako ★★$$$$ Fine food is served in a pleasant setting, with family-style seating on tatami mats at low tables. The menu includes *shabu-shabu* (cook-it-yourself soup), good tempura, *teppanyaki* items grilled at the table, and a wide variety of other Japanese favorites. ♦ Japanese ♦ Daily dinner. Reservations recommended. 923.1555

56 Colony Surf Hotel $$$$ The 21-story, 90-room hotel was closed for renovations as we went to press. ♦ 2895 Kalakaua Ave (just south of Sans Souci Beach Park). 923.5751; fax 922.8433

Within the Colony Surf Hotel:

Michel's ★★★$$$$ Owned by restaurateur Andy Anderson, who owns the renowned **John Dominis** restaurant (see page 142), this place was featured on "Lifestyles of the Rich and Famous." The dining room has a setting few restaurants can match. Literally on the beach, the oceanside halves of the three large dining rooms are kept completely open except during storms, and diners lucky enough to secure the best tables are within a linen napkin's toss of the beach. The decor is lavish, with candlelight, crystal, and chandeliers. The front-row views of the sunset and Waikiki's glittering lights can prove mesmerizing. The cuisine is supposed to be French, but the menu actually emphasizes local seafood and a legendary rack of lamb. ♦ French/Seafood ♦ Daily dinner. Reservations required. 923.6552 ₺

57 Diamond Head Beach Hotel $$$ A small European-style establishment with 26 suites and 31 luxury rooms, this hotel features fully equipped kitchens (there's no restaurant), complimentary continental breakfast, and lanais overlooking the Pacific. It's a charming hostelry on a minuscule wedge of white sand on Diamond Head Beach. Guests can jog, play tennis and soccer, or fly kites in **Kapiolani Park** just across the street. Ask about the special 50-percent discount. ♦ 2947 Kalakaua Ave (south of Sans Souci Beach Park). 922.1928, 800/367.2317; fax 924.8980

58 Diamond Head Beach Park A narrow, rocky beach stretching for two acres along Diamond Head Road, this beach is dangerous for swimming and surfing and is best used for meditating or fishing. Check out the view from the overlook. The trail leads to tide pools. Although there's unlimited access, parking is tricky. ♦ Beach Rd (off Diamond Head Rd)

59 Diamond Head If you fly into Hawaii, chances are the first thing you'll see (at least if you're seated on the right side of the plane) is this landmark, a volcanic crater that's been dormant for an estimated 150,000 years. Early Hawaiians called it "Leahi" (referring to the forehead of an *ahi* tuna) because its lines resemble the profile of a fish. But when sailors found diamondlike crystals here in the 1800s, they nicknamed it "Diamond Head" (the crystals turned out to be calcite). The crater's walls are 760 feet high; a 40- to 60-minute climb (roughly one mile) up the inside slopes to the top is rewarded by a stunning view of Honolulu. The park is open daily from 6AM until 6PM; bring flashlights for the climb, which goes through a tunnel. Entrance and parking lot off Diamond Head Rd (near 18th Ave)

60 Queen Kapiolani Hibiscus Garden Pathways meander around dozens of varieties of hibiscus, free for the looking but not for picking. This showcase garden thrives on conscientious care from its curator and manure from the nearby **Honolulu Zoo**. ♦ Free. Daily. Off Paki Ave (between Monsarrat and Kapahulu Aves) ₺

Hang Ten

Surfing was introduced to the Hawaiian islands by Polynesians, who brought the sport with them when they migrated from the South Seas around AD 500. Hawaiian chants from the 15th century refer to surfing exploits and contests, and when Captain James Cook arrived on Oahu in 1778, he found Hawaiian men and women riding waves on wooden

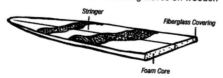

Stringer
Fiberglass Covering
Foam Core

planks and canoe fragments. At that time, surfing was the sport of Hawaiian royalty, who not only got the best surfboards (made of choice lighter woods) but also enjoyed exclusive rights to the top surfing beaches. In fact, commoners who trespassed on the "royal" surfing spots faced the death penalty.

The sport all but disappeared during the missionary era and wasn't

Body Board

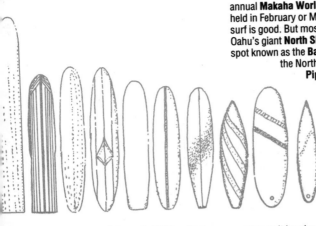

annual **Makaha World Surfing Championships** are held in February or March, depending on when the surf is good. But most of the attention is focused on Oahu's giant **North Shore** waves and a turbulent surf spot known as the **Banzai Pipeline.** Every December the North Shore hosts the **Marui Pipeline Masters,** the **Hard Rock Cafe World Cup of Surfing,** and the **Hawaiian Professional Surfing Classic**—collectively known as the **Triple Crown**—to determine who will reign as the next surfing champion.

Many surfers declare the Banzai Pipeline the home of the perfect wave. The word "pipeline" describes the tube-shaped form a wave

officially reestablished until the early 1900s, when Duke Kahanamoku, a champion Hawaiian swimmer and surfer, formed Waikiki's first surfing club. Kahanamoku was a major force in popularizing surfing throughout the world, demonstrating his prowess in competitions from Atlantic City to Australia.

As new materials were developed, surfboards became lighter and easier to ride. The first "modern" board was made in the mid-1940s from balsa wood sheathed in fiberglass. Today, boards are made of lighter synthetic foam. Professional boards are cut, shaved, and sanded by hand, and are of the highest-quality fiberglass and resin, offering the ultimate in speed and control.

Hawaii's professional surfing events established the foundation for the world circuit, in which the island surfers still reign supreme. In the 1950s the **Makaha International** was the only major worldwide surfing event. Some of Hawaii's prime surfing conditions are still found on **Oahu** at **Makaha Beach,** where the

creates as it breaks; "banzai" is a Japanese war cry favored by the kamikaze surfers who challenge the waves here. Larger tube-shaped waves exist, but none is as ferocious as the pipeline wave during the winter months; it was believed to be unrideable until the 1960s. Surfers tackling a pipeline wave have about 5 to 10 seconds to soar from one end of the tube to the other before they're buried under swirling sand or caught by the "guillotine"— the name for the wave's falling edge (known for breaking surfers' necks). The only thing surfers see as they race through the pipeline is a trickle of light at the other end. If a surfer fails to get through the tube and manages to survive the fall, the next 10 to 60 seconds of hurtling through the water are even more terrifying; once the water starts to pull back, the coral bottom can be a worse enemy than the crashing tube.

Petroglyphs on lava near the Banzai Pipeline suggest that Polynesian surfers were perhaps the first to ride a pipeline wave. However, the first known person to ride a pipeline was Phil Edwards in 1961, and the filmed event, called *String Hollow Days,* was a forerunner of the movie *Endless Summer.* Edwards used a 10-foot board; today the most common boards measure 7 feet and shorter.

If you're eager to test your prowess on the waves, a good way to start learning is by bodyboarding— a combination of bodysurfing and surfing (known in the less hip circles as "boogie-boarding"). The bodyboarder lies down on a three-foot board and rides the waves—an experience that's much easier (and safer) than surfing. If you're ready to try true surfing, however, the widest, longest boards, called mini-tankers, are best for beginners; they catch the waves earlier, giving you more time to get balanced before the wave grows too steep. Many surf shops rent surfboards for beginners and can arrange private lessons.

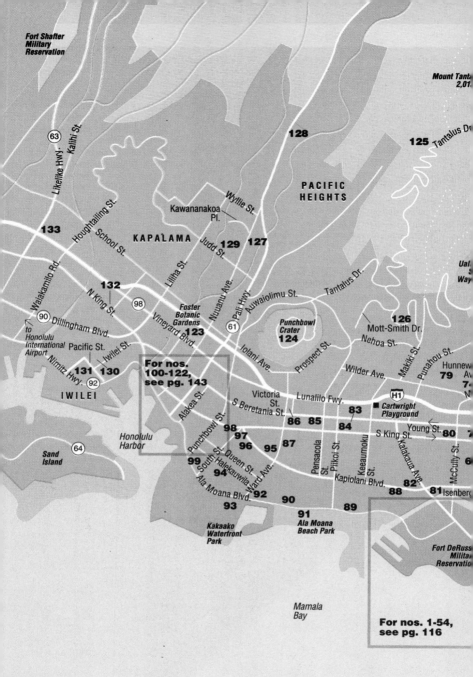

Fort Shafter
Military
Reservation

Mount Tanta
2,01

128

125 Tantalus Dr

Likelike Hwy.

63

Kalihi St.

Houghtailing St.

133

Wyllie St.

Kawananakoa
Pl.

**PACIFIC
HEIGHTS**

KAPALAMA

School St.

Judd St.

129 **127**

Ual
S
Way

Waiakamilo Rd.

132

N King St.

98

Liliha St.

Nuuanu Ave.

Pali Hwy.

Auwaiolimu St.

Tantalus Dr.

126
Mott-Smith Dr.

Nehoa St.

90

Dillingham Blvd.

to
Honolulu
International
Airport

Pacific St.

Foster
Botanic
Gardens

Vineyard Blvd.

123

61

**Punchbowl
Crater**
124

Prospect St.

Wilder Ave.

Makiki St.

Punahou St.

Hunnew
Av

7
N

Nimitz Hwy.

Iwilei St.

131 **130**

92

For nos.
100-122,
see pg. 143

Alakea St.

Iolani Ave.

Victoria
St.

Lunalilo Fwy.

S Beretania St.

H1

■ Cartwright
Playground

IWILEI

Honolulu
Harbor

64

Sand
Island

Punchbowl St.

South St.

Queen St.

Halekauwila

98
97
96

95

99

Ward Ave.

87

86 **85**

84

83

Pensacola
St.

Piikoi St.

Keeaumoku
St.

S King St.

Young St.

80

Kalakaua Ave.

McCully St.

6

94

92

Ala Moana Blvd.

93

Kakaako
Waterfront
Park

90

91
Ala Moana
Beach Park

Kapiolani Blvd.

82

88

89

81 Isenberg

7

For nos. 1-54,
see pg. 116

Fort DeRuss
Milita
Reservatio

Mamala
Bay

Pacific
Ocean

N

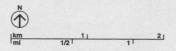
km
mi
1/2   1
1   2

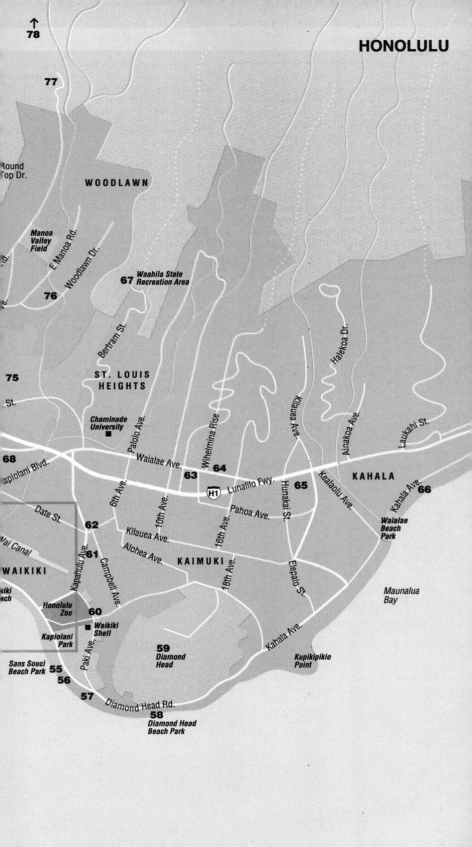

HONOLULU

↑
78

77

Round
Top Dr.

WOODLAWN

Manoa
Valley
Field

E Manoa Rd.

Woodlawn Dr.

76

67 Waahila State
Recreation Area

Bertram St.

Halekoa Dr.

75

St.

**ST. LOUIS
HEIGHTS**

Chaminade
University ■

Patolo Ave.

Wilhelmina Rise

Kilauea Ave.

Ainakoa Ave.

Laukahi St.

68

Kapiolani Blvd.

Waialae Ave.

63 **64**

KAHALA

Date St.

6th Ave.

10th Ave.

H1 Lunalilo Fwy.

Pahoa Ave.

Hunakai St.

65

Kealaolu Ave.

Kahala Ave.

66

Waialae
Beach
Park

62

Kilauea Ave.

16th Ave.

Wai Canal

Kapahulu Ave.

61

Campbell Ave.

Alohea Ave.

KAIMUKI

WAIKIKI

18th Ave.

Elepaio St.

Maunalua
Bay

kiki
ach

Honolulu
Zoo

60

■ Waikiki
Shell

Kapiolani
Park

Paki Ave.

59
Diamond
Head

Kahala Ave.

Kupikipikio
Point

Sans Souci
Beach Park

55

56

57

Diamond Head Rd.

58
Diamond Head
Beach Park

Honolulu

The Honolulu beyond the tourist paradise of **Waikiki** is a modern metropolis, a center of commerce between the Far East and Australia and the United States, and the legislative and executive capital of the 50th state. This is a working city, but it has much of interest to the traveler, such as **Iolani Palace,** the only royal palace in the United States. The historic harbor area, once a seedy sailors' port and now revamped and restored, has a marketplace filled with shops and restaurants, new piers to accommodate giant cruise ships, and a narrated boat tour. There are art and historical museums, cultural centers, parks, botanical gardens, numerous places to shop (including **Ala Moana Shopping Center,** the largest in the state, and the upscale **Tower Marketplace),** and lots of fine places to eat and drink (such as **Restaurant Row,** a collection of trendy eateries near the waterfront).

There's also **Chinatown,** which preserves the traditions of one of the city's major ethnic groups. Centered on **Maunakea Street** and its cross streets, Chinatown's multiracial population actually includes Chinese, Filipinos, Hawaiians, and, more recently, Vietnamese and Laotian immigrants. Urban renewal has provided a face-lift, and the seedy bars, pool halls, and rooming houses are now outnumbered by noodle factories, open-air markets, herb shops, bakeries, clothing and jewelry stores, art galleries, and restaurants.

A tour through Honolulu gives visitors a greater understanding of Hawaii's history, its diverse cultures, and its place in the world today.

61 Bailey's Antiques and Aloha Shirts
Pre-statehood aloha shirts and other clothing combine with antique bottles and local memorabilia to make this a must stop on any souvenir-shopping itinerary. ♦ Daily. 517 Kapahulu Ave (near Herbert St). 734.7628

62 Keo's ★★★$$$ The family that used to own **Mekong** in Honolulu created such a following that they converted this former strip joint into a large, orchid-drenched restaurant. (Owner Keo Sananikone decorates the ornate room with fresh orchids and stalks of jungle greens.) A magnet for celebrities and the otherwise chic, the place is regularly voted in magazine polls as one of Hawaii's most popular restaurants. The menu is enormous. Highlights include Evil Jungle Prince (a blend of chicken, lemongrass, coconut milk, Chinese cabbage, and red chilis), green papaya salad, prawns in a sweet peanut sauce, and delicious spring rolls. Sananikone grows his own herbs, bananas, and produce

on the North Shore. This is a star in the island's ethnic dining scene, and deserving of its fame. ♦ Thai ♦ Daily dinner. Reservations recommended. 625 Kapahulu Ave (between Mooheau Ave and Williams). 737.8240

63 Hale Vietnam ★★$ The specialty here is *pho,* a steamy Vietnamese soup prepared in nearly two dozen ways—and voted the best in town by *Honolulu Magazine. Pho* lovers come here from all over the island to linger over hot bowls of soup or light, piquant spring rolls. ♦ Vietnamese ♦ Daily lunch and dinner. No reservations. 1140 12th Ave (at Waialae Ave). 735.7581

64 3660 On The Rise ★★$$$ Following on the heels of other successful trendy establishments, this small yet elegant restaurant specializes in "Euro-Island" cuisine. Its patrons are for the most part wealthy locals who come for the well-rounded menu of uniquely prepared veal, steak, lamb, and seafood, including farm-raised catfish tempura with *ponzu* sauce (a citrusy soy sauce) and steamed *opakapaka* (pink snapper) with black bean sauce. The location is somewhat removed from the tourist scene, but it's certainly worth the short drive for lunch or dinner. ♦ Pacific Rim ♦ Tu-F lunch and dinner; Sa-Su dinner. 3660 Waialae Ave (at Wilhelmina Rise). 737.1177 ♿

65 Kahala Mall The **Ala Moana Shopping Center** may be larger, but this shopping center has more character. Located in Oahu's wealthiest neighborhood, the mall houses standard merchandisers—**Liberty House, The Gap, Banana Republic,** and **Woolworth** —as well as many unique specialty shops that warrant serious browsing by visitors and residents alike. ♦ Daily. 4211 Waialae Ave (at Kilauea Ave). 732.7736

Within Kahala Mall:

California Pizza Kitchen ★★$$ It serves up exactly the same fare as the Waikiki restaurant, and likewise packs 'em in with pizza and pasta specials. ♦ Pizza/Pasta ♦ Daily lunch and dinner. 737.9446 ♿. Also at: 1910 Ala Moana Blvd (at Ena Rd), Waikiki. 955.5161

Yen King ★$ The specialty is Szechuan cuisine, with nearly a hundred items on the menu, most of which are reasonably priced. If you like spicy dishes, try the garlic chicken, lemon beef, or sizzling rice shrimp. ♦ Chinese ♦ Daily lunch and dinner. 732.5505 ♿

66 Waialae Country Club One of Hawaii's most exclusive and private country clubs is home to the **Hawaiian Open** golf tournament, held every February. Built in 1927 in a then-remote part of Oahu, the flat 18-hole course (par 72, 6,651 yards) borders the ocean and offers vicious doglegs, deep bunkers, and nearly 2,000 palm trees—many of them centuries old—to challenge even the most skilled golfers. ◆ Daily. Members and guests only. 4997 Kahala Ave (east of Kealaolu Ave). 732.1457

66 Kahala Mandarin Oriental Hotel $$$$ Formerly the **Kahala Hilton**, this high-end of high-end Hawaiian resorts underwent a change of ownership and multimillion dollar renovation in 1996 and now is up and running in high style. Designed by **Edward Killingsworth**, the 10-story hotel has 371 rooms and suites, some at the edge of a lagoon filled with large sea turtles, tropical fish, and cavorting bottlenose dolphins (lagoon units must be booked far in advance). Set on six and a half acres well removed from the congestion of Waikiki, it also offers a wide private beach (excellent for swimming) surrounded on three sides by the greenery of the **Waialae Country Club**, a pool, and lush landscaping. Quiet pathways wind through tropical foliage, passing tiny streams, miniature waterfalls, and flowering gardens. Amenities include a fitness center with Jacuzzi, sauna, weights, and massage therapists for ultimate indulgence. Many of the guests are Hollywood stars, producers, agents, and writers who appreciate the privacy here. The staff keeps a record of repeat guests and their preferences. ◆ 5000 Kahala Ave, Kahala. 734.2211, 800/367.2525; fax 739.8800 ♿

Within the Kahala Mandarin Oriental Hotel:

Hoku ★★$$$ Dramatic is the word for this newly renovated Asian restaurant, which features a spectacular ocean view and interesting menu selections such as wok-seared Hawaiian prawns on Asian vegetables with a basket of tomato goat-cheese pesto bread. An open kitchen and sushi and oyster bar add an element of fun, as does a pianist playing jazz during the dinner hour. ◆ Euro-Asian ◆ M-Sa lunch and dinner; Su brunch and dinner. Reservations recommended. 734.2211

67 Waahila State Recreation Area Residents who want to escape the heat drive to this cool, elevated retreat at the top of residential St. Louis Heights. Picnic facilities (including barbecue grills) are available under the Norfolk pines and ironwoods, and there's a great strawberry guava grove that's open to all pickers when the fruit is in season. ◆ At the end of Bertram St

Hail to the Chiefs

In 1795, after years of civil war, the Hawaiian Islands (except **Kauai** and **Niihau**) were united under Kamehameha the Great (Kamehameha I). His ascension to the throne gave birth to a dynasty that would last nearly a century and forever change the way of life of his subjects. After his death in 1819, Kamehameha the Great was succeeded by seven monarchs; the last was Queen Liliuokalani, the first female ruler of Hawaii, overthrown in 1893. Here is a list of Hawaii's mighty monarchs and the years they ruled the islands:

Kamehameha I (1795-1819)

Kamehameha II (1819-24)

Kamehameha III (1825-54)

Kamehameha IV (1855-63)

Kamehameha V (1863-72)

William C. Lunalilo (1873-74)

David Kalakaua (1874-91)

Liliuokalani (1891-93)

68 Down to Earth Natural Foods Store Everything from fresh organic produce to "Tom's of Maine" toothpaste is stocked in this natural foods store, including a fine selection of vitamins, pasta, Indian chutney, grains, nuts, greeting cards, health-conscious cosmetics, cheese, and other products sold in bulk. Within the store is the **Down to Earth Deli**, a vegetarian mecca dispensing healthful salads, chili, tabbouleh, pastries, and pastas. It's de rigueur to bring your own bag for groceries. ◆ Daily 8AM to 10PM. 2525 S King St (between Kapaakea La and Hausten St). 947.7678 ♿

69 Maple Garden ★★$ A longtime favorite for spicy Mandarin and Szechuan cuisine, this establishment is usually crowded and noisy with chatter and platter-clatter. Specialties include smoked Szechuan duck and eggplant with spicy garlic sauce. ◆ Chinese ◆ Daily lunch and dinner. Reservations recommended. 909 Isenberg St (between Kapiolani Blvd and S King St). 941.6641 &

70 Chiang Mai Northern Thai Restaurant ★★★$$ If you didn't know about this Honolulu find, you'd never notice it among the other glitzier options. Don't let the innocuous storefront exterior deceive you—inside all is simple and serene. Stop in for papaya salad, Cornish game hen, or a plate of curried local fish, and find out why many locals are having their mail forwarded here. ◆ Thai ◆ M-F lunch; daily dinner. Reservations recommended. 2239 S King St (between Isenberg St and Makahiki Way). 941.1151 &

71 Quilts Hawaii Hawaiian quilts are the specialty here, most of them in the four-digit price range. There's also a smattering of other Hawaiiana, including fine koa furniture and bowls, handbags, jewelry, pillows, and quilt kits. ◆ M-Sa. 2338 S King St (between Isenberg St and Hoawa La). 942.3195 &

71 India Bazaar Madras Cafe ★$ You've probably had better Indian food, but this is a decent deal (it's popular with college students, if that's a clue). There are six entrées to choose from: four vegetarian selections and two chicken curries with rice; all come with a choice of two vegetable side dishes. ◆ Indian ◆ Daily lunch and dinner. No credit cards accepted. 2320 S King St (between Isenberg St and Hoawa La). 949.4840 &

72 Philip Paolo's ★★$$ One of Honolulu's better Italian restaurants is found in a remodeled colonial-style house with wood floors, high ceilings, and a patio overlooking the garden. Menu highlights include chicken Marsala, oven-baked fish, and steak Capri. ◆ Italian ◆ Tu-Su lunch and dinner. Reservations recommended. 2312 S Beretania St (between Isenberg and Griffiths Sts). 946.1163

73 Anna Bannana's ★$ During the day you'll still see the occasional Harley-Davidson motorcycle parked in front of this unpretentious social pub. In the 1960s and 1970s, it was the hangout for beer-guzzling students from the nearby university campus. Now, it's better known for serious dartboard tournaments and substantial and colorfully named sandwiches like the Rick Nelson (roast beef with melted cheese, dijon mustard, cream cheese, and bean sprouts) and Gary's Superturkey (sliced turkey with bacon bits, cheese, and salad dressing). Reggae bands play to a crowded house Friday and Saturday nights, and there's live blues and rock music on Thursday and Sunday evenings. It's also a great place to use the rest room (you'll see). ◆ American ◆ Cover after 9PM. Daily 11AM-2AM. 2440 S Beretania St (between Kaialiu and Isenberg Sts). 946.5190

74 Manoa Valley Inn $$ Under the direction of T-shirt magnate Rick Ralston (owner of the local **Crazy Shirts** chain), this two-story 1920s structure survived impending destruction and was designated a historical home. Ralston furnished the inn, which consists of seven bedrooms and a cottage, from his extensive collection of antiques and period furnishings, including brass beds. Marc Resorts took over the inn in 1994; while not up to its former splendor in terms of service and comfort, it continues to offer guests continental breakfast, afternoon cheese, wine, and fruit, and other amenities—though there's no restaurant. It's precariously close to the bustling university, there's no pool, and not all rooms have TVs and phones. Still, the inn is a good choice for the price and the ambience. ◆ 2001 Vancouver Dr (west of University Ave). 947.6019, 800/535.0085; fax 946.6168

75 University of Hawaii (UH) Probably the ugliest collection of unrelated architectural styles in Hawaii is on the university's 300-acre campus, although the extensive landscaping provides some relief. The center for higher education opened in 1908 with 12 teachers and five full-time students. Now 20,000 full-time students attend the Manoa campus, with another 30,000 enrolled at the Hilo campus and in the university's statewide community college system. The university earned its reputation with strong international studies, marine biology, tropical agriculture, and oceanography programs, along with specialized programs in the travel industry and hotel management. It's also in the forefront of astronomy research and the world search for alternative energy sources. ◆ 2444 Dole St (between St. Louis Heights and University Ave). 956.8111

Within the University of Hawaii:

East-West Center In 1960 this institution and the surrounding 21 acres were dedicated by Congress to promote better relations, both cultural and technical, between the US and the countries of Asia and the Pacific. Funded by various nations and private companies, the center contains several artistic treasures from the Far East, including murals, paintings, sculptures, and tapa hangings from China, Korea, Thailand, and Japan in the exhibition hall. Friends of the **East-West Center** offer hour-long tours by appointment, or you're welcome to browse solo. Be sure to stroll through the landscaped grounds; look for the Japanese garden. ♦ Free. M-F. 1601 East-West Dr. 944.7111 ⌖

76 Coffee Manoa ★$ A popular gathering place for university students, this small cafe sells dozens of varieties of coffee beans. Or, if you prefer, you can take home a bag of your favorite gourmet blend ground on the premises. Banana poi and ginger pumpkin muffins are available, as well as other breads, scones, and assorted pastries. ♦ Cafe ♦ M-F breakfast, lunch, and dinner; Sa-Su breakfast and lunch. Manoa Marketplace, 2752 Woodlawn Dr (between Kaloaluiki and Kolowalu Sts). 988.5113 ⌖

77 Lyon Arboretum Taro, orchids, bromeliads, ferns, cinnamon, coco, koa, kava, palms, coffee, yams, bananas, and hundreds of other plant species can be found in these lush botanical gardens, only a short drive from downtown Honolulu. The arboretum is closely associated with Beatrice Krauss, an ethno-botanist who has taught here for decades. Crafts, gardening, and cooking workshops, plant sales, special outings, and many other activities are offered here, and mosquito repellent is provided. Also on the property are a bookstore and a gift shop. ♦ Donation. M-Sa 9AM-3PM for self-guided tours. One-hour guided tours are offered on the third Saturday of the month at 10AM. Reservations required for guided tours. 3860 Manoa Rd (in the Honolulu Watershed Forest Reserve). 988.7378

78 Manoa Falls Tired of the Waikiki hustle? Escape to this cool, quiet forest fragrant with ginger and tropical blooms. It's the perfect place for a long picnic followed by a swim in the freshwater pool underneath the falls. To get here, take the trail that begins at the end of Manoa Road (look for the brown trail marker and park just past it). It's about a 30-minute hike (one mile) to the falls. ♦ Waihi Stream (seven-tenths of a mile north of Lyon Arboretum).

79 Punahou School Hawaii's most famous private school opened in 1841 for children whose parents were Congregationalist missionaries and Hawaiian *alii* (royalty). The grounds were donated by Queen Kaahumanu, Kamehameha I's favorite wife and one of the mission's noteworthy converts. The alumni list reads like a *Who's Who of Hawaii*, and new generations of missionary descendants,

joined by Honolulu's nouveau riche, perpetuate the exclusivity of the kindergarten through high-school enrollment. ♦ 1601 Punahou St (at Wilder Ave). 944.5711

80 King Tsin ★★$$ The Joseph Wang family oversees the kitchen, which specializes in remarkably creative Szechuan dishes. Try the beggar's chicken baked in clay pots (half-day advance notice is required), or if you're not planning that far ahead, the spare ribs in orange-honey sauce. ♦ Chinese ♦ Daily lunch and dinner. 1110 McCully St (between S King and Young Sts). 946.3273

81 Hard Rock Cafe ★★$$ Like all restaurants of the same name, this place seems to sell more T-shirts than dinners. It's all here—loud music, central bar, wood and brass decor—but Hawaiian icons (surfboards) are mixed in with the rock 'n' roll memorabilia (including John Lennon's Starfire 12 guitar). The all-American fare—Texas-style ribs, barbecued chicken, chili, burgers, and steaks—is served carhop style. Don't bother looking for free parking; it's not worth the trouble. ♦ American ♦ Daily lunch and dinner. No reservations. 1837 Kapiolani Blvd (between McCully St and Kalakaua Ave). 955.7383 ⌖

82 Hawaii Convention Center The construction in progress at the intersection of Kapiolani and Kalakaua Avenues at the site of the old **Aloha Motors** dealership will one day be the $200-million, million-square-foot convention center that Hawaii's politicos have been fighting either for or against for the last decade. Designed by prominent local architects **Wimberly, Allison, Tong and Goo**, in tandem with a Seattle firm, the center will have an exhibit hall, ballroom, theaters, alfresco courtyards, and dozens of meeting spaces. Completion is expected by 1998. ♦ Kapiolani Blvd and Kalakaua Ave

83 Mekong I ★★★$ The first of a now well-established family-run chain, this tiny restaurant offers a long list of Thai specialties. Those who come here are strictly interested in the menu, which includes curries, spring rolls, ginger fish, satays, and Evil Jungle Prince (a blend of chicken, lemongrass, coconut milk, Chinese cabbage, and red chilis). Alcohol isn't served, but you're welcome to bring beer or wine. ♦ Thai ♦ M-F lunch; daily dinner. No reservations. 1295 S Beretania St (between Keeaumoku and Piikoi Sts). 591.8841 ⌖

Restaurants/Clubs: Red   Hotels: Blue
Shops/ Outdoors: Green   Sights/Culture: Black

139

83 Sada Restaurant ★★$$$ You can order off the Japanese menu, but most folks come for the sushi, prepared with the freshest fish and seafood (though the sake doesn't hurt either). The quality can be inconsistent, but on a good night, it's one of the best sushi bars in town. ♦ Japanese ♦ Daily lunch and dinner. 1240 S King St (between Keeaumoku and Piikoi Sts). 949.0646

84 Wisteria ★$$ A longtime local favorite, this is one of those word-of-mouth places you'd never discover on your own. The cuisine is Japanese (sushi, shrimp tempura), with some American selections (spaghetti, barbecued chicken). Don't try to get in on a Friday night without reservations. ♦ Japanese/American ♦ Daily breakfast, lunch, and dinner. Reservations required Friday nights only. 1206 S King St (at Piikoi St). 531.9276 &

85 Auntie Pasto's ★$$ If you're in the mood for a quiet, relaxing dinner, keep looking. But if you want decent Italian food at very reasonable prices and are willing to endure some noise, this is the place (voted "Best Place for a Meal under $15" by *Honolulu Magazine*). Start with an order of basil bread, then try the eggplant Parmesan or fish stew. Save room for the delicious mud pie. ♦ Italian ♦ M-F lunch and dinner; Sa, Su dinner. 1099 S Beretania St (at Pensacola St). 523.8855

86 Honolulu Academy of Arts The 30 galleries here display world-renowned European and American masterpieces, a permanent Oriental collection, and the best of Hawaii's art. The handsome, tile-roofed building, which opened as a museum in 1927, encloses landscaped courtyards filled with plants and sculptures. The academy was founded by avid art collector Mrs. Charles Montague Cooke, whose family home had been on this site. New York architect **Bertram Goodhue** designed the structure, a blend of Hawaiian, Oriental, and Western styles. ♦ Donation requested. Tu-Sa 10AM-4:30PM; Su 1PM-5PM. Tours are offered Tuesdays through Saturdays at 11AM and Sundays at 1PM. 900 S Beretania St (between Victoria St and Ward Ave). 532.8700; fax 532.8787 &

Within the Honolulu Academy of Arts:

Garden Cafe ★$ This canopied cafe serves commendable but modestly sized salads, sandwiches, and bowls of soup for lunch, but since it's a fund-raising venture for the academy, operated mostly by volunteers, who would dare complain about quantity, especially in such a pleasant garden setting, surrounded by sculptures and hanging plants? (A bonus: the volunteers often share family recipes with the cafe; try the warm goat cheese sandwich, for example.) ♦ Cafe ♦ Tu-Sa lunch. Reservations recommended. 532.8734 &

87 Neal S. Blaisdell Center (NBC) Formerly the **Honolulu International Center (HIC)**, this $12.5-million complex was renamed in the 1970s for a popular Honolulu mayor who served from 1955 to 1968. The 8,000-capacity arena plays host to basketball, boxing, and sumo wrestling, as well as conventions, rock concerts, circuses, ballet performances, and major theatrical productions. ♦ 777 Ward Ave (between Kapiolani Blvd and S King St). 591.2211 &

88 Ala Moana Hotel $$ At 36 stories high, this 1,169-room hotel is the tallest building in the state. Better yet, it's linked by a footbridge to the **Ala Moana Shopping Center** (see below). The rooms feature such nice extras as Jacuzzi tubs, lanais, and Japanese robes. There's also a pool, sundeck, and business center. ♦ 410 Atkinson Dr (at Mahukona St). 955.4811, 800/367.6025; fax 947.7388 &

Within the Ala Moana Hotel:

Royal Garden ★★$$ Traditional Chinese fare (try the lobster with garlic sauce, the Peking duck, or the shark fin soup) is served until very late at night in this eatery, a favorite among local Chinese-Americans. For lunch, the waitresses cart dim sum from table to table. ♦ Chinese ♦ Daily lunch and dinner. Third floor. 942.7788 &

Nicholas Nickolas ★★$$$$ Enjoy fabulous views of Waikiki while dining on steak or seafood. Fish lovers should consider the *opakapaka* (pink snapper) with lemon butter and capers or the *ahi* (tuna) with spinach, feta cheese, and hollandaise sauce. This is among the most popular places for sophisticated after-dinner dancing, nightly until 3AM. ♦ Continental ♦ Daily dinner. Reservations required. 36th floor. 955.4466

89 Ala Moana Shopping Center The granddaddy of all malls, this is the largest shopping complex in the state, with more than 200 stores and restaurants and four levels of open-air walkways alongside carp-filled ponds. When it opened in 1959, it was the biggest shopping center in the world. **Palm Boulevard,** on the upper level, is its snobby subsection, a mini-version of Beverly Hills' Rodeo Drive, with **Chanel, Gucci, Dior, Tiffany & Co.,** and **Cartier.** Other stores include **The Nature Company, Sharper Image, Ralph Lauren, Benetton,** and **Crazy Shirts,** a locally owned chain of T-shirt shops. **Liberty House,** the major local department store, and **Sears** are the anchors. Among the interesting gift and crafts shops are **Hawaiian**

Island Creations and **Irene's Hawaiian Gifts.** The center is slated for renovation; a new wing will be added (look for **Nordstrom's** to anchor it), as well as more space for parking. More than 60 million shoppers come here every year, and state residents pile in from the outer islands to shop, but you may find it no more interesting than your local mall. ◆ Daily. Free parking. 1450 Ala Moana Blvd (between Atkinson Dr and Piikoi St). 946.2811 ♿

Within the Ala Moana Shopping Center:

Makai Market $ If hunger strikes while you're shopping, stop at this carnival of fast-food establishments. Among the tasty choices are pizzas at **Sbarro's,** Korean plate lunches at **Yummy's,** Cantonese cuisine at **Patti's Chinese Kitchen,** Szechuan favorites at **Panda's,** and much more, including Japanese and Thai food to go, hot dogs, hamburgers, deli items, baked potatoes, and salads. ◆ Fast food ◆ Daily. Street level

Byron II Steak House ★$$$$ Grilled New York steak is the best choice on the menu at this business-lunch hangout. It's the only true restaurant at the shopping center and stays open even after the stores have closed. ◆ Steaks ◆ Daily lunch and dinner. Reservations recommended. Street level. 949.8855 ♿

90 Ward Centre Located on the Diamond Head side of **Ward Warehouse** (see page 142), this trendy mall has restaurants and fast-food establishments upstairs and almost three dozen shops downstairs. ◆ Daily. 1200 Ala Moana Blvd (between Auahi St and Kamakee Sts). 591.8411 ♿

Within Ward Centre:

Keo's Thai Cuisine ★★$$ Another offshoot of Keo Sananikone's restaurant dynasty, this establishment offers patrons a choice of dining in an air-conditioned room or in the open-air courtyard amid orchids and Thai art. The menu offers a limited selection compared to Sananikone's popular Kapahulu establishment, but it's still a pleasant place to enjoy Evil Jungle Prince (a popular entrée of chicken, lemongrass, coconut milk, Chinese cabbage, and red chilis), spring rolls, and Danang seafood curry. ◆ Thai ◆ M-Sa lunch and dinner; Su dinner. First level. 596.0020

Honolulu Chocolate Company The owners fill their largest shop with toys (including stuffed animals they make themselves), gift boxes, preserves, teas, and sinful sweets. Indulge in the apricots or ginger dipped in dark chocolate, truffles, liqueur-flavored candies, macadamia turtles, and more. ◆ Daily. First level. 591.2997 ♿. Also at: Restaurant Row, 500 Ala Moana Blvd (between South and Punchbowl Sts). 528.4033 ♿

Borders Books & Music *Honolulu Weekly* readers voted this the best new store in town

in 1996—and for good reason. More than 150,000 books and 50,000 CDs and cassettes line the shelves at this branch of the national chain; there's even a coffeehouse upstairs where friends and family members can go for refuge while the book buyer browses.◆ M-Th 9AM-11PM, Fri-Sa 9AM-12PM, Su 9AM-9PM First level. 591.8995

Mocha Java Espresso & Fountain ★$ With a wide selection of gourmet blends and pastries, this is the best coffeehouse in the area. The espresso milk shakes are great for an afternoon boost. In addition, the expanded menu includes treats like dijon chicken crepes and whole wheat tortillas with beans, garlic, eggs, cheese, potatoes, green peppers, and onions. ◆ Coffeehouse ◆ M-Sa breakfast, lunch, and dinner; Su breakfast and lunch. First level. 597.8121 ♿

A Pacific Cafe Oahu ★★★$$$ Jean-Marie Josselin's first eatery, on Kauai, was such a runaway hit that he and wife Sophie, who designed the restaurant, have expanded to three islands. The ceiling of this uptown eatery is curved and colored to resemble a wave, the furnishings are bamboo, and the overall ambience is one of sophisticated languor. Signature dishes include tower of lamb loin with pine nut and watercress crust, and grilled Portobello mushroom and roasted baby vegetable risotto with smoky tomato broth at dinner; Vietnamese noodle soup with shrimp miso, Hawaiian fish, and tempura shrimp for lunch; and firecracker salmon rolls with tsukemono salad and hot-and-sour dip *pupus* (appetizers). Much of the produce used in Josselin's culinary creations comes from his organic garden on Kauai.◆ Hawaiian Regional ◆ M-F lunch, daily dinner. Reservations recommended. Second level. 593.0035

Compadres Mexican Bar and Grill ★$$ Enjoy a pitcher of margaritas with complimentary tortilla chips and salsa. A few fish and American entrées have slipped onto the basically Mexican menu, and you can't go wrong ordering the all-American burger or the *pollo* burger (broiled chicken sandwich), which come with a huge pile of curly fries. Specialties include baby back ribs and *pollo borracho* (literally "drunk chicken"—chicken cured in tequila, rock salt, and herbs for 24 hours and grilled to a crisp). Live music is featured on Thursday and Friday nights. ◆ Mexican ◆ Daily lunch and dinner. Second level. 591.8307 ♿

Ryan's Bar & Grill ★$$ Extremely popular for the affordable menu, which includes sandwiches (we like the Thai chicken one), fish, salads, pastas (opt for rigatoni basillica, with sweet peppers, sausage, and seasoned ricotta), and *pupus* (appetizers), this restaurant is also a well-known singles bar, with a wide selection of beer and fresh oyster shooters. ♦ American ♦ Daily lunch and dinner. Reservations recommended. Second level. 591.9132 ⧉

91 Ala Moana Beach Park Protected by an offshore reef, this beach is safe for swimming year-round, with lifeguards on duty during peak hours. It's also equipped with picnic facilities, public bathrooms, a snack stand, and tennis courts. ♦ Ala Moana Park Dr (off Ala Moana Blvd)

92 Ward Warehouse A variety of family restaurants (everything from pizza and sandwiches to seafood), boutiques, and specialty stores are found in this two-story mall. ♦ M-Sa 10AM-9PM; Su 10AM-5PM. 1050 Ala Moana Blvd (between Kamakee St and Ward Ave). 591.8411 ⧉

Within the Ward Warehouse:

The Old Spaghetti Factory ★$ Part of the popular mainland chain, this is the perfect place for feasting on inexpensive carbohydrates. ♦ Italian ♦ Daily lunch and dinner. Second level. 591.2513 ⧉

Dynasty II Restaurant ★$$ Gourmet Chinese dishes such as shark fin soup and chicken with black bean sauce are served in an elegant setting of rosewood furniture and pink tablecloths. There are two **Dynasty** restaurants under the same ownership; the other is a smaller and simpler establishment, so don't confuse them when making reservations. ♦ Chinese ♦ Daily lunch and dinner. Reservations recommended. Second level. 531.0208 ⧉ Also at: Discovery Bay Center, 1778 Ala Moana Blvd (at Hobron La), Waikiki. 947-3771 ⧉

Nohea Gallery This eclectic gallery features crafts by Hawaiian artists. You'll find paintings, lithographs, ceramics, sculpture, woodwork, glasswork, prints, and jewelry. ♦ Daily. First level. 596.0074 ⧉

Pomegranates in the Sun Innovative island clothing and jewelry designs are carried here, plus a small selection of children's clothes. *Honolulu Magazine* awarded the boutique top marks for its variety of excellent merchandise. ♦ M-F 10AM-9PM; Sa 10AM-5M. First level. 591.2208 ⧉

93 John Dominis ★★$$$$ Named after an early governor of Oahu, the oceanside restaurant beckons from a spectacular point in Kewalo Basin; floor-to-ceiling windows showcase the exceptional view (if you can stop gawking at an indoor lagoon filled with stingrays and manta rays). Loyal customers return for the variety of fish and seafood, definitively prepared by chef Greg Paulson. Favorites include the fish-and-prawns dish and the macadamia cream pie. This restaurant is also a fabulous, albeit high-priced, choice for Sunday brunch, with omelettes, pasta, and waffles prepared to order at different food bars. ♦ Seafood ♦ Daily dinner; Su brunch. Reservations recommended. 43 Ahui St (between Olomehani St and Ala Moana Blvd). 523.0955 ⧉

94 Hawaiian Bagel ★$ This modest bagel factory bakes them as fresh as they get. Sandwiches, quiche, and a limited selection of deli items are also available. ♦ Bagels/Deli ♦ M-Sa breakfast and lunch. No reservations. No credit cards. 753-B Halekauwila St (between Ahui and South Sts). 596.0638 ⧉

95 Yanagi Sushi ★★★$$ Serving some of the freshest sashimi and sushi in Hawaii, the shoji-screened restaurant packs in locals as well as tourists and celebrities (photos and autographs of the latter adorn the walls). ♦ Sushi bar ♦ Daily lunch and dinner. Reservations recommended. 762 Kapiolani Blvd (between Ward Ave and Cooke St). 537.1525 ⧉

96 Columbia Inn ★$ Every city has a spot that caters to the media, and this is Honolulu's. Adjacent to the **News Building,** which houses both of the state's daily papers, the restaurant and bar opened the day the Japanese bombed Pearl Harbor. Journalists and public relations people choose from the mixed menu of basic American and Japanese cuisine, with assorted local favorites thrown in for good measure. Order a burger, saimin (a spicy noodle soup), or the sizzling steak platter. Kids eat free on Mondays and Tuesdays. ♦ Japanese/American ♦ Daily breakfast, lunch, and dinner. No reservations. 645 Kapiolani Blvd (at Curtis St), Honolulu. 596.0757 ⧉

97 News Building Home of Hawaii's two daily newspapers, this green building with a red-tile roof is also a gallery where local artists' work is shown. Liberty Newspapers runs the *Honolulu Star-Bulletin,* the afternoon publication, and Gannett Corporation owns the *Honolulu Advertiser,* the more successful morning paper. ♦ Free. Open to the public M. 605 Kapiolani Blvd (at South St). 525.8000 ⧉

98 Mission Houses Museum The first frame house in the islands was built in 1821 for newly arrived Congregationalist missionaries. Two coral-block buildings were soon added to the prim white-frame structure: the **Frame House**

is where printer Elisha Loomis established Hawaii's first press; the **Chamberlain House** was for the mission's purchasing agent. Now operated by the **Hawaiian Mission Children's Society** (descendants of the missionaries), **Mission Houses Museum** is a repository of mementos from Hawaii's early history. A visitors' center houses a gift shop, a library holds a substantial collection of Hawaiiana, and a 14-minute video tells the story (part of it, anyway) of Hawaii's past. ♦ Admission (includes a 45-minute guided tour). Tu-Sa 9AM-4PM. 553 S King (at Kawaiahao St). 531.0481

99 Restaurant Row The selection of trendy restaurants and bars near the Honolulu waterfront make this an "in" place for discriminating singles and yuppies. ♦ 500 Ala Moana Blvd (between South and Punchbowl Sts)

Within Restaurant Row:

Sunset Grill ★★$$ The noise level tends to get out of hand in this high-ceilinged restaurant, but that hasn't made it any less popular, especially for lunch. The menu offers a pleasant selection of pasta, salads, grilled fish, and meat, with tempting appetizers to start. Try the mozzarella cakes, Anaheim peppers, and roasted garlic and goat cheese. And if you've room for dessert, treat yourself to an ice-cream concoction. Sunday brunch is bright and cheery with eggs, waffles, pancakes, and pasta. ♦ Pacific Rim ♦ M-Sa lunch and dinner; Su brunch and dinner. 521.4409 ♿

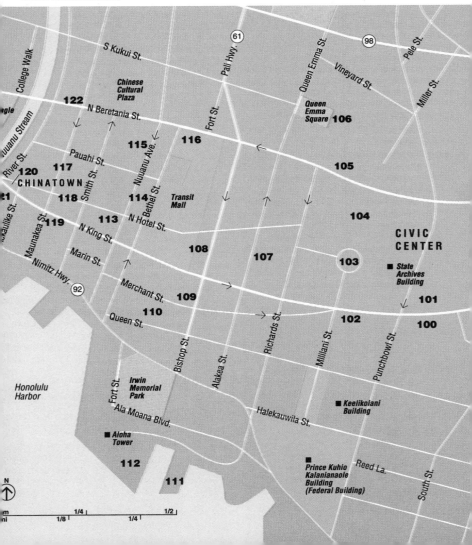

Ruth's Chris Steak House ★★$$$$
Twenty-four-ounce T-bone steaks and 14-ounce ribeyes as well as other entrées like chicken breast broiled with lemon and herbs are served in an atmosphere enhanced by padded booths and white linen. Everything is à la carte, so dinner can get pricey real quick. ♦ Steaks ♦ Daily dinner. Reservations recommended. 599.3860 ♿

100 Kawaiahao Church Completed in 1842, more than 20 years after the first New England missionaries arrived aboard the *Thaddeus,* this handsome structure took five years to build, using 14,000 coral blocks that the congregation cut from ocean reefs. The walls of **Kawaiahao,** which means "freshwater pool of Hao" (the ancient spring), have witnessed royal marriages, coronations, and funerals. The 10:30AM Sunday service, conducted in Hawaiian and English, is noted for its stirring sermons, first-rate choir, and organ music. Visitors may take a self-guided tour. ♦ Open daily; call for hours. 957 Punchbowl St (at S King St). 522.1333

On the grounds of the Kawaiahao Church:

King Lunalilo's Tomb The tomb can be seen near the entrance to the church. Lunalilo was the only Hawaiian monarch who refused to be interred in the **Royal Mausoleum** in Nuuanu Valley, asking on his deathbed to be buried closer to his people at **Kawaiahao**. The churchyard is also the resting place of several missionaries and converts.

101 Honolulu Hale (Honolulu City Hall) The gracious California Spanish-style design of the city hall, built in 1929, provides a nice contrast to **Iolani Palace** and the **State Capitol** (see below). Italian sculptor Mario Valdastri designed the bronze-sheeted front doors, which weigh 1,500 pounds each; the 4,500-pound chandeliers in the terra-cotta–tiled courtyard, patterned after one in the 13th-century Bargello Palace in Florence, Italy; and the columns and balconies made of coral and crushed Hawaiian sandstone. Two three-story wings in the original style were added in the early 1950s. A belt of green space links the city hall to the colonial-style **Mission Memorial** buildings and the gray concrete **Honolulu Municipal Building.** ♦ 530 S King St (at Punchbowl St). 523.4385

102 King Kamehameha I Statue The gold-and-black statue of the spear-carrying chief wearing a feather cloak and helmet (see illustration on page 137) stands outside **Aliiolani Hale** (the State Judiciary Building). King Kamehameha I, who conquered and then united the islands, is regarded as Hawaii's greatest warrior. This statue is a replica, however; the original stands in front of the **Kapaau Courthouse** in Kohala on the Big Island, where Kamehameha was born and reared and where he first came to power. Visit

here in June during the King Kamehameha Day celebration, when the statue's outstretched arms are filled with dozens of leis. ♦ 417 S King St (between Punchbowl and Mililani Sts)

103 Iolani Palace In an attempt to keep the highly polished Douglas fir floors scuff-free, America's only royal palace (pictured on page 145) provides guests with booties to cover their shoes. The palace, whose name means "the hawk of heaven," epitomizes King Kalakaua's preoccupation with emulating the royal courts of Europe. Aptly nicknamed "The Merry Monarch," Kalakaua had a penchant for surrounding himself with material goods. With construction costs topping $360,000, the palace was completed in 1882, eight years after Kalakaua was crowned king. The design, the work of architects **Thomas J. Baker, Isaac Moore,** and **C. J. Wall,** provided the perfect backdrop for Kalakaua's elaborate court life. The palace was filled with period furniture shipped around Cape Horn or painstakingly copied by local artisans. Royal guards were outfitted in dazzling uniforms that weighed entirely too much for the tropics.

Following Kalakaua's death in 1891 and the coup that toppled the monarchy in 1893, the palace became Hawaii's seat of government. Until 1969, when the new **State Capitol** (see below) was built, the Senate met in the palace's royal dining room and the House of Representatives in the throne room. Since then, some $6 million has been spent restoring the palace to its former glory. The nonprofit **Friends of Iolani Palace** conducts 45-minute tours. ♦ Admission. Tours W-Sa 9AM-2:15PM, every 15 minutes. Reservations recommended. 364 S King St (between Punchbowl and Richards Sts). 522.0822 ♿

103 Iolani Banyan What appears to be a massive tree is really two banyans that have been intertwined for a century. Said to have been planted by Queen Kapiolani, the banyan provides a shady canopy for passersby. ♦ Between the State Archives Building and Iolani Palace

103 Coronation Bandstand King Kalakaua wanted a fitting site for his coronation, so in 1883 he built this gazebo and crowned himself and Queen Kapiolani in a lavish ceremony. The copper dome of the wedding cake–like pavilion is the original, but the rest of the structure was rebuilt of concrete after termites had weakened it. Eight pillars symbolizing Hawaii's major islands support the dome. Kalakaua was the only king crowned here, but the bandstand also serves as a stage for gubernatorial inaugurations and weddings. In 1993 it was the site of a Hawaiian sovereignty rally, which drew thousands of spectators. Each Friday, the Royal Hawaiian Band, established in 1836 by King Kamehameha II, gives a free concert at noon. ♦ On the grounds of Iolani Palace

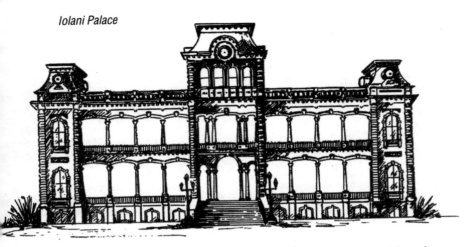

Iolani Palace

04 Queen Liliuokalani Statue Hawaii's last monarch is memorialized in a bronze sculpture at the entrance to the **State Capitol**, where she was imprisoned following her overthrow. Unveiled in 1982, the eight-foot statue by Marianne Pineda shows the queen standing erect, her left hand holding the proposed constitution of 1893 (which cost her the throne) and a page of "Aloha Oe," the islands' traditional song of farewell. Her right hand is extended in friendship. ♦ S Beretania St (between Punchbowl and Richards Sts)

104 State Capitol Designed to take advantage of the views of the ocean, city, and mountains, the capitol (pictured above) features a four-story atrium that lets natural light fill the center of the structure. The interior trim, paneling, and furnishings are koa wood, and the courtyard is paved with Molokai sand, a nice Hawaiian touch. The state legislature and the governor moved into the $24.5-million building in 1969, after being headquartered in **Iolani Palace**. The sign on the governor's doors reads *E komo mai* (Please come in). Visitors are free to sit in on regular sessions of the Senate and the House of Representatives, which are held from January through April. While the laws of parliamentary procedure are followed on the floor, proper English tends to crumble in favor of local pidgin (Hawaiian slang) during heated debates. The capitol's most festive occasion is the traditional opening of the legislature the third Wednesday of every January. On that day, both the legislators and their desks are covered with flowers and leis. Morning festivities include hula dancing, songs, and even comedy

routines by leading island entertainers. At noon, everyone adjourns to lavish buffets. ♦ Open to the public M-F; courtyard open daily 24 hours. 415 S Beretania St (between Punchbowl and Richards Sts). 586.2211 &

104 Father Damien Statue Belgian priest Damien Joseph de Veuster, who has been nominated for sainthood, lived and worked among the lepers of Molokai for 16 years before dying of leprosy (now called Hansen's disease) in 1889. He is memorialized in this bronze statue by Marisol Escobar. The work drew a great deal of criticism when it was unveiled in 1969 because it portrays the priest in his dying days, when his features were deformed by the disease. ♦ State Capitol courtyard

105 Washington Place When the American naval captain who built this estate in 1846 was lost at sea, his son, John Dominis, moved into the mansion with his wife, Lydia Kapaakea, the future Queen Liliuokalani. After Dominis's death and the overthrow of the monarchy in 1893, Liliuokalani returned to **Washington Place** (named after George Washington) and lived here until her death in 1917. The governor of Hawaii now resides in the stately two-story mansion, and the ground floor, most of which has been restored to look as it did originally, is used for state receptions. Past governors have hosted dinners here for visiting dignitaries, including Queen Elizabeth and the late Emperor of Japan. The upstairs rooms are private quarters for the governor and his family. ♦ Not open to the public except on special occasions such as inauguration celebrations. S Beretania St (between Punchbowl and Queen Emma Sts). 538.3113

Hawaii depends on imported petroleum, primarily crude oil from Alaska, for 90 percent of its energy.

106 St. Andrew's Cathedral Shortly after the traumatic death of his four-year-old son Albert, King Kamehameha IV converted to the Church of England and founded **St. Andrew's.** The king died a year later at age 29, but construction of this Episcopalian headquarters began in 1867 under the direction of his widow, Queen Emma. The uniformed students on the premises go to **St. Andrew's Priory,** at the back of the cathedral. ◆ Queen Emma Sq (off Queen Emma St). 524.2822 ♿

107 Young Sing ★$$ Lunch conversations reverberate off the high ceiling of this popular and crowded Chinese restaurant. The extensive menu includes outstanding dim sum (Chinese dumplings of beef, pork, and seafood). ◆ Chinese ◆ Daily lunch and dinner. No reservations. 1055 Alakea St (between Hotel and S King Sts). 531.1366 ♿

108 Tamarind Park Bring a brown-bag lunch and enjoy one of the frequent noontime concerts held in this green, open space fronting the **Pauahi Tower** office building. Henry Moore's *Upright Motive No. 9,* an 11-foot bronze statue in the reflecting pool, was executed in 1979. Loosely based on the human form, it draws its inspiration from the prehistoric monoliths at Stonehenge, North American Indian totem poles, and Polynesian sculpture. ◆ Bishop St (between S King and S Hotel Sts)

109 Alexander & Baldwin Building This distinctive corporate headquarters (pictured below) opened in 1929. Alexander and Baldwin founded the youngest of the "Big Five" companies (the others are C. Brewer & Company, Theo. H. Davis & Company, Amfac Inc., and Castle & Cooke Inc.), a group of corporations that ruled the islands economically until Hawaii became a state (and that still have quite a bit of influence). Architects **C. W. Dickey** and **Hart Wood** designed the structure with Dickey's trademark Hawaiian roof; the subtle Chinese influence was Wood's signature. At the time, the building was one of only two Honolulu

structures made completely of concrete and steel. Admirers praised its workmanship and details, particularly the murals, terra-cotta ornamentation, and black Belgian marble in the first-floor reception area. A floating mezzanine has been added to the building, but many original details remain. ◆ Open to the public M-F. 822 Bishop St (between Merchant and S King Sts). 525.6611 ♿

110 C. Brewer Building Constructed in 1930, this last and smallest of the "Big Five" headquarters built in downtown Honolulu looks more like a mansion than a corporate office. Chief architect **Hardie Phillips** gave the two-story structure a Mediterranean flavor with Hawaiian motifs. Details include wrought-iron rails and grillwork that represent sugarcane and light fixtures that recall sugar cubes. ◆ Open to the public M-F. 827 Fort St (between Queen and S King Sts)

111 Hawaii Maritime Center Trace the role of the sea in life on the islands, from Polynesian migration by canoe to the whaling days and the era of Matson steamships. Three thousand years of maritime history are displayed. The ship docked outside, *Falls of Clyde,* is part of the one-hour tour. ◆ Admission. Daily 8:30AM-5PM. Pier 7, Honolulu Harbor. 536.6373 ♿

At the Hawaii Maritime Center:

Falls of Clyde The last of its kind, this square-rigged, four-masted, iron-hulled ship used to sail into Honolulu Harbor more than a century ago, when the docks were lined with similar vessels and sailors could virtually step from one ship to another. Built in Scotland, the wooden ship was purchased in 1898 by the Matson cruise line to serve on the route between San Francisco and Hawaii. The ship was restored in 1963 and is now a museum.

112 Aloha Tower Marketplace Passengers who sailed Matson steamships to Hawaii decades ago will remember the **Aloha Tower** as an imposing architectural landmark—it was the tallest structure on the waterfront. The 10-story, 184-foot-high tower, designed in 1921 by **Arthur Reynolds,** doesn't seem

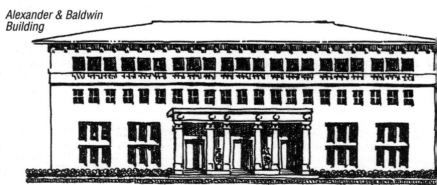

Alexander & Baldwin Building

tall at all any more compared to the steel-and-glass high-rises of downtown Honolulu. But it's the centerpiece of Honolulu's newest gathering place, a $100-million collection of 120 shops and restaurants designed to attract visitors to the historic port area of town. ◆ Pier 9, Honolulu Harbor. 537.9260 ♿

Within the Aloha Tower Marketplace:

Big Island Steak House ★★$$$ This restaurant was transplanted from the Big Island and looks to have survived the move fairly well, except that, unlike the original, it doesn't metamorphose into a nightclub at 10PM. A romantic interlude over lobster or filet mignon is the specialty of the house. ◆ Steaks/Seafood ◆ Daily lunch and dinner. No reservations. 537.4446 ♿

Buffalo Bud's Bar & Grill ★$$ An ocean view is the biggest draw at this casual Southwestern-themed eatery, but the blackened *ahi* (tuna) and barbecued chicken hold their own among the battery of offerings at the popular **Marketplace.** ◆ Southwestern. ◆ Daily lunch and dinner. No reservations. 536.6868 ♿

Scott's Seafood ★★$$$ Floor-to-ceiling windows, stainless steel table tops, and a heart-stopping view of Honolulu Harbor would make this seaside bistro popular even if the fresh mahimahi, pork chops, and filet-and-lobster combos didn't draw diners from the mall. ◆ Steak/Seafood ◆ Daily lunch and dinner. Reservations recommended. 537.6800 ♿

113 Lai Fong Inc. Low rents and interesting storefronts and spaces have attracted art dealers to Honolulu's Chinatown, resulting in a number of galleries clustered within several blocks of Nuuanu Avenue. This is one of our favorites. While you could easily mistake it for a thrift shop, what with the musty mounds of Chinese bric-a-brac, real treasures lurk in the shadows here: carved jade buttons, *cheongsams* (fitted Chinese dresses), funky ivory jewelry from pre-statehood days, and garish Chinese statues of folk gods. ◆ M-F 11AM-4PM, Sa 11AM-3PM. 1118 Nuuanu Ave (at N Hotel St). 537.3497

114 Hawaii Theater After a 10-year, $21-million restoration process orchestrated by a mainland firm and paid for with both public and private funds, the 1,400-seat beaux-arts theater hosts art shows and theatrical and musical performances in an auditorium that features mosaics, columns, and bas reliefs with Shakespearean themes. 1130 Bethel St (between S Hotel and Pauahi Sts). 528.0506

115 Pegge Hopper Gallery One of Hawaii's best-known artists, Pegge Hopper paints canvases of huge Hawaiian women in Gauguin colors. Their various poses create a feeling of calm serenity. You can also buy greeting cards, calendars, and T-shirts featuring her work. A small, koa-framed print might sell for about $75. ◆ M-F 11AM-4PM; Sa 11AM-3PM.

1164 Nuuanu Ave (between Pauahi and N Beretania Sts). 524.1160 ♿

116 Cathedral of Our Lady of Peace The first Catholic priests came to Hawaii in 1827 from France, but this cathedral wasn't dedicated until 1843, when opposition to Catholicism had died down. Three years later, the first pipe organ on the islands was played here. Mass is held on both Saturdays and Sundays. ◆ Transit Mall, 1184 Bishop St (at S Beretania St). 536.7036 ♿

117 Maunakea Street Lei Stands Along a few blocks of Maunakea Street you'll find small storefronts selling leis, with workrooms behind the refrigerated flower cases. The scents of carnation, maile, *puakinikini*, ginger, pikake, and tuberose fill the air as women string the leis with long, thin needles. These shops offer some of the best prices and selections of leis. **Cindy's Lei and Flower Shoppe** (1034 Maunakea St, 536.6538) is a family-run landmark that has been around for generations. Also recommended are **Lita's Lei and Flower Shoppe** (59 N Beretania St, 521.9065), **Aloha Leis and Flowers** (1145 Maunakea St, 599.7725), **Jenny's** (65 N Beretania St, 521.1595), and **Sweetheart's** (69 N Beretania St, 537.3011). ◆ Maunakea St (between Nimitz Hwy and N Beretania St)

117 Maunakea Marketplace If you're cruising through Chinatown, don't miss this marketplace and don't eat before you come here. A permanent conglomeration of stands, set up county-fair style, sells food from all over the world—the Philippines, Japan, Singapore, Malaysia, China, Hawaii, Thailand, Korea, Italy, India, and Vietnam. After you're filled to the brim, waddle through the huge Asian market and gaze upon the myriad foodstuffs for sale. ◆ Daily. Maunakea St (between N Hotel and Pauahi Sts)

118 Hotel Street Hawaii's version of skid row isn't what it was during World War II, when servicemen frequented the area's red-light establishments. James Jones documented the seediness of these few downtown blocks in his novel *From Here to Eternity*. You can still buy a cold beer at any of the bars, and ladies of the night continue to beckon from the street corners, but the city is making an effort to clean up the area (as is indicated by the police station on one of the side streets). Restaurants and groceries operated mainly by immigrants from Southeast Asia are gradually replacing the bars and X-rated businesses. ◆ Between Bishop and River Sts

On Hotel Street:

Wo Fat ★$$ Hawaii's oldest restaurant, established in 1882, is a landmark and an institution. In its heyday, the monumentally ornate establishment was the choice locale for banquets and celebrations among the Chinese community. It was closed in 1995 and reopened under new management. It's worth a stop for lunch or dinner, especially if you're experienced at ordering from a Cantonese menu (try the ginger chicken or Peking duck). ♦ Chinese ♦ Daily lunch and dinner. No reservations. 115 N Hotel St. 524.1628 ♿

119 Wong and Wong Restaurant ★★$ Wonderful down-home cooking characterizes this modest restaurant. The trick is to order the specials, listed on signs hanging from the walls. The steamed fish, especially the mullet, is prepared Chinese style with a soy sauce, ginger, and green-onion sauce. You may be able to walk in for lunch, but dinner reservations are a good idea. ♦ Chinese ♦ Daily lunch and dinner. Reservations recommended for dinner. 1023 Maunakea St (at N King St). 521.4492

120 Ba-le Sandwich Shop 1 ★$ Some of the best French baguettes in the islands (and great French coffee, too) are made and sold by the Vietnamese owners of the **Ba-le** concessions around Honolulu. This little coffee shop—the **Ba-le** headquarters— serves Vietnamese dim sum, spring rolls, 20 noodle dishes, and sandwiches that hint of the flavors of Saigon. ♦ Vietnamese ♦ Daily breakfast and lunch. No credit cards accepted. 150 N King St (at River St). 521.3973 ♿

121 Oahu Market

Every morning this large, bustling market illustrates how busy Chinatown was before supermarkets came into existence. The regular customers obviously prefer to select their fresh fish and roasted pork from butchers who know their names. You'll hear Cantonese, Vietnamese, and other Asian languages as prices are agreed upon. When in season, mangoes and litchis are sold here, but you'll have the most fun buying *char siu* (barbecued pork). The butcher will chop the meat into bite-size pieces so you can nibble as you browse. ♦ M-Sa 6:30AM-4:30PM; Su 6:30AM-noon. 145 N King St (at Kekaulike St). 841.6924

Sans Souci (French for "without a care") Beach, located near the volcanic crater Diamond Head on Oahu, was the favorite haunt of author Robert Louis Stevenson.

Check out Oahu's North Shore in November and December, when some of the gnarliest surfers in the world come to ride the choicest waves in Hawaii.

122 Doong Kong Lau-Hakka Restaurant ★★$ The food here (ginger chicken, shrimp with broccoli, et al) is as superb as the decor is simple. Hakka cuisine isn't as spicy as Szechuan, but it's just as good. Some of the more popular selections arrive at your table on sizzling platters. ♦ Chinese ♦ Daily breakfast, lunch, and dinner. No reservations. 100 N Beretania St, Ste 110 (between Maunakea and River Sts). 531.8833

123 Foster Botanic Gardens Feel free to picnic and wander in this 13.5-acre green domain at the edge of downtown Honolulu. A plethora of orchids and other plants (5,000 species of tropical flora in all) flourishes in the oldest botanical garden in the state. A gallery and bookstore also are on site. ♦ Nominal fee. Daily; tours at 1PM. Reservations required for tours. 50 N Vineyard Blvd (between Maunakea St and Nuuanu Stream). 522.7065 ♿

124 Punchbowl Crater (National Memorial Cemetery of the Pacific) Centuries ago, human lives were sacrificed here to appease the gods (hence the dormant volcano's Hawaiian name, *Puowaina,* which means "Hill of Sacrifice"). The crater's 114-acre floor is now the final resting place for veterans of World Wars I and II, the Korean and Vietnam Wars, and the Persian Gulf War, as well as their dependents. Some 34,000 white pillars in neat rows line the velvet expanse. The first rays of sun that probe the rim of the crater at dawn create a powerful effect, especially during the sunrise service on Easter Sunday. World War II journalist Ernie Pyle is buried here among the soldiers he immortalized, as is Ellison Onizuka, the astronaut from Hawaii who was killed in the Challenger space-shuttle disaster in 1986. ♦ Free. Daily. 2177 Puowaina Dr (south of Auwaiolimu St, follow the green-and-white signs), Honolulu. 566.1430

125 Tantalus Drive If you start to get the feeling that the Honolulu area is short on natural beauty, make your way down this scenic route. Start on Puowaina Drive (on the north side of Punchbowl Crater), which eventually turns into Tantalus Drive and winds through some incredible real estate almost to the top of Mount Tantalus (2,013 feet), with pull-offs every mile or so to let you admire the view of Honolulu. At the top of Tantalus Drive, pull over and wander along the trails that meander through the valley, then head back down Round Top Drive, stopping at the **Puu Ualakaa State Wayside** to snap a few photos.

126 The Contemporary Museum A cultural oasis in a city where cartoonlike portraits of flippers, fins, and sunsets often pass for art, this museum in a stunning 3.5-acre setting exhibits works by artists of international reputation, including David Hockney and George Rickey. The main building, a former estate of Mrs. Charles Montague Cooke, consists of five interconnected galleries and a separate pavilion, although some of the most interesting works—large contemporary sculptures by Rickey, Robert Arneson, Tom Klesselmann, Charles Analdi, and others—are displayed on the impeccably landscaped grounds. The prints sold at the adjacent **Museum Shop** make wonderful gifts. ♦ Admission. Tu-Sa 10AM-4PM; Su noon-4PM. 2411 Makiki Heights Dr (between Makiki St and Mott-Smith Dr). 526.0232 &

Within The Contemporary Museum:

The Contemporary Cafe ★★$ If you are anywhere near the Makiki Heights area, stop at this chic cafe and choose from a wide selection of salads, gourmet sandwiches, daily specials (hope for escargot mezzanine, with sun-dried tomatoes, pesto butter, and wine sauce), and homemade desserts. On a sunny day, the outdoor seating surrounded by sculpture is unbeatable. ♦ Cafe ♦ Tu-Su lunch. No reservations. 523.3362 &

27 Royal Mausoleum The most important burial place in the islands holds the remains of Kings Kamehameha II, III, IV, and V, King Kalakaua, Queen Liliuokalani, and other royalty and favored friends of their courts. (King Kamehameha I's body has never been discovered, though historians presume it's hidden in a secret burial cave on the Big Island, where he died in 1891.) The other Hawaiian monarch who isn't buried here is King Lunalilo, who requested a private tomb on the grounds of **Kawaiahao Church** (see page 143). King Kamehameha V chose the mausoleum's three-acre site in 1865, and royal remains were moved from an old, overcrowded tomb on the **Iolani Palace** grounds. The cross-shaped chapel was designed by the islands' first professional architect, **Theodore Heuck**. ♦ Free. M-F. 2261 Nuuanu Ave (between Oahu Cemetery and Pali Hwy). 536.7602

28 Queen Emma Summer Palace This cool summer retreat in Nuuanu Valley belonged to Queen Emma and her husband, King Kamehameha IV. When the Duke of Edinburgh visited Hawaii in 1869, Emma had the elegant **Edinburgh Room** built to accommodate a lavish gala for him (a party that he, unfortunately, failed to attend). The Hawaiian government purchased the palace in 1890, after Emma's death, and the **Daughters of Hawaii** have maintained it as a museum since 1915. The grand rooms contain many personal belongings of the royal family, including the koa wood cradle of Emma and Kamehameha's son, Albert, heir to the throne and Queen Victoria's godson, who died at the age of four. Self-guided tours are available. ♦ Admission. Daily. 2913 Pali Hwy (between Laimi and Puiwa Rd). 595.3167

129 Alexander Cartwright's Tomb The man who some believe invented baseball (others credit Abner Doubleday) was buried in Honolulu on 12 July 1892, and his pink granite tomb is in **Oahu Cemetery** (to the right of the road, a few hundred feet from the entrance). Alexander Cartwright was chairman of the committee that drew up the rules for baseball in 1845, and he fixed the base paths at 90 feet. He also umpired in the first official game, held 19 June 1846 between the **New York Knickerbockers Baseball Club** (which later became the basketball team that plays today) and the **New York Nine** in Hoboken, New Jersey. Later, on a trip to the islands, Cartwright became so enamored of Honolulu that he moved here and began to teach baseball. (He also founded the city's first volunteer fire department.) **Cartwright Playground** in Makiki is where he is said to have laid out Hawaii's first baseball diamond. ♦ 2162 Nuuanu Ave (between Judd St and Robinson La). 538.1538

130 Dole Cannery by Horizon In the old days, the cloying smell of pineapple filled the air as you neared the cannery in the Iwilei District. Two million pineapples a day were processed here, each inspected by women in white aprons, gloves, and caps. Now the buildings house brand-name outlet stores, including Levi Strauss, Big Dog Sportswear, and Hawaiian Island Gems, along with photos and artifacts from the pineapple's heyday. The shopping center has expanded exponentially and is hard to miss—it's painted seven shades of yellow. A free multimedia show on the history of pineapple production in Hawaii goes on every half hour from 9:30AM to 3:30PM. A two-story, $40-million aquarium is slated to be the property's next big attraction, open by late 1998. ♦ Free. Daily. 650 Iwilei Rd (between Sumner and Pacific Sts). 531.2886 &

131 Hilo Hattie Garment Factory Every month, more than 30,000 aloha garments (shirts, dresses, shorts, and the like) are cranked out here. Busloads of tourists come to watch the garments being made by dozens of workers toiling at their machines. The outlet store, Hawaii's largest, is a great place for alohawear souvenirs. ♦ Free. Daily. Guided tours by appointment only. 700 N Nimitz Hwy (at Pacific St). 537.2926 &

Tourism was introduced to Oahu in the late 1920s, when Matson Navigation Company steamships dropped off the first mainlanders in Waikiki.

Restaurants/Clubs: Red   **Hotels:** Blue
Shops/♥ Outdoors: Green   **Sights/Culture:** Black

Tall Tales and Matters of Fact

Scour them six months before your trip or page through them between catnaps on the beach; either way, you're sure to find something of interest in each of the following books about the Hawaiian Islands:

The Atlas of Hawaii (1983; Department of Geography, University of Hawaii Press) The authors of this book must know everything about Hawaii. Their book is crammed full of fun facts like what plants grow where on what islands and how long it takes to drive from place to place on each isle.

Hawaii to Da Max! by Douglas Simonson, Ken Sakata, and Pat Sasaki (1992; Bess Press) The subtitle—"Everything You Always Wanted to Know About Hawaii, But Didn't Have a Local Friend to Tell You"—says it all. Written half in English, half in pidgin, this casual, chatty guide gives visitors a behind-the-scenes look at their vacation paradise.

Hawaiian Hiking Trails by Craig Chisholm (1994; Fernglen Press) This useful book includes photos, basic maps, and tips on hiking some of Hawaii's better-known trails, from **Maui**'s 45-minute **Waikamoi Ridge Trail** to the four-day trek into the **Kalalau Valley** on **Kauai**.

Hawaii by James Michener (1959; Random House) This epic novel was published the year Hawaii became a state. It's hard to put it down—and easy to forget that it's only fiction.

Maui's Hana Highway: A Visitor's Guide by Angela Kay Kepler (1987; Mutual Publishing of Honolulu) Pick up this book before you drive to **Hana**; it will lead you down side roads that you'd drive right by otherwise. (And side roads are the heart and soul of the Hana adventure.)

Letters from Hawaii by Mark Twain (1975; University of Hawaii Press) Mark Twain was one of three well-known 19th-century authors (the others: Robert Louis Stevenson and Jack London) to take a turn at immortalizing the island chain in print. This book is fairly hard going, but it gives readers an idea of daily life in what was to Twain a foreign country.

Travels in Hawaii by Robert Louis Stevenson (1973; University of Hawaii Press) The writer and his family arrived in Hawaii on the chartered yacht *Casco* in 1889 and stayed five months. These are stories of Stevenson's adventures on the **Big Island** and **Molokai,** with a handful of poems included.

The Many Splendored Fishes of Hawaii by Gar Goodson (1985; Stanford University Press) If you plan to snorkel, take this paperback along. If you don't plan to snorkel, this overview of the islands' marine life might change your mind.

Shoal of Time by Gavan Daws (1968; University of Hawaii Press) This is one of the most definitive—and most readable—books on Hawaiian history in print.

Stories of Hawaii by Jack London (1965; University of Hawaii Press) John Griffith London (1876-1916) sailed his self-designed ketch *Snark* from San Francisco to **Honolulu** in 1907 and spent half a year touring the islands. He learned to surf, met with the deposed Queen Liliuokalani, checked out dormant **Haleakala** and active **Kilauea Volcano,** and chronicled his adventures and misadventures in this easy-to-read volume.

132 Tamashiro Market Look for a hot-pink building and the faded landmark sign (a pinkish-orange crab), and start hoping for a parking space. The market is worth a visit, especially if you love seafood, as it offers a wide selection of fresh island fish as well as favorites from the mainland and other parts of the world. The kids will enjoy watching the live crabs, frogs, and lobsters crawling around in tanks, and you'll marvel at the extraordinary beauty of some of the sea's starnge bounty. A huge board hanging over one of the fish counters lists the Hawaiian and mainland names for fish. If you're not squeamish, there's a first-rate selection of *poke* (raw fish). ♦ Daily. 802 N King St (at Palama St). 841.8047 ♿

HOP MUSEUM

CELEBRATING A
CENTURY OF DISCOVERY

33 Bishop Museum When Charles Reed Bishop founded this museum in 1889 in honor of the Hawaiian heritage of his wife, Princess Bernice Pauahi, he hoped it would rank among the great museums on earth. No doubt he would be proud to know that it now not only houses the world's greatest collection of Hawaiian cultural and natural-history artifacts but is a highly regarded center for Pacific-area studies. The museum's success is largely attributable to its director, W. Donald Duckworth, who came to Honolulu in the early 1980s and continues to expand the exhibition and publication programs.The museum's centerpiece is **Hawaiian Hall**—three floors of carved war gods and feather cloaks, mementos of the 19th-century monarchs, valuable Polynesian artifacts, and more. The **Hall of Hawaiian Natural History** offers fascinating displays on the islands' geological origins, including a lava tube with its own ecosystem. Children can touch lava or try making a grass hut in the **Hall of Discovery,** across the lawn from the main gallery building. Next door is the **Planetarium** and the **Shop Pacifica,** which stocks numerous of books on Hawaiian and Polynesian history. You can also purchase authentic reproductions of museum pieces, such as bags and hats woven from *lauhala* (the leaves of the pandanus tree), and Hawaiian quilts. ♦ Admission. Daily. Tours M-F 10AM, noon. Planetarium shows M-Th, Su 11AM, 2PM; F-Sa 11AM, 2PM, 7PM. Observatory F-Sa 7PM-9PM, weather permitting. 1525 Bernice St (between Houghtailing St and Likelike Hwy). 847.8200; information about current programs 848.4129; planetarium reservations 847.8201

Southeast Oahu

Not far from the hurly-burly of Honolulu, the southeast section of Oahu is a quiet, natural region of uncrowded white-sand beaches, dramatic lava rock coastline, and jagged cliffs. In the late 1980s public outcry halted proposed development here, and thus far the area has escaped encroaching civilization. Sandy Beach and Makapuu Beach are considered two of the best bodyboarding spots on the island, and the calm, clear waters of Hanauma Bay make it easy for snorkelers to observe the colorful residents of the underwater state park there.

34 Swiss Inn ★★$$$ Fans of Martin Wyss's cooking love this restaurant for its affordable menu and first-rate cuisine. Red napkins top white tablecloths at this out-of-the-way "in" spot; go early to snag one of the wooden booths lining the walls. The veal dishes (Wiener schnitzel, veal medaillons, Holstein schnitzel) are very popular, and there's also pasta, chicken, seafood, and fondue. ♦ Swiss/German ♦ W-Sa dinner; Su brunch and dinner. Niu Valley Shopping Center, 5730 Kalanianaole Hwy (near Halemaumau St), Kuliouou. 377.5447 &

135 Roy's Restaurant ★★★★$$$ Roy Yamaguchi was a leader in establishing a regional Hawaiian/California cuisine, and his consistently innovative creations keep it interesting. He calls his cuisine "Euro-Asian," and specialties include seafood pot stickers; ravioli of lamb, goat cheese, and pesto; lobster in macadamia nut butter sauce; rack of Niihau lamb; and grilled Lanai venison in a basil and port sauce. The hundreds of other selections change regularly, depending on what's in season. The place is wildly successful, although the noise level in the trendy dining room is distracting to conversationalists, and the restaurant is in an odd location on the outskirts of the Hawaii Kai suburb. Contemporary Hawaiian music is performed on Fridays and Saturdays after 8PM. ♦ Euro-Asian ♦ Daily dinner. Reservations recommended. 6600 Kalanianaole Hwy (at Keahole St), Hawaii Kai. 396.7697 &

136 Hanauma Bay Nestled against a volcanic crater that's missing a chunk on one side, the bay is a beautiful snorkeling spot, with waves so gentle even nonswimmers feel safe. The fish in this underwater state park are protected by law from spearhunters and anglers, which means snorkelers often find themselves nose-to-nose with brilliantly colored reef fish boldly going about their business (they're accustomed to stares). Food for the fish can be purchased at the concession stands, where snorkel gear is rented too. The best spot for swimming (but not snorkeling) here is the **Keyhole,** a sandy-bottomed section at the far end of the park. Nonswimmers will enjoy the **Toilet Bowl,** a hole in the rock where waves shoot out at regular intervals. The bay's downside is that it gets pretty crowded; try to avoid the afternoon rush. The preserve is closed on Wednesday until noon to give the marine life some private time. This bay may look familiar to film buffs; this is where Elvis Presley starred in *Blue Hawaii,* and directors used it for beach scenes in *From Here to Eternity* (the Burt

Lancaster–Deborah Kerr clincher, however, was shot near Makapuu Beach). ♦ Hanauma Bay Rd (off Kalanianaole Hwy)

137 Halona Blowhole A powerful gush of water spews into the air whenever ocean waves shooting through the lava tube here cause enough pressure to build. (You may hear a honking sound too.) On clear days, the islands of Molokai and Lanai are visible on the horizon, and on those rare, exceptionally fine days, you may see Maui between them. ♦ Off Kalanianaole Hwy (east of Hanauma Bay, at the Hawaii Visitors Bureau marker)

138 Sandy Beach You may see people playing in the surf, but it can be dangerous to swim at this beach because the waves break in shallow water. While they offer some of the island's best tubes for bodysurfing, only experts should tackle these waves—many swimmers and bodysurfers have suffered broken necks here throughout the years. A safer activity is kite flying, which is also popular here. Picnic and public facilities are available, and a lifeguard is on the lookout. ♦ Off Kalanianaole Hwy (northeast of Hanauma Bay)

139 Makapuu Beach Park Although this is a dangerous swimming spot, there is excellen[t] bodysurfing for experts. The lookout point above Makapuu offers a breathtaking view o[f] the windward coastline, outlying Sharkfin an[d] Rabbit Islands, and bodysurfers in the wave[s] below. Public facilities and lifeguards are he[re] too. ♦ Off Kalanianaole Hwy (east of Sea Life Park)

140 Sea Life Park Paying to see fish and sea mammals in tanks and pools seems ridiculou[s] when you're surrounded by water full of thes[e] saltwater denizens. But this park (see the ma[p] below) is well worth the price of admission fo[r] anyone who likes to watch dolphins, not to mention schools of tropical fish, monk seals, penguins, and other marine life—more than 4,000 creatures in all. The **Touch Pool** is grea[t]

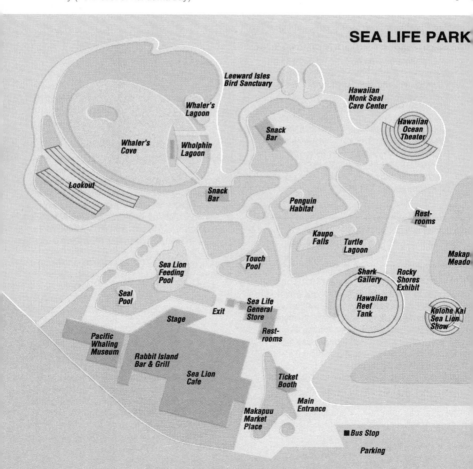

SEA LIFE PARK

Leeward Isles Bird Sanctuary

Hawaiian Monk Seal Care Center

Whaler's Lagoon

Snack Bar

Hawaiian Ocean Theater

Whaler's Cove

Wholphin Lagoon

Lookout

Snack Bar

Penguin Habitat

Rest-rooms

Kaupo Falls

Turtle Lagoon

Makap[uu] Meado[w]

Sea Lion Feeding Pool

Touch Pool

Shark Gallery

Rocky Shores Exhibit

Seal Pool

Hawaiian Reef Tank

Kelohe Kai Sea Lion Show

Exit

Sea Life General Store

Stage

Pacific Whaling Museum

Rabbit Island Bar & Grill

Rest-rooms

Sea Lion Cafe

Ticket Booth

Main Entrance

Makapuu Market Place

Bus Stop

Parking

for kids, who can run their fingers across the sea cucumbers, starfish, shells, giant worms, and other interesting sea animals in a shallow pool. The **Rocky Shores Exhibit** re-creates the surfswept intertidal zone of Hawaii's shoreline, and the **Hawaiian Reef Tank** simulates an offshore reef three fathoms below sea level, with live sharks, eels, sea turtles, and fish. A Pacific bottlenose dolphin rides a boogie board at the **Hawaiian Ocean Theater,** where you can also meet Kekaimalu, the world's only "wholphin" (a cross between a whale and a dolphin) on the guided tour. A new interactive exhibit allows kids to come face to face with dolphins and other sea life (for an additional fee). The park's setting is perfect for swimming, sunbathing, and picnicking. ♦ Admission. Daily. 41-202 Kalanianaole Hwy (southeast of Waimanalo Beach). 259.7933 ♿

Within Sea Life Park:

Pacific Whaling Museum This privately owned museum has the largest collection of whaling artifacts and scrimshaw in the Pacific. The 36-foot-long skeleton suspended from the ceiling is from a sperm whale that became stranded and died off Oahu in 1980. There's also a museum shop. ♦ 259.7933 ♿

41 Bueno Nalo ★★$ Don't be surprised to find people waiting outside this humble establishment; the Mexican food here is *muy buena,* and they can only seat 20 or so at a time. If you don't mind eating early you can avoid the wait, but otherwise join the party in line. Specials include steak fajitas and chicken chimichangas. There's no liquor license, so BYOB. ♦ Mexican ♦ Daily lunch and dinner. No reservations. 41-865 Kalanianaole Hwy (at Puuone St), Waimanalo Beach. 259.7186 ♿

42 Bellows Field Beach Park You can ride the gentle bodysurfing waves at this rural beach, which is part of the **Bellows Air Force Station,** but only from noon Friday to Sunday evening, since war games are played here the rest of the week. ♦ Off Kalanianaole Hwy (look for the Bellows AFS sign), Waimanalo

Windward Oahu

excursion to Windward Oahu is an enjoyable ange of pace for people vacationing in Waikiki d elsewhere in Honolulu. Most people on this le of the island live in **Kailua,** a Honolulu bedroom mmunity, or **Kaneohe,** an attractive suburb that's me to the Kaneohe Marine Corps Air Station. ilua's main attraction is its wide, sandy beach— rfect for swimming and a top windsurfing spot. neohe has a number of beachside and cliffside uses and an offshore reef where numerous lorful creatures hang out. Both towns have some od restaurants. To get an overview of the vast een arena known as Windward Oahu—Kailua and neohe, the ocean, farms, and cliffs—stop at the

Nuuanu Pali Lookout, about 15 minutes from downtown Honolulu. The area also boasts a number of tourist attractions.

143 Olomana Golf Links Waimanalo boasts a short, relatively easy 18-hole course (par 72, 6,326 yards) as well as a small restaurant on Oahu's northeast shore. ♦ Inexpensive greens fees. Daily. 41-1801 Kalanianaole Hwy (between Waimanalo and Kailua). 259.7926

144 Koolau Farmers Stop at this nursery just outside of Kailua for freshly cut flowers and potted plants. Colorful hibiscus, bougainvillea, heliconia, anthuriums, and orchids contribute to the fragrance in the air. Longtime customers rave about the personal service. ♦ Daily. 1127 Kailua Rd (at Ulumanu St), Kailua. 263.4414 ♿

145 Mid-Pacific Country Club The club offers a long, tight, and challenging 18-hole course (par 72, 6,784 yards) on the windward side of the island. Lessons are available for $50 an hour, and there's a snack shop on the premises. ♦ Expensive greens fees. No credit cards accepted. Daily; walk-ons allowed when possible. 266 Kaelepulu Dr (off Aalapapa Dr), Kailua. 261.9765

145 Buzz's Original Steak House ★$$$ One of Oahu's first surf-and-turf restaurants, this **Buzz's** is the original **Original Steak House.** At lunch you order off the menu, and for dinner there's a selection of specials, including the usual fresh fish and steaks, and a salad bar that's better than most. ♦ Steaks/Seafood ♦ M-F lunch; daily dinner. Reservations recommended. 413 Kawailoa St (across from Kailua Beach Park), Kailua. 261.4661 ♿. Also at: 98-751 Kuahao Pl (at Kaahumanu St), Pearl City. 487.6465 ♿

146 Kailua Beach Park A family-oriented windward beach with generous stretches of white sand, this spot is safe for swimming and bodysurfing, but look out for windsurfers recklessly zipping about. The southeastern section of the park is a stretch of white sand known as Lanikai Beach, which fronts the tony Lanikai neighborhood. Picnic and public facilities are available, and there's a lifeguard on duty. ♦ Off S Kalaheo Ave, Kailua

147 Casablanca ★$$ The Benalis, two brothers from Morocco with experience at a number of local restaurants, including **Rex's Black Orchid** and the now-defunct Hajiibaba's, took over a neighborhood Mexican restaurant and transformed it into Kailua's (and Hawaii's) only Moroccan dining establishment. This is about as culinarily adventurous as the bedroom community of Kailua gets; *pastilla* (chicken pie) and couscous with vegetables are menu highlights. ♦ Moroccan/N. African ♦ M-Sa dinner. 19 Hoolai St (off Kailua Rd), Kailua. 262.8196 &

148 Pali Golf Course This verdant 18-hole course (par 72, 6,524 yards) is located at the foot of the Koolau Mountains. ♦ Inexpensive greens fees for both residents and visitors. Daily; call a week ahead for reservations.45-050 Kamehameha Hwy (between Pali Hwy and H-3), Kaneohe. 266.7610

148 Nuuanu Pali Lookout Follow the signs or the busloads of tourists along the Pali Highway to this lookout and hold on to your hat. It's one of the most blustery spots in Hawaii—a place where gentle trade winds turn into formidable gusts. Civilization hasn't improved the panorama (that's the **Pali Golf Course** you're looking at). Still, at 1,000 feet, it's a great place to view windward Oahu. Legend has it that the **Battle of Nuuanu Valley** was fought here in 1795, with Kamehameha the Great and his forces pushing the opposing army over the palisades to their deaths. ♦ Nuuanu Pali Dr (off Pali Hwy)

149 Haiku Gardens Pathways wind through the landscaped grounds of this tropical garden at the base of the misty Koolau Mountains. Site of the occasional wedding, it's also a favorite spot for pleasant strolls. ♦ Haiku Rd (off Kahekili Hwy), Kaneohe

Within Haiku Gardens:

Chart House ★$$$ The food isn't the best at this member of the steak-and-seafood chain, but romantics could certainly do worse than book a table in the atmospheric garden dining room and put in a couple of orders for coconut crunchy (tempura fried) shrimp or a 20-ounce prime rib with Santa Fe spice and firecracker onions. ♦ Steaks/Seafood ♦ M-Sa lunch and dinner; Su brunch and dinner. Reservations recommended. 247.6671 &. Also at: 66-011 Kamehameha Hwy (at Haleiwa Rd), Haleiwa. 637.8005 &

In 1974 Democrat George Ariyoshi became the first American of Japanese descent to govern an American state. After three terms, Ariyoshi passed the office to another Democrat, John Waihee, the first person of native Hawaiian ancestry to serve as governor of the islands. The flame was passed to Governor Ben Cayetano in 1994; Cayetano is the first Filipino man to govern an American state.

The first automobile in Hawaii was a Wood Electric, delivered to H. A. Baldwin of Honolulu in 1899.

150 Byodo-in Temple Built in 1968 to honor Hawaii's first Japanese immigrants, the replica of a 900-year-old Buddhist temple in Japan is situated serenely in the **Valley of the Temples Memorial Park,** a huge cemetery at the foot of the Koolau Mountains. A Buddha statue (illustrated above) near a pond filled with swans and carp is an imperturbable presence as peacocks stroll by and visitors ring the three-ton bronze bell. ♦ Nominal admission. Daily. 47-200 Kahekili Hwy (at Hui Owa St; look for the Valley of the Temple Shopping Center), Kaneohe. 239.8811 &

151 Kahaluu Drive Highway 836, from Kaneohe to Kahaluu, is a pleasant coastline detour around Kahekili Highway (Highway 83). If you don't wish to see the **Haiku Gardens** or **Byodo-in Temple,** take this alternative scenic route. ♦ Hwy 836 (from Kaneohe to Kahaluu)

152 Senator Fong's Plantation and Gardens Former US Senator Hiram Fong retired to devote more time to this 725-acre botanic garden, which opened to the public a few years ago. There are more than a hundred varieties of fruits and flowers, and sweeping ocean views from a 200-acre section of the garden, which visitors explore on a guided tram tour. The plantation **Adventure Center** offers a variety of activities, including horseback riding, lei making, and hiking. The gift shop holds a selection of Hawaiian-made souvenirs. ♦ Admission. Daily; last tram tour 3PM. 47-285 Pulama Rd (off Kahekili Hwy), Kahaluu. 239.6775

North Shore

The drive along the northern coast of Oahu is memorable. On one side of the road are small ranches and farms with banana trees, papayas, taro, orchids, and anthuriums backed by the green **Koolau Mountains.** On the other side is the Pacific, often rolled in the awe-inspiring waves, several stories high, that make this the most famous surf spot in the world. Many wealthy residents of Honolulu and the mainland own vacation homes along the North Shore beaches.

153 Paniolo Cafe $$ Fifty-five years ago, this establishment was a truck stop for cane truckers hauling their goods between Kahuku and Punaluu. The hacienda-style restaurant now is owned by none other than Don Ho and serves local favorites like Portuguese bean soup and *laulau* (banana leaf–wrapped pork). ♦ Polynesian ♦ Daily lunch and dinner. 53-146 Kamehameha Hwy, Punaluu. 237.8020 &

54 Polynesian Cultural Center If you haven't been to the South Seas, this is a good introduction to the cultures of Polynesia: Hawaii, Fiji, Tonga, Samoa, Tahiti, and the Marquesas. It's a kind of Disney-goes-Pacific, with each culture's traditions demonstrated by students from the nearby **Brigham Young University (BYU)** campus, many of them Polynesian. Watch as they pound poi, string leis, husk coconuts, and make tapa cloth from mulberry bark. Set aside a whole day to drive from Waikiki (it's about an hour and a half each way), tour the various areas devoted to individual islands and island groups, and take in all the demonstrations (the canoe pageant is at 2:30PM; the evening show is at 8PM). You may be exhausted and overwhelmed, but the narration is as entertaining as it is corny. Each evening there's a buffet dinner show. (You can buy a general admission ticket, which includes daytime activities and the dinner show, or an admission-only ticket, which doesn't include the evening buffet.) With more than 30 million guests, the center has been one of Hawaii's leading visitor attractions since the **Church of Jesus Christ of Latter-day Saints** opened it in 1963. And though there's controversy about the integrity of the production, which has provided more than $100 million for **BYU,** it's still an educational experience. ♦ Admission. M-Sa 12:30PM-9:30PM. 55-370 Kamehameha Hwy, Laie. 293.3333

155 Mormon Temple Since 1864, the Mormon headquarters has occupied 6,000 acres in the community of Laie, where 95 percent of the population is Mormon. The **Church of Jesus Christ of Latter-day Saints** built the temple, a comely white edifice in impeccably landscaped grounds, in 1919. Visitors are not allowed to enter the structure, but are welcome to tour the surroundings, which are dotted with reflecting pools. A visitors' center features a large statue of Christ, a genealogy center, and several films. ♦ Free. Grounds open daily 9AM-8PM. 55-600 Naniloa Loop (off Kamehameha Hwy), Laie. Visitors' Center 293.2427 &

155 Tiare Puroto Pareus Just down the street from the **Mormon Temple** is the home and business of Ura Behling, a charming and talented designer and fabricator of colorful pareus (wraparound skirts). You can't miss the place when it's in full operation; dozens of brightly colored sheets stretch across the driveway as solar power and patterned cutouts create tropical impressions through fading. The prices here are the best around, and the service can't be beat, which explains the occasional tourist bus unloading at the doorstep. ♦ Daily. 55-533 Naniloa Loop (off Kamehameha Hwy), Laie. 293.5893

156 Malaekahana State Recreation Area Just past Laie, right before you reach the former plantation town of Kahuku, you'll find postcard-perfect Malaekahana. On weekdays the arc-shaped beach is usually empty except for a few fishermen casting their nets. There's good swimming and bodysurfing, but no lifeguard on duty. Remember to lock your car and keep valuables out of sight, then take your time strolling down the wide white-sand beach or picnicking under the ironwood trees on the south end. There's a bathhouse with cold showers, and camping by permit. ♦ Off Kamehameha Hwy (3 miles north of Laie)

Turtle Bay

Golf and Tennis Resort

157 Turtle Bay Hilton and Country Club $$$$ More than an hour's drive from Waikiki, this 808-acre resort is for people who really want to get away from everything. There's not much to do here but test your skill on the two Arnold Palmer–designed golf courses (one 18 holes and one nine), sunbathe by the two pools, or hit the beach. It can get pretty windy on Kuilima Point, where the hotel's 371 guest rooms, 32 suites, and 96 cabanas are located, but that makes the beach next door popular with surfers. Sit back and watch them ride the waves, or roust yourself to play tennis, ride horses, or windsurf. If you rent a car, Waimea Bay, Sunset Beach, or the town of Haleiwa are nice day trips. ♦ 57-091 Kamehameha Hwy, Kawela. 293.8811, 800/445.8667; fax 293.9147 &

Within the Turtle Bay Hilton and Country Club:

Sea Tide Room ★$$$$ The Sunday brunch buffet here draws local residents for the bountiful selection, including the omelette bar, fish table, and dessert station, and the fine beach view. ♦ Continental ♦ Su brunch. No reservations. 293.8811 &

Hawaii is ranked fourth in the nation in terms of amount of coastline, with a total of 450 miles. (It's way behind the state with most coastline—Alaska, with 6,640 miles.)

Child's Play

Entertaining the kids usually isn't hard in Hawaii, since the beach is only a short drive away from almost everywhere. But should you get a dose of "liquid sunshine" (i.e., rain) or want a change of pace, here are 10 alternative activities that are sure to delight everyone in the family:

1 Swim with the dolphins at the **Hilton Waikoloa Village** on the **Big Island.**

2 Visit **Sea Life Park** on **Oahu.** Small children will be happy for hours at the **Touch Pool,** running their fingers over patient marine life like sea cucumbers and starfish, while even jaded big kids will love Kekaimalu, the only "wholpin" (a cross between a whale and a dolphin) in captivity.

3 Spend a day at the **Molokai Ranch Wildlife Park,** home to about 1,000 wild animals, from giraffes to exotic greater kudus.

4 Bike down **Haleakala.** Kids have to be four feet, eight inches tall to take on the 10,023-foot-high dormant volcano on **Maui,** but all those who qualify will love the 38-mile ride, downhill all the way.

5 Tour **Iolani Palace,** the only royal palace in America, located in **Honolulu,** Oahu. Older children (and their parents) will be intrigued by stories about the Hawaiian royals, including the extravagant King Kalakaua and the beloved Queen Liliuokalani, who was made a prisoner in her own home.

6 Hike to the top of **Diamond Head,** the volcanic crater just outside Oahu. It's supposed to take an hour, but the kids will probably run up in half that time. This is a fun excursion for all ages, but the littlest hikers may be scared by the tunnel that stretches for a few hundred feet en route, so bring a flashlight.

7 Walk the **Kau Desert Trail** at **Hawaii Volcanoes National Park** on the Big Island. The two-hour hike leads to footprints in lava made by 18th-century Hawaiian warriors trying to escape a 1790 eruption of **Kilauea.** The trail also winds through the Big Island's only desert; be sure to bring water.

8 Go to the **USS Arizona Memorial,** which memorializes those who died in the Japanese raid on **Pearl Harbor,** Oahu, on 7 December 1941. A free boat tour to the site is given daily by the Navy, but young history buffs will also be interested in the documentary film shown at the visitors' center.

9 Ride the waves on **Waikiki Beach.** Several beachfront outfitters offer surfing and body-boarding lessons.

10 Take a ghost tour of **Waikiki.** Kids of all ages will be thrilled to hear about the dozens of spirits that are said to haunt this modern metropolis. **Honolulu Time Walks** (922.5277) offers this and other walking tours.

Turtle Bay Hilton Golf Courses These oceanside courses are known for their ferocious winds, but that doesn't keep golfers away from the 18 holes of the championship **Kuilima** course (par 72, 7,199 yards) or the regulation nine-hole course (par 36, 3,164 yards). Legend says that Mickey Mantle, with the wind at his back, drove a ball over the 357-yard fourth hole using a No. 4 wood, though George Fazio designed the course with wind in mind. ◆ Expensive greens fees. Daily. Preferred starting times and rates for Turtle Bay Hilton guests. 293.8811

158 Sunset Beach It's a world-famous North Shore site for winter surfing contests, but year-round high waves and strong currents make this beach dangerous for swimmers. When the sets of 10-story-high waves come in, head this way and join the mesmerized crowd. It's a good beach for strolling and sunbathing during spring and summer, but don't ever turn your back on the winter waves. ◆ Off Kamehameha Hwy (6 miles northeast of Haleiwa), Sunset Beach

159 Ke Iki Hale $$ This is the Hawaii everyone dreams of—palm trees silhouetted against the sunset, golden beaches stretching for miles, whales cavorting in the winter, and cozy little cottages with large picture windows to take it all in. Only eight duplexes occupy this acre and a half of oceanfront property, from single bedrooms on the street side to one- and two-bedroom adjoining units facing the ocean. Simplicity and serenity are the operative words here, with a deliberate absence of modern-day luxuries: no Jacuzzi, room service, restaurant, TVs, or even telephones (there's a pay phone nearby, though, and the amenities of Haleiwa are only minutes away). The exteriors of the hotel buildings could use a new coat of paint, but the cottages are immaculate inside, with full kitchens and patios. The property is on Ke Iki, one of Oahu's best beaches, a broad expanse of white sand and palm trees that partially recedes during the winter, when thundering 10-foot waves crash on the reefy shoreline. Rinse off under a shower that's been fastened to a palm tree, then lie in a hammock or picnic at tables near the sand. You could easily stay in your swimsuit all day, "talking story" with aloha-spirited owner Alice Tracy and not caring one whit about the rest of the world. ◆ 59-579 Ke Iki Rd (off Kamehameha Hwy), Waimea. 638.8229, 800/377.4030

160 Puu-o-Mahuka Heiau (Escape Hill Temple) For an incredible view of the North Shore and Waimea Bay, drive up Pupukea Road to this *heiau* (ancient temple), where humans once were sacrificed as part of the Hawaiian religion. The temple remains a sacred place, and offerings of ti leaves and stones are still made here. ◆ Pupukea Rd (off Kamehameha Hwy; look for the Hawaii Visitors Bureau marker), Waimea

0 Waimea Falls Park The lush grounds of the 1,800-acre park across the street from Waimea Beach include an arboretum and more than 30 botanical gardens, with thousands of tropical and subtropical species. Ride through the park in an open-air minibus or take a guided walking tour. Be sure to see the cliff divers jumping four times daily from the 45-foot falls that give the park its name, and **Halau O Waimea**, the park's resident hula troupe, which performs the *kahiko* (ancient hula) in the upper meadow immediately following each dive. The **Proud Peacock Restaurant** (638.8531) serves palatable (but unexceptional) steak, seafood, and pasta dinners. There's also a snack bar and picnic area—and plenty of peacocks. ◆ Admission. Daily. 59-864 Kamehameha Hwy (4 miles north of Haleiwa). 638.8511 ♿

1 Waimea Beach Park The waters are calm during the summer, when local kids play "king of the mountain" on the huge rock in the bay. But it's an entirely different beach in November, when enormous waves pound the shore. This is one of the world's premier surfing spots, lined with spectators in the winter when the expert surfers are out. There are lifeguards and public facilities. ◆ Off Kamehameha Hwy (4 miles north of Haleiwa)

2 Haleiwa Beach Park There's good swimming and snorkeling here during the spring and summer, but surfing should be left to the experienced. ◆ 62-449 Kamehameha Hwy (just north of Haleiwa)

3 Jameson's by the Sea ★★$$$ This is *the* roadside stop for seafood and pasta at sunset. Baked stuffed shrimp and fresh *opakapaka* (pink snapper) are served in the upstairs dining room. Downstairs, at the informal open-air lanai, *pupus* (appetizers) and drinks flow all day. ◆ Seafood ◆ Daily lunch and dinner; W-Su lunch and dinner upstairs. Reservations recommended. 62-540 Kamehameha Hwy (across from Haleiwa Beach Park). 637.4336 ♿

4 Chart House at Haleiwa ★★$$$ With indoor and outdoor dining right next to Haleiwa Harbor, the popular seafood-and-steak chain is a local hot spot. Service may be spotty, but the salad bar is always good

(especially the Caesar salad) and the fish menu is ample. Try the *ahi* (tuna) or *ono* (wahoo). ◆ Steaks/Seafood ◆ Daily dinner. 66-011 Kamehameha Hwy (at Haleiwa Rd), Haleiwa. 637.8005. Also at: Haiku Gardens, 46-336 Haiku Rd (west of Kahekili Hwy), Kaneohe. 247.6671 ♿

164 H. Miura Store & Tailor Shop Walking into this store is like stepping back in time to the days when Haleiwa was a plantation town. The friendly family—now in its third generation of shopkeeping—can tell you about that era because they opened their place in 1918. The secret to their success is making swim trunks and walking shorts for the surfers who frequent the North Shore every winter. The names and measurements of their regular customers are kept in a ledger, but the Miuras never forget a face. ◆ Daily. 66-057 Kamehameha Hwy (just south of Haleiwa Rd), Haleiwa. 637.4845 ♿

164 S. Matsumoto Shave Ice Store For generations, Haleiwa has been the home of a favorite local treat: finely shaved ice flavored with fruit syrups served modestly in a paper cone. Comparing "shave ice" to a snow cone would be an injustice, though; even the finest snow cone couldn't compete. The best establishments, like **Matsumoto**'s, make their own syrups and offer variations with vanilla ice cream (delicious) and sweet *azuki* beans. Three flavors in one cone is the norm. ◆ Daily. 66-087 Kamehameha Hwy (just south of Haleiwa Rd), Haleiwa. 637.4827

164 Rosie's Cantina ★$ Surfers meet here for the hefty breakfasts, good margaritas, standard Mexican cuisine, and friendly environment. Order a margarita and a plate of sizzling fajitas or a "Triple Crown" (one beef, one chicken, and one cheese enchilada) and let the hassles of everyday life recede. ◆ Mexican ◆ Daily breakfast, lunch, and dinner. No reservations. Haleiwa Shopping Plaza, 66-165 Kamehameha Hwy (between Waialua Beach and Haleiwa Rds), Haleiwa. 637.3538 ♿

164 Pizza Bob's $ With small booths and a bustling surfer atmosphere, this is a typical beer and pizza joint. ◆ Pizza ◆ Daily lunch and dinner. No Reservations. Haleiwa Shopping Plaza, 66-165 Kamehameha Hwy (between Waialua Beach and Haleiwa Rds), Haleiwa. 637.5095 ♿. Also at: Restaurant Row, 500 Ala Moana Blvd (between South and Punchbowl Sts), Honolulu. 532.4602 ♿

Hawaii, the southernmost state in the US, is the only island state in the country. It is larger than Rhode Island, Delaware, and Connecticut combined.

Paddlemonium!

What soccer is to Mexico and hockey is to Canada, outrigger canoe paddling is to Hawaii: a sport of heritage. Not only is it Hawaii's official team sport, it's one of the oldest organized sporting events in the Pacific.

Outrigger canoe paddling may seem simple and straightforward to the spectator, but it actually takes years for individual paddlers to develop and execute the perfect stroke and rhythm, then incorporate it into a team effort (which is why an individual's paddle is as respected as a shortstop's favorite glove). Competition among—and even within—teams is fierce, especially at advanced levels, but sportsmanship and camaraderie always prevail.

Although outrigger canoes have played a role in Hawaiian history since the Polynesians arrived centuries ago (they used to paddle out to fish, then race back to port to get the best price), modern competition didn't formally begin until 1908, when Alexander Hume Ford founded the **Outrigger Canoe Club.** Ford's club led to the first regatta devoted to canoe racing, held in 1933 on the **Big Island.** Since then, paddling's popularity has

exploded; each major island has its own association and member clubs competing on local, state, and international levels.

The Superbowl of all races is the **Bankoh Molokai Hoe** (which means "The Bank of Hawaii Molokai Paddle"), the annual Molokai-to-Oahu men's world championship, held on the second Sunday of October. Hundreds of athletes from around the world paddle the 40.8 miles from **Hale o Lono Harbor** on Molokai to **Waikiki Beach** on Oahu, braving canoe-splitting waves and treacherous currents. The women's championship competition, **Bankoh Na Wahine O Ke Kai** ("Women Against the Sea"), is held on the last Sunday of September.

M. BLUM

165 Kua Aina Sandwich Shop ★★$ The hamburgers here are so juicy they'll literally drip down your elbows, the french fries actually taste like potatoes, and the sandwiches are *onolicious*, especially those with creamy avocados. The only thing that needs work is the less-than-amiable service. ◆ Sandwiches ◆ Daily lunch and dinner. No credit cards. No reservations. 66-324 Kamehameha Hwy (between Twin Bridge and Opaeula Rds), Haleiwa. 637.6067

165 Coffee Gallery ★★$ We wouldn't drive here from Honolulu for a cup of java, but if you're in Haleiwa you'd be insane not to stop in for the olfactory rush, an "aesthetically correct cup of coffee" (according to the business card), and a pesto-veggie sandwich. Soup, desserts, sandwiches, waffles, and bagels are served in a covered patio setting, with Grateful Dead tunes in the background. ◆ Coffeehouse ◆ Daily breakfast, lunch, and dinner. No reservations. 66-250 Kamehameha Hwy (between Twin Bridge and Opaeula Rds), Haleiwa. 637.5571 &

165 Kaala Art Artist/owner John Costello paints his dreams on canvases while brother Kevin keeps the racks stocked with T-shirts and

scads of imported casualwear from Thailand and Bali. Colorful pareus (Polynesian wraparound skirts) line the walls—they're the perfect tropical gift. ◆ Daily. 66-456 Kamehameha Hwy (between Twin Bridge and Opaeula Rds), Haleiwa. 637.7065

166 Sugar Bar A cool, blue oasis in a desert of tourist traps, this bar may be Oahu's last bastion of local beer-guzzling solidarity. Described as your basic down-home country bar by owner Peter Birnbaum, a patron of the arts and possessor of what must be Hawaii's only bust of Beethoven, this place is a second home to the people of sleepy Waialua. Packs of bikers tether their hogs here on the weekends and proceed to gorge on the sausages and drinks, always under the watchful, scowling eye of ol' Ludwig V. Rumor has it that somewhere on the memorabilia-lined walls—if you look hard enough and drink long enough—you'll find the answer to the meaning of life. ◆ Daily 11AM-2AM. 67-069 Kealohanui St (between Farrington Hwy and Waialua Beach Rd), Waialua. 637.6989 &

Central Oahu

Land in the center of Oahu is devoted to agriculture and the military. Pineapple and sugarcane fields stretch as far as the eye can see, and ensconced in those fields are the **Schofield Barracks,** headquarters for the US Army's 25th Infantry Division. **Wahiawa,** near the military base, was once a picturesque plantation town. Now it's a seedy spot with a few grocery stores, fast-food outlets, and rough bars.

67 Dole Plantation Sink your teeth into a piece of pineapple while viewing the display on the fruit's history. The pavilion is in the heart of Hawaii's pineapple country, surrounded by neat pineapple fields and red soil so rich it'll stain your white sneakers. The gift shop carries replicas of old Dole labels, now collector's items. Free self-guided tours take about 45 minutes. ◆ Daily. 64-1550 Kamehameha Hwy (6 miles south of Kamooloa). 621.8408 ♿

68 Schofield Barracks The US Army's 25th Infantry Division headquarters are here, right beside the sugarcane and pineapple fields that Japanese bombers flew over to raid Pearl Harbor. The barracks are named for Major General John M. Schofield, the Army's Pacific military division commander, who came to Hawaii in the 1870s on the pretext of vacationing but spent his time around the Pearl River Lagoon, as Pearl Harbor was then called, investigating its suitability as an American military enclave. ◆ Kolokole Rd (off Hwy 99)

69 Mililani Golf Club Located in the suburbs of leeward Oahu, this course (par 72, 6,455 yards) is shaded by trees on former sugarcane fields. ◆ Moderate greens fees. Daily. 95-176 Kuahelani Ave (at Kamehameha Ave), Mililani. 623.2254

eeward Oahu

is is the least touristy section of Oahu—in fact, u won't find any hotels, fancy restaurants, or rist-oriented shops here at all. A large community native Hawaiians and other Pacific Islanders lives re, working small farms in the broad valleys. West ast residents have a reputation for being unfriendly the people they consider intruders, and in the past re have been incidents of vandalism and even lence against tourists, although the situation has proved in recent years. This is the dry, leeward le of the island, where the days are usually hot and sty. The beaches can be dangerous for swimmers m October to April, with strong currents and dertows, but they are great for surfing. **Makaha ach,** the most famous on the **Waianae Coast,** has en the site of the **Makaha World Surfing ampionships** since 1952.

70 Keawaula Bay It's easy to find—just keep driving until you run out of road. A popular surf spot (called "Yoke's"), this is also a great beach for soaking in the rays. The waves are too big to allow swimming in winter; snorkeling here isn't recommended because of poor visibility year-round. ◆ At the end of Farrington Hwy

71 Sheraton Makaha West Course This uncrowded, 18-hole championship golf course (par 72, 7,077 yards) is set against the green cliffs of the Waianae range. The fairways have great views of the Pacific coastline, especially at sunset. ◆ Expensive

greens fees. Daily. Shuttle service from Sheraton hotels in Waikiki is available. 84-626 Makaha Valley Rd (east of Farrington Hwy), Makaha. 695.9544

172 Makaha Beach Park Professional surfing originated here. It subsequently shifted to the North Shore, but Makaha still hosts the annual **Makaha World Surfing Championships,** which include the **Buffalo Big Board Surfing Classic,** a championship tournament for surfers whose long, elegant boards first put the sport on the map. The competition is held in February or March, depending on when the surfing conditions are best. As with most other beaches along the Waianae Coast, this isn't the most hospitable place for tourists, so keep a low profile and lock your car. ◆ Off Farrington Hwy, Makaha

173 Pokai Bay Beach Park Being the only fully sheltered beach along the Waianae Coast makes this place unique. Unfortunately, this part of the island doesn't cater to tourists. To avoid vandalism, be sure to lock your car. Picnic and public facilities are available, and lifeguards are on duty. ◆ Off Farrington Hwy, Waianae

Kapolei and Pearl City

In the southwest corner of Oahu, Kapolei is a new urban area that stands where there were acres of gently waving sugarcane just a few years ago. The mini-metropolis is being billed as Oahu's "Second City," and developers have high hopes of someday rivaling Waikiki dollar for visitor-industry dollar. Right now, however, Kapolei consists of a hotel, a restaurant, and a golf course right in the middle of nowhere.

East of this new resort area is middle-class Pearl City, the site of **Pearl Harbor.** The **USS Arizona Memorial,** which honors those who died in the Japanese attack of the harbor on 7 December 1941, has drawn respectful visitors for decades.

174 Koolina Resort This $3-billion development, with a hotel, a classy Mediterranean restaurant, and an 18-hole golf course, is located in the newly created resort area of Kapolei. ◆ Aliinui Dr (off Farrington Hwy), Kapolei

Within the Koolina Resort:

Ihilani Resort and Spa $$$$ This resplendent 387-room hotel is removed from the usual visitor attractions, but it offers many of its own, including a white-sand beach, two pools, a spa, five restaurants, and six tennis courts. Rooms come equipped with such extras as CD players and three phones. ◆ 92-1001 Olani St (at Aliinui Dr), Kapolei. 679.0079, 800/626.4446; fax 679.0295 ♿

Restaurants/Clubs: Red	**Hotels:** Blue
Shops/ 🌳 Outdoors: Green	**Sights/Culture:** Black

Azul ★★$$$$ No children under seven are allowed in this elegant and intimate cherry wood–adorned dining room at the **Ihilani Resort and Spa.** Select from such specialties as marinated rack of lamb, veal tenderloin, and ragout *onaga* (red snapper in a saffron and white-wine sauce). ◆ Mediterranean ◆ Dinner M, Tu, and Th-Sa. Reservations recommended; shirts with collars required for men. 92-1001 Olani St (at Aliinui Dr), Kapolei. 679.0079 ⚬

Koolina Golf Course Cascading waterfalls and ocean views add to the appeal of this Ted Robinson–designed 18-hole course (par 72, 6,867 yards). There's a free shuttle for guests of the **Ihilani Resort and Spa.** ◆ Expensive greens fees, discounted for resort guests. Daily. Across from the Ihilani Resort and Spa. 676.5300

175 Waikele Center In 1995, shopping centers in the US averaged $261 in sales per square foot; the new Waikele Center grosses $800 a year for every square foot of store space. That's because of all the great outlet stores on the grounds, including **The Sports Authority** (677.9933), **The Saks Fifth Avenue Clearinghouse** (676.1773), and **OshKosh B'Gosh** (676.8080), and other well-known names like **Borders Books & Music** (676.6699). ◆ M-F 9AM-9PM, Sa 10AM-6PM. The center is accessible by bus or take H-1 to Exit 7, Waipahu. 676.5858 ⚬

176 Pearl Country Club A country club in name only, this public 18-hole course (par 72, 6,230 yards) overlooks Pearl Harbor; a forest of trees patiently awaits your hooks and slices. ◆ Expensive greens fees. Daily. 98-535 Kaonohi St (off Kamehameha Hwy), Pearl City. 487.3802

177 Pearlridge Center The two sections of this air-conditioned mall are connected by monorail. **Liberty House, JC Penney,** and **Sears** are the anchor stores; there are also boutiques and specialty shops, 16 movie screens, and numerous restaurants, including **Bravo Restaurant and Bar** (487.5544) for pizza and **Monterey Bay Canners** (483.3555) for grilled fish at affordable prices. On the corner of the busy intersection leading to the mall is **Anna Miller's** (487.2421), a coffee shop with winning pies; look for a circular building separate from the center. There's also a miniature golf course called **Jungle River** (488.8808) that keeps nonshoppers busy. ◆ Daily. 98-1005 Moanalua Rd (at Kaonohi St), Pearl City. 488.0981 ⚬

178 Aloha Stadium **Charles Luckman & Associates** designed the 50,000-seat stadium, home of the **University of Hawaii Rainbows,** the state's only college football team. The real excitement is when the **Hula Bowl, Aloha Bowl,** and **Pro Bowl** football games are televised from here every winter.

The stands can be moved to transform the football field to a baseball field. Unfortunate it seems that the stadium is slowly rusting because of the salty environment. ◆ 99-500 Salt Lake Blvd (between H-1 and Kamehameha Hwy). 486.9300 ⚬

178 Aloha Stadium Flea Market Wednesday and weekends the stadium parking lot is a gia flea market, with new and secondhand goods Vendors sell jewelry, kids' clothes, food, muumuus, aloha shirts, slippers, and toys, among other things. Shuttles pick up passen gers at the major hotels for a fee. ◆ Nominal for entry. W, Sa-Su 6AM-3PM. Aloha Stadium 99-500 Salt Lake Blvd (between H-1 and Kamehameha Hwy). 955.4050 ⚬

179 USS Bowfin Submarine & Park Explore the living and working spaces of a restored World War II US submarine, one of fewer th 20 still in existence, on a 40-minute self-guided tour. The museum also offers an impressive collection of sub-related artifacts and a small theater screens submarine-themed videos. ◆ Admission (no children under four allowed). Daily. 11 Arizona Memorial Dr (off Kamehameha Hwy), Pearl Harbor. 423.1341

179 USS Arizona Memorial It was early Sunda morning, 7 December 1941, and most of Honolulu was still sleeping when the **Pearl Harbor Naval Base** was bombed by Japanese planes. The attack caught the US Pacific fleet by surprise, leaving it devastated: 2,395 military personnel and civilians died, 188 planes were destroyed, and 18 major warship were sunk. The *USS Arizona* sank at its mooring blocks in 40 feet of water, becoming the tomb for 1,177 officers and sailors.

In 1962, a gracefully arched white structure was built over the *USS Arizona.* Designed by Honolulu architect **Alfred Preis,** the memorial is a national shrine, with the names of the 1,177 US Navy men and Marines killed on the *Arizona* engraved on a marble plaque, and on of Hawaii's most popular tourist attractions. Before boarding a Navy shuttleboat to the memorial, walk through the $5-million **Visitors' Center,** where the "day of infamy" is recounted. The National Park Service tour, including a documentary film and shuttle to the memorial, lasts about 75 minutes. ◆ Free. Tickets to the day's launches are issued on a first-come, first-served basis; before noon there's often a one- to three-hour wait. Visitors' Center daily 7:30AM-5PM. Shuttlebo 8AM-3PM (weather permitting). Shirts and shoes required. Arizona Memorial Dr (off Kamehameha Hwy), Pearl Harbor. 422.0561 ⚬

0 Pearl Harbor Naval Ship Tours On the first Saturday of every month, the US Navy opens one of its ships anchored in Pearl Harbor to the public for the afternoon. Visitors have free rein to explore the ship's cannon deck and to poke around the fascinating, puzzle-like maze of rooms and berths belowdecks. ♦ Free. First Saturday of every month noon-4PM. Enter through the Nimitz Gate at the end of Hwy 92, Pearl Harbor. 476.0281

1 Honolulu International Country Club This 18-hole private course (par 71, 5,987 yards) was designed in part by Arnold Palmer. ♦ Daily. Members and guests only. 1690 Ala Puumalu Pl (off Ala Hahanui), Honolulu. 833.4541

182 Moanalua Gardens Huge monkeypod trees dominate this sprawling 26-acre playground that is open to the public. The Prince Lot Hula Festival is held here each July to honor the prince (who became King Kamehameha V) for reviving the ancient hula during his 1863-72 reign, after more than four decades of a missionary-imposed ban. The only remaining buildings are a cottage where Kamehameha V used to entertain his friends and the **Chinese Hall** built in the early 1900s by Samuel Mills Damon. Nearby Moanalua Valley features petroglyphs and other historic sights. ♦ Daily 7:30AM-3PM. Nature hikes into the valley twice monthly; call for dates and reservations. Off Moanalua Fwy (Moanalua Gardens exit), Honolulu. 833.1944

ests

eorge Mavrothalassitis
xecutive Chef, Four Seasons, Maui

My favorite restaurant is **Chiang Mai Northern Thai Restaurant,** a family-style restaurant in Honolulu. The food is great.

trolling down the ocean sidewalk along the **South Shore** between the **New Otani Kaimana Beach Hotel** and **Kapahulu Avenue.** Try it at sunset.

The **Contemporary Museum** in Honolulu. Visit the pavilion displaying a set from the opera *L'Enfant et es Sortilèges.*

The authentic Hawaiian music at the **Sheraton Moana Surfrider** on Sunday afternoons.

Roy Yamaguchi
Chef/Owner: Roy's Restaurant, Roy's Nicolina, Roy's Kahana Bar & Grill, Roy's Poipu Bar and Grill, Roy's Tokyo, Roy's Guam, Roy's Waikoloa, Roy's Aoyama, Roy's Pebble Beach, Roy's New China Max, Roy's Restaurant Cebu

Hiking **Upper Tantalus,** and visiting the **Bishop Museum,** the **East-West Center,** and the **Lyon Arboretum,** all on Oahu.

Haleiwa and **Waimea Bay** on Oahu's **North Shore.**

A romantic dinner at the beautiful **La Mer** restaurant at the **Halekulani Hotel** in Waikiki, Oahu.

Hiram L. Fong
Retired US Senator/Attorney/Chairman of the Board, Finance Enterprises, Ltd., Honolulu

Take a scenic drive, stopping at the **USS Arizona Memorial,** a monument built in tribute to those who died aboard the *USS Arizona* on 7 December 1941. The US Navy offers a free boat tour of **Pearl Harbor** and the memorial.

Visit **Waimea Falls Park,** a 1,800-acre arboretum on the North Shore; the **Polynesian Cultural Center** in Laie, whose re-created villages represent seven ancient cultures; **Senator Fong's Plantation and Gardens,** a 725-acre garden estate with lush tropical forests and exotic flowers and fruit trees;

and **Sea Life Park** in Makapuu, an oceanside display of marine life.

Take **Tantalus Drive** to the **Puu Ualakaa State Wayside** for a spectacular view by day or night.

Walk along famous **Waikiki Beach;** see the animals and collections of tropical birds at the **Honolulu Zoo;** take a historic walking tour of **Downtown Honolulu** and visit **Iolani Palace,** the only palace in America, the **Mission Houses Museum, Kawaiahao Church, Washington Place,** and our **State Capitol;** or walk through **Chinatown,** where you can shop at the open markets.

Joyce Matsumoto
Relations Director, Halekulani Hotel, Honolulu

May Day Twilight Celebration with the Brothers Cazimero at the **Waikiki Shell Amphitheater** (don't miss the lei exhibition, either).

Sunset cocktails and traditional Hawaiian entertainment at the **Halekulani Hotel**'s **House Without a Key** in Waikiki.

A rainbow-colored shave ice at the **S. Matsumoto Shave Ice Store** on the North Shore.

Celebrating Christmas with the **Honolulu Boys Choir.**

Brett A. Uprichard
Editor, *Hawaii Drive Guides*; Associate Editor, *Honolulu Magazine*

Sunset drinks at the **Sheraton Moana Surfrider**'s **Banyan Veranda**—very relaxing and beautiful, with views of surfers and canoes.

A morning hike to the top of **Diamond Head Crater**—the very best view of Waikiki and the beach.

Any Hawaiian luau at an old beachside house. *Kalua* pig never tastes as good anywhere else, and the amateur entertainment is usually terrific.

A midnight stroll on **Lanikai Beach** (near **Kailua Beach Park**) during a full moon.

Teriyaki steak on a stick at the **Punahou** or **McKinley High School** carnivals.

Kauai

A rainbow rising over a sugarcane field. A trio of laughing girls riding their horses through a small town. A Japanese man with a weathered face selling produce from his fields. These are the sorts of memorable vistas and vignette seen around every other bend on the 553-square-mile island of Kauai (kuh-wah-*ee*).

Nicknamed "The Garden Island," Kauai can lay claim to many superlatives. It's the oldest major island in the Hawaiian chain, believed to have been the original home of the volcano goddess Pele. Its cliffs and canyons, unduplicated on any of the other islands, are the result of the persistent workings of streams and ocean waves on once-bleak volcanic craters and cinder cones. At the dead center of this roughly circular isle, 5,148-foot **Mount Waialeale** draws the most rainfall of anywhere in the world, an average of 440 inches a year. It's here (some believe) that a race of tiny people called "menehune" fashioned impossibly intricate structures overnight. Kauai was also the first island visited by English explorer Captain James Cook in 1778 (with tragic results). This island has many more miles of sandy beach (40) than any other in the Hawaiian chain—and, finally, Kauai is the only Hawaiian island from which no other land can be seen.

But it isn't just the island's historical, geographical, or geological attributes that distinguish it from its counterparts. Kauai's people are extraordinary too. When Hurricane Iniki hit in September 1992, there were few criminal incidents; instead, the island's 50,000 residents pooled their energy and skills to put the island back together—and to make it better than before. A Mayor's Conference on Tourism was formed, and islanders set about creating a structure for planned growth that focuses on ecotourism and Hawaiian cultural programs rather than megaresorts and golf courses.

While tourism on the island is still 25 percent below pre-Iniki figures, and several major hotels and a few stores remain boarded up with no plans to reopen, travelers to Kauai will see few reminders of 1992's devastating natural disaster. Some returning visitors may notice that the foliage is slightly less lush but first-timers will find it hard to imagine that things could be more green.

There's still much on Kauai to attract a traveler's interest and admiration. On the island's verdant **North Shore**, there's the nouveau-chic town of **Hanalei;** the deluxe **Princeville** resort; **Lumahai Beach,** where Mitzi Gaynor endeavored to wash a man out of her hair in the movie *South Pacific;* the mythical island of Bali Hai, actually a series of misty mountain peaks seen from **Haena State Beach Park** and transformed by clever camera angles in that same movie; and the postcard-perfect cliffs of **Na Pali Coast.** On Kauai's dramatically different southern coast, sun lovers bask on the beach in the **Poipu** resort area. And in the heart of the isle, there's the awe-inspiring 10-mile-long, two-mile-wide **Waimea Canyon,** where meandering rivers and earth-colored canyon walls rob even the veteran traveler of facile descriptions

Na Pali Coast

Valley of the Lost Tribe

29 Polihale State Park

Mana

50

Kaumualii Hwy.

Kokee Rd.

55

Kekaha

Waimea Canyon Dr.

550

Waimea River

550

25

Waimea

Waimea Bay

24 Russian Fort

Kaulakahi Channel

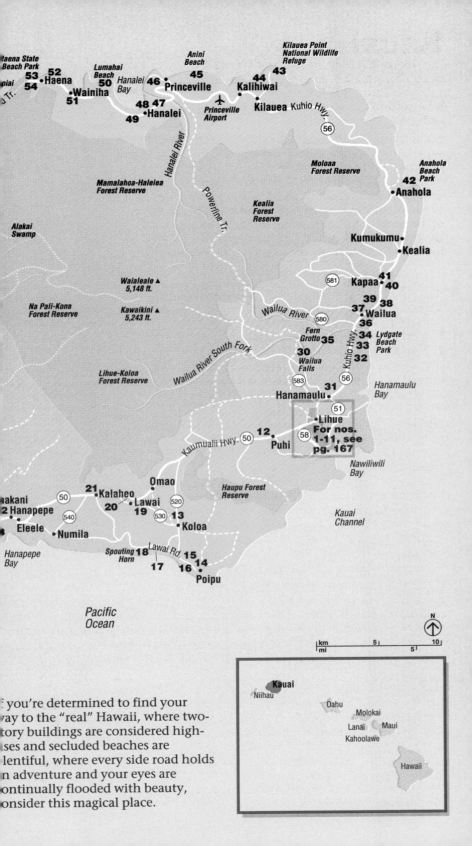

Haena State Beach Park

53 • Haena 52
54 51
• Wainiha

Lumahai Beach 50
Hanalei Bay 46 • Princeville 45
Anini Beach

48 47
49 • Hanalei

Princeville Airport

44 • Kalihiwai 43
• Kilauea
Kilauea Point National Wildlife Refuge

Kuhio Hwy.

56

Moloaa Forest Reserve

Anahola Beach Park
42
• Anahola

Mamalahoa-Haleiea Forest Reserve

Hanalei River

Kealia Forest Reserve

Kumukumu •
• Kealia

Alakai Swamp

Waialeale ▲ 5,148 ft.

Powerline Tr.

581 Kapaa • 41
40

Na Pali-Kona Forest Reserve

Kawaikini ▲ 5,243 ft.

Wailua River

580

39 38
37 36
• Wailua

Fern Grotto 35
30 Wailua Falls

34 Lydgate Beach Park
33
32

Wailua River South Fork

Lihue-Koloa Forest Reserve

583
31

Kuhio Hwy.

56

Hanamaulu •

51

Hanamaulu Bay

Kaumualii Hwy.

50 12
• Puhi

• Lihue
58 **For nos. 1-11, see pg. 167**

Nawiliwili Bay

21 • Kalaheo
Omao

Haupu Forest Reserve

Kauai Channel

50
aakani
2 Hanapepe
20
19 • Lawai
520

540
530 13

Eleele • Numila
• Koloa

Hanapepe Bay

Spouting Horn 18 Lawai Rd 15
17 16 14
• Poipu

Pacific Ocean

km
mi
5
5
10

N

Kauai
Niihau
Oahu
Molokai
Lanai Maui
Kahoolawe
Hawaii

f you're determined to find your
ay to the "real" Hawaii, where two-
tory buildings are considered high-
ises and secluded beaches are
lentiful, where every side road holds
n adventure and your eyes are
ontinually flooded with beauty,
onsider this magical place.

Area code 808 unless otherwise noted.

Getting to Kauai

Airports

Lihue Airport

Two miles east of **Lihue**, this small, island-style airport has an open-air terminal and car-rental booths—period. All arrivals and departures are interisland.

Airport Services

Information	246.1440
Lost and Found	246.0253
Parking	245.8716

Airlines

Aloha Airlines	245.3691, 800/367.5250
Hawaiian Airlines	245.1813, 800/367.5320
Mahalo Air, interisland	246.3500, 800/277.8333
from the mainland	800/4-MAHALO

Getting to and from Lihue Airport

By Bus

The **Kauai Bus** (241.6410) charges $1 for travel between **Kekaha** and Lihue or Hanalei and Lihue.

By Car

To get to Lihue, head west on **Ahukini Road (Highway 570)** or south on **Kapule Highway (Highway 51)**.

The following car-rental firms have booths at **Lihue Airport**.

Alamo	246.0646, 800/327.9633
Avis	245.3512, 800/331.1212
Budget	245.1901, 800/527.0700
Dollar	245.3651, 800/421.6868
Hertz	245.3356, 800/654.3131
National/Interrent	245.5636, 800/227.7368

By Taxi

There's a cab stand across from the baggage claim area. The fare to Lihue is about $7, to the **Wailua/ Kapaa** area, about $16, and to Poipu resorts, $30.

Princeville Airport

Two miles east of **Princeville** on Kauai's **North Shore,** this small airport has one terminal (no phone) that's closed when flights are not arriving or departing. At press time, no commercial flights were using the airport, although there was talk of several smaller carriers stepping in to offer these services.

Interisland Carriers

Aloha Airlines makes direct hops on Boeing 737s to **Lihue Airport** from the **Honolulu International Airport** on Oahu and **Kahului Airport** on Maui. **Hawaiian Airlines** flies nonstop DC9s to Lihue from **Honolulu International** only, as does **Mahalo Air**.

Getting Around Kauai

Bicycles

Although some of the roads tend to be a bit narrow on the North Shore, Kauai is a great place to travel on two wheels. **Pedal and Paddle** in Hanalei (at the **Ching Young Shopping Village,** 826.9069), rents mountain bikes and Kauai cruisers (old, beaten-up bikes) on a daily and weekly basis, with locks and helmets included.

Buses

The **Kauai Bus** (241.6410) runs between Hanalei and Kekaha from 5:30AM to 6PM Mondays through Saturdays. Passengers can ride quite a distance for just a $1 fare.

Driving

One main road follows the island's coastline. From Lihue west it is called **Kaumualii Highway (Highway 50)**; from Lihue north it is called **Kuhio Highway (Highway 56)**. Roads are generally good and drivers normally courteous.

Avoid driving between Lihue and Kapaa during rush hours. Otherwise, driving on the island is easy; the road that skirts the coast will get you almost everywhere you want to go. Be sure to explore some of those intriguing side roads that extend off the highway, however. Some of Kauai's most beautiful and untouched spots are off the beaten path but well worth seeking out.

Hiking

Some of the finest hiking trails in Hawaii can be found on Kauai. Headliners include treks across Waimea Canyon, and the 13-mile **Powerline Trail**, a ridge trail that connects the North Shore with Wailua. But the quintessential Kauai hike is the 11-mile **Kalalau Trail** from **Kee Beach** along the Na Pali Coast to an unparalleled stretch of white sand. For the lowdown on this and other trails, order a copy of *Hiking Kauai* by Robert Smith (Booklines Hawaii; $10.95).

Parking

Parking in Kauai is as easy as *lilikoi* (passion fruit) pie. Rarely will you have to feed a meter (if you do, a quarter will generally buy half an hour). There are no parking garages.

Taxis

Cabs aren't easily hailed here, but they come (eventually) when called. Try **ABC Taxi** (822.7641) or **North Shore Cab** (826.6189). The regulated fare is $2 when the flag drops and 25¢ per eighth mile.

Tours

Kauai doesn't suffer from any shortage in the tour department, from adrenaline-producing adventures to tame rides in horse-drawn carriages. A fascinating departure from the humdrum is offered by **Oceanic Society Expeditions'** (800/326.7491) diving, fishing, and natural history tour to one of the 125 atolls that make up Hawaii: Midway Island. Three-, four-, and en-night packages are available. And no roll call ours would be complete without a mention of **ialeale Boat Tours** (822.4908), which offers artures every 30 minutes on slow-moving power ts to the well-known **Fern Grotto. Polynesian venture Tours** (246.0122) runs full- and half-tours of Waimea Canyon, **Wailua River,** and North Shore. **Captain Zodiac Raft Expeditions** 6.9371) operates daily trips along the athtaking Na Pali Coast in inflatable rafts. another kind of water sightseeing, **Outfitters uai** (742.9667) provides kayaks, equipment, guides for coastal tours in the lightweight ts. History buffs will enjoy the tours offered by ntation Carriages (246.9529); participants hear v sugar was and is cultivated on the island during 0-minute cane-field ride in a wagon pulled by desdales. Flightseeing tours are offered by **:k Harter Helicopters** (245.3774) and **Na Pali licopters** (245.6959), among others.

alking

lking is the transportation mode of choice in small vns like Hanalei, Kapaa, **Koloa,** and **Hanapepe,** but ween towns something a bit faster and more ged is in order.

YI

opping

e biggest mall is **Kukui Grove Center** (245.7784) _ihue, with branches of **Penthouse** (245.7751) for counted alohawear, and **Kauai Products Store** 6.6753), featuring goods made by local artisans. e **Coconut Plantation Marketplace** (822.3641) in paa is home to 69 stores, among them **Tropic suals** (823.8327), which stocks island attire for men, and **Island Surf Shop** (822.6955), with ean gear for all ages. But the most fun place to op is probably Hanalei town, site of more unusual claves like the **Ching Young Shopping Village** 6.7222), where the merchandise runs to lonesian beads and koa wood figurines.

sitors' Information Centers

e **Kauai Visitors' Bureau** (KVB; 3016 Umi St, ue, HI 96766, 245.3971; fax 246.9235) is open m 8AM to 4:30PM Mondays through Fridays.

hone Book

nergencies

nbulance/Fire/Police	911
ntal Emergency	246.8811
spital (Wilcox Memorial Hospital)	245.1100
cksmith	245.8004
armacy	822.4918
ison Control	800/360.3585
lice (nonemergency)	241.6711

Lihue

On the southeast coast of Kauai, Lihue is the commercial and governing center of the island and the point of arrival for most visitors. Although it in many ways remains a quiet old plantation town (there's still an operating sugar mill here), recent development projects—restoration of portions of the town, renovation of the **Lihue Shopping Center** as a sleek civic center, new housing, and a shopping center—have given Lihue a somewhat more modern aspect. The town's streets reflect its changing nature, with banged-up old pickups parked behind shiny new sports cars. The heart of "downtown" Lihue is a little square lined with government offices, a small museum, and the county court. **Nawiliwili,** the island's main harbor, is two miles distant, and **Kalapaki Beach** is at the ocean end of the harbor. Lihue offers some interesting sights, good restaurants, and a quirky charm.

1 **Hamura's Saimin Stand** ★$ If you haven't experienced the saimin sensation, hunker over a bowl of the traditional Hawaiian noodle soup (the ethnic equivalent of burgers and fries) here with the locals. A modest place with narrow Formica counters, this eatery spoons out some of the best saimin on Kauai. Try the teriyaki beef version. ◆ Hawaiian/Japanese ◆ Daily breakfast, lunch, and dinner. No reservations. No credit cards. 2956 Kress St (between Kalena and Rice Sts). 245.3271

2 **Kauai Museum** The story of the islands of Kauai and Niihau, from the first volcanic eruptions more than six million years ago through the 19th century, is told in a permanent exhibit in the **William Hyde Rice Building,** named for the last appointed governor of Kauai under the Hawaiian monarchy. In the **Albert Spencer Wilcox Building** (illustrated above), named for the son of missionary teachers, you'll find changing exhibits of Kauai art and historical artifacts. To see some of the generally inaccessible sights of the island without boarding a chopper, watch the film that was shot during a helicopter tour. ◆ Admission. M-Sa. 4428 Rice St (at Eiwa St). 245.6931 &

Restaurants/Clubs: Red		**Hotels:** Blue
Shops/ ♥ Outdoors: Green		**Sights/Culture:** Black

TIP TOP

3 Tip Top ★$ Known by locals and visitors from the outer islands as *the* breakfast place in Lihue, this eatery serves up stacks of macadamia nut and banana pancakes, side orders of spicy Portuguese sausage, and eggs with papaya. A favorite meeting place of Kauai's movers and shakers, it's also renowned for its fresh-baked cookies, cakes, and pies. The cafe is connected with a low-budget motel, but that isn't recommended. ♦ Japanese/American ♦ Tu-Su breakfast, lunch, and dinner. 3173 Akahi St (at Hardy St). 245.2333 &

si Cisco's

4 Si Cisco's ★$$ Big portions of south-of-the-border fare are served here; house specialties include tamales, fajitas, and mason-jar margaritas. The food isn't great, but it's a good deal for the price. ♦ Mexican ♦ Daily lunch and dinner. No reservations. Kukui Grove Center, Old Nawiliwili Rd (at Kaumualii Hwy). 246.1563 &

5 Grove Farm Founded in 1864 by George N. Wilcox, a descendant of New England missionaries, this self-contained sugar plantation is a slice of the real Kauai. When Mabel Wilcox, George's niece and the last Wilcox to live on the plantation, died in 1978, it became a nonprofit educational organization dedicated to preserving the history of plantation life on the island. Well-versed guides conduct tours of the main plantation home, the cottages in which George lived and guests stayed, and the workers' camp houses. Miss Mabel's clothes hang in her closet, her sister Elsie's silver-handled hairbrushes remain on her dresser, and their uncle's collection of canes and hats is in his cottage. Housekeepers dust the furniture, replace the flowers, bake cookies, and make iced tea for visitors. This is one of the most fascinating attractions on Kauai. ♦ Admission. Tours M, W, Th 10AM and 1PM. Reservations required (sometimes one week in advance); no tours on rainy days and national holidays. 4050 Nawiliwili Rd (between Lala Rd and Aheahe St). 245.3202

According to the 1994 state census, the population of "full-blooded" native Hawaiians (defined as those with four pure Hawaiian grandparents) on Kauai is 46.

6 JJ's Broiler ★★$$$ Even *Gourmet* magazine couldn't wrest the recipe for the secret sauce on this eatery's famous garlic-flavored Slavonic steak from owner Jim Jasper. Mahimahi and lobster join the beefy stars served in this handsome establishment. ♦ Steak/Seafood ♦ Daily lunch and dinner. Reservations recommended. In the Anchor Cove complex, 3416 Rice St (near Kalapaki Rd). 246.4422 &

7 Kauai Chop Suey ★★$ The enormous menu here has a following among the lunchtime crowd hungry for chow mein, shrimp with black beans, or one of the dozen of other Cantonese offerings. Kauai chow mein—a steaming plate of noodles, chicken, shrimp, *char siu* (barbecue pork), and lots of vegetables on cake noodles—is the house specialty. ♦ Chinese ♦ Tu-Su lunch and dinner. No reservations. No credit cards. Pacific Ocean Plaza, 3501 Rice St (near Lala Rd). 245.8790 &

7 Cafe Portofino ★★$$$ Wood beams, ceiling fans, and an open-air terrace overlooking Kalapaki Beach all contribute to this eatery's charm. The gourmet Italian menu features such unusual dishes as rabbit in wine sauce with black olives, and veal Portofino—sauteed with shrimp and scallops in a lemon sauce. Treat yourself to an afternoon cocktail or an espresso at the bar or stop by for one of the occasional live jazz performances. ♦ Italian ♦ M-F lunch and dinner; Sa-Su dinner. Reservations recommended. Pacific Ocean Plaza, 3501 Rice St (near Lala Rd). 245.2121 &

8 Kauai Marriott $$$$ The island's largest hotel, this property, formerly the **Westin Kauai**, recently underwent a $28-million refurbishment that placed special emphasis on things Hawaiian, from the plants used to landscape the grounds to the animals living on islands created by a 2.1-acre reflecting lagoon in the center of the 800-acre property. There are five towers with 356 well-appointed guest rooms and suites, 232 one- and two-bedroom time-share units, four restaurants, a health spa, and hammocks and cabanas on the beach. The hotel's swimming pool is one of the largest in Hawaii, with 26,000 square feet of water surface and a lining of 1.8 million blue-and-white mosaic tiles. It's hard to go wrong at this place—under any management. ♦ Kalapaki Beach. 245.5050, 800/228.9290; fax 245.5049 &

Within the Kauai Marriott:

Duke's Canoe Club ★★$$ The theme of this statewide restaurant chain is Hawaii's "Ambassador of Goodwill," surf star Duke Kahanamoku. At this branch, the walls are made of elegant koa wood, photos of the Duke adorn the walls, and there's a spectacular ocean view. The steak and lobster or shrimp scampi over linguine aren't half bad either. Check out the bands that play after the dinner hour Wednesday through Saturday. ◆ Casual American ◆ Daily lunch and dinner. Reservations recommended. 245.5050 ♿

9 Kauai Lagoons Golf Club The championship 18-hole **Kiele Course** (par 72, 6,674 yards) was created for tournament play, and the traditional links-style 18-hole **Kauai Lagoons Course** (par 72,

6,578 yards) is for all levels; all 36 holes were designed by Jack Nicklaus. The club also has a swimming pool, health spas, and eight tennis courts, including a stadium court. ◆ Expensive greens fees. Daily. 3351 Hoolaulea Way (adjacent to the Kauai Marriott). 241.6000, 800/634.6400

10 Nawiliwili Beach Park The beach here is superb for swimming, thanks to its sheltered cove and sandy bottom, and the waves are suitable for novice surfers. Old-timers will remember the days when Hawaiian beachboys steered their canoes through the surf here. ◆ At the end of Nawiliwili Rd

11 Alakoko Fish Pond (Menehune Fish Pond) According to folk legend, the menehune were two-foot-tall people who occupied Kauai long before the Polynesians and accomplished enormous physical feats, the remains of which are still visible. The menehune are credited with making this

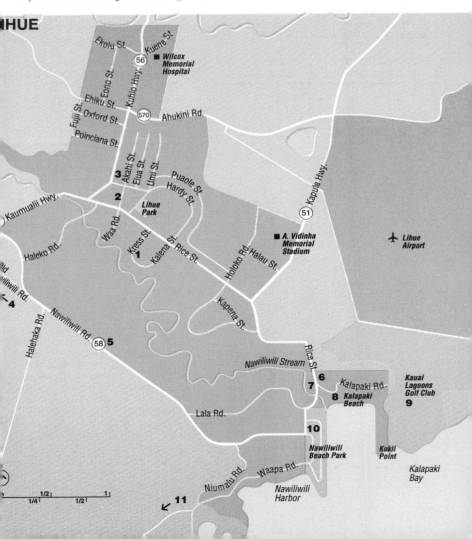

mullet pond by building a 900-foot-long wall to cut off a bend in the Huleia River. Legend has it that a princess and her brother asked the menehune to undertake this task, and they agreed as long as the two didn't watch them build it. Naturally, they did watch, and, quite unnaturally, they were turned to stone as a result. The twin pillars near the fish pond are said to be the curious siblings. ♦ Overlook on Hulemalu Rd (off Niumalu Rd)

South Shore

Hot and nearly always sunny, with broad, white beaches, generally calm seas, and a profusion of tropical plants and trees, the southern coast of Kauai has been one of the most popular destinations on the island; vacationers flocked to the resorts at **Poipu** to enjoy tennis, good restaurants, and luxurious lodgings as well as excellent swimming, snorkeling, scuba diving, and surfing. Recovery from the hurricane has been slow for area resorts, but many are once again busy; the coast's natural attributes have pretty much returned to their pre-hurricane splendor, so the area is gradually resuming its place as Kauai's most popular vacation spot.

Beyond the Poipu resorts and the gentrified plantation town of **Koloa,** southern Kauai is still a quiet, rural place where people depend on sugarcane rather than tourism for their livelihoods.

12 Kilohana Estate Gaylord Parke Wilcox, a relative of **Grove Farm** founder George N. Wilcox (see page 166) and at one point head of the **Grove Farm** plantation, probably never imagined that the Tudor-style dream house (pictured above) he built in 1935 would one day be a shopping complex, with his office serving as a jewelry store. The original woodwork and furnishings now adorn an Art Deco gallery, shops, and restaurants. The master bedroom is a gallery featuring the works of leading Hawaiian artists. Carriage rides and sugarcane tours are available for a fee. ♦ Daily. 3-2087 Kaumualii Hwy (Hwy 50), Puhi. 245.5608 &

Electronic windows that change from clear to frosted at the flick of a switch are installed in every room at the Princeville Resort on Kauai. When the power is off, a thin layer of crystals sandwiched between two plates of glass diffuses light rays, creating a "frosted" effect. When the switch is flipped, the crystals align themselves and voilà—instant room with a view.

Restaurants/Clubs: Red   **Hotels:** Blue

Shops/ ♥ Outdoors: Green   **Sights/Culture:** Black

Within Kilohana Estate:

Gaylord's Restaurant ★★$$$ Named after Gaylord Wilcox of the prominent missionary family, this restaurant offers alfresco dining in some of the most pleasing surroundings on the island. A courtyard overlooks the sprawling lawns of the estate while a private dining room retains the luxury and splendor of its plantation-era heyday. Continental specialties include fresh seafood, prime rib, and lamb with exotic chutneys. ♦ Continental ♦ Daily lunch and dinner; Su brunch and dinner. Reservations recommended. 245.9593

13 Old Koloa Town Bodysurfing and sun worshiping aren't the only attractions in the Poipu area. This $2-million restoration project was the brainchild of Robert H. Gerell of **Koloa Town Associates.** Gerell negotiated a 67-year lease from the **Mabel P. Waterhouse Trust** and acquired three acres and about a thousand feet of frontage road in Koloa, then set to work refurbishing the weathered, termite-ridden storefronts that creaked from one end of Koloa to the other, outfitting them in 19th-century style. Some of the historical structures that were restored are a stone mill stack from **Grove Farm;** the **Koloa Hotel,** Kauai's first hostelry, built in 1898; and the 1900 **Yamamoto Store.** Dozens of businesses also have opened behind renovated storefronts, including **Lappert's Ice Cream** (742.1272) and **Crazy Shirts** (742.7161). Unfortunately, the restoration jacked up the rents in town, and several *kamaaina* (longtime residents) were forced to leave their cozy hometown storefronts. ♦ Koloa Rd (Hwy 530)

Within Old Koloa Town:

Koloa Broiler ★$$ Save some money and broil your own steaks and burgers at this casual, quaint little restaurant (illustrated above). Fish and chicken are also reasonably priced. Meals include salad bar, rice, and baked beans. ♦ Steaks ♦ Daily lunch and dinner. No reservations. 5412 Koloa Rd. 742.9122 &

14 Poipu This area was the hardest hit by Hurricane Iniki. What wasn't demolished by 30-foot waves was blown apart by 180-mph winds; entire houses, some priced in the millions, were gutted or ripped off their foundations. A trip to the sunny South Shore and **Poipu Beach** is once again a popular excursion from the Wailua or Lihue areas, though; most folks will hardly see any trace of the damage. The **Tunnel of Trees,** a grove of eucalyptus trees that forms a natural archway along Highway 520, is a distinctive landmark along the way. **Poipu Beach Park,** hard hit by the hurricane, attracts sun lovers and whale watchers as before, and quality bodysurfing can still be found at **Brennecke Beach.** The area's most famous natural attraction, beyond the fine beaches, is **Spouting Horn** (see page 171), a geyserlike lava tube. ♦ At the end of Poipu Rd (Hwy 520)

Within Poipu:

Poipu Beach Park Considered the best swimming beach on the island and one of the most beautiful on Kauai before being hammered by Iniki, Poipu Beach has mostly recovered from the hurricane, although its public bathhouse was still in ruins at press time. The sunny stretch of sand is good for swimming, snorkeling, and whale watching (in winter). ♦ Hoone Rd (from Poipu Rd take Hoowili Rd south for a quarter of a mile)

Outrigger Kiahuna Plantation Condominiums $$$ This first-class resort has plantation-style buildings right beside Poipu Beach. It is an excellent place to settle while enjoying Kauai's sunniest shoreline. The 36-acre property is generously landscaped with broad, manicured lawns, trees, and bougainvillea, with pathways and tiny Japanese-style bridges leading to the beach. While the most popular of the 333 units are those on the shore, the ones fronted by lawns are equally pleasant. There's a pool, a restaurant, and 10 tennis courts. Each unit has a full kitchen and is equipped with a TV and VCR. ♦ 2253 Poipu Rd. 742.6411, 800/688.7444; fax 742.1698 &

15 Roy's Poipu Bar and Grill ★★★$$$ This was Midas-fingered restauranteur Roy Yamaguchi's fourth eatery (there are now 11 scattered throughout the Pacific Rim). The place is packed with diners putting away meals like *kiawe*-grilled hibachi-style salmon and herb-grilled fillet of beef. ♦ Euro-Asian ♦ Daily dinner. Reservations recommended. 2360 Kiahuna Plantation Dr (off Poipu Rd), Poipu. 742.5000; fax 742.5050 &

15 Kiahuna Golf Course Poipu's first championship 18-hole course (par 70, 6,336 yards), designed by Robert Trent Jones Jr., was completed in 1983. It's since been eclipsed by several island courses, but is less expensive and challenging, so it still attracts eager golfers. ♦ Moderate greens fees. Daily. 2545 Kiahuna Plantation Dr (off Poipu Rd), Poipu. 742.9595

16 Sheraton Kauai $$$$ At press time the property was scheduled to reopen late in 1997. More than $100 million is being

pumped into the renovation, but progress is slow. ♦ 2440 Hoonani Rd (off Lawai Rd), Poipu. 742.1661, 800/325.3535; fax 742.9777 &

16 Hyatt Regency Kauai $$$$ Kauai's second-largest resort sits on 48 acres of choice oceanfront property. Although Iniki inflicted $55 million worth of damage, the completely restored hotel reopened only six months after the 1992 hurricane. Designed by Honolulu architects **Wimberly, Allison, Tong and Goo** and Santa Monica interior decorators Hirsch-Bedner & Associates, the structure is splendidly landscaped with a re-created shipwreck and a five-acre lagoon that faces Keoneloa Bay, commonly called "Shipwreck's Beach." The remarkable architecture draws inspiration from island homes, with gorgeous, handcrafted koa wood furnishings. Five restaurants are on the property, from the lagoon-side **Dock** to **Tidepools,** a seafood spot. Scuba diving, snorkeling, tennis, and catamaran sailing are among the many sports guests can enjoy, plus there's an 18-hole Robert Trent Jones Jr. golf course and a driving range. Sailing, horseback riding, kayak excursions, and helicopter tours are all nearby. In addition, the hotel's "Discover Kauai" program, run under the auspices of the **Kauai Historical Society** and **Na Hula O Kaohi Kukapulani,** offers a range of activities (free to guests), including presentations on the history and lore of hula (with demonstrations) and a dune walk focusing on the endemic plants and sea life of the Poipu Beach area. ♦ 1571 Poipu Rd, Poipu. 742.1234, 800/742.2353; fax 742.6265 &

16 Poipu Kai Condominiums $$$ The comfortably appointed condominium resort has 235 units (100 managed by Colony Hotels & Resorts) on 110 lavishly landscaped acres adjacent to the beach. Each unit is a home away from home with a full kitchen, a washer/dryer, a TV set, and fans; there's also a restaurant that serves dinner (so it's not *too* much like home). Six swimming pools, nine tennis courts, and two championship golf courses are on opposite sides of the property. ♦ A two-day minimum stay is required. 1941 Poipu Rd, Poipu. 742.6464, 800/777.1700; fax 742.7865

Mokihana, a rare, fragrant plant that grows only on Kauai, is used to make exotic leis; however, *mokihana* leis cannot be worn against bare skin because the berry-size fruit is so potent it can burn your flesh.

Making Waves:
Smart Steps to Snorkeling Safely

Thanks to the warm, clear water and the relatively shallow coastline, Hawaii boasts some of the top snorkeling beaches in the world. Snorkeling is also one of the cheapest and most rewarding activities Hawaii has to offer. For less than three dollars a day, anyone who can float or swim can rent snorkel gear and spend hours gawking at the colorful sea life that inhabits the offshore coral reefs.

Snorkeling conditions change daily depending on the weather and surf, so your best bet is to ask a rental-shop employee where to go (try to avoid overrated spots such as **Molokini Island,** unless you don't mind swimming over and under other bodies to catch a glimpse of some fish). If you're fearful of taking the plunge, keep in mind that those who are afraid to try snorkeling (and you know who you are) usually are the ones who enjoy it the most. No matter where you decide to jump in, remember that the number-one safety rule is to snorkel with a partner.

Tips for Staying on Top

Make sure your mask fits properly. Check it by trying to inhale through your nose—you shouldn't be able to. (If you have a mustache, water may leak through your mask; apply Vaseline to your upper lip to help form a seal that will keep the water out.)

To test the fit of a full-foot fin, lean forward while standing up. The back of your foot should not slip out.

A wet suit is optional in Hawaii's warm waters, and it does tend to inhibit your ability to dive underwater.

Apply waterproof sunblock to your face, ears, neck, arms, back, and legs.

Defog your mask properly to avoid condensation. De-Fog, which is sold as a liquid spray or drops, works best, but saliva will suffice in a pinch. Thoroughly rinse your mask with water immediately after using it; never let it dry out with saltwater on it.

Put your fins on just before you enter the water (otherwise they may sink, and you'll never find them); lean on your buddy for support.

Enter the water walking backwards, with your mask on and the snorkel in your mouth, keeping a constant eye on the waves. When you're chest-deep into the water, turn and face the waves and start kicking.

Do not use your arms to swim. Keep them at your sides and let your legs and fins do the work.

Avoid looking straight down or your snorkel will fill with water; instead, look slightly ahead. If water enters your snorkel, don't panic. Just tilt your head back and blow out the water. If you're caught without any breath, lift your head above water, remove the snorkel from your mouth, and drain it.

Don't touch the marine life unless you're absolutely sure it's safe, and stay off the coral. Coral is a fragile, living animal that can die easily from careless human contact. Furthermore, coral may look soft, but it isn't. Not only can it easily scrape off your skin, it can also cause a nasty infection, so make sure each scrape is washed and rinsed thoroughly with fresh water.

Periodically check the shoreline to confirm that you're not on your way to Tahiti. Currents can be very deceiving.

If you're nervous, bring along a boogie board to hold on to. Holding hands with your partner is also calming.

A small plastic fish chart (available at most snorkel shops) is a great way to identify the various species.

If you feel adventurous and want to swim underwater, remember to pinch your nose and blow it gently whenever you feel even the slightest pressure in your ears. If you fail to do this, you may blow a hole in your eardrum.

To exit the water, walk out backwards (so you're always facing the waves).

Clean and rinse all of the rental equipment in fresh water before returning it.

17 The Beach House ★★★$$$ At a table overlooking the water at sunset, with a sizable order of *ahi* (tuna) *au poivre* or wok-charred, sesame-crusted tiger-eye sashimi, even the most craven holiday cynic would be hard-pressed not to enjoy him- or herself. ♦ Pacific Rim ♦ Daily dinner. Reservations recommended. 5022 Lawai Rd, Kukuiula. 742.1424 &

18 Spouting Horn Poipu's top tourist attraction is a gush of ocean water that explodes through a lava tube when the waves roll in, sometimes causing a moaning sound. Legend has it that the groan is from a lizard trapped in the tube. Note: The lava tube's reputation far exceeds its actual performance. ♦ Lawai Rd (near Camp 18 Rd), Kukuiula

19 National Tropical Botanical Garden Since it opened in 1971, this garden has survived several storms, and Hurricane Iniki proved no exception. Restored to its original splendor, this 186-acre botanical jewel continues to protect and propagate plants that otherwise might become extinct, adding some 1,000 plants to its inventory each year.

In 1938, Robert Allerton, the son of a pioneer Chicago cattleman, and his son, John Gregg Allerton, began to transform the **Allerton Estate** (formerly a vacation domicile of Queen Emma, wife of Kamehameha IV) into a garden showplace. With the help of hired gardeners, Allerton and his son spent 20 years clearing jungle growth to create sweeping gardens around reflecting pools, fountains, and statues. Kauai's *kamaaina* (locals) gave them cuttings and seeds, and the Allertons scoured the islands of the South Pacific for varieties never before seen on Kauai. Today visitors are able to tour the garden and **Allerton Estate.** ♦ Admission. Tours Tu-Sa 9AM, 1PM. Reservations required (sometimes six months in advance); call 332.7361 or write to Box 340, Lawai, HI 96765. Hailima Rd (off Hwy 530)

20 Mustard's Last Stand ★★$ If you're anywhere near the area, stop at this red-and-yellow kiosk for hot dogs, hamburgers, or fish-and-chips. Surfboard benches, daily specials, and friendly service are enough to keep the joint busy. ♦ American ♦ Daily 10AM-5:30PM. Kaumualii Hwy (Hwy 50, at Hwy 530), Lawai. 332.7245 &

21 Brick Oven Pizza ★$$ It's the best-known name in pizza on the island and one of the few places to eat on the way to Waimea Canyon.

Selections include pineapple and vegetarian pizza on whole-wheat dough (made fresh daily). Sandwiches, salads, and take-out orders are also available. ♦ Pizza/Deli/Takeout ♦ W-Su lunch and dinner. 2-2555 Kaumualii Hwy (Hwy 50), Kalaheo. 332.8561 &

22 Green Garden Restaurant ★★$$ Sue Hamabata and her daughter Gwen continue a family tradition started in 1948 by serving abundant amounts of delicious Asian, American, and Hawaiian food in the greenery-filled dining room that was once the family's home. Draped in her signature cascade of Niihau-shell leis, Sue greets guests, helps with the serving, and offers advice on meals tailored to your taste and budget. Start with a fresh *lilikoi* (passion fruit) daiquiri, indulge in butter-brushed filet mignon or broiled peppercorn chicken, and don't dare leave without finishing a piece of the famous *lilikoi* chiffon pie. ♦ Asian/American/Hawaiian ♦ M, W-Su breakfast, lunch, and dinner. Hana Rd (off Kaumualii Hwy), Hanapepe. 335.5422 &

22 Lappert's Ice Cream The Kauai-pie ice cream—a concoction of coffee and fudge with a hint of coconut and macadamia—is one of the irresistible flavors created by ice-cream wizard Walter Lappert, who came to Kauai to retire in 1981 and instead found himself churning out this creamy dessert. Soon the hobby snowballed into a 13,000-gallon-a-month business. His sweet success is spreading to local merchants as well, who supply him with crates of papayas, guavas, coconuts, pineapples, and mangoes, and about 8,000 pounds of macadamia nuts a month, not to mention the pure cane sugar, which he whips into more than 70 flavors of ice cream. You can buy Lappert's ice cream from this small white factory and shop, as well as throughout the islands. ♦ Daily. 1-3555 Kaumualii Hwy (Hwy 50, just west of Hanapepe). 335.6121, 800/356.4045 &

23 Salt Pond Beach Park This beach is named for the nearby ancient ponds where the Hawaiians harvested salt from drying beds. Every year the **Hui Hana Paakai O Hanapepe** (The Hanapepe Association of Salt Workers) lets ocean water dry in the ponds, collecting the prized salt crystals for use at home or for gifts. Sometimes referred to as "Hanapepe salt," it has a reddish tint and is coveted by Hawaiians, who consider the colored salt superior for healing and seasoning. However, because of state health regulations, it can't be sold commercially. There is also good swimming, fishing, and shelling at the beach, as well as picnic and public facilities. ♦ At the end of Lele Rd (off Kaumualii Hwy)

West Kauai

The main attractions on the western side of Kauai are natural ones. The highlight is **Waimea Canyon,** a spectacular 10-mile-long gash cut by the **Waimea River.** A few miles beyond the canyon is **Kokee State Park,** a 4,345-acre nature reserve that delights picnickers, hikers, campers, and others who just appreciate nature at its purest. Also pristinely beautiful are the white-sand beaches that stretch between **Mana** and **Polihale State Park.**

24 Russian Fort (Fort Elizabeth) In 1817 a German doctor named Georg Anton Schaeffer was sent to Kauai as a Russian agent. His mission was to negotiate the return of some furs lost in a Russian shipwreck off Kauai, and while he was at it, to convince Kauai's King Kaumualii to allow Russia to establish a military presence on the island in return for military assistance. The plan was eventually derailed by Kamehameha I, the ruler of the other Hawaiian isles. Wary of Russia, he forced Kaumualii to send Schaeffer away, but not before this star-shaped Russian-style fort, named for Czar Nicholas's daughter, was built on the banks of the Waimea River. Remnants of the lava stone fort are buried in the brush. ♦ Off Kaumualii Hwy (Hwy 50, at Waimea River)

25 Waimea Plantation Cottages $$$ If you wanted to immerse yourself in the real island lifestyle, you would get yourself one of the 47 one- to five-bedroom cottages (oceanfront, if possible) and settle into a rocking chair on the lanai. These cottages, on 27 acres in laid-back Waimea, are recommended for true R&R seekers only, as there isn't much in the way of entertainment (unless you include Waimea Canyon) nearby. However, there is a pool on the premises and a restaurant serving dinner on Fridays and Saturdays. One caveat: There is no air-conditioning and Waimea is hot in the summer. ♦ 9400 Kaumaulii Hwy, Waimea. 338.1625, 800/9.WAIMEA ♿

26 Menehune Ditch Kauai schoolchildren learn shortly after they can talk that if they don't want to be held responsible for something that goes wrong, they can always blame it on the menehune. Some say the menehune were a pygmy-size class of Polynesian laborers brought to Kauai by the old Hawaiians. Others say they are only a myth, the Hawaiian version of the leprechaun. True romantics credit the mysterious, mischievous people with magical powers and maintain that the ones who left Kauai did so on a floating island. This prodigious work is probably the menehune's most famous. The fitted stonework, not found anywhere else in

Hawaii, is said to be the remains of an aqueduct built by the menehune at the request of a Kauai king who wanted to irrigate nearby taro patches. Legend holds that the king was so pleased with their work he rewarded the menehune with a feast of shrimp, along with their favorite foods: sweet potatoes and *haupia* (coconut pudding). ♦ Menehune Rd (off Kaumualii Hwy in Waimea)

27 Waimea Canyon Plummeting 3,657 feet at its deepest point, the 10-milelong canyon is a rough, inhospitable cut—only goats and birds can manage the jagged terrain. For lack of a better comparison, it is often called the "Grand Canyon of the Pacific"—a worn-out exaggeration. Although no match for the Grand Canyon, it is still one of Hawaii's most photographed attractions. The main overlook offers a sprawling landscape, where white-tailed birds soar overhead and the echoes of bleating feral goats can often be heard. Colors range from gold to purple, red, and green, and when the canyon depths are clouded by mist, the effect is even more dramatic.

Hardy hikers may want to tackle the trails that zigzag down the canyon's wall, while the **Iliau Nature Loop** north of the lookout is a nice path for casual strollers. If you're staying in Lihue or Poipu, set aside an entire day for this excursion; although the canyon is only about 35 miles from Lihue, there are interesting towns along the way and slow-moving traffic occasionally causes delays. Once there, you'll want to continue on to **Kokee State Park** (see below) for a peek into the verdant and mysterious Kalalau Valley. Check your gas gauge before heading up to the out-of-the-way canyon, and bring a sweater—it's cool because of the higher elevation. ♦ Waimea Canyon Dr (the canyon lookout, marked by a Hawaii Visitors and Convention Bureau sign, is 5.6 miles past the junction of Hwys 55 and 550)

28 Kokee State Park Three miles from the canyon lookout, the park has a cool climate that attracts islanders tired of the same perfect weather day in and day out. At a 3,600-foot elevation, the 4,345-acre park is a brisk, nature-lover's bonanza, with rare honeycreepers, native flora, and burbling streams. The hiking trails are abundant (they cover 45 miles), and there's one for just about every level of expertise. From the end of June through August, the park's island-famous plums are free for the picking, and anglers (with licenses) can fish for rainbow trout in Kokee's cool streams from August through September. The fish eggs were flown in from the mainland, hatched on Oahu, and released for sportfishing here. You'll also find **Kokee Lodge** (see below), a gift shop, a bar and restaurant, and an information center in this idyllic forest setting. ♦ End of Hwy 550

Within Kokee State Park:

Kokee Lodge $ These 12 rustic cabins sleep four to six people in extremely simple style. There's one bathroom per cabin, and each bed has a blanket and a sheet, but that's about it for amenities. There's a restaurant open daily for breakfast and lunch. ♦ Book well in advance. Write to: Kokee Lodge, Box 819, Waimea, HI 96796. 335.6061 ⭑

Kokee Natural History Museum Informative and well managed, the museum features displays, videos, and photographs about **Waimea Canyon** and **Kokee State Park.** Trail information also is available. ♦ Donation. Daily. At the 15-mile marker on Hwy 550. 335.9975; fax 335.6131 ⭑

28 Kalalau Valley Lookout Timing is everything at this 4,000-foot-high vantage point, where the vista is usually clear in the early morning but obscured by mist and clouds by afternoon. Sightseers often make the long ascent to Kalalau only to find the fabled view hidden by the clouds. But when the clouds part, even if just for a moment, the effect is startlingly beautiful. Honeycreepers feed on lehua blossoms; waterfalls and fluted cliffs stand before you. Until early this century, the valley—the largest on the Na Pali Coast—was occupied by hundreds of Hawaiians who lived on the abundant fruits and vegetables grown here. No one lives in this remote area now. Experienced hikers can reach Kalalau from Haena on the North Shore, but there is no trail from the lookout because of the dangerous terrain.

29 Polihale State Park This is the most remote beach on Kauai that can be reached by car. There's good summer swimming, but it's rough the rest of the year. Rest rooms, showers, and barbecue grills are provided. ♦ End of Kaumualii Hwy (Hwy 50)

ast Kauai

dway up the east coast of Kauai are the resort eas of **Wailua** and **Kapaa.** Once the private eserve of Hawaii's *alii* (royalty), this is now the ost popular tourist area on the island (and the ly place that has any traffic to speak of). It offers uperb beach, a river that winds through tropical rests hiding grottoes and waterfalls, and depend- le weather all year. In recent years the two towns of ailua and Kapaa have grown together, linked by velopment along **Kuhio Highway (Highway 56).** th have some fairly good restaurants, numerous

souvenir and dive shops, and hotels and condominiums that line miles of white-sand beach.

30 Wailua Falls If there's been substantial rain, you'll see two exquisite falls (*wailua* means "twin waters") tumbling over the 80-foot cliff. Hawaiian chiefs used to dive down this precipice to prove their courage. Skip the lookout for the falls, which is four miles west of Kapaa, unless you don't mind the monotonous ride to get there. ♦ End of Maalo Rd (Hwy 583)

31 Hanamaulu Cafe & Tea House ★★ $$ Kick the Kauai salad-bar habit and spend a unique island evening in one of the garden rooms at this Japanese/Chinese restaurant, a local favorite for more than 60 years. The nine-course dinners (including snow-crab claws, spareribs, and ginger-seasoned fried chicken) are memorable, and the lobster—baked in a rich butter sauce with bread crumbs—has a unique flavor. ♦ Japanese/ Chinese ♦ Tu-F lunch and dinner; Sa-Su dinner. Reservations required for the garden rooms only. 3-4296 Kuhio Hwy (Hwy 56), Hanamaulu. 245.2511 ⭑

32 Outrigger Kauai Beach Hotel $$ Although it rests on a Hawaiian burial site (which is considered unlucky), this property rode out Hurricane Iniki relatively unscathed. In 1996, a $1.8-million renovation polished the rooms further. The series of five-story buildings is oriented toward the ocean and a long strip of sandy beach, which is suitable only for sunning because of the undertow. Three swimming pools more than compensate, though; the main pool is particularly elaborate, with caves, trickling waterfalls, fountains, and lots of greenery. The hotel has 346 guest rooms with lanais, cable TV, and refrigerators. There are two restaurants on the property. The **Wailua Golf Course** (see below) is a short ride away. ♦ 4331 Kauai Beach Dr (off Kuhio Hwy). 245.1955, 800/688.7444; fax 245.3956 ⭑

33 Wailua Golf Course The low greens fees make this one of the best golf bargains in Hawaii. Extending more than a mile along Wailua Beach, the 18-hole course (par 72, 6,585 yards) was built in 1920 among sand dunes and ironwood trees. The ocean comes into play on three holes, and the demanding back nine is highlighted by the famous Sea Beach Hole at the par-three 17th, where too much club will guarantee a Pacific-bound ball. ◆ Inexpensive greens fees. Daily. 3-5350 Kuhio Hwy (Hwy 56). 241.6666

33 Aston Kaha Lani Condominiums $$ Secluded on nine acres of beachfront property in Wailua, the 75 individually owned and decorated units have ocean-view lanais and are managed by the always reliable Aston Resorts. There's a pool and a tennis court (but no restaurant) on the premises; a golf course is nearby. A $4-million renovation completed in 1996 might give Aston fans added incentive to investigate. ◆ 4460 Nehe Rd (off Leho Dr). 822.9331, 800/922.7866; fax 822.2828

34 Lydgate Beach Park Local families and visitors enjoy this pleasant combination of beach, protected pools, sophisticated playground, picnic pavilions, and a tree-shaded park beside the Wailua River. There are public facilities on the premises. ◆ Off Kuhio Hwy (Hwy 56), Wailua

35 Fern Grotto The Wailua River, the best-known river in Hawaii, leads to this visitor attraction that has achieved the status of a "must-do" (it's a "must-not-do" if you don't like crowds or a circuslike atmosphere). The grotto is reached via boxy cruise boats that glide upriver as entertainers do the hula and perform standard Hawaiian tunes to ukulele accompaniments. After the boats land, you'll walk through jungle to a truly impressive cave filled with giant cascading ferns. Inside, the hired help recount legends with background music. The return trip is highlighted by a Hawaiian sing-along. The grotto is a popular site for weddings, complete with the traditional "Hawaiian Wedding Song." ◆ Cruise fee. Boats leave from Wailua Marina, off Kuhio Hwy (Hwy 56), Wailua. Smith's Motor Boat Service 821.6892; Waialeale Boat Tours 822.4908 ⑃

36 Wailua Marina Restaurant $$ Crowded with **Fern Grotto** tourists during the day, this huge, very touristy place has a little more breathing room during dinner hours. Dishes such as baked stuffed pork chops, fried chicken, and *ahi* (tuna) stuffed with crabmeat carry reasonable price tags. ◆ American ◆ Tu-Su lunch and dinner. Wailua Marina, 5971 Kuhio Hwy (Hwy 56, at Wailua River). 822.4311

37 Kintaro ★★$$$ Sleek, elegant, and authentically decorated with kimonos and Japanese screens, this restaurant offers an impressive selection of sashimi, sushi, *zaru soba* (buckwheat noodles), *nabemono* (seafood soup), *teppanyaki* (items grilled at tableside), and other exquisite delicacies. Be adventurous and try freshwater eel grilled with sweet sauce over rice. ◆ Japanese ◆ M-Sa dinner. Kuhio Hwy (Hwy 56, near Haleilio Rd) Wailua. 822.3341 ⑃

38 Coconut Plantation This resort development comprises four hotels and the **Coconut Plantation Marketplace**, with some 70 shops (most of them touristy), several restaurants, and a movie theater. ◆ Off Kuhio Hwy (Hwy 56), Waipouli. 822.3641

Within Coconut Plantation:

Aston's Kauai Beachboy Hotel $$ The highlight of this establishment is its setting on a milelong stretch of Waipouli Beach, which is actually better suited for wading and beachcombing than for swimming. The 233 lackluster rooms have refrigerators and lanais with ocean or mountain views. Serious shoppers are well located here, within walking distance of the **Coconut Plantation Marketplace.** There's also a pool, two tennis courts, and a spartan restaurant on the premises. ◆ 4-484 Kuhio Hwy (Hwy 56). 822.3441, 800/922.7866; fax 822.0843 ⑃

Kauai Coconut Beach Resort

COCONUT PLANTATION

Kauai Coconut Beach Resort $$$ Set in nearly 11 acres of coconut trees along Waipouli Beach, all 311 rooms and suites in this resort have lanais, most with ocean view. Stained-glass windows and tapestries in the public areas are accented by a 40-foot water-fall cascading into a reflecting pool. The beach is scenic but often windy, and swimming isn't recommended because of the rocks; the Jacuzzi at poolside is a good alternative. The restaurant on the grounds is only fair (though a deal for families, as kids under 12 eat free), but the nearby town of Kapaa offers appealing dinner options. ◆ Kuhio Hwy (Hwy 56). 822.3455, 800/222.5642; fax 822.1830 ⑃

38 The Bull Shed ★$$$ Many swear by it and others swear at it, but there's no argument over the choice location on the windy eastern shore, with the waves marching toward the windows. A heroic cut of prime rib stands out on the short menu of beef, lamb, chicken, and fish dishes; there's also a salad bar. This local favorite is usually crowded; service can be haphazard. ♦ American ♦ Daily dinner. No reservations. 796 Kuhio Hwy (Hwy 56, across from McDonald's), Waipouli. 822.3791 ঙ

39 Aloha Diner ★$ Strictly local-style, this small diner serves the best saimin and Hawaiian food on Kauai. The small family operation is an institution—folks line up for fried *akule* (scad), *lomilomi* salmon (chopped with tomato), *laulau* (pork in taro and ti leaves), and poi (taro root). Don't get your hopes up if you're a *malihini* (newcomer), as Hawaiian food is usually an acquired taste. ♦ Hawaiian ♦ Tu-Sa lunch and dinner. No reservations. No credit cards. 971-F Kuhio Hwy (Hwy 56) (in the Waipouli Complex). 822.3851 ঙ

39 Kauai Village This shopping center houses a sorely needed **Safeway** grocery store plus **Waldenbooks** and a **Longs** drugstore. There are also a few restaurants, including **Papaya's Natural Foods** (823.0190) and **Panda Garden Chinese Restaurant** (822.0092). ♦ Kuhio Hwy (Hwy 56), Waipouli. 822.4904

Within Kauai Village:

A Pacific Cafe ★★★★$$$ When owner/chef Jean-Marie Josselin, formerly of the **Hotel Hana-Maui** and the **Coco Palms Resort,** opened this stylish restaurant, he lost no time boosting his already considerable reputation. Pacific Rim cuisine takes on new life in his able hands; try the wok-charred mahimahi with garlic-sesame crust and lime-ginger sauce or sea scallops in caramelized pineapple vinaigrette. Local farmers truck in the fresh produce daily—all the vegetables served here are grown on the island. The decor is tropical, with ceramic plates made by Josselin's wife, Sophaonia. ♦ Pacific Rim ♦ Daily dinner. Reservations recommended. 822.0013 ঙ

40 Ono Family Restaurant ★$ Famous first for its charburgers, this popular place has expanded its offerings. The prices are low (compared to the resort areas), and the food is American, from fresh fish to meat loaf. A bit more exotic are the one-of-a-kind buffalo burgers and buffalo steaks, made from bison raised in Hanalei on the North Shore. There's takeout too. ♦ American ♦ Daily breakfast and lunch. 4-1292 Kuhio Hwy (Hwy 56, south of Kukui Rd), Kapaa. 822.1710 ঙ

41 Kountry Kitchen ★$ From the Polynesian omelette with Portuguese sausage and kim chee (spicy, pickled cabbage) to the quarter-pound burgers on sesame-seed buns and the complete steak, chicken, and fish dinners, this dependable little diner keeps big eaters happy without devouring their wallets. ♦ Country-style ♦ Daily breakfast and lunch, W-M dinner. 4-1485 Kuhio Hwy (Hwy 56), Kapaa. 822.3511

42 Anahola Beach Park Because of Anahola's shallow waters, the swimming is excellent here. It's a popular spot for families and fishers, and the northern end is Hawaiian Homestead land (set aside for people who are at least 50 percent Hawaiian). Picnic facilities are available. ♦ Off Aliomanu Rd (near Anahola)

North Shore

Beautiful and remote, the northern coast of Kauai has an embarrassment of riches: white-sand beaches; luminous **Hanalei Bay;** numerous waterfalls; a wide fertile valley of taro fields; funky resort communities with lots of unusual shops and interesting restaurants; luxurious resort hotels; and places to camp, hike, swim, surf, snorkel, sail, fish, golf, play tennis, and ride horses. Movie aficionados may recognize some spots here—parts of *Jurassic Park* were filmed on the North Shore, and this was also the setting for *South Pacific.* In the northwest is the extravagantly beautiful and nearly inaccessible **Na Pali Coast,** 14 miles of cliffs so rocky and valleys so steep and narrow that the road that follows the perimeter of the island can't traverse them.

On the down side, the towns of **Princeville** and **Hanalei** are decidedly quiet, and the weather can be wet in winter. But the uncrowded beaches, expanding range of activities, and authentic Hawaiian ambience have begun to attract more and more travelers to this spectacular tropical setting.

43 Kilauea Point National Wildlife Refuge Lighthouses are usually found in rugged, unspoiled areas, and this one is no exception. When the **Kilauea Lighthouse,** which is on the National Register of Historic Places, was built in 1913, it could be seen 20 miles from shore. The US Coast Guard stopped operating it when an automated light was installed in 1974; the US Fish and Wildlife Service now runs the 106-acre preserve. A $6-million renovation has been completed since Hurricane Iniki hit in 1992, sprucing up the visitors' center with new exhibits and building a half-mile trail to a volcanic crater. Look for red-footed boobies and wedge-tailed shearwaters soaring above; from the lookout point, try to spot sea turtles and porpoises. Nene geese, Hawaii's endangered state bird, and the Laysan albatross are to be found here too. From December through April, this nature-lover's refuge is a wonderful vantage point for humpback-whale watching. ♦ Nominal admission. Daily. Kilauea Point Lighthouse Rd (off Kolo Rd). 828.1413 ঙ

An average of 80,000 tourists bump elbows daily in Waikiki, Oahu.

44 Magical Ocean Front Retreat $$$$ A book called *The Best Places to Kiss in Hawaii* lists this cottage on an 11-acre gated estate as a perfect choice for romantics. Amenities include an indoor-outdoor shower, barbecue area, VCR, stereo, CD player, and TV. The hideaway has no restaurants on site but is only minutes from the Princeville area. ♦ A three-night minimum stay is required. Off Kuhio Hwy (Hwy 36), Kilauea 828.2662

45 Anini Beach There's a protective reef 200 yards offshore, making this white-sand beach safe for swimming and a favorite with beginning windsurfers. The picnic area makes the beach popular with families, and shell seekers also find it rewarding. Polo matches are held here on summer weekends and **Anini Beach Windsurfing** (826.9463) offers three-hour-long introductory and advanced windsurfing lessons, as well as equipment rental. On either side of the main beach are numerous secluded coves. ♦ Anini Rd (off the northern Kalihiwai Rd)

46 Princeville Resort In the summer of 1969, while flower children were making their way from one end of the US to the other in VW vans, Eagle County Development Corporation was breaking ground on what two decades later would be a 9,000-acre resort area, complete with beaches, two golf courses, two hotels, a shopping center, a health club, an airport, condominiums, and numerous restaurants. ♦ Ka Haku Rd (off Kuhio Hwy)

Within the Princeville Resort:

Chuck's Steak House ★$$$ A notch or two above the Surfer Joe ambience of the chain's earlier restaurants, this place has a smart design and an interesting menu. Ask for a table on the lanai and settle in for a fish sandwich or an enchilada at lunch; sautèed *opakapaka* (pink snapper) and prime rib are the specialties at night. ♦ Steaks/Seafood ♦ M-F lunch, daily dinner. Princeville Shopping Center, 5-3420F Kuhio Hwy. 826.6211 ♿

Princeville Condominiums $$$ Although the **Princeville Hotel** (see below) garners more attention, some of these condominiums on the bluffs above Hanalei Bay are exceptionally roomy. The main attractions here are the **Makai** and the **Prince Golf Courses,** as well as the gorgeous beaches and dramatic mountain scenery of the Hanalei area. All of the condominiums have pools, plus there are two tennis courts, riding stables, and good beaches nearby (though access to them is somewhat difficult). Many real estate companies handle vacation rentals of condos and homes in the Princeville area. ♦ 5-4280 Kuhio Hwy. Pacific Paradise Properties 826.7211, 800/800.3637 fax 826.9884 ♿

Within the Princeville Condominiums:

Winds of the Beamreach ★★$$ Mountain views and expertly prepared Hawaiian fare await at this eatery. The casual, airy decor is accented by nature's art outside the large windows. Try the Hawaiian fish (steamed in ginger and sesame oil), macadamia-nut chicken, or stir-fried vegetables with either chicken or beef. Don't miss the smooth-as-silk guava chiffon pie. ♦ Steak/Seafood ♦ Daily dinner. No reservations. 826.6143

Princeville Hotel $$$$ In 1985 Sheraton decided to venture where others feared to tread: the extraordinary setting but sometimes unreliable climate of Kauai's North Shore. Situated on the Hanalei Bay lookout point, the hotel holds the plum location in the Princeville development.

The architects originally designed a simple hotel, which descended the face of Puu Poa Point in a series of three terraces. But the Sheraton corporation wanted more upscale accommodations and more ocean views, so the architects came up with a $100-million renovation, which was completed in 1991. All 241 rooms, 11 suites, and public areas, including the lobby, lounge, and restaurants, now offer a clear view of the 23-acre site. Each of the **Prince Suites,** about one-and-a-half times the size of the king and double rooms, boasts a formal entry hall, a living room, an oversized bathroom with a spa tub, a bedroom with floor-to-ceiling bronze mirrors, and 18th-century Italian-style furniture throughout. Special extras include butler and valet service, 24-hour room service, and complimentary transportation to the two nearby golf courses, health spa, and six tennis courts.

Also on site are an Italian restaurant; a luxurious pool; an exercise room; a beauty salon; and beach kiosks for snorkeling and windsurfing. Guests have preferred starting times and charge privileges at the adjacent **Princeville Resort** facilities, including the tennis courts and **Makai** and **Prince Golf**

Courses. ♦ 5520 Ka Haku Rd (off Kuhio Hwy). 826.9644, 800/826.4400; fax 826.1166 &

Hanalei Bay Resort and Suites $$$
Originally built as an exclusive condominium project, this 200- to 300-unit property was converted into a hotel complete with a full-service restaurant, stunning landscaping, and all the romance of Bali Hai. Two- and three-story buildings with one- to three-bedroom suites overlook Hanalei Bay. The spacious units offer all the conveniences of home—living room, dining room, full kitchen, and washer/dryer. With eight tennis courts, an on-site tennis pro, and the Princeville golf courses nearby, this is an attractive choice for golf and tennis buffs. There are two pools, daily maid service, and air-conditioning. ♦ 5380 Honoiki Rd (off Liholiho Rd). 826.6522, 800/827.4427; fax 826.6680 &

Within the Hanalei Bay Resort and Suites:

Bali Hai ★★$$$ The airy dining room, beautifully embellished with batik banners, overlooks the tennis courts, with the Pacific Ocean in the distance. Baked salmon, grilled chicken with raspberry sauce, scampi, and smoked tofu stir-fry are among the extensive selections. ♦ American ♦ Daily breakfast, lunch, and dinner. Reservations recommended. 826.6522 &

Princeville Golf Courses These sensationally scenic 45 holes of golf (18 holes at the **Prince Course**, 27 holes at the **Makai Course**) were designed by Robert Trent Jones Jr., who owns a home in nearby Hanalei. The courses are spread out on a lush plateau high above Hanalei Bay with a view of Mount Waialeale, plunging waterfalls, and the ocean. The ocean holes are the most spectacular, but the lake and woods holes offer superb blends of golf and scenery. The only drawback is the threat of rain, especially during winter and spring. The **Prince Course** is, par 72, 7,309 yards. The **Makai Course** consists of the **Ocean Course** (nine holes, 3,157 yards), the **Lake Course** (nine holes, 3,149 yards), and the **Woods Course** (nine holes, 3,208 yards); play two for a full par 72 round. The **Prince Golf and Country Club,** which serves the **Prince Course,** has its own restaurant, health spa, and lounge. ♦ Expensive greens fees. Daily. Preferred starting times and rates for Princeville Resort guests. 5-3900 Kuhio Hwy. 826.5000

47 Hanalei to Haena Drive The drive begins when you cross the Hanalei River on the Hanalei Bridge (built in 1912) and dead-ends nine miles later at **Haena State Beach Park** (see page 180). Along the way you'll rumble across the 10 little bridges of Hanalei Valley, some of them wooden and most only one lane wide. Taro fields fan out across the valley, then the road swings closer to the steep cliffs. The Na Pali Coast is rich with eucalyptus, paperbark, giant tree ferns, and banana and coconut trees. You'll also see a succession of sandy beaches nuzzled by foamy waves, and waterfalls plunging hundreds of feet down the mountain slopes. Cattle graze in green valleys that extend from the base of the mountains, and side roads dart off through tunnels of trees leading to silent beaches. There are wet caves and dry caves, tumbledown green clapboard houses with saddles straddled across porch rails, and chalet-style vacation homes trying to hide in the thickly wooded areas that guard the long, empty beaches. The only consolation in reaching the end of the road is that you'll get to turn around and drive the same beautiful route all over again.

48 Tahiti Nui ★★$$$ If you're in Hanalei on a Wednesday or Friday night, don't even consider going anywhere else. Just plunk down your $40 and indulge in a practically authentic Hawaiian/Tahitian all-you-can-eat luau, complete with *kalua* pig cooked in the traditional *imu* (underground oven). The rest of the week the menu features items like chicken teriyaki, fresh pan-grilled *ono* (wahoo), and fried rice—not as good as the luau, but still a taste of the real Hawaii. ♦ Polynesian ♦ Daily breakfast, lunch, and dinner. Reservations required. Off Kuhio Hwy (Hwy 560), Hanalei. 826.6277 &

48 Zelo's Beach House Restaurant and Grill ★★$$$ Currently the "in" place in the "in" town on Kauai, this restaurant charms diners with alfresco seating, as well as shellfish tacos, sun-dried tomato pesto rigatoni, beer-battered fish and chips, and the like. ♦ Nouvelle ♦ Daily lunch and dinner. Off Kuhio Hwy (Hwy 560), Hanalei. 826.9700 &

Because Kauai is the only island without a carnivorous mongoose population, the *moa*, or Hawaiian chicken, is ubiquitous here. A descendant of domesticated birds brought to Hawaii by Polynesian settlers centuries ago, the *moa* is fair game for anyone's dinner table, but most residents don't care for the taste of it.

Kauai didn't get its first traffic lights until 1973, when they were installed in Lihue at the intersection of Rice and Umi Streets, near the Kauai Museum.

Many Hawaiians—especially those of Japanese ancestry—believe the bird of paradise is a sign of good luck. They often plant this exotic flower in their front yards in hopes of bringing good fortune to the household. The variety with orange blossoms grows up to five feet tall, while those with white blossoms can reach heights of 20 feet.

Taking the Plunge

To see Hawaii only from above the sea is to see only half of paradise. Below the turquoise-blue depths is an unearthly, dreamlike world that, thanks to Jacques Cousteau and his Self-Contained Underwater Breathing Apparatus (also known as SCUBA gear), is accessible to just about anyone. In fact, more than 20,000 visitors and residents are happily blowing bubbles around Hawaii's islands every day—and among tourists it's an even more popular pastime than surfing.

Hawaii offers some of the best—and least expensive—dive programs in the world. Most hotels either have their own dive program or will recommend a nearby dive center. Hotel-run programs usually offer free 30-minute pool lessons in an attempt to sell an introductory dive (for about $100 to $120) and eventually a SCUBA certification course (prices for certification range from $150 to $400, depending on where the dives take place). Five-day certification courses usually last a few hours each morning, whereas three-day courses take all day. Both are equally educational, although five-day courses tend to be more fun and relaxed. If you aren't sure whether diving is the sport for you, it's now possible to test the waters by signing up for a one-time introductory ocean dive with an instructor without having to take classes or purchase gear.

Diver's Dress Code

Buoyancy Control Device (BCD) This inflatable and deflatable vest enables you to maintain neutral buoyancy underwater and keeps you afloat when you're at the water's surface. Can be inflated by mouth or with the air tank.

Dive Knife It's hardly ever used, but a knife is good for banging on the tank to get your partner's attention.

Fins The fins provide a diver with his or her sole means of propulsion. The large surface area and stiff material increases swimming efficiency and decreases effort, making arm movement unnecessary.

Gauges These important pieces of equipment show you how much air remains, the depth of the water, the direction in which you're headed (compass directions), and how much nitrogen you've absorbed (via a dive computer).

Mask A properly fitted mask is essential to safe diving because it allows your eyes to focus underwater. Almost all masks are made of silicon, which lasts longer than rubber. For those who have sight problems, prescription masks are available.

Regulator This crucial device automatically regulates the air flow and pressure from tank to lungs. You have complete control over the amount of air you breathe.

Tank Made from aluminum, steel, or alloy, a full size-80 tank holds enough air (at ±3000 psi) to fill a phone booth. Rate of air consumption depends on various conditions (depth, current, experience), but beginning certified divers can normally stay 60 feet underwater for about 40 minutes.

Weightbelt Literally a belt with weights attached to it, this item compensates for the buoyancy of the tank and wet suit. It's easily removable in case of emergency.

Fins **Wet Suit** A full- or half-body dive suit is recommended for maintaining body heat (yes, even in Hawaii's warm waters) and for protection against cuts and scrapes.

Dive Knife

Wet Suit

Tank

Gauges

Weightbelt

Buoyancy Control Device

Mask

Regulator

48 Ching Young Shopping Village This eclectic collection of shops gets top marks for its ingenious array of goods; plan to fritter away at least an hour here. ♦ Daily. 5-5190 Kuhio Hwy (west of Aku Rd), Hanalei. 826.7222

Within the Ching Young Shopping Village:

On the Road to Hanalei Character oozes from every pore of this 13-year-old, 1,000-square-foot emporium, where anything from a pareu (wraparound Polynesian outfit) to locally made jewelry, to Hawaiian antiques, to a child's toy may be found. The real secret to the place, though, is that the fun is in the looking. ♦ Daily. 826.7360 ♿

48 Captain Zodiac Raft Expeditions A Zodiac raft ride is a unique and thrilling experience that offers a spectacular view of the soaring Na Pali Coast cliffs. You'll also weave in and out of sea caves and ride around (and sometimes through) waterfalls that spill into the ocean. Captain Zodiac (aka Clancy Greff) and his band of enthusiastic guides know every inch of the coast, and their narration is a mix of Hawaiian history, legends, and even gossip about the local celebrities. Dolphins or sea turtles might swim alongside the raft, and you can get even closer to the marine life on one of the snorkel-and-raft trips. Be forewarned that the front of the raft hits all the bumps, so sit at the rear if you want a smoother ride. From May through September the company also offers drop-off and pick-up raft service to backpackers hiking the beautiful 11-mile trail through the **Na Pali Coast State Park** (see page 180) from Haena to Kalalau Valley. Raft trips are sometimes canceled when the weather's rough, particularly during the winter months. ♦ Fee. Reservations required. Excursions leave from Bali Hai Beach (also called Tunnels Beach), Haena. 826.9371, 800/422.7824; fax 826-7704

48 Hanalei Bay A stunning, picture-perfect arc of sand cradled by the sharp flanks of Mount Waialeale, this beach is popular for picnics, sunbathing, and local beach gatherings, and sought after by Hollywood, which caught it in all its splendor in the movie *South Pacific.* Swimming is dangerous here during the winter. There are public facilities and a quaint pier. ♦ Weke Rd (west of Aku Rd), Hanalei

48 Hanalei Gourmet ★★$$ Teachers at the old Hanalei Elementary School might have been surprised to know that students' desks would someday be replaced by elegant tables and the head of their classrooms morphed into a long bar facing a series of mountain waterfalls in what is now one of the town's most popular restaurants. Menu highlights here include such fare as eggplant sandwiches, shrimp boil, and artichoke dip. ♦ American/Hawaiian Regional ♦ Daily breakfast, lunch, and dinner. 5-5161 Kuhio Hwy, Hanalei. 826.2524 ♿

49 Waioli Mission House Museum This two-story cottage was brought to Hawaii in prefabricated sections in 1836 by New England missionaries who didn't want to go native. It's undergone a year-long renovation post-hurricane and looks better than ever. Period furniture fills all of the rooms. There used to be a pole-and-thatch meeting house on this site in the early 1830s, when traditional, prehistoric tools were still used and made in Hanalei. Lovely gardens flourish in the back. ♦ Donations welcome. Tu, Th, Sa 9AM-3PM. Kuhio Hwy (Hwy 560), Hanalei. 245.3202

50 Lumahai Beach It's one of the most photographed beaches in Hawaii, and you probably won't be able to resist taking your own snapshot of the place where Mitzi Gaynor washed that man out of her hair in *South Pacific.* There are actually two beaches; the one farther west is more dangerous, especially if the surf is up. ♦ Off Kuhio Hwy (Hwy 560, to get to the first swimming area, turn right off Kuhio Hwy after Hanalei Bay, then follow the unmarked trail; the second beach is farther west by the river)

51 Wainiha General Store "The Last Store on the North Shore" is alive and well and still selling snacks and sodas at "last store" prices. Check out the T-shirts or rent snorkeling gear. ♦ Daily. 5-6607 Kuhio Hwy (Hwy 560), Wainiha. 826.6251 ♿

Kauai was the first Hawaiian island discovered by Captain James Cook, who anchored there in 1778.

The tally of extinct species in Hawaii is a sobering 100 plants, 88 invertebrates, and 24 birds; endangered species total 41 invertebrates, 29 birds, 19 plants, eight marine mammals, two reptiles, and one land mammal.

Waialeale, which gets 40 feet of rain per year, holds the world record for the most rainy days in a year—350.

52 Charo's ★$$ The effervescent entertainer of "cuchi-cuchi" and Xavier Cugat fame bought a house on the North Shore and liked it so much that she set up her own restaurant here, a lovely little place on the beach at Haena with a view of the surf. Drop in for *pupus* (appetizers) and frozen drinks, a fresh-fish burger, chicken Barcelona, or paella (the owner's secret blend of seafood, chicken, and aromatic Spanish saffron). ♦ Continental/Spanish ♦ Daily lunch and dinner. Reservations recommended. 5-7132 Kuhio Hwy (next to the Hanalei Colony Resort), Haena. 826.6422 &

52 Hanalei Colony Resort $$$ Spread along four acres of coastline, this is the only resort in the majestic Hanalei Valley. The scenic, isolated hideaway has 48 newly renovated two-bedroom condominiums, a pool, and a beach, but no restaurant, TVs, phones, or air-conditioning. ♦ 5-7130 Kuhio Hwy, Haena. 826.6235, 800/628.3004; fax 826.9893

53 Haena State Beach Park A set designer couldn't create a more beautiful beach than this one, curving sensuously among palm trees backed by mountains. This Kauai legend was used for the Bali Hai setting in the movie *South Pacific*. Swimming is unsafe here in the winter because of strong currents. There are picnic and camping facilities, though. ♦ Off Kuhio Hwy (Hwy 560), Haena

53 Kee Beach Kauai's famous "end of the road" also marks the beginning of the hiking trail into spectacular Kalalau Valley. This is a good place to swim year-round, and during summer months, when the waters are calm, the snorkeling is excellent. At the end of the

road near the beach are the ruins of the **Hula Heiau,** a spot sacred to the ancient Hawaiian and the former site of a traditional Hawaiian school. ♦ End of Kuhio Hwy (Hwy 560), Haen

54 Maniniholo Dry Cave The first of a trio of caves past **Haena State Beach Park,** it is actually a mile-long lava tube running under a cliff. ♦ Hwy 560 (across from Haena State Beach Park), Haena

54 Waikapalae and Waikanaloa Wet Caves According to Hawaiian legend, the fir goddess Pele made a vain attempt to find a home on the North Shore of Kauai, but all she found were these two wet caves. Water was the last thing she needed, so she packed her flames and went to Kilauea on the Big Island. Some people swim in the caves—or even scuba dive—but it can be dangerous. It's worth a quick stop to see their exteriors, though. Hwy 560 (across from Haena State Beach Park), Haena

55 Hanakapiai Beach The mildly arduous two-mile hike from Kee Beach offers spectacular views at every turn. Pandanus, wild watercress, guava, fragrant *lauae* ferns, *kukui,* and countless other plants are fed by mountain streams and tiny springs. White-tailed tropic birds circle against the cliffs and dolphins can sometimes be seen when the trail is close to sea level. This trail reveals the marvels of erosion and the beauty of Na Pali, one of Hawaii's unforgettable natural sights. Be careful of the strong riptides at the beach; swimming is not recommended here for less than strong swimmers and at any other time but summer. Also: In the winter, Mother Nature robs the beach of sand, which she graciously returns around the end of April. ♦ Kalalau Trail (2 miles west of Kee Beach)

56 Na Pali Coast State Park The history of the area is as fascinating as the hike to it. Hawaiians lived here in large numbers from the 1400s through the 1800s. Later, a lepros victim named Koolau hid from officials with his wife and child in these precipitous hills.

Na Pali Coast

And in the 1960s, flower children maintained the tradition by hiding from their families and the law in remote corners of the Na Pali Coast, building love shacks in which to turn on, tune in, and drop out. Today the area is a state park, but it's still a place to go when you want to feel far away from the world as you know it. **Hanalei Sea Tours** (826.7254) and **Captain Zodiac Raft Expeditions** (826.9371) both offer a hiker's drop-off raft service for the 11-mile hike to Kalalau in the calmer summer months. Be forewarned that the **Kalalau Trail** isn't a cakewalk—even the first two miles require a lot of uphill walking. ♦ No prior arrangements are needed to hike the first two miles to Hanakapiai Beach, but hiking the remaining nine miles and camping requires a permit. For more information about hiking and camping permits, contact the Department of Land and Natural Resources, 3060 Eiwa St (at Hardy St), Lihue, 274.3444. ♦ Kalalau Trail

Bests

Susan Dixon
Managing Editor, *Kauai Times*

The best of Hawaii is Kauai, a 555-square mile, rainbow-tinged Eden at the northernmost end of the Hawaiian archipelago.

This island, with nothing that can be called a city and no road wider than two lanes, has twice been voted by world travelers as the friendliest visitor destination in America. But its ultimate draw is its secrets.

The island's 113-mile shoreline contains 40 miles of sand beach, which means that on almost any day, one can claim a private place in the sun. My favorite is a cove on **Anini Beach,** near Hanalei, which is generally deserted and a few miles down the road from the more populated beach park.

The **Hula Heiau** sacred ruins near **Kee Beach** at the end of the road is a place of incredible beauty and haunting inspiration. High on a cliff overlooking the ocean and at the entrance to the awesome **Na Pali Coast,** it is well worth the short hike.

Then there is the **Hanalei Bay Resort and Suites** at sunset. This was the scene of *South Pacific* and it is located, of course, on **Hanalei Bay** within the **Princeville Resort.**

Kokee State Park, high above **Waimea Canyon,** offers the opportunity to get cold in Hawaii. A few days in a cabin with a fire burning in the stove is a grand diversion. And while you're at it, hike the magnificent Kokee trails.

Tour helicopter rides, as well as **Na Pali Adventures** boat trips along the Na Pali Coast, are spectacular.

Dining on the lanai at **Tahiti Nui** in Hanalei is always a feel-good experience.

But what's best about Kauai is something that can't be articulated. If you accept its invitation and allow it to embrace you, you will know what we mean when we say that this island, still ruled by the capricious forces of nature and the whims of ancient gods, is a place where wounded spirits and bruised bodies can be healed.

JoAnn A. Yukimura
Former Mayor, County of Kauai

A walk through old **Hanapepe Town,** one of the small-town treasures of our west side, filled with the history and spirit of Kauai's people.

The view of **Hanalei Bay** as you descend into the **Hanalei Valley.** The **Hanalei Pier** is a picturesque landmark on the bay.

The **Wailua** area on the east coast of the island is a storehouse of Hawaiian history and culture. Several *heiaus* (ancient temples) are located within the area, and many legends and events of historical significance are centered here.

If you're interested in Hawaiian history: The **Kauai Museum** is located in Lihue; the **Waioli Mission,** built and furnished by missionaries in 1834, is in Hanalei Valley; and **Grove Farm,** with an operating diesel engine and other artifacts, is in Lihue.

M. BLUM

Niihau

The mysterious island of Niihau (*nee-ee-how*), located 17 miles off the leeward coast of Kauai, holds as much intrigue for the residents of Hawaii's neighboring islands as it does for tourists, both of whom are denied access. Strict controls on travel to and even information about this privately owned, 73-square-mile island have given rise to its nickname, "The Forbidden Island."

Niihau operates on a very simple doctrine, established by its owners, the Robinson family, to maintain the island's role as a haven for indigenous Hawaiians: No one is allowed on the island unless invited, and though residents are free to travel off the island with permission from the Robinsons, those who leave the island to marry may not return with their spouses and can arbitrarily be refused access.

By modern standards, life on Niihau would best be described as primitive, and that's how the residents intend to keep it. The island's 225 inhabitants, most of them pure-blooded Hawaiians, have an abundance of transistor radios and a couple of generators, but few modern appliances and no hotels, telephones, indoor plumbing, or jails. They spend their days fishing, swimming, shelling, and herding cattle or sheep on horseback. A few pickup trucks provide the only modern modes of transportation, and entertainment occasionally includes gathering around a portable television. Most of the residents born and raised on Niihau speak fluent Hawaiian, and the children attend the island's one public school, then move to Kauai for the upper grades. Ironically, few Niihau students return to live here permanently once they've experienced the modern world.

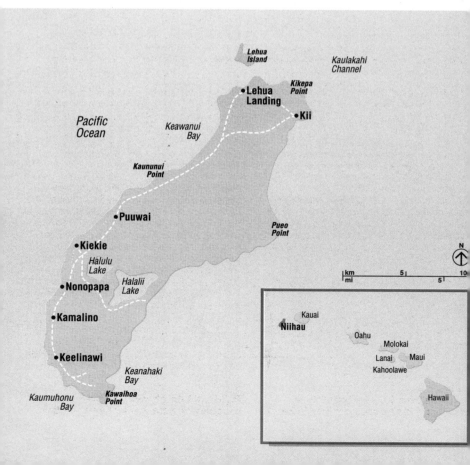

The history of Niihau reads like a James Michener novel. In 1863, Eliza Sinclair, the daughter of a wealthy Scottish merchant and widow of a New Zealand rancher, loaded her family and all their possessions (including sheep, cattle, and prize Arabian horses) aboard a 300-ton bark canoe and set out to find an island for her clan. After turning down an invitation to purchase a swampy area later known as Waikiki, she persuaded King Kamehameha IV to sell Niihau to her for $10,000 and proceeded to build a rambling 20-room house, as well as barns for her animals. Her ranch flourished, and Hawaiian laborers hired from nearby Kauai quickly established a small community. These ranch hands are the ancestors of Niihau's current residents.

Sinclair's descendants, the Robinson family (who reside on nearby Kauai but still own Niihau), have refused all offers by outside agencies, including the state, to buy the island (in the general plebiscite of 1959, Niihau was the only precinct in Hawaii to reject statehood). Aside from a few modest bungalow-type dwellings, the island remains in its natural state, with miles of white-sand beaches, mostly arid land, and two large natural lakes. The people of Niihau are employed by the Robinsons to work on the ranch lands. In return, they pay no rent, do no grocery shopping (food and other supplies are brought to the island regularly by boat), and have little to worry about. A traditional pastime among the women is the gathering of tiny, rare shells that wash up only on Niihau's windward beaches and are fashioned into the famous Niihau shell leis. These delicate, ornate, and very expensive leis are often of museum quality and coveted by private collectors. In fact, Niihau shell leis are some of the most treasured possessions of the Hawaiian people.

Since the profit the ranch produces is inconsequential compared to the amount the Robinsons could make selling the island for commercial development, it is apparent that their motive for sustaining its unique lifestyle is not monetary. Yet because no newcomers are allowed to settle on Niihau, and the children seldom return to live out their lives on this archaic isle, the future of Niihau is uncertain at best. It's widely believed that the Robinsons will never bow to commercial interests and sell their rights to Niihau, but a change seems inevitable—even on an island whose people are dedicated to resisting it.

Pass the Pork, Please

The only thing rarer in Hawaii than an authentic Hawaiian native is an authentic luau, where family and friends bearing food arrive as the host puts the finishing touches on the *imu* (underground oven), in which a whole pig is slowly baked. In ancient times, a luau was a special event, held as a tribute to the gods for a bountiful harvest, or to celebrate a momentous occasion such as the crowning of a chief or a victory in battle. Today, family luaus are held on all of the major Hawaiian islands to celebrate the birth of a first child or to bless a new house or marriage. Besides giving everyone a reason to get together, a luau reinforces community friendships and is viewed as a gift from the luau host to neighbors and family. The modern commercial luau bears little resemblance to the genuine event, but this doesn't necessarily make it any less entertaining. Most tourists probably wouldn't enjoy themselves at a real luau anyway, since the festivities consist primarily of conversation and the food (apart from the pork) is raw seafood and the ubiquitous poi (cooked taro root, which is a popular Hawaiian staple). To compensate for different tastes, tourist-oriented luaus provide constant entertainment (such as scantily clad male and female dancers and singers); a wide range of very non-Hawaiian food and a smattering of traditional, local dishes, including the famous baked pig; plus a nonstop flow of watered-down mai tais. A luau usually costs between $35 and $45, and it's a good idea to research who is currently offering the best show in town, since quality varies. Truth be told, though, even at the tackiest Hawaiian luau almost everyone seems to have a good time.

History

Hawaii's history, packed with kings, queens, hurricanes and volcanic eruptions, reads like a fairy tale. What follows are highlights in the state's colorful past.

In the beginning According to *Kumulipo* (the Hawaiian version of Genesis), in the beginning of time there was darkness. Out of the darkness, Wakea (father sky) and Papa (mother earth) united and gave birth to **Hawaii**, then **Maui, Kahoolawe,** and the other islands. Plant and animal life were placed on the islands in preparation for the appearance of Kumulipo (the first man) and Po'ele (the first woman). Happy with the fruits of their labor, Wakea and Papa bestowed royal titles on the children of Kumulipo and Wakea and made them rulers of the islands. All subsequent Hawaiian *alii* (royalty) claim their legitimacy as rulers from Wakea and Papa.

300-750 AD Polynesians from islands 2,000 miles to the south discover and eventually settle in the Hawaiian Islands. They abandon cannibalism and human sacrifice and develop a farming culture built around the worship of Lono, the fertility god.

1100 A wave of Tahitian warriors invades the islands, causing profound changes in the Hawaiian religious and social system. The practice of human sacrifice resurfaces (cannibalism does not), and a rigid social and religious system called *kapu* is introduced. Like European feudalism, *kapu* requires allegiance of peasants to local chiefs who control the land. In return, the chiefs protect the peasants from other chiefs. This system lasts 700 years. Over the years, upper, middle, and lower classes form. The *alii* (kings and queens) are the ruling class, the *kahuna* (doctors, navigators, and other professionals) make up the middle class, and fishermen and laborers are at the bottom of the social order.

1778 While searching for the fabled Northwest Passage across the North American continent, English explorer Captain James Cook of the *HMS Resolution* sails into **Kauai's Waimea Bay.** Cook is mistaken for the god *Lono,* who is expected to return to earth in a vessel with a tall crossbeam hung with great white sheets. Cook names the archipelago the **Sandwich Islands** after his patron, John Montague, fourth Earl of Sandwich, then sails for Alaska.

1779 Frustrated by the Alaskan winter and his fruitless search, Cook returns to Hawaii. Cook's officer, William Bligh (of *HMS Bounty* fame), draws the first maps of Maui's coastline. Soon the *kahuna* conclude that, if not Cook, certainly most of the English sailors are mere mortals. Following a series of mishaps, Cook is killed by a Hawaiian mob. Hawaii's population is estimated at about 300,000.

1784 The Hawaiian Islands are divided into three kingdoms. Kalaniopuu controls Hawaii and part of Maui; Kahekili rules most of Maui, **Lanai,** and **Oahu;** his brother, Kaeo, controls **Kauai.** The three kingdoms are constantly at war with one another.

1788 In his dying days, Kalaniopuu names his nephew Kamehameha heir to his throne.

1790 Captain Simon Metcalfe of the US merchant ship *Eleanora* kills scores of Hawaiians in the Olowalu

Massacre on Maui. Kamehameha captures the *Fair American* and two sailors, Isaac Davis and John Young. Using the *Fair American*'s cannons and the military expertise of Davis and Young, Kamehameha begins a bloody campaign to unite the islands.

1810 After years of war and thousands of deaths, Kamehameha captures Kauai, the last island not under his control. For the first time, all of Hawaii is ruled by one king, with **Lahaina** on Maui the capital.

1819 Kamehameha I dies. His son and heir Liholiho adopts the title Kamehameha II and begins to dismantle the *kapu* system. At a gathering of island royalty and foreign dignitaries, Kamehameha II violates one of the oldest and most sacred *kapu* by having women at his table and allowing them to eat freely. The feast becomes known as *Ai Noa* (free eating) and signals the collapse of the old order.

1820 Fourteen Calvinist missionaries arrive from Boston. Kamehameha II grants them permission to establish a mission. The missionaries establish schools and develop the Hawaiian alphabet; their impact on Hawaiian life will be profound and lasting.

1823 Kamehameha II's mother converts to Christianity. Following her lead, most of the island's royalty converts.

1824 Kamehameha II dies on a state trip to England and is succeeded by his nine-year-old son, who is crowned Kamehameha III.

1825 The first coffee seedlings are planted in **Mano Valley.**

1831 **Lahainaluna School** is established. It is the first American school west of the Rockies.

1834 *The Torch of Hawaii,* the first Hawaiian-language newspaper, is printed.

1840 Kamehameha III replaces his absolute rule with a constitutional monarchy.

1845 The capital is moved to Honolulu.

1846 Lahaina is the undisputed whaling capital of the world. Almost 600 whaling ships anchor in its port each year.

1848 Kamehameha III introduces the practice of private ownership of land. He divides Hawaii into three land groupings: crown land belonging to the king; government land belonging to the chiefs; and public land belonging to the peasants who cultivate it. Hawaiians are unaccustomed to the concept of private property, and much of these lands will be sold by their owners in the next decade.

1849 The first sugar refinery is built in Maui.

1850 The **Masters and Servants Act** allows the importation of foreign labor to work on the new sugar plantations. Chinese laborers are the first immigrants to arrive, followed a decade later by Japanese. The stage is set for the growth of large commercial sugar estates with strong links to the US. Meanwhile, the influx of diseases previously unknown on the islands

s taken a toll on the natives, whose population has
•n reduced to about 50,000.

54 Kamehameha III, the last of the powerful
narchs, dies. His successor, Kamehameha IV
axander Liholiho), resists pressure for annexation
he US. The plantation owners' increased influence
:ompanies a decline in the power of the crown and
Protestant advisors.

63 Kamehameha IV dies childless. The throne
sses to his brother, Lot Kamehameha, who
:omes Kamehameha V.

72 Kamehameha V dies without leaving a direct
scendant, thus ending the Kamehameha dynasty.
e next king, William Lunalilo, is elected by the
islature but soon dies childless.

74 Kalakaua, known as the "Merry Monarch," is
cted king. He pushes for even closer ties to the US.
akaua is also responsible for the compilation of
mele, Hawaii's great oral history tales.

76 In exchange for long-term leasing rights to
arl Harbor, the **Reciprocity Act** exempts Hawaiian
jar from US import duties, thus linking US
ategic and Hawaiian commercial interests.

90 The native population is now about 40,000.

91 Kalakaua dies during a visit to the US and is
:cceeded by his sister, Liliuokalani. A critic of
erican influence in Hawaii, she will be the last
waiian monarch.

93 Liliuokalani is overthrown in a bloodless coup
by plantation owners and sanctioned by members
he US Congress. President Benjamin Harrison
nds a Marine contingent from the *USS Boston*
ore to guarantee order. Sanford B. Dole heads the
ovisional government and immediately seeks
nexation by the US. However, the annexation treaty
s in the Senate and President-elect Grover
veland, a strong opponent of expansionism,
eatens to reinstate Liliuokalani.

94 The provisional government of Hawaii
fts a constitution placing strict
operty requirements on voting rights,
s limiting the native vote. On 4 July
94 Sanford B. Dole reads the
clamation declaring Hawaii a
ublic.

98 The Spanish-American
r and fears of Japanese
pansionism feed a surging
pansionist sentiment in the US.
7 July President William
Kinley signs an agreement to
nex the Hawaiian Islands. Five
eks later, the formal transfer
sovereignty takes place and
nford B. Dole becomes the
st official governor of the
wly established territory of
waii (population 154,000).

00 The first golf course is
ilt on Oahu.

01 The **Moana,** the first hotel in
aikiki, opens.

1903 The **Hawaii Visitors and Convention Bureau**
opens its first office on Oahu.

1906 James Dole purchases **Lanai,** the smallest of
the Hawaiian isles, and establishes the world's
largest pineapple plantation and fruit cannery.

1911 **Pearl Harbor** is officially inaugurated. The US
military presence in Hawaii grows steadily.

1912 Duke Kahanamoku is the US Olympic
swimming champion.

1936 Pan American Airlines flies to Hawaii from
California. The trip takes 20 hours. Commercial air
service spurs the growth of tourism.

1941 The Japanese bomb the Pearl Harbor Naval
Base on Oahu on 7 December. The US enters World
War II; martial law is declared in Hawaii.

1945 During World War II, Hawaii's population
grows from 400,000 to 900,000.

1959 Hawaiians vote 17-to-1 in favor of statehood in
an islands-wide referendum. In March, Congress
ratifies the Hawaiian State Bill. President Eisenhower
signs the bill on 21 August, making Hawaii the 50th
state. Owen Douglas Jr., the winner of the first
Hawaiian Open International Golf Tournament,
receives a $150 award (today's prize is over
$100,000). James Michener's *Hawaii* is published.

1964 The average number of tourists in Hawaii on
any given day is 16,037.

1973 The first **Honolulu Marathon** is held; in less
than a quarter-century it will be the third-largest
26.2-mile race in the country.

1983 The long-dormant **Kilauea** volcano erupts on
the **Big Island.** Hawaii's population reaches one
million; the annual tourist count, five million.

1985 Japanese investment in Hawaiian real estate
explodes. By the end of the decade, Japanese
investment accounts for 80 percent of the total
foreign investment in Hawaii.

1989 The average number of tourists in Hawaii on
any given day is 169,670.

1990 Democrat John D. Waihee III is elected
the first native Hawaiian governor in the
United States.

1991 Tourism accounts for one-third of
Hawaii's $30-billion economy. Carolyn
Suzanne Sapp is the first Miss Hawaii to
be named Miss America.

1992 On 11 September, Hurricane Iniki
ravages Kauai, causing $2.5 billion dollars
in damage.

1993 US Congress issues an official
apology for its involvement in the coup
that overthrew Queen Liliuokalani 100
years earlier.

1994 Democrat Benjamin Cayetano is
elected the first Filipino governor in the
United States.

1996 Hawaii's lower court becomes the
first in the nation to find no compelling
interest to deny the rights of marriage to
same-sex partners.

JENNIFER LEONARD

Index

Index

Restaurants

Only restaurants with star rating
are listed below. All restaurants
listed alphabetically in the main
(preceding) index. Always call in
advance to ensure a restaurant
not closed, changed its hours, o
booked its tables for a private pa
The restaurant price ratings are
based on the average cost of an
entrée for one person, excluding
tax and tip.

★★★★ An Extraordinary
            Experience
★★★ Excellent
★★ Very Good
★ Good

$$$$ Big Bucks ($25 and up
$$$ Expensive ($15-$25)
$$ Reasonable ($10-$15)
$ The Price Is Right
    (less than $10)

★★★★

The Canoe House $$$$ **27**
Dining Room at the Lodge at Ko
    $$$$ **99**
Gerard's $$$$ **71**
Haliimaile General Store $$$ **84**
Kona Village Luau $$$$ **30**
La Mer $$$$ **123**
A Pacific Cafe (Kauai) $$$ **175**
Prince Court (Maui) $$$$ **81**
Roy's Restaurant $$$ **151**
Seasons $$$$ **80**